THE GROUNDING OF MODERN FEMINISM

NANCY F. COTT THE GROUNDING
^{OF}MODERN
FEMINISM

YALE UNIVERSITY PRESS   NEW HAVEN AND LONDON

Photo credits: facing Intro., NWP Papers, LC;
chap. 1, George Middleton Papers, LC; chap. 2,
NWP Papers, LC; chap. 3, *The Suffragist,* VIII:8
(Sep. 1920), p. 222, and VIII:9 (Oct. 1920), p.
255; chap. 4, the Cleveland Museum of Art, gift
of Amelia Elizabeth White; chap. 5, *American
Magazine,* Oct. 1932, p. 1; chap. 6, *Survey* 57
(Dec. 1, 1926); chap. 7, *Vanity Fair,* June 1925,
p. 67; chap. 8, Mary Anderson Coll., SL;
Conclusion, *Survey* 57 (Dec. 1, 1926).

Designed by Sally Harris
and set in Caledonia type by
Graphic Composition, Inc.,
Athens, Georgia.
Printed in the United States of America by
Vail-Ballou Press, Binghamton, New York.

Library of Congress Cataloging-in-Publication Data

Cott, Nancy F.
    The grounding of modern feminism.

  Includes index.
    1. Women in politics—United States—History.
2. Women's rights—United States—History.
3. Women—Suffrage—United States—History.
4. Feminism—United States—History. I. Title.
HQ1236.5.U6C68   1987   305.4'2'0973
87–10642
ISBN 0–300–03892–5 (cloth)
        0–300–04228–0 (pbk.)

The paper in this book meets the guidelines for
permanence and durability of the Committee on
Production Guidelines for Book Longevity
of the Council on Library Resources.

to Josh and Emma

History may be a compilation of lies;
nevertheless, it contains a few truths, and
they are the only guides we have for the future.

Emma Goldman
"The Traffic in Women," 1909

CONTENTS

ACKNOWLEDGMENTS

Near the end of a long project it is a pleasant fantasy to envision composing the acknowledgments. Actually writing this very last item, when a few words seem so inadequate to match what is owed, is much more difficult. Nonetheless I hope to express here some fraction of my gratefulness to Lee Cott, for his patience, loving care, morale-boosting confidence in me, and gift of play, all of which sustained us through my long *charrette*. I also am deeply indebted to those friends who read the whole first draft of this book: Judith Butler, Bill Chafe, Alan Dawley, Steve Fraser, Linda Gordon, and Martha Minow. Each offered astute and constructive commentary which enabled me to embark on revision. At different points over the more years than I like to remember that I have been at work on this project, Joyce Antler, Mari Jo Buhle, Ellen DuBois, Joan Jensen, Alice Kessler-Harris, Juliet Mitchell, Elizabeth Pleck, Leila Rupp, and Judith Smith read drafts of chapters or portions; it is a pleasure to acknowledge the benefit of their opinions and their inspiriting interest and suggestions. I especially appreciate Ellen DuBois's comradely enthusiasm and longstanding willingness to share her knowledge about the history of early twentieth-century feminism. My particular thanks to Alex Keyssar and to Ellen Rothman for supplying confirmation, consolation, or encouragement at the right times.

I am obliged for the skillful and efficient help given to me by research assistants at different points over several years: Leora Auslander, Dana Frank, Cynthia McLaughlin, Michael Melcher, Jane Schultz, and Linda Watts have aided me along the way; Linda Anderson, Alesia Bone, Allison Coleman, and Natalie Danford of the Women's Studies Program office at Yale readily delivered on my requests for library tasks. I would like to thank Judith Schwarz, too, for locating the Heterodoxy flyer, and Roland Marchand both for loaning me a negative and for very timely and helpful advice about copyright permissions. For expert typing of my yellow lined pages (before I entered the word-processor era) I am indebted to Lorraine Estra, Patricia DeNault, Nimfa Gehman, Kathleen Marotta, and Betty Paine; and especially to Deborah Carroll O'Connor, who was also a generous and effective teacher of software mysteries.

My research and writing have been supported in part by a Rockefeller Foundation Humanities Fellowship in 1978–79, a Radcliffe Research Scholarship (funded by the Andrew W. Mellon Foundation) at the Arthur and Elizabeth Schlesinger Library on the History of Women in America in the spring of 1982, and by a John Simon Guggenheim Memorial Foundation Fellowship and residence at the Charles Warren Center for Studies in American History in 1985, all of which I gratefully acknowledge.

Without the help of curators and librarians at the archives I consulted in several states, this study would have been impossible. I appreciate their granting me permission to quote from documents in their collections. I wish especially to thank Paul Heffron and James Hutson at the Library of Congress, Jean Soderlund at the Swarthmore College Peace Collection, Eleanor Lewis at the Sophia Smith Collection, and Richard Ogar at the Bancroft Library for answering my mail inquiries so helpfully, and, as always, the staff at the Schlesinger Library, Eva Moseley, Kathy Kraft, Anne Engelhart, Betsy Shenton, Barbara Haber, and Karen Morgan, for their splendid and neverfailing support. The talents and conscientiousness of everyone I have dealt with at Yale University Press have made the process of publication a pleasure, which I acknowledge with thanks.

ACRONYMS

AAUW: American Association of University Women
ACW: Amalgamated Clothing Workers of America
AFL: American Federation of Labor
BVI: Bureau of Vocational Information
CPPA: Conference on Progressive Political Action
CU: Congressional Union
DAR: Daughters of the American Revolution
ERA: Equal Rights Amendment
GFWC: General Federation of Women's Clubs
IWSA: International Woman Suffrage Alliance
LWV: National League of Women Voters
NAACP: National Association for the Advancement of Colored People
NACW: National Association of Colored Women's Clubs
NAWSA: National American Woman Suffrage Association
NCCCW: National Committee on the Cause and Cure of War
NCL: National Consumers' League
NCNW: National Council of Negro Women
NCPW: National Council for Prevention of War
NCW: National Council of Women
NFBPW: National Federation of Business and Professional Women's Clubs
NWP: National Woman's Party
PTA: National Congress of Parents and Teacher Associations
WCPA: Women's Committee for Political Action
WCTU: Woman's Christian Temperance Union
WCWD: Women's Committee for World Disarmament
WILPF: Women's International League for Peace and Freedom
WJCC: Women's Joint Congressional Committee
WONPR: Women's Organization for National Prohibition Reform
WPU: Women's Peace Union of the Western Hemisphere
WSPU: Women's Social and Political Union
WTUL: National Women's Trade Union League
YWCA: Young Women's Christian Association

INTRODUCTION

National Woman's Party suffragists from New York, picketing the White House, January 26, 1917

T his book is about the time when the word *feminism* came into use
in the United States, and the women who used it. The appearance of
Feminism in the 1910s signaled a new phase in the debate and agitation
about women's rights and freedoms that had flared for hundreds of years.
People in the nineteenth century did not say *feminism*. They spoke of
the advancement of woman or the cause of woman, woman's rights, and
woman suffrage. Most inclusively, they spoke of the woman movement,
to denote the many ways women moved out of their homes to initiate
measures of charitable benevolence, temperance, and social welfare and
to instigate struggles for civic rights, social freedoms, higher education,
remunerative occupations, and the ballot. Nineteenth-century women's
consistent usage of the singular *woman* symbolized, in a word, the unity
of the female sex. It proposed that all women have one cause, one movement.

But to twentieth-century ears the singular generic *woman* sounds awk-
ward, *the woman movement* ungrammatical. At the very point in the
1910s—the height of the suffrage campaign—when *the woman movement* began to sound archaic, the word *feminism* came into frequent
use.[1] Its proponents explicitly distinguished it from suffragism, despite
their vital connections with the suffrage movement. The meaning of
Feminism (capitalized at first) also differed from the woman movement.
It was both broader and narrower: broader in intent, proclaiming revolution in all the relations of the sexes, and narrower in the range of
its willing adherents. As an *ism* (an ideology) it presupposed a set of
principles not necessarily belonging to every woman—nor limited to
women.

This shift in vocabulary has not been noticed by recent historians,
who, like most users of the English language, readily adopted the neo-
logism *feminism* and applied it retrospectively and generally to claims for
women's rights. The vocabulary of feminism has been grafted onto the
history of women's rights, which has been dominated by the history of
gaining the ballot; the chronology of the suffrage movement has thereby
come to determine judgments about the rise and fall of feminism as well
as to rule our perception of the larger woman movement. Understandable though it is, historians' tendency to lump together the woman movement, the chronology of the suffrage movement, and the vocabulary
of feminism has been misleading for our comprehension of the early

3

twentieth century. In any recent history of women in the United States, you are likely to find comment on the demise of feminism in the 1920s rather than recognition that the name and phenomenon had just recently cropped up.[2] Although continuity in the suffrage campaign obscured the important transition, the new language of Feminism marked the end of the woman movement and embarkation on a modern agenda. Women's efforts in the 1910s and 1920s laid the groundwork and exposed the fault lines of modern feminism.

These days, when the word feminism is regularly used and abused, encompassing a range of understandings and distortions as great as that adhering to, say, *liberalism*, I find it important to root the term in history without unnecessarily limiting its current applications. Feminism is hard to define. It is tempting to use it to denote all the long past efforts to advance women's status, as the *Oxford English Dictionary* did when it first included the modern word (not until its 1933 supplement): "the opinions and principles of the advocates of the extended recognition of the achievements and claims of women; advocacy of women's rights."[3] The term resists boundaries; unlike the nineteenth-century vocabulary, *feminism* allows a range of possible relations between belief and action, a range of possible denotations of ideology or movement.

My current working definition of feminism is not tied down to specific historical time. It has three core components, none of them highly exact; each might admit contest within it. First is belief in what is usually referred to as sex equality but which might be more clearly expressed in the negative, as opposition to sex hierarchy. Equality is such a difficult quantity to apply to human beings (because it is colloquially taken to mean sameness) that the point is served better by expression in terms of opposition to ranking one sex inferior or superior, or opposition to one sex's categorical control of the rights and opportunities of the other.[4] Second, feminism in my working definition presupposes that women's condition is socially constructed, that is, historically shaped by human social usage rather than simply predestined by God or nature. Although the concept has only recently been given vocabulary in the distinction of gender from the biological category of sex, the perception that women's status vis-á-vis men (whatever its natural or divine origins) has been purposefully shaped and thus can be reconstructed has long been essential to efforts to gain women rights or freedoms.[5] If women's condition were entirely determined by its natural or divine origins, then there would be no possibility for change.

My third point, tied to the second, is about gender group identity.

Feminism posits that women perceive themselves not only as a biological sex but (perhaps even more importantly) as a social grouping. Related to that understanding is some level of identification with "the group called women," some awareness that one's experience reflects and affects the whole. The conviction that women's socially constructed position situates us on shared ground enables the consciousness and the community of action among women to impel change.[6]

Of course such conviction is not necessarily held by all women. (Nor only by women—it was no small innovation that feminism allowed men to join where the *woman* movement could not.) Simone de Beauvoir disputed women's consciousness of themselves as a group when she declared in her magnum opus of 1949, *The Second Sex,* that "women do not say 'we.'" In her observation, "proletarians" and "Negroes" did, but women did not display the common consciousness of saying *we,* "except at some congresses of feminists or similar formal demonstrations; men say 'women,' and women use the same word in referring to themselves. They do not assume authentically a subjective attitude." What it means to belong to "the group called women" has been subject to myriad interpretations. At the same time that de Beauvoir wrote, the historian Mary Ritter Beard expressed it as succinctly as possible: "Women can't avoid being women whatever they do."[7]

It might be objected that my definition of feminism is a modern one, shaped in the twentieth century, and most relevant to the modern world. That, however, is the crux of this book: considerations about women's identity and consciousness as a group that became visible in the 1910s when Feminism did are with us still. The 1910s and 1920s revealed paradoxes which had hovered around efforts to obtain women's rights earlier but which became defining elements of feminism in the twentieth century. Feminism asks for sexual equality that includes sexual difference. It aims for individual freedoms by mobilizing sex solidarity. It posits that women recognize their unity while it stands for diversity among women. It requires gender consciousness for its basis yet calls for the elimination of prescribed gender roles. These are paradoxes rooted in the actual situation of women, who are the same as men in a species sense, but different from men in reproductive biology and the construction of gender. Men and women are alike as human beings, and yet categorically different from each other; their samenesses and differences derive from nature *and* culture, how inextricably entwined we can hardly know. Furthermore, because of the constitution of human individuality and the way that men and women are situated in the world, women, however much "the same" we are as a gender group distinguished from men, differ from one another, because the self and gender are shaped by other characteristics such as race, culture, class, and age. These paradoxes vivified feminism when it was first named, and continue to. The ruling fiction of feminism, the conception "all women," is—like the ruling fiction "all men" in democratic theory—always observed in the breach.

That feminism is a theory about equality appears most visibly in its goal; as many have argued, feminism can be seen as a demand to extend to women the individualistic premises of the political theory of liberalism. A cardinal aim has been to end "specialization by sex," in the language of the 1910s—that is, to free women from sex-typing and allow them individual choices, or to "let them be sea captains, if you will," as Margaret Fuller had put it sixty years earlier.[8] Yet feminism is also a theory about sexual difference, as can be seen in its method of mobilization, for it posits that women, *as* women, will feel the collective grievances to push forward toward equality.[9] As much as feminism asserts the female individual—by challenging delimitation by sex and by opposing the self-abnegation on behalf of others historically expected of women—pure individualism negates feminism because it removes the basis for women's collective self-understanding or action.

These seemingly abstract and general considerations jump forward if one looks seriously at the historic turning point of the 1910s and 1920s. The very culmination of the woman movement brought into high relief the paradoxes outlined above regarding women's social sameness to and difference from men, women's social sameness to and difference from each other, and the self-destructive potential of a movement which makes individuation of its members a principal goal. The singular conceptualization of *woman* in the woman movement came into crisis: the more women gained the rights and access it had pressed for, the less operable its premise of unity.

The nineteenth-century woman movement had dealt with the tensions engendered by women's actual diversity (of ascriptive character, achieved status, and opinion) in several different ways. One (and the least successful in mobilizing a mass movement) was white, Protestant, bourgeois women's tendency to consider themselves, *their* movement, as *the* woman movement (in other words, to ignore diversity). Another, more inclusive strategy was to concentrate ideologically and rhetorically on the character and conditioning that women of all sorts were presumed to share by virtue of attachments to home, family, and childrearing, a

portrayal which resembled reality sufficiently to be more widely persuasive. The woman movement operated from firm convictions about wom-
en's own ground of expected domesticity while aiming toward goals of
equality between the sexes: equality of access to education, a single sexual standard, equal suffrage. A third approach, successful in mobilizing
mass support by the 1910s, was the focus on the ballot, which enabled
groups of very different women to build coalitions toward a common
goal. The gathering force of the woman movement had by the early
twentieth century encouraged into voice women who spoke out not only
about disfranchisement by sex, but about disfranchisement explicitly informed by racial, political, or economic loyalties: black women, white
Southern women, socialist women, trade union women. The diversities
among women came to the fore in the 1910s in overt ways that could not
be contained in the principles or organizations that had been handed on
from the nineteenth century—except, importantly, in the renewed suffrage agitation. The vote appealed instrumentally to different subgroups
for various reasons, while they had their common disenfranchisement to
unite them. The common goal of the ballot harmonized emphases on
women's equality to men with emphases on women's difference from
men; suffragists argued on both grounds.[10]

By the 1910s the nineteenth-century woman movement had gained
entry to, although not transformation of, many avenues of social, economic, and political power from which women had felt excluded. As girls
and women swarmed on to terrain culturally understood as male—the
street, factory, store, office, even the barbershop—the domestic definition of women became obsolescent. Some women practiced law, voted,
held political, judicial, and civic office; some women managed capital,
explored the globe, held the highest academic degrees possible; some
women smoked in public and others flaunted their sexuality on the silent
screen, belonging to no man. These were, we would now say, tokens,
not representative women. Nonetheless, that achievement of token access undermined sweeping claims about the limitations placed on womanhood. So long as "woman's sphere" bound women, they had a circum-
stantial unity; once women were formally (though ambiguously)
unbound, joining together on behalf of their sex required a new delib-
erateness and ideology, which the appearance of the word Feminism
symbolized. A new understanding was needed, which Feminists proposed by making individuality and heterogeneity among women their
principles and yet holding these in abeyance by acting in sex solidarity.

Women who took up the term Feminism made certain innovations and new emphases, stressing not only equal citizenship but also economic independence and what they called "sex rights." Most innovative, along with the expectation of political solidarity they made the variability among women—the awareness that women did not necessarily operate in or from one domestic sphere—a principle of their outlook. Feminists offered no sure definition of who woman was; rather, they sought to end the classification *woman*. They posited a paradoxical group ideal of individuality. Insofar as they opposed specialization by sex they gave free rein to individualism; but Feminism relied on a solidarity deeded down from the woman movement and reinforced by suffragists' emphasis on women's common disenfranchisement. In the 1910s, a period of cultural and social upheavals of several sorts beside the culminating campaign for the vote, the movement of consciousness called Feminism flourished as much because of as despite its paradoxes. The suffrage coalition temporarily concealed the fact that the "cause of woman" had been called into question. Was there a common "advancement of woman"? Or was the advance of some individuals or some groups of women at odds with that of others? Did some women advance at the expense of other women? As more kinds of women took public roles than in the past these questions quickened, and came to the fore in the 1920s. Then women grappled with translation of the paradoxical doctrine of Feminism into political mobilization, social policy, and economic action. The divisions apparent among women in the 1920s manifested competing conceptions of gender equality and gender difference, and variant strategies for reconciling women's range of needs with their common interest in ending sexual subordination. The uniting goal of the vote accomplished, women faced the difficult realization of the larger goals of Feminism: individuality, full political participation, economic independence, "sex rights." They did so in the context of internal diversity and lack of consensus among women themselves, in an era of assertive business enterprise, bureaucratization of organizational life, and professionalization, an era in which phenomena as different as the decline in voting and the rise of social scientific standards of femininity measured the increased participation of women and shaped feminism.

As a history of feminism, this book is not about all women's situation, nor about all outstanding political, social, or economic initiatives by women. I have been selective and have undoubtedly neglected things that could arguably be related to feminism—for instance, individuals who were "firsts" or groups which may have ignored or rejected feminism in name but which may be seen in retrospect to have furthered

women's rights or freedoms. Defining feminism ever more narrowly, as
if to find its very qualifications, risks losing sight of relevant episodes;
but expanding it to cover every worthy or new endeavor women take up
equates the term with "what women did" and renders it meaningless. I
have taken as my guide the usage of women who themselves claimed the
name of "woman's" cause or feminism, although I think there is a systematic prejudice in that usage. The woman's rights tradition was historically
initiated by, and remains prejudiced toward, those who perceive themselves first and foremost as "woman," who can gloss over their class,
racial, and other status identifications because those are culturally
dominant and therefore relatively invisible. The privilege—or self-
deception—of making gender more important than its attendant attributes has not been available, most obviously, to women of color in the
United States, where race has been such a crucial marker, but neither
does that angle of vision wholly match most women's experience, in
which gender joins religious group, class background, regional culture,
political opinion, and other ascribed and achieved characteristics. Nonetheless, that perception of "womanhood" as defining one's identity has,
at times in history, galvanized women of diverse sorts, and it has been
the essential element of coalitions based on sex solidarity.

This is principally a study of consciousness—women's willingness or
reluctance to say *we*—a study of feminist intentions and the ways they
do or do not materialize. Feminist intents and attempts to mobilize
women act dynamically in their social environment, generating and re-
sponding to hostility and resistance as well as enthusiasm. Since feminism aims to alter power relationships between men and women, it
meets resistance not only from male self-interest, and the self-interest of
entrenched holders of power, but also from human leanings toward commitment, acculturation, or resignation to the established forms in which
gender relations are enmeshed. I have tried to set feminist claims in the
context of the conditions for and against their accomplishment, which
involves questions of leadership and organization, but this book is not
principally a study of leaders or of women's organizations. My interest is
less in bringing renown to the little-known names of the women herein
than in exploring their outlooks in order to suggest what was possible
and likely among a larger generality of women.

Rather than fixing itself in some particular locale my study proposes a
national scope, which means that it mainly brings forward the big-city,
well-educated, white, usually Protestant, gainfully employed or politically active women who showed up in national media and in national

women's organizations. My focus far underrepresents the heterogeneity of women's experience in the United States, although conflicts of allegiances vigorously emerge within its limits. A study intending national scope can offer, at this point when local studies remain to be done, an interpretive framework. A new framework for understanding the early twentieth century is needed. Rather than strictly marking 1920 as the end of an era, we should recognize the surrounding decades as a period of crisis and transition. The modern feminist agenda—to enable female individuals with several loyalties to say *we* and to achieve sexual equality while making room for sexual difference between women and men—was shaped then. What historians have seen as the demise of feminism in the 1920s was, more accurately, the end of the suffrage movement and the early struggle of modern feminism. That struggle was, and is, to find language, organization, and goals adequate to the paradoxical situation of modern women, diverse individuals and subgroups who "can't avoid being women whatever they do," who inhabit the same worlds as men, not in the same way.

1

THE BIRTH OF FEMINISM

WHAT IS FEMINISM?
COME AND FIND OUT

FIRST FEMINIST MASS MEETING

at the PEOPLE'S INSTITUTE, Cooper Union

Tuesday Evening, February 17th, 1914, at 8 o'clock, P. M.

Subject: "WHAT FEMINISM MEANS TO ME."

Ten-Minute Speeches by

ROSE YOUNG	GEORGE CREEL
JESSE LYNCH WILLIAMS	MRS. FRANK COTHREN
HENRIETTA RODMAN	FLOYD DELL
GEORGE MIDDLETON	CRYSTAL EASTMAN BENEDICT
FRANCES PERKINS	EDWIN BJORKMAN
WILL IRWIN	MAX EASTMAN

Chairman, MARIE JENNEY HOWE.

SECOND FEMINIST MASS MEETING

at the PEOPLES' INSTITUTE, Cooper Union

Friday, February 20th, 1914, at 8 o'clock, P. M.

Subject: "BREAKING INTO THE HUMAN RACE."

The Right to Work.—
RHETA CHILDE DORR

The Right of the Mother to Her Profession.—
BEATRICE FORBES-ROBERTSON-HALE.

The Right to Her Convictions.—
MARY SHAW.

The Right to Her Name.—
FOLA LA FOLLETTE.

The Right to Organize.—
ROSE SCHNEIDERMAN.

The Right to Ignore Fashion.—
NINA WILCOX PUTNAM.

The Right to Specialize in Home Industries.—
CHARLOTTE PERKINS GILMAN.

Chairman, MARIE JENNEY HOWE.

ADMISSION FREE.   *NO COLLECTION.*

Handbill for Feminist Mass Meeting, 1914

"T he time has come to define feminism; it is no longer possible to ignore it," the lead editorial in the *Century*, a general feature magazine, proclaimed in the spring of 1914. "The germ is in the blood of our women. The principle is in the heart of our race. The word is daily in the pages of our newspapers. The doctrine and its corollaries are on every tongue." The *Century* hardly lagged in fixing on the term, for *feminism*—a word unknown to Elizabeth Cady Stanton and Susan B. Anthony—had blossomed into use by writers, intellectuals, and radicals just a year or so before. Feminism was "something so new that it isn't in the dictionaries yet," a 1913 proponent announced, something revolutionary that aimed "to alter radically the mental attitudes of men and women." "We need an appropriate word which will register this fact . . . that women are changing," declared Marie Jenny Howe, an acknowledged leader among New York City women ebulliently fostering such change. "The term feminism . . . foisted upon us," she wrote, "will do as well as any other word to express woman's effort toward development."

Only a rare quirk prior to 1910, usage of *feminism* became frequent by 1913 and almost unremarkable a few years later.[1] Both men and women brought it into common parlance. In 1913, when a caustic male reviewer for the political journal the *Nation* was criticizing nine books by and about women under the heading "The Feminist Mind," Floyd Dell, a Greenwich Village cultural radical recently become coeditor of a brash new serial called the *Masses,* published a small volume championing *Women as World Builders,* subtitled *Studies in Modern Feminism.* Henrietta Rodman, a schoolteacher who had bobbed her hair and was leading a fight against the New York school system for its policy of dismissing women teachers who married, founded a group called the Feminist Alliance in 1914. In short order, "vamp" star of the silent screen Theda Bara declaimed "I am in effect a feministe"; Republican presidential candidate Charles Evans Hughes in 1916 worried about a "distinct feminist movement constantly perfecting its organization to the subversion of normal political issues," and the Missouri Anti-Suffrage League warned that "Feminism advocates non-motherhood, free love, easy divorce, economic independence for all women, and other demoralizing and destructive theories."[2]

What did use of the new term feminism signify? In its early uses—usually capitalized—the word had shock value and an encompassing yet unspecified referentiality. All who used it felt they had to define it to some extent and yet, curiously, assumed their listeners would know what they were talking about. One writer in the lively *Harper's Weekly*, noting at the end of 1913 that "within a year the Feminist Movement has become of interest to everyone," saw it as "the stir of new life, the palpable awakening of conscience." Well-known public figures who were favorably disposed toward Feminism tended to be general when called on for a definition: thus the usually voluble theoretician Charlotte Perkins Gilman declared it to be "the social awakening of the women of all the world," and Carrie Chapman Catt, the organization woman soon to lead the National American Woman Suffrage Association to victory, defined Feminism in 1914 as a "world-wide revolt against all artificial barriers which laws and customs interpose between women and human freedom"—"an evolution, like enlightenment and democracy" with "no leaders, no organization," and local variation in its specific objects.[3]

Prior uses of the word gave little solid guidance. *Feminism* came into English from the French *feminisme*, first used in the 1880s by a determined advocate of political rights for women, Hubertine Auclert, founder of the first woman suffrage society in France. When republishing in 1907 a letter she had written twenty-five years earlier in which she had used *feminisme* and *feministe*, Auclert thought the terms original enough to italicize both and to take credit for having coined them. During the 1890s *feminisme* began to be used more regularly in the titles of French women's groups and publications, but moderate advocates of *les droites des femmes* felt it necessary to insist they were more *feminine* than *feministe*. It required a decade or more for a broad spectrum of French suffragists to find the term generally acceptable. The term feminism migrated to England in the 1890s, when detractors more than advocates used it—usually surrounded by quotation marks—to refer more often to unwanted Continental doctrines than to English developments. The authoritative *Oxford English Dictionary* finds none but depreciating remarks with which to document early usages: for instance a notice from the *Daily News* of 1897 that Goldwin Smith had "alluded . . . somewhat disparagingly to that phase of feminism which is so curious a feature of the present day," and an account in the 1908 *Daily Chronicle*, "in Germany feminism is openly socialistic."

In the United States, the first references pointed to Europe. Perhaps the earliest journalistic use was in the title "Feminism in Some European Countries," appearing in 1906 in the New York offshoot of the London *Review of Reviews*. The article dealt principally with Madeleine Pelle-

tier, a socialist who would shortly initiate "militant" suffrage tactics
in France. (Pelletier—like Hubertine Auclert—drew comparisons between class oppression and sex oppression but went beyond Auclert to
link the two.) Tying the Latin root *femina* (woman) to the modern concept of an *ism,* and yet also connected with socialism in early English-
language usages, the term initially inspired confusion in the United
States: was this an ideology that men could join or a separate and antagonistic politics for women only, perhaps even threatening men with feminization? A very curious early reference appeared in the *American Suffragette,* a serial briefly published in New York by suffrage enthusiasts
pioneering new tactics. There, an essayist distanced the mysterious doctrine in a short piece of December 1909 called "Suffragism Not Feminism," which began, "the right to vote is not based on contrasts between
the sexes nor on animosity of one sex against the other, nor do we take
refuge in any perverse theories." Characterizing feminists as "men and
women who . . . wish to force womanly attributes on the man," it assured
the reader that suffragists, in contrast, wished "no animosity between the
sexes, but willing cooperation on the common ground—the Public Welfare."[4]

Feminism burst into clear view a few years later because it answered
a need to represent in language a series of intentions and a constituency
just cohering, a new moment in the long history of struggles for women's
rights and freedoms. In part it was a semantic claim to female modernism. "We have grown accustomed . . . to something or other known as
the Woman Movement. That has an old sound—it *is* old," one proponent
tossed off. "But Feminism!" she exulted. "A troop of departures from the
established order of women's lives" all marched under "one great spreading canvas labeled 'Feminism.'" In part it was an explicit and semantic
effort to exceed the bounds of—to insist on goals more profound than—
the rising advocacy of woman suffrage. "All feminists are suffragists, but
not all suffragists are feminists," explained a participant. To Feminists,
she went on, the vote was only a tool. The real goal was a "complete
social revolution": freedom for all forms of women's active expression,
elimination of all structural and psychological handicaps to women's economic independence, an end to the double standard of sexual morality,
release from constraining sexual stereotypes, and opportunity to shine in
every civic and professional capacity.[5] Despite the early muddle, the
very rapid and intense gravitation toward the term Feminism about 1913
suggests that it was not merely convenient but marked a new phase in
thinking about women's emancipation. But as much as proponents felt

Feminism diverged from the generations in the woman movement who had come before, and the suffrage movement in the midst of which it was born, it was greatly indebted to both.

The nineteenth-century woman movement—the rubric used at the time to indicate women's strivings to improve their status in and usefulness to society—handed on a complex legacy to women of the twentieth century. Nineteenth-century women of various kinds, times, and places had perceptively analyzed the circumstances of their sex. As individuals and in groups they had sought diverse means and ends to assert their share in directing the world's public as well as private destinies. They had sought to gain access to the rights and prerogatives men had, and to reevaluate and re-value women's nature and abilities. In the woman movement three arenas of effort can be distinguished, although within each variations abounded. One, begun very early in the century, lay in service and social action, motivated variously by noblesse oblige or by neighborly or altruistic intent; this included benevolent, charitable, social welfare, and (eventually) civic reform efforts in which women, seeing a special mandate for themselves because of their gender, discovered new strengths in collectivity and forms for self-assertion. Another comprised more overtly self-interested, more focused campaigns for "woman's rights"—rights equivalent to those that men enjoyed on legal, political, economic, and civic grounds. The third included more amorphous and broad-ranging pronouncements and activity toward women's self-determination via "emancipation" from structures, conventions, and attitudes enforced by law and custom. These three arenas displayed not simply smaller and larger visions of the same thing—although they often overlapped—but also potentially conflicting visions, the first more, the second less loyal to the existing social order, the third not loyal at all. To put it most simply, benevolent women's activities sought ameliorative measures to preserve, women's rights advocates sought to reform by making more sexually egalitarian (nonetheless to "join") the existing order, whereas proponents of women's emancipation sought to unseat or at least to radically transform it.[6]

Participants in these efforts, while linked by their attempts to revise gender relations, drew on more than one intellectual, philosophical, and political tradition.[7] The tradition that most obviously nourished woman's rights advocates was Enlightenment rationalism, its nineteenth-century political legacy liberalism, and its social representation bourgeois individualism. That tradition of ideas about the natural rights and liberties of all humans underlay women's demands for the removal of social barriers "arbitrarily" designated by sex, provoked environmentalist analyses of gender differences, and justified claims to liberties and opportunities equal to men's. Another important generator and legitimator of women's social assertions was Protestant faith. As much as orthodox Protestantism insisted on customary gender differences as a bedrock of social and religious order and strove to limit woman's proper role to a certain circumscribed benevolence, the proselytizing churches elevated and endorsed women's moral character and social role. Evangelical Protestantism in the nineteenth century supported the notion that women were morally superior to men and thus encouraged women to value themselves and their own contribution to social life. Quakerism and more antinomian varieties of Protestant belief, with their stress on the equal importance of all human beings before God, inspired some of the most eloquent and powerful nineteenth-century spokeswomen for equal rights and freedoms. The third major intellectual seedbed for the woman movement lay in socialist critiques of the inequities inherent in industrial capitalism organized on a competitive and individualist basis. Less Karl Marx's historical materialism and model of class conflict than the utopian socialist visions of Henri St. Simon and Charles Fourier early in the century, the ideas for a cooperative commonwealth held by the Knights of Labor after the Civil War, and the effortlessly harmonious corporatist proposals of Edward Bellamy's Nationalism at the end of the century supplied models of alternative social organization taken up by women in the United States. The communitarian socialist tradition was a resource for women who wanted to make the sexual division of labor and the relation of the private household to the rest of society matters for examination and change rather than resigned acceptance.

Taking up "the cause of woman" meant differing from and to some extent going back on, or beyond, intellectual kin and mentors from all three traditions, however. Women railed against the insufficiencies of liberal political discourse even as they seized it for themselves; they apprehended Protestant teachings at a different angle from that intended by most ministers; and they adapted socialist models to their own purposes. Leaders' and spokeswomen's own loyalties zigzagged and were subject to more than one interpretation. They were eclectic in their selection of mentors and resources, and due to historical change and generations of leaders, the gravity of the woman movement shifted more than once. Participants operated on a number of fronts, including education, employment, legal and civic rights, social reform, personal behavior. They invented and supported women's institutions: homes for widows and orphans, normal schools and colleges, health institutes and medical schools, mothers' organizations, clubs of all sorts, wage-earners' protective leagues, settlement houses. They tirelessly made speeches and published books and pamphlets, petitioned and lobbied state authorities, brought cases before courts, occasionally even dared direct action techniques and civil disobedience. The process brought forward eloquent speakers and leaders and theoreticians of tremendous insight who in turn educated others.

Any attempt to sum up the meanings and accomplishments of the nineteenth-century woman movement inevitably betrays the several strands of interests and approaches and convictions, as well as conflicts, within it. Even within the groups most clearly identifiable and best documented—that is, the national and state associations formed to pursue the specific goal of woman suffrage—changing composition, shifting priorities, and fateful alliances can easily be pointed out. The issues of whether to ally—and if so with whom—perpetually recurred. The post–Civil War rift between Elizabeth Cady Stanton and Susan B. Anthony and their colleagues in abolition and women's rights Lucy Stone and Henry Blackwell, over the relative priority of black male suffrage and woman suffrage, is well known. The change over time from Stanton's and Anthony's fiery leadership in the late 1860s to the NAWSA leadership in 1900, indebted to temperence and social purity advocates, is now often stressed in histories of the woman suffrage movement.[8] These represent only a fraction of the controversies and tensions, the different emphases in ideology, means, and alliances among constituents of the aggregate woman movement.

As much as nineteenth-century participants and observers oversimplified by speaking of *the* woman movement, however, that language spoke a substantial truth. The rubric acknowledged that discussion and demands and actions raised by women constituted an integral spectrum crosscutting other political and intellectual views, even when indebted to them. The individuals and intents involved, although analytically distinguishable, also intertwined and overlapped. They shared and forwarded the perception that the gender hierarchy of male dominance and female submission was not natural but arbitrary. Author Mary Austin remembered the confidences shared by women along the suffrage trail: "'Well, it was seeing what my mother had to go through that started me'; or 'It was being sacrificed to the boys in the family that set me going'; or 'My father was one of the old-fashioned kind.' . . . women of high intelligence went white and sick telling how, in their own families, the mere whim of the dominant male member . . . had been allowed to assume the whole weight of moral significance." Such recollections of women who became suffragists during the latter half of the nineteenth century revealed a common thread of rage at the injustice of male dominance and the arbitrariness of male privilege, and some jealousy of male prerogatives even when—perhaps because—they affirmed female character.[9]

Nineteenth-century women protesting against male dominance or refuting it in their actions did not choose to argue simply on the basis of women's human character (that is, likeness to men) or simply on the basis of women's unique sexual character (that is, difference from men). Women voiced these two kinds of arguments in almost the same breath. The underlying theme that women were variable human beings as men were, had the same human intellectual and spiritual endowment as men, and therefore deserved the same opportunities and rights to advance and develop themselves, persistently surfaced. Elizabeth Cady Stanton voiced it before the New York state legislature in the mid-1850s: "Here, gentlemen, is our difficulty: When we plead our cause before the lawmakers and savants of the republic, they can not take in the idea that men and women are alike; . . . we ask for all that you have asked for yourselves in the progress of your development, since the *Mayflower* cast anchor beside Plymouth rock; and simply on the ground that the rights of every human being are the same and identical." On the other hand, Stanton and other women argued that their sex differed from the male: whether through natural endowment, environment, deprivation, or training, human females were moral, nurturant, pacific, and philosophically disinterested, where males were competitive, aggrandizing, belligerent, and self-interested. Jane Frohock, a contemporary of Stanton's, wrote in the reform journal *Lily,* "It is woman's womanhood, her instinctive femininity, her highest morality that society now needs to counter-act the excess of masculinity that is everywhere to be found in our unjust and unequal laws." It followed from that articulation of womanhood that both sexes would benefit if women were to gain *equal* access to education, work, and citizenship, so as to represent themselves and balance society with their characteristic contribution.[10]

By the close of the century the spectrum of ideology in the woman movement had a see-saw quality: at one end, the intention to eliminate sex-specific limitations; at the other, the desire to recognize rather than quash the qualities and habits called female, to protect the interests women had already defined as theirs and give those much greater public scope. A tension stretched between emphasis on the rights that women (like men) deserved and emphasis on the particular duties or services that women (unlike men) could offer society, as also between the claim that women had to act for their own advantage or for the benefit of others. No collective resolution of these tensions occurred and seldom even did individuals permanently resolve them in their own minds. Although shifts in emphasis over time can be discerned, the woman movement as a whole maintained a functional ambiguity—rather than a debilitating tension, it was a stereographic or double-lensed view, bringing reality into three-dimensional focus. As phrased at the founding of the International Council of Women in 1888 by Zerelda Wallace (an ardent temperance worker whose sense of frustration in that cause led her to demand full political rights), women had organized in order "to plead for freedom for themselves in the name of and for the good of humanity."[11]

Nineteenth-century feminists could (and did) argue on egalitarian grounds for equal opportunity in education and employment and for equal rights in property, law, and political representation, while also maintaining that women would bring special benefits to public life by virtue of their particular interests and capacities. In part the duality was tactical. Advocacy in the woman movement was always in dialogue with those hostile to its aims. Attacked for "unsexing" women, activists might stress enduring female virtues. Ridiculed on the basis of women's incompetencies, they might stress their indubitably human endowment. Excluded from arenas designated as male or accused of proposing strong-minded women's ascendency over men, they might argue the injustice of excluding humans who happened to be female or emphasize the benefits to society of women's contributions. Mary Austin's retrospect on small-town America's expectations in the 1880s illuminated the motivation women had to battle on every front, to adopt (lawyerlike) every possible relevant defense. "There was a human norm," she recalled, "and it was the average man. Whatever in woman differed from this norm was a *female* weakness, of intelligence, of character, of physique."[12] But there were deeper than tactical roots to the varying emphases on women's special strengths and on their full human endowment. "Woman's sphere" was both the point of oppression and the point of departure for nineteenth-century feminists. "Womanhood" was their hallmark, and they insisted it should be a human norm, too.

The nineteenth century woman movement thus deeded to its successors a Janus face. Many early twentieth-century activists embraced the whole image. Suffragist Harriet Burton Laidlaw, for instance, succinctly reasoned on behalf of the ballot in 1912 that insofar as women were like men they deserved the same rights, and insofar as they differed, women ought to represent themselves. Advocates who conjoined women's rights to the agenda of Progressive social reform frequently weighted the end of the see-saw stressing women's gender differences from men, women's need to protect their established interests, women's duties owed and services to be offered to society. Arguments for women's advance based on natural rights had less purchase by that time, in part because exclusionary barriers in education and employment, and the legal disabilities of married women, had already been successfully challenged. On the other hand, the renewed rhetoric of social justice and democratic representation in Progressive politics and the assault on entrenched oligarchic interests in the muckraking journalism of the time infused the discourse of women seeking change on their own behalf. Thus a New Hampshire suffragist applauded a recent college-age recruit in 1907 because she was one of the "few American college girls who care to understand the great problem of human rights as applied to an unpopular cause."[13]

The woman movement at the turn of the century was manifesting groundswells of change resulting from the increasing differentiation and heterogeneity among women in America. As the consolidation of industrial capitalism in the late nineteenth century had widened the distance and agitated the visible conflict between capital and labor, waves of European immigration, migration from farms to cities, and consequent rapid urban growth had not only revealed extremes of wealth and poverty but also multiplied religious and cultural variety and created broader ranges of educational sophistication, cosmopolitan privilege, and occupational distinction. Through growth in population and exploitation of resources, through war, diplomacy, and economic force the United States was asserting itself as a national power to be reckoned with in the hemisphere and the world. The industrial infrastructure of the nation built, almost two-thirds of Americans at work no longer labored on the farm but found their occupations on railroads or construction sites, in factories or trades, in shops, offices, or banks, in hospitals, schools, libraries, government ranks, or more innovative institutions. The rise of the "tertiary" sector—those people who neither grew something from the land nor created something with their hands nor owned property but managed, corresponded, communicated, serving among people rather than products—was as apparent as was the corporation as the ascendant business entity. Through recent mergers and consolidation the control of almost all major industries rested in a handful of companies. The innovations of electricity, gas lighting, telegraph, photograph, and telephone belonged to the nineteenth century; the twentieth quickly introduced the automobile, airplane, wireless, moving picture, electric railway, and even radioactivity. Science applied its force to technology and industrial management; its mystique reigned in philosophy and literature. Individuals' attempts to grasp hold of their changed world broke through the surface of time-worn expectations in assertions of the value of the "new."[14]

These were important years for women's educational, occupational, and professional advance. Obvious to all were the growing numbers of women wage-earners in urban industries and services (their ranks swelled by waves of immigration from Europe), and the inchoate army of white-collar workers, from telephone operators to shop-girls in shirtwaists, who went to and from stores and offices every day. By 1905, despite sex segregation in the labor market, those who publicly objected to women's wage-earning as often envisioned competition between women and men for jobs as they feared destruction of womanliness in the work world. Female college graduates gained proportion on male graduates, and some male bastions of graduate and professional training were opened to women. College graduates invented careers for themselves by founding social settlement houses and evolving social work practice. As the twentieth century opened, one could find women doctors and lawyers, women public health officers and social investigators, women architects and planners, newspaperwomen as well as women novelists, and women teachers not only in the grammar schools but on the faculties of research universities.[15] More than one generation now collided, those who had been brought up in "woman's sphere" (of varying cultural traditions) and those whose experience was just as much shaped by factory or office, coeducational schooling, urban social life, municipal reform efforts, or political action in clubs, unions, temperance or socialist associations.[16] The growing frequency of women's new experiences in public, organizational, and occupational life marked one of the ways in which the outlines of twentieth-century America were already taking shape.

The noticeable growth of single women's employment outside the home, the diversification of living patterns and family relationships that implied, and the emergence to social concern of a new type of woman leader, educated in college and perhaps graduate school and trained to analyze social problems, set the stage for a new era in the woman movement. Local women's associations multiplied and joined in state and national federations, in their form manifesting the larger scale and typical consolidation of institutional life of the era, in their purposes reflecting the more frequent involvement of women in the economic arena outside the home. The two competing national suffrage associations consolidated in 1890 into the National American Woman Suffrage Association, although the most vigorous suffragist activity continued to take place at the local level. Women's clubs across the nation joined in a General Federation in 1892. The National Association of Colored Women, reflecting the color line drawn by the "General" Federation, brought black women's clubs together in 1896. The National Consumers' League, aiming to educate and organize consumers to oppose manufacturers' exploitation of workers, formed in 1899 from a base in New York. In major cities women college graduates founded settlement houses in sprawling immigrant quarters, becoming resident social researchers and sympathetic neighbors and aides at the same time. In 1903, settlement house workers and trade unionists created the National Women's Trade Union League to urge women workers into unions and to inform the public about their needs.

The gathering momentum of change in women's lives displayed itself most vividly in the labor movement and the suffrage movement, themselves reciprocally influential. Between 1905 and 1915, in New York City, Philadelphia, Chicago, and lesser cities, more than a hundred thousand women in the needle and garment trades walked off their jobs, demanding for themselves "Bread and Roses!" and appealing to middle-class women to support their protest and "Make Sisterhood a Fact!" Wage-earning women—most of them Jewish and Catholic immigrants—filled the streets of cities on picket lines, packed union halls, and marched in parades, asking for economic justice through collective bargaining, for an end to deadly sweatshop conditions, for decent wages and some hours of leisure. Young, unskilled, and putatively transient workers, wage-earning women were generally overlooked if not actively discouraged by AFL-affiliated male craft unionists; only a tiny fraction of women in industrial occupations were unionized in the first decade of the twentieth century. Hired into industrial occupations at a time of de-skilling through rapid mechanization, women were valued by employers chiefly insofar as they were unorganized and would accept low wages. Employers used the full range of techniques to prevent women workers from unionizing, from employee associations and corporate welfare schemes to spies and blacklists, promotion of ethnic and racial conflicts among employees, disruption of meetings, and police intimidation and

violence. Nonetheless, the strike wave that began among shirtwaist mak-
ers in New York and Philadelphia in 1909 and jumped to Chicago, Mil-
waukee, Cleveland, Kalamazoo, Lawrence, and Rochester over the next
five years not only announced to the world women's wage-earning presence but also proved their militance on behalf of unionization.[17]

It was time to insist that "women were permanent factors in industry,
permanent producers of the world's wealth, and . . . must hereafter be
considered as independent human beings and citizens rather than adjuncts to men and to society," as journalist Rheta Childe Dorr, who took
it upon herself to investigate various lines of women's industrial work,
put it.[18] The link between women's economic roles outside the home and
their civic and all other rights was thenceforward inescapable. A chief
beneficiary of women's efforts to be recognized as "permanent producers" was the movement for woman suffrage. At the time Dorr wrote,
settlement house workers and WTUL members who were also ardent suffragists were urging the NAWSA to include in its circle the immigrant and
wage-earning population. "These women of the trade unions who have
already learned to think and vote in them would be a great addition and
a great strength to this movement," Gertrude Barnum, Hull House resident and WTUL organizer, proposed at the 1906 NAWSA convention. In
1907 the WTUL itself established a Suffrage Department. To the new
generation of leaders in the suffrage movement, such as Harriot Stanton
Blatch, daughter of Elizabeth Cady Stanton, the connection between
women's economic roles in society and their justification and need for
the ballot was crucial. Taking up activity in the New York state suffrage
campaign in the mid-1890s after two decades of married life in England,
Blatch stressed that women's productive labor of all sorts, their contribution to social life and well-being, required a political voice. A college
graduate, she expected that education, expertise, and professional attainment, rather than wealth or gentility, would fit women for political
leadership. She veered away from her mother's reliance on natural rights
arguments for the ballot by emphasizing that economic and political obligations and prerogatives were reciprocal. "It is with woman as a worker
that the suffrage has to do. It is because she is the worker the state
should have the value of her thought," she reasoned.

Joining the WTUL in New York in 1905 sparked a new current in
Blatch's woman suffrage work. There, her acquaintance with wage-
earning women of earnest trade-union spirit and their independent-
minded, independently wealthy or self-supporting allies cemented in
her mind the connection between the organized power of labor and the

enfranchisement of women and inspired her to found early in 1907 a new suffrage organization, the Equality League of Self-Supporting Women. From an initial meeting attended by two hundred women the Equality League within a year and a half claimed almost twenty thousand members, including divisions from the Typographical Union, Bookbinders' Union, and the Inter-Borough Association of Women Teachers. It enlisted leading women trade unionists such as the Jewish capmaker Rose Schneiderman and the Irish former collarmaker and garment worker Leonora O'Reilly, both strong presences in the WTUL. Among its self-supporting women were socialist intellectuals and Greenwich Village radicals passionately engaged in challenging the world around them, including lawyers and social investigators Madeleine Doty, Ida Rauh, and Jessie Ashley, and nurse Lavinia Dock of the Henry Street Settlement House. Under Blatch's leadership the new group immediately arranged for trade-union women to testify before the New York state legislature on behalf of full woman suffrage (while the long-standing New York Woman Suffrage Association was still championing a property-based municipal ballot for women). At the session, garment-union organizer Clara Silver protested that the state, by holding forth to bosses and male unionists the lesson of female inferiority, was countermanding working women's struggle for justice in industry. "To be left out by the State just sets up a prejudice against us," she said.[19]

In the spring of 1908, the Equality League brought across an English "suffragette," Anne Cobden-Sanderson, to speak of the exploits of the Women's Social and Political Union, soon to be made world-famous by Emmeline and Christabel Pankhurst. Reciprocal influence between women in the U.S. suffrage movement and their counterparts in Britain and Europe reached a peak in the decade before World War I, as illustrated by the founding of the International Woman Suffrage Alliance in 1904 and its subsequent biennial conventions in European capitals until war broke out. Woman suffrage was indeed an international movement, in all the industrialized countries, especially the Protestant ones. When Finland in 1906 became the first European nation to grant women unrestricted suffrage, campaigners in surrounding countries intensified their endeavors. Socialist networks as well as the International Woman Suffrage Alliance served as international couriers after the Congress of the Second International in 1907 issued a directive for member parties to undertake campaigns for universal suffrage.[20]

British suffragettes were the great newsmakers of the time. The Pankhursts' Women's Social and Political Union had its origins in 1903 among

Lancashire working-class women. It was of those beginnings, and the working-class leader Annie Kenney, that Cobden-Sanderson spoke in New York's Cooper Union in 1908.[21] Like the contemporaneous arousal of woman suffrage activity in the United States, the English innovations relied on women's roles as economic producers supporting their claims to political freedom. The tactics of the WSPU included street demonstrations, mass marches, and disruption of male politicians' meetings, which led to explosive clashes with police. In 1906 the Pankhursts moved to London, where their "shocking outrages" catapulted them—the "militant women"—to international headlines. They led public demonstrations in the mud and rain, thrust banners from the gallery in Parliament, addressed passersby on street corners (and were arrested for obstruction), sent deputations to see the Prime Minister, and heckled members of Parliament. Intensifying their moral pressure to physical violence in 1909, members of the WSPU smashed windows and assaulted guards at No. 10 Downing Street and other government buildings. Sent to jail, they refused to eat. Hunger-striking became their regular practice when they were imprisoned in consequence of their renewed onslaught of property destruction. The Pankhursts' autocratic command lost them most of their followers, however, who formed the Women's Freedom League in 1907 and took a path they called "constitutional militance"— tax protests, census boycotts, and other creative forms of civil disobedience short of physical violence.[22]

The staging of sensational events, the use of nonviolent civil disobedience, and the disruption of government as usual that came to be called militance in the woman suffrage movement were tactics adopted from an inventory available in working-class, socialist, and nationalist politics. The Pankhursts said they had learned their most extreme militance— destruction of property, arson, and physical assault—from Irish nationalists. (Those tactics were shunned by virtually all other suffragists.) The class origin of militant tactics was illustrated by the international fact that few middle- and upper-class suffragists partook beyond the level of appearing on the street, that itself being a significant affront to respectability. Among German suffragists, even mass parades never caught on.

In the United States, however, because of the example of the British suffragettes and women workers on strike, and the contributions of Socialist women, woman suffrage activity after 1907 blossomed with techniques planted by the political left. European and American delegates attending the IWSA meeting in London in 1909 came face to face with militance, which caused a slight but noticeable ripple effect. Carrie

Chapman Catt, a leader in the International group, was impressed but not converted. A significant handful of American suffragists who would become principals in the Congressional Union and its successor, the National Woman's Party—including Alice Paul and Lucy Burns, Alva Belmont, Inez Haynes Irwin, Rheta Childe Dorr, and Anne Martin—witnessed or joined the English actions between 1906 and 1911. Mrs. Pankhurst undertook a speaking tour to the United States in 1909, during which she ignited followers and inspired new leaders, such as Katherine Houghton Hepburn and Emily Pierson in Hartford, Connecticut. Perhaps there was a greater taste for what could be called "democratic" pageantry in the American republic; at any rate, once speeches and meetings in the open air were begun, they proved necessary in order to accommodate large crowds. Prepared outdoor demonstrations went just one step further. New leaders advocating attention-getting methods (like Blatch) were bold and persuasive, helped by the interest of sensation-seeking news media.[23]

As "girl strikers" in the garment trades milked for publicity purposes the contradiction between the standard image of gentle womanhood and the harsh conditions of the assembly line and picket line, suffragists who became militant relied for attention on their tactics confronting or even assaulting predictable models of femininity. The Progressive Union for Woman Suffrage in New York, the first to attempt a street parade (in 1908), prided itself on being theatrical, although its leader insisted that women found such public tactics "distasteful" and only took them up by necessity, in the "divine spirit of self-sacrifice."[24] The new tactics had a spiraling effect within the suffrage movement and also made waves outside it. Such action in a common cause increased women's solidarity. Partakers in norm-defying behavior (such as speaking outdoors on a soapbox to a mixed audience, subject to men's jeers) were kept at razor's edge awareness and forced to reconsider internal and external constraints dictated by gender. Then, if one norm were crossed, why not another? Ironically, because of its origins, the usefulness of suffrage militance was biased toward the elite; the wealthier its proponent was—the more ladylike she was supposed to be—the greater the effect of her subversion of the norm.

Suffragists searching for new constituents invigorated old groups or established new ones, among them the Political Equality League in Philadelphia, the Boston Equal Suffrage Association, the Hartford Equal Franchise League, the Chicago Political Equality League, and the San Francisco Wage Earners' Suffrage League. Within a year or two not only in New York but also in Baltimore, Boston, San Francisco—even in Boone, Iowa—suffragists showed new imagination and urgency, making up or adapting from British examples such publicity-generating practices as vigils, parades, trolley-car and auto speaking tours.[25] These were consciously modern stunts, relying on and taking advantage of the existence of mass media. Adopting the view of government as a broker of interests among which women's points of view had to be consulted, local suffrage groups secured wider audiences with their new methods of publicity. In New York, under Carrie Chapman Catt's leadership, the Woman Suffrage Party got under way early in 1910, purposely mimicking Tammany Hall in its organization of the whole city into precincts and districts for effective oversight. Aiming for a statewide municipal suffrage bill in 1909, the Illinois Equal Suffrage Association ran a Suffrage Special train from Chicago to the state legislative session in Springfield, where twenty-five women each gave three-minute speeches from varying points of view.

In California, many local groups (some specialized for college women, temperance workers, wage-earners, or socialists) worked together in the successful state referendum campaign of 1911. They canvassed door-to-door and held street meetings in cities and towns, took auto trips to rural areas to put on skits and songs, posted billboards and held high school essay contests. The California Equal Suffrage Association in the north reported issuing three million pages of literature, and the California Political Equality Association in the south reported more than a million leaflets and pamphlets. That victory, on the heels of one in Washington the year before, touched off rising expectations nationwide. "Best of all," California suffragist Katherine Phillips Edson reflected upon the 1911 success, "something has happened within woman herself—an increased self-respect—a feeling of honor for herself and for her sex. She is no longer treated as a dependent person, but . . . [is] to think her own thoughts—right or wrong—in the policy of her state."[26]

The new vigor was expressed in multiple, sometimes rival suffrage organizations at the grassroots, formed around neighborhoods, colleges, trades, professions and clubs. The energy was sprouting up from below. At that very time a NAWSA officer admitted to members of her board, "In large places, the National is now hardly known to exist. The local suffragists are absorbed in local work and care only for such work." Intense internal conflicts over leadership, finances, and tactics racked the top levels of NAWSA; the Reverend Olympia Brown, who had been a suffragist since Civil War days, pronounced the "shallow false talk of love excellence harmony &c" amidst the ongoing warfare "so false that it makes me vomit." By 1912, however, NAWSA made two major policy changes that reflected the influence of the grassroots suffrage movement: the open-air meeting was accepted as policy, and officers of the organization, previously held to strict nonpartisanship, were freed to work for the political parties of their choice.[27]

By the 1910s woman suffrage was a platform on which diverse people and organizations could comfortably, if temporarily, stand. The nineteenth-century view of the ballot as representing the self-possessed individual had been joined by new emphasis on the ballot as the tool of group interests. City and state machine politics unmistakably conveyed the message that votes enabled self-identified groups to have their needs answered or their intents manipulated. Population growth and immigration, industrialization and the rise of great cities were compelling people to reenvision the state as the arena in which differing group interests might be calculated and conciliated. Americans turned to political reforms in the 1910s to address the conditions brought on by industrialization, immigration, and urbanization: dissident Republicans produced the Progressive Party, and the Democrats the "New Freedom"; the Socialist Party made unparalleled electoral gains. The political arena was seen as the forum in which the competing wants of differing economic, ethnic, and regional groups might be accommodated, in which cooperation on concrete reforms could be engineered without groups losing their particular identities. In synchronous parallel, voting appeared as a more pressing need for women, and diverse kinds of women could see the vote as a concrete goal around which to form a coalition.[28] Since both male and female reformers had been pushing for more than a decade for government investigation and regulation of housing, factory conditions, and community health and safety, suffragists could argue that modern conditions bridged the chasm between the realm of politics and woman's conventional realm of the home. Where in the mid-nineteenth century the proposal of female enfranchisement profoundly threatened the ideology of woman's sphere, by the 1910s the need as well as right to vote in order to ensure domestic welfare could be persuasively presented as part of women's duties as wives, mothers, and community members.[29] By that time, suffragists were as likely to argue that women deserved the vote *because* of their sex—because women as a group had relevant benefits to bring and interests to defend in the polity—as to argue that women deserved the vote *despite* their sex.

Because the vote was recognized as a tool of group interests as well as a symbol of equal access of citizens to self-government, the demand for equal suffrage could be brought into accord with the notion that women differed from men. In fact, the more that women's particular interests were stressed—so long as the premise of equal access was sustained— the better the argument for woman suffrage. Thus, when Carrie Chapman Catt summed up "Why Women Want to Vote" early in 1915, she gave two kinds of reasons. The first had to do with justice, rights, women's sameness to men, and democracy: since women are people and in America the people are supposed to rule, she wrote, the vote is woman's right, and disenfranchisement on the basis of sex is unjust. Her second, equally emphatic line of reasoning had to do with women's duties, talents, and difference from men: the vote was woman's duty because the United States government, competent in areas where men shone (such as business, commerce, and the development of natural resources), was inadequate in areas where mothers' skills were needed, such as schooling, caring for criminals, or dealing with unemployment.

The vote harmonized the two strands in foregoing woman's rights advocacy: it was an equal rights goal that enabled women to make special contributions; it sought to give women the same capacity as men so they could express their differences; it was a just end in itself, but it was also an expedient means to other ends. "Sameness" and "difference" arguments, "equal rights" and "special contributions" arguments, "justice" and "expediency" arguments existed side by side. Although the gender differences marked out were conventional—defining women as mothers, housekeepers, and caregivers—turning these stereotypes to serve goals of equal access and equal rights minimized their constraints. Not simply accommodationist or conservative in its willingness to point out the need for political representation of women's differences from men, the suffrage movement of the 1910s encompassed the broadest spectrum of ideas and participants in the history of the movement.[30]

That was the only decade in which woman suffrage commanded a mass movement, in which working-class women, black women, women on the radical left, the young, and the upper class joined in force; rich and poor, socialist and capitalist, occasionally even black and white could be seen taking the same platform. Socialist Party members concentrated on rousing working-class support for woman suffrage, taking vigorous and efficacious parts in the western state campaigns and in New York. In 1910 not only workplace organizers and union militants but working-class women of many sorts were demonstrating new audacity and forms for cooperation, which were strengthened by and further fueled the suffrage movement. In Providence, Rhode Island, Jewish immigrant housewives "declared war against the kosher butchers," picketing the shops to enforce their collective boycott, because prices rose too high and customers were not receiving "respectable treatment." In Chicago, a group of Bohemian women edited and printed their own newspaper, campaigning forcefully for woman suffrage and aiming to broaden the horizons of working women. Just after woman suffrage passed in Washington, the *Seattle Union Record,* the city's principal labor newspaper, transformed its Woman's Department from a page on food, home, and fashion to a Magazine Section covering suffrage victories and other national and international events. Its new woman editor connected the position of "stay-at-home" wives to that of their employed sisters. The new section reported on wage-earning women's strikes and struggles to organize for the eight-hour day, highlighted women's advances into professions and other formerly male occupations, and leavened the loaf with anecdotes of women besting men at various jobs. The Women's Card and Label League, a formerly halting union auxiliary organized through the Seattle Central Labor Council, pronounced itself a contributor to the woman movement as well as the labor movement, and began to flourish.[31] National leaders in the WTUL turned their interests more intensively to gaining the ballot, believing that women had to be able to assert and protect their economic interests in the political arena. "Working women must use the ballot," cried a garment maker, testifying before the New York State Senate in the wake of the disastrous fire that killed over 140 women employed at the Triangle factory, "in order to abolish the burning and crushing of our bodies for the profit of a very few." White-collar workers—saleswomen at Filene's department store in Boston, for example—also joined the movement. Before 1909 "the girls in the offices in which I worked . . . were nearly all opposed to women suffrage," a former clerical worker recalled, but within a few years "the desire for the vote was nearly universal with them."[32]

Black leaders and black women's organizations spoke up for woman suffrage in increasing numbers, claiming that the enfranchisement of black women would address and help to redress the forcible disenfranchisement of black men in the South. Although the woman suffrage movement had never been without some black contributors and innovators, black women's participation intensified during the 1910s. The major national organizations, the National Association of Colored Women, the National Federation of Afro-American Women, and the Northeastern Federation of Colored Women's Clubs, threw themselves actively into

the movement despite the color line drawn by many of their white counterparts. At the local level black women's clubs, like the Alpha Club
established by Ida Wells-Barnett in Chicago, worked effectively in state
campaigns. They mobilized to promote not only gender justice but also
race progress, while aware of Southern white suffragists' contentions that
white women's votes would outnumber the votes of all blacks. Southern
white women had become visible in the national suffrage movement in
the 1890s but their participation too did not burgeon until after 1910.
Atlanta, for instance, harbored two white woman suffrage groups in 1910
and eighty-one in 1917.

Interestingly, both black supporters and white opponents maintained
that enfranchised black women would somehow resist the Southern
Democratic treachery that had deprived black men of their votes. Within
two years of its founding in 1910, W. E. B. DuBois's journal the *Crisis*
carried a symposium of black spokesmen and women endorsing woman
suffrage, and it published a second in 1915. Throughout these years
DuBois kept up a running commentary on the progress of the movement—including egregious affronts by white women to black—while remaining a vociferous supporter. Black women argued for the ballot on
the basis of both rights and duties, as did white women. Adella Hunt
Logan of the Tuskegee Woman's Club deftly put it, "Women who see that
they need the vote see also that the vote needs them." Black women
often argued that the ballot would bring within their reach long-sought
and not conventionally political aims: it would enable them to preserve
their interests as workers, improve their chances for education, rally
against black male disfranchisement, and also protect themselves against
the bane of sexual exploitation by white men. "She needs the ballot, to
reckon with men who place no value upon her virtue, and to mould
healthy sentiment in favor of her own protection," wrote Nannie Helen
Burroughs, an educator of black girls and promoter of domestic science.
Instrumental as this reasoning was, it underscored the point that Katherine Edson had made in a different way, that the ballot in this era symbolized private self-respect and public dignity for women.[33]

Women at both ends of the economic spectrum had new appetite for
political organization. Suffrage groups found ready recruits not only
among wage-earners but also among prosperous women formerly indifferent or opposed. Perhaps the best index was the swing in club women's
attention. Before 1904 the GFWC maintained a "nonpartisan" position on
suffrage, seeing its theater in benevolence rather than politics; but that
year's convention gave space to a NAWSA speaker, and by 1910 members

lined the aisles for a convention debate on suffrage, gripped with the topic. College women formerly devoted to social uplift or social life now joined the political movement. The College Equal Suffrage League united college groups from fifteen states in 1908 and began dispatching its own organizers to campuses. One wrote home from Nebraska in 1909 the news that women students were now "not afraid of antagonising the men or losing invitations to parties by being suffragists." In large cities, upper-class women—"society" women of great names and fortunes—newly entered the suffrage movement, thereby making it "fashionable" as it had never before been. They entered at the top, as their resources permitted: in New York in 1910 Alva (Mrs. O. H. P.) Belmont, inheritor of both Vanderbilt and Belmont fortunes, and Mrs. Clarence MacKay, wife of the founder of International Telephone and Telegraph, headed their own suffrage societies; in Chicago the upper-class women of the Chicago Women's Club established the Political Equality League in order to exert their leadership in the movement. "Polite up-town rich ladies mingling with free and democratic spirits with us poor wage slaves of the slums," was the way labor radical and journalist Mary Heaton Vorse breezily characterized her publicity committee of the New York Woman Suffrage Party in 1915.[34]

An important inspiration for privileged women's political activism in this period, and for their search for cross-class alliances, was their sense that wage-earners (especially trade unionists) were exemplars of independent womanhood. To a self-selected minority of educated women seeking validation of their own social usefulness, women wage-earners—despite the exploitative conditions under which they labored—represented not simply victims to be assisted but a vanguard to be emulated. Thus suffragist Harriet Burton Laidlaw sought to mollify WTUL leader Leonora O'Reilly, whose temper sometimes lashed out scornfully at the class blindness of her wealthy "allies": "surely if we who can do less than you, we who are not so close to vital things, can learn anything from you, do you not know that we are teachable?" As far back as 1890 Jane Addams had evocatively attributed "The Subjective Necessity for Social Settlements" to her own and similarly privileged young women's disquieting sense of living life at a remove. Not an infrequent temperament of the times, such longing of the pampered or the intellectual to be in touch with vital things was found among men as well as women and expressed in reactionary as well as rebellious politics, but for educated women in particular it was an expression of their alienation from the restricted genteel world conventionally allowed them.

By 1910 more than a few educated and prosperous women intensified their search for real "life and labor"—the name chosen in 1910 by the WTUL for its journal—by aligning themselves with wage-earning women who were visibly manifesting insurgent spirit. For instance, Maud Younger, born to wealthy parents in San Francisco, educated in private schools, and sent to Europe, began a stint at the College Settlement in New York in 1901, on an impulse. "I went to see it Monday, and Tuesday went to stay. I went for a week but stayed five years." There she was converted to trade unionism, woman suffrage, and protective labor legislation. Later in life, when Alice Paul (who had done similar work) criticized the relationship between settlement house residents and the tenement community—calling it "artificial" because the residents formed a "favored class"—Younger had to assent, but at the time she simply saw herself as united to working women's struggle for justice. She joined the WTUL's efforts in 1904 and signed up with the Waitresses Union in 1907 when she took a wage-earning job herself (and wrote about it for *Mc-Clure's Magazine*). Returning to San Francisco in 1908, she led in forming a Waitresses Union there. In the California campaign for woman suffrage, she organized the Wage Earners' Equal Suffrage League, which she represented on the five-member state Central Campaign Committee while she was the delegate of the Waitresses Union on the Central Trades and Labor Council. Effective in the successful contemporary effort to obtain an eight-hour law for women workers in California, when she came back East in 1912 she picketed with the White Goods strikers in New York and lobbied with the WTUL for protective labor legislation in the nation's capital.[35] Between suffragists' demonstrations and working women's self-assertions, a reciprocally influential escalation was taking place. All across the country, women seemed determined to extend the boundaries and raise the stakes of the woman movement.

In that percolating environment Feminism, the revolution of rising expectations, came forth. Here were its envoys:

> They are all social workers, or magazine writers in a small way. They are decidedly emancipated and advanced, and so thoroughly healthy and zestful, or at least it seems so to my unsophisticated masculine sense. They shock you constantly. . . .They have an amazing combination of wisdom and youthfulness, of humor and ability, and innocence and self-reliance, which absolutely belies everything you will read in the story-books or any other description of womankind.

They are of course all self-supporting and independent, and they
enjoy the adventure of life; the full, reliant, audacious way in which
they go about makes you wonder if the new woman isn't to be a very
splendid sort of person. . . . They talk much about the "Human Sex,"
which they claim to have invented, and which is simply a generic
name for those whose masculine brutalities and egotisms and feminine pettinesses and stupidities have been purged away so that
there is left stuff for a genuine comradeship and healthy frank regard
and understanding.

Thus a perceptive young Columbia University graduate, the *New Republic* essayist Randolph Bourne, described a feminist "salon" of young
women who lived in Greenwich Village. One of the cohort of progressive
intellectuals in New York, Bourne perhaps more readily identified with
the rebellious "outsider" status women felt because his physical stature
as a hunchbacked dwarf put him outside the male norm.[36]

The women who lifted the banner of Feminism had, by and large,
already welcomed the idea of radical and irreverent behavior in the labor
movement, art, or politics. Although it was a worrisome diversion from
class analysis for Marxists, Feminism was born ideologically on the left of
the political spectrum, first espoused by women who were familiar with
advocacy of socialism and who, advantaged by bourgeois backgrounds,
nonetheless identified more with labor than with capital and hoped for
the elimination of exploitation by capital and the intervention of a democratically controlled state. They considered themselves socialists or progressives leaning toward socialism and had, unlike most of the American
population, a tolerance for "isms." They embedded their critique of gender hierarchy in a critique of the social system. Feminism appealed to
them in part because of their awareness of contemporary socialism, and
because of seeming analogies between feminism's and socialism's analyses of group oppression and proposals of social transformation. In the
New Review, a journal of socialist intellectuals just starting in 1914, Mary
White Ovington (who five years earlier had been one of the white co-
founders of the NAACP) paired Feminism with Socialism, calling them
"the two greatest movements of today."[37]

A powerful model of disruption was also provided by the English militants, with whom feminists welcomed identification as much as the
NAWSA leadership feared it. Staid U.S. journals reflected the English
situation in titles such as "How to Repress the Suffragettes" or "What
Should Be Done with the Wild Women," but when Emmeline Pank-

hurst, just out of prison, crossed the Atlantic to raise money for her cause, her detention at Ellis Island at the British government's request drove U.S. suffragists to furious empathy. Once she was released, she received an overwhelming reception, Harriot Stanton Blatch recalled. Edna Kenton saw the English "militant women" as a symbol of the "spiritual militancy" developing more widely in women, "a highly significant part of the general unrest that is burrowing beneath old codes, undermining old values and ideals, and tossing them up into unsteady mountains of broken sepulchers and moldy rubbish." Mary Heaton Vorse cheered their violence, writing to a friend, "I cannot imagine anything that would affect better the moral health of any country than something which would blast the greatest number of that indecent, immoral institution—the perfect lady—out of doors and set them smashing and rioting."[38]

Feminism partook of the free-ranging spirit of rebellion of the time, which exploded in many forms, from the Ashcan School of painting to the "one big union" idea of the Industrial Workers of the World. The joyfully self-important motive to flout convention, épater les bourgeois, belonged to Feminism as well as to other contemporaneous forms of cultural blasphemy. Feminism severed the ties the woman movement had to Christianity and conventional respectability. "Am I the Christian gentlewoman my mother slaved to make me? No indeed," Genevieve Taggard catechized herself while a student at the University of California at Berkeley in the 1910s, already a socialist familiar with the literary radicals in San Francisco; "I am a poet, a wine-bibber, a radical; a non-church-goer who will no longer sing in the church choir or lead prayer meeting with a testimonial." As a joke, on the suffrage campaign trail, the young Nebraskan Doris Stevens wrote to her Oregon friend Sara Bard Field—who had divorced her husband, a minister, against his resistance—inquiring if she believed in prayer and if so would she invoke a deity ("to follow the conventional habit of men") at an upcoming suffragist convention. Field responded that she had "quit the prayer-business some years ago" and "had no speaking acquaintance with any deity and hence could not supplicate him her or it."[39]

Like the radicalism of contemporary male intellectuals, Feminism infused political claims with cultural meaning and vice-versa. Feminism was a "revolt against formalism" (in the phrase of a historian of contemporary intellectual trends): a refusal to heed the abstraction of womanhood as it had been handed down, a refusal intrinsic to the "conscious attempt"—as radical Edna Kenton put it—"to realize Personality," to achieve self-determination through life, growth, and experience. Feminism was a revolt "as much against Woman as Man—both of those are capitalized impersonalities!" Not the "source of all evil," not "more deadly than the male"—not, indeed, summarizable in any such abstract and formal shibboleth—women must be acknowledged to be "people of flesh and blood and brain, feeling, seeing, judging and directing equally with men, all the great social forces," Mary Ritter Beard, trade-union supporter and avid suffragist, insisted. Charlotte Perkins Gilman described the Feminist: "Here she comes, running, out of prison and off pedestal; chains off, crown off, halo off, just a live woman."[40]

As a movement of consciousness, Feminism intended to transform the ideas of submission and femininity that had been inculcated in women; the suffrage movement provided a ready vehicle for propagating this vision with imagination and ingenuity. Feminism relied on the existence and the communications networks of the suffrage agitation to become a movement. With nothing specific to sign, nothing specific to join, it was not a movement whose numbers are easily recoverable, but it quickly spread from New York to other urban locales wherever intellectuals and activists grasped the term to name their uncharted assertions and yearnings not expressed in palpable goals such as the suffrage. So far as Feminism's changing of consciousness depended on creating a community of struggle, the suffrage movement provided a ready community—though depending on their predilections, suffragists of different sorts took or left the connections Feminists drew between woman suffrage and more radical transformation of women's status. The suffrage movement, larger in numbers, and Feminism, larger in intents, were separable yet overlapping and reciprocally influential. Feminists' presence in the suffrage movement broadened its margins, while the suffrage campaign gave them a platform.

Yet to some extent Feminism was a reaction against an emphasis in the woman movement itself, the stress on nurturant service and moral uplift. A "restless woman" would brag that she was "doing the world some good" but just as important, "having a better time than any woman in the world ever had before." When the woman movement of the 1910s stressed woman's duties, Feminists reinvigorated demands for women's rights. They took as a mentor the democratic theorist Mary Wollstonecraft and revered her for her norm-defying sexual life as well as for her vindication of the rights of women. Feminists forthrightly demanded "the removal of all social, political, economic and other discriminations which are based upon sex, and the award of all rights and duties in all fields on the basis of individual capacity alone," in the language of the Feminist Alliance led by Henrietta Rodman.[41] Under their witty treatment the conception of woman's rights underwent luxuriant growth. At a feminist mass meeting in New York in 1914, on a program entitled "Breaking into the Human Race," Rheta Childe Dorr spoke on the right to work; Beatrice Forbes-Robertson Hale, author of the 1914 book *What Women Want: An Interpretation of the Feminist Movement,* on the right of a mother to follow her profession; actress Mary Shaw on the right to one's convictions; Fola LaFollette (also an actress, the daughter of Wisconsin's Senator Robert LaFollette) on the right to keep one's name; Rose Schneiderman on the right to organize; Charlotte Perkins Gilman on the right to specialize in home industries; and Nina Wilcox Putnam on the right to ignore fashion.

That mass meeting was a project of a group of women gathered under the leadership of Marie Jenny Howe, who named their circle Heterodoxy because it "only . . . demanded of a member that she should not be orthodox in her opinions," as one recalled. Beginning with twenty-five women in 1912, Heterodoxy epitomized the Feminism of the time. Howe, a middle-aged nonpracticing minister and the wife of noted Progressive municipal reformer Frederic C. Howe, started the group shortly after she moved to New York from Cleveland. Authors Dorr and Inez Haynes Gillmore were both early members, and so were journalist Mary Heaton Vorse, psychologist Leta Stetter Hollingworth, anthropologist Elsie Clews Parsons, socialist trade unionist Rose Pastor Stokes, lawyer Elinor Byrns, and many other equally spirited souls. The first "feminist mass meeting" called by Heterodoxy had featured schoolteacher Rodman, who spoke on her cooperative living scheme to solve the problem of professional women's housework; Frances Perkins (later secretary of labor under FDR), at that time an industrial investigator who had kept her "maiden" name when she married, like many Village Feminists; and Crystal Eastman, a lawyer, social investigator, and political and cultural radical. Several men sympathetic to Feminism also spoke, including Floyd Dell, his coeditor at the *Masses* Max Eastman (who was Crystal Eastman's brother and the husband of Ida Rauh), publicist George Creel, dramatist George Middleton (husband of Fola LaFollette), and nationally known newspaper columnist Will Irwin (who would marry Inez Haynes Gillmore). Heterodoxy provided "a glimpse of the women of the future, big spirited, intellectually alert, devoid of the old 'femininity,'" said member Elizabeth Gurley Flynn, a socialist and organizer for the Industrial Workers of the World.

"We thought we discussed the whole field," Dorr reflected on the years from 1912 to 1917, "but we really discussed ourselves."[42] At regular Saturday meetings, through speakers and raging discussions, Heterodoxy members learned about cultural, political, and scientific innovations— "twilight sleep" during childbirth, the progress of the Socialist Party, psychoanalysis, or a new play—and assessed how these affected them as women. A consciousness-raising group before the term was invented, Heterodoxy illustrated how far Feminism, born in an era of social tumult as an ideology of women's social awakening, was nonetheless inward-looking and individualistic. Together with Feminism's manifestations in social action in the 1910s individual psychic freedom stood as its central aim, reiterating a principle of long standing in the women's rights tradition. From Elizabeth Oakes Smith's emphasis on women's "singleness of thought" in the 1850s to Elizabeth Cady Stanton's evocation of "The Solitude of Self" in the 1880s, nineteenth-century spokeswomen had voiced women's individuality of temperament, unpredetermined by gender or by family role, as at least a minor and sometimes a major theme.[43] Individualism—in the sense of self-development—became much more pronounced in the Feminism of the 1910s, as the Heterodoxy title "Breaking into the Human Race" implied.

"We intend simply to be ourselves," Howe declared, "not just our little female selves, but our whole big human selves." By the early twentieth century it was a commonplace that the New Woman stood for self-development as contrasted to self-sacrifice or submergence in the family. Individualism for women had come of age, so to speak. The material conditions of wage-earning and urban settlement made it feasible for a significant minority of women to distinguish themselves from the lot of women, to assert individual choice in livelihood, personal relationships, and habit of dress and living. None did this more fully than Feminists themselves. Elsie Clews Parsons even drolly foresaw the day when her 1914 volume on female customs and taboo would be gathered up in a Woman's Museum with "specimens of women's industries and arts . . . the first law brief or the first novel written by her," to show "to a doubting posterity that once women were a distinct social class." For the moment, however, the suffrage agitation clearly marked how far women did constitute a distinct social class, a disfranchised political class. Self-proclaimed Feminists held individualism in dynamic tension with their political and social identification as women. "What a Unity this group of free-willed, self-willed women has become," the Heterodoxy members— who called themselves "the most unruly and individualistic females you ever fell among,"—reflected on their own paradox.[44] They moved toward

a definition of women's common political task and consciousness that relied less on that staple of the nineteenth-century woman movement, the
uniting theme of motherhood, than on the themes of deprivations and
rebellions felt in common by women of various sorts.

Even in the turbulent political environment of the prewar years, the
profound ambitions and ambiguities of Feminism required an exceptional wrench from the status quo that only a minority could conceivably
make. Despite the economic changes that had brought women into the
paid labor force, despite the improving rates of women's entry into
higher education and the professions, and despite the collective and political strengths women had shown through voluntary organization, the
vast majority of the population understood women not as existential subjects, but as dutiful daughters, wives, and mothers. The effort to find
release from the "family claim," which settlement leader Jane Addams
had eloquently described in the 1880s, was being painfully repeated decade after decade. Even a college graduate struggling to establish an independent life and work for herself might have to record ruefully, as
Hilda Smith did, that "our families make us feel like murderers instead
of joyous adventurers."[45]

Feminism, as the Heterodoxy membership and interests made clear,
was the province first of all of women highly educated, either formally in
colleges and graduate schools or informally in the labor or socialist movement, women busy with worldly, not domestic, occupations. The strong
presence of women who had been to college and even graduate or
professional school among early Feminists—as among the new generation of leaders in the suffrage movement, especially those who endorsed
militance—was remarkable in an era in which only a tiny proportion of
women or men had higher education. The proportion of eighteen- to
twenty-one-year olds in the United States enrolled as undergraduates in
degree programs was on the increase, from under 4 percent of all in 1900
to nearly 8 percent in 1920. Women comprised a growing proportion of
these students—40 percent in 1910, almost half in 1920. This small proportion did not come from the highest levels of wealth—upper-class
women did not go to college—but were a self-selected minority of those
just below and into the solid middle class. Going to college in this period
was certainly a badge of class privilege and yet for women it was also a
badge of aspiration beyond the ordinary horizons of one's sex.[46]

The education or training of these early Feminists was one very significant measure of their unusual status; the independent livelihoods they
were pursuing was another. The principle of freedom to choose one's

work regardless of sex and regardless of marriage was a central tenet for Feminists. Their most influential mentor in this effort was Charlotte Perkins Gilman (herself a Heterodoxy member). Since the 1890s, from California to the East Coast, as a soul-stirring speaker and a prolific writer, Gilman had been conveying her critique of the "sexuo-economic" relation that she saw binding women to men, molding women to exaggerate sex-specific characteristics and to rely on men as economic providers. Gilman elevated into a theory of social evolution the changes that perspicacious women saw happening around them; she urged women to move in the direction already pointed out, by leaving their ancient unspecialized home occupation, following the path marked by modern industry and professions, and exercising their full human capacities in useful work of all sorts. She proposed, furthermore, the socialization of remaining home employments such as cooking and laundry and argued that housecleaning and childcare would be better performed by specialized paid employees than by housewives and mothers not necessarily suited and not paid for the tasks.[47]

Gilman's themes were reinvigorated when Olive Schreiner, a white South African novelist renowned for her *Story of an African Farm*, published her magnum opus, *Woman and Labor*, in the United States and England in 1911. "We take all labor for our province!" Schreiner declaimed. In compelling and timely prose—for in 1910s women made not only unique gains in unionization but also unique inroads into the male-dominated professions—Schreiner lambasted female "parasitism," her denotation of women's economic subordination to and reliance on men. She dignified women's self-expression and social contribution through their chosen work, and her focus found many adherents in the United States. In Seattle, when the formerly cautious members of the Card and Label League announced that they were "commencing to think for themselves," they cited Schreiner's critique of parasitism. Deciding to widen their horizons beyond the household, they turned the league into a "training school for women" and barred men from their afternoon meetings.

Schreiner was also a prophetess of women's sexual release. As youths in England in the 1880s she and Havelock Ellis, the budding philosopher of sex, were intimates, sharing the belief that women's sexual passions were no less than men's. In Schreiner's *Women and Labor*, economic freedom went hand in glove with heterosexual attraction and intimacy. Schreiner saw the free play of women's talents and intellectual powers as a stimulus rather than a burden to love between the sexes. More emphatically than Gilman (who also foresaw finer marriages once women shook off the sexuo-economic bond), Schreiner promised that economic independence would bring a "closer, more permanent, more emotionally and intellectually complete relation between the individual man and woman."[48]

That vision combining equality of economic choice with heterosexual intimacy was essential to Feminism in the 1910s. Severing the ties the woman movement had to Christianity, Feminism also abandoned the stance of moral superiority, which was tied to sexual "purity," and evoked instead women's sexuality. Again redefining rights, Feminism asserted "sex rights on the part of women"—as Inez Milholland, recent graduate of Vassar and law school and a dazzling and adventurous suffragist, put it. The younger women who claimed the name of Feminists marched off the path long trod by women critics of the double standard. Unlike a long line of Anglo-American evangelical women, who insisted that men adhere to the same canon of sexual respectability that governed women—and unlike Christabel Pankhurst, whose demand for a single standard of morality was epitomized in her notorious slogan "Votes for Women and Chastity for Men"—they urged a single standard balanced in the direction of heterosexual freedom for women. Feminists were determined to be "frank" about sex, which meant (to them) to acknowledge openly that sexual drives were as constitutive of women's nature as of men's. They reformulated in terms of principle the loosening of sexual behavior that had preceded them not among purposive women reformers (except for a handful of late nineteenth-century "free lovers") but among working-class adolescents, bohemians, and entertainers.[49]

Sex outside of marriage in the 1910s was outlawry befitting Feminist aims to explode the understructure of conventional society. It involved a transvaluation of values, erasing the boundaries between the "pure" and the "fallen" woman. It was a personal form of direct action as risky, as thrilling, as full of a paradoxical sense of play and deadly responsibility as throwing a bomb. Philadelphian Miriam Allen de Ford, a college graduate and suffragist, composed an "Apologia" to mark her sexual initiation at age twenty-six:

> Why am I writing this? The world of conservatives will never understand it; the world of radicals needs no explanation. To the world at large I am an outcast, and it is true I have deliberately excommunicated myself. . . .
>   If I have any justification, it is this:—

I was being sapped, strangled, exploited, blinded by a decaying civilization. A man came, and tore the bindings from me and showed me freedom and the light of day. No matter *what* happened, that was my soul's salvation. I have taken it and embraced it all—the Social Revolution, the life of rebellion, the certainty of misunderstanding, slander and heartbreak. Fate made my chance come just when I was most bound to the old and had to break most bonds to get free. I had to take it when I could get it, or else be stifled forever by the horrible, sugar-coated world of reform and philanthropy in which I lived. Besides, I owed a certain debt to the man who had shown me this awful truth, not to keep from him any longer the happiness he could find in me. . . .

If the man who gave me this vision had no love-connection with me; if he were to leave me tomorrow; if the whole question of my personal relations with him were eliminated; I should do just as I am doing. . . . The world's honor is my degradation; the world's condemnation must be my pride and victory.[50]

De Ford may have been given to self-dramatization. Another Feminist offered a more casual view of women's sexual adventures outside marriage in an anthropological spoof called "Marriage Customs and Taboo Among the Early Heterodites." "Three types of sex relationships may be observed, practiced by those who call themselves *monotonists, varietists,* and *resistants,*" it recorded. "Most of the *monotonists* were mated young and by pressure of habit and circumstance have remained mated. The *varietists* have never been ceremonially mated but have preferred a succession of matings. The *resistants* have not mated at all. (Note: True resistants are rare. As virginity is an asset outside of monotony many varietists assume an outward resistancy. I recall one resistant who had cleverly concealed 18 varieties of mating, because as she confessed her economic status depended upon her virginity.)" And so on, regarding the "marriage union label," Sangerism, deceptive ring wearing, and other parodic descriptions.[51]

Yet Feminists did not make very clear what were meant by women's sex rights beyond the basic acknowledgement of erotic drives, which might be said by 1912 to be a staple of sophisticated urban discourse. (Even a *Nation* reviewer that year maintained, "As for the right of women to a frank enjoyment of the sensuous side of the sex-relation . . . no sensible person now disputes that right, but only, as in the case of men, the right to make it a subject of common conversation.") They did not make clear how sex rights related to marriage, or monogamy, or homosexual as well as heterosexual relationships. Certainly their aims stemmed from a generally critical attitude toward the failings of bourgeois marriage, not only for harboring male tyranny but for dull predictability and emotional barrenness. Louise Bryant, a Portland, Oregon, radical, reported scornfully to Sara Bard Field in 1916 that the town was full of gossip about herself and John Reed, "discussing our most intimate affairs and saying, 'Of course Jack won't marry her.' As if *marriage*, that most diabolic law of all laws—could *purify* anything!" She described their relationship, in contrast, as "so free": "We don't interfere with each other at all, we just sort of supplement, and life is very lovely to us—we feel like children who will never grow up." As Bryant implied, their drift was less to destroy monogamy than to restore it to value, based in egalitarian companionability and mutual desire, whether blessed by the state or church or not. But even the most restless women at this time found the theory of nonmarital sex easier to swallow than the continued practice of it. Feminists who found male partners did marry (and divorce and remarry), often keeping their maiden names, trying for egalitarian relationships. "I am trying for nothing so hard in my own personal life as how not to be respectable when married," was Mary Heaton Vorse's compromise.[52]

Not only was there no consensus on these questions but feminist suffragists more or less agreed that experimentation involving these issues should be kept separate from the campaign for suffrage, so, although one heard about sexual freedom "on all sides," as Mary Austin recalled, "one heard about it in connection with prominent suffragettes, but not directly. There was a disposition to keep such matters to one's self." Older suffragists hastened to disavow any connection between the vote for women and sexual promiscuity, for free love was a bogey that anti-suffragists had been warning about for decades. Indeed, anti-suffrage writers of the early 1910s very quickly discerned that Feminism was even more alarming than suffragism because of its combined emphasis on women's economic independence and sex rights along with the vote. To opponents of women's self-assertion, the vision of women deploying their own sexuality appeared just as aggressive as their claim to support themselves, and just as threatening to men as insistence on male chastity was. Regardless of Feminists' pursuit of heterosexual adventures and their promises that men would have more fun, they were accused of "sex-antagonism." By ancient cultural tradition, the loosing of women's sexual desire from men's control released the fiendish contents of Pandora's box. In the very years that feminists were articulating this threat, the thrill and the fear female sexual assertiveness posed to male control was translated into mass culture by the vamp star of the silent screen, Theda Bara. She reigned supreme from 1913 to 1916, her role emblematic of the simultaneous allure and threat to the social order contained in the female erotic. In Bara's own view, her role expressed female assertiveness unseating male hegemony. "Women are my greatest fans," she said, "because they see in my vampire the impersonal vengeance of all their unavenged wrongs. . . . I am in effect a feministe."[53]

Feminists assigned more liberatory meaning and value to passionate heterosexual attachment than did any woman's rights advocates before them. Seeing sexual desire as healthy and joyful, they assumed that free women could meet men as equals on the terrain of sexual desire just as on the terrain of political representation or professional expertise. Inauthenticity seemed a greater danger than sexual exploitation. As pioneers of heterosexual freedom, Feminists were far from acknowledging publicly the potential for submergence of women's individuality and personality in heterosexual love relationships, or the potential for men's sexual exploitation of women who purposely broke the bounds of conventional sexual restraint. In private they saw, inevitably, travesties of their ideal. "I am sure the emancipated man is a myth sprung from our hope and eternal aspiration," Doris Stevens admitted to Sara Bard Field in a blinding moment of truth. Relationships with women were the consoling counterpoint and sometimes the replacement for relationships with men. The liberatory value that they assigned to heterosexual affairs did not prevent them from valuing as much or more their emotional relationships with women. The members of Heterodoxy included heterosexual, bisexual, and lesbian women, who coexisted harmoniously in apparent respect for each others' choices. The letters of women on the suffrage trail spoke passionately of their appreciation for one another, regardless of their heterosexual involvements and sometimes in explicit comparison to them. Doris Stevens and Sara Bard Field, for example, both were deeply involved with men and yet Stevens wrote to Field that despite her lover's being "devotion personified," Sara was "the only human in my life whom I love without reservation"; "my love for Dudley doesn't touch yours." Both perceived the omnipresent potential for domination in loving men. Field, despite her fervent devotion to her lover, conceded that "he covers me as a man *can* love," and Stevens responded that this "made me quite sad for I know it's true. Even dear unselfish Dudley hems me in so that it is he or no one."[54]

The difficulties that sexuality brought to the Feminist agenda were highlighted in the influential work of Ellen Key, a Swedish writer. In 1912 Key was regarded as a "tremendous radical," and "everybody who used to read Charlotte Perkins Gilman was now reading [her]," Rheta Childe Dorr remembered, although her "very name was anathema to most suffragists." Key was one of many European theorists to whom American rebels looked for justifications of changing sex morality. Havelock Ellis, one of the English New Moralists, who had assaulted the Victorian notion that women were sexually anesthetic and given new scientific attention and spiritual relevance to sex, was read avidly in the United States at the turn of the century. Ellis was the mentor sought out by birth control pioneer Margaret Sanger in 1914 when she traveled to England to escape U.S. prosecution. By that time Sigmund Freud's revolutionary ideas about sexuality and the unconscious were burning a path among vanguard intellectuals in Greenwich Village. Key magnetized women in particular, however, because she was a woman and she wrote all about *female* sexual fulfillment. Key's *Century of the Child* was translated and published in the United States in 1910, her *Love and Marriage*—which *Harper's Weekly* editor Norman Hapgood judged "probably had a profounder influence in this field than any other book since John Stuart Mill's *Subjection of Women*"—in 1911, *The Woman Movement* in 1912, and *Renaissance of Motherhood* in 1914.[55]

Like Ellis (who wrote the introductions to the American editions of her books), Key romanticized female eroticism and, like most apostles of sexual liberation of the time, linked erotic life to bodily health and spiritual harmony. She claimed that women's true fulfillment was sex-specific, intrinsically bound to the nurturance expressed in maternity—just as nineteenth-century conventions had it—but she broke through the Victorian separation between motherhood and female eroticism and linked "motherliness" to heterosexual desire, itself sacred and self-validating. She argued that women should be free to form love relationships and should be able to end marriages which did not bring them sexual satisfaction. Only those marriage that consummated and enshrined sexual love were valid, in her view.

Refusing to bow to respectability or to legal or patriarchal authority for women's sexual activity, Key was a radical. She repudiated the concept of illegitimate birth and championed unwed mothers. A socialist opposed in principle to the economic dependence of women on men, she argued that marriage when joined was an economic partnership in which the wife/mother earned and should own half of her husband's wages or assets. For single mothers she advocated state subsidy or "motherhood endowment" by which the state would recognize maternal labor. Incorporating many of Key's ideas, the Bund für Mutterschutz und Sexualreform, founded in 1904 in Leipzig (with Key in attendance), aimed to equalize the legal rights of husband and wife, to legitimize "free unions," to bring state support to unmarried mothers, and (in a significant policy advance beyond Key) to make birth control legal and available. As it generated both tremendous resistance and eager support, the New Morality espoused by Mutterschutz proponents was the central issue in the German women's movement in the early twentieth century. Its political leaders, Adele Schreiber and Helene Stocker, vigorously challenged the patriarchal family for subjugating women and the state for failing to support and acknowledge mothers' (including unmarried mothers) work of childrearing. In Scandinavia, too, Key's ideas were reformulated into social policies pushed through by women reformers. Norwegian legislation of 1915, for example, regularized the status of and allowed state support for the unwed mother's child.

Some American women were deeply impressed with Scandinavian and German women's efforts of this sort and saw them as far more fundamental than the aim for political rights, far more radical because they "would change not only law but custom, would reverse the attitude of mind towards marriage," so Chicago philanthropist and philosopher Ethel Sturges Dummer thought. Her friend Katherine Anthony, a Heterodoxite and the author of a social investigation of employed working-class mothers, agreed that the European women's emphasis on the "triumph of volitional motherhood over sex slavery" was essential to feminism. Anthony researched and published in 1915 a book on *Feminism in Germany and Scandinavia*. In her view, those movements aimed to steer clear of the property relations of patriarchal marriage, while enabling women to express their sexuality in "possessionless sex."

Key's ideas posed problems to Feminists because she envisioned a sex-specific destiny for women, where they looked for the "human sex." Anti-sentimental and anti-patriarchal, Key nonetheless glorified the redeeming value of motherhood and believed that women who achieved the satisfaction of heterosexual love should fulfill themselves as mothers. Katherine Anthony called Key a "wise fool," admitting that there was much "dross" in her "genius" but continuing to admire the Mutterschutz feminists for attempting a "new science of womanhood" neither observant of old gender constraints nor emulative of men. Dorr baldly judged Key a "reactionary" except for her assault on the double standard of sexual morality.[56]

Many women, however, seem to have taken what they wanted to hear

from Key's message, making her principally an apostle of women's sexual
liberation and secondarily a voice urging women not to adopt the male
as a model. Of Feminist spokeswomen of the 1910s, birth control agitator
Margaret Sanger most wholly incorporated Key's ideas. When she
founded her law-defying newspaper, the *Woman Rebel*, in the spring of
1914, Sanger located the "basis of Feminism" less in "masculine-domi-
nated" concerns such as employment than in "the right to be a mother
regardless of church or state." Not only her contempt for marriage law
but also her view of erotic desire as sacred and her championing of a
"feminine element" or "absolute, elemental, inner urge of womanhood"
bespoke Key's and Ellis's influence. The birth control movement in the
1910s, however, appealed to Feminists on many counts and was the most
obvious political form their ideas on sexuality took. Stirred up by anarchist and labor leaders such as Emma Goldman, the birth control movement challenged conventional respectability both by speaking of sex and
by linking sex oppression to class oppression. It spoke for women's exercise of their sexuality and control of their reproductive capacity free of
state interference. Neither the economic independence nor the heterosexual freedom on the Feminist agenda were possible without birth control. Acknowledging the range of opinion within Feminism, Crystal Eastman insisted, "Birth Control is an elementary essential in all aspects of
feminism. Whether we are the special followers of Alice Paul, or Ruth
Law, or Ellen Key, or Olive Schreiner, we must all be followers of Margaret Sanger."[57]

Key argued that the American emphasis on women's right to work outside the home was misplaced, since women's freedom and happiness
were not to be gained through emulation of or competition with men in
the economic or political arena. (In the 1890s she had even opposed
woman suffrage, though she switched to support in 1905.) Charlotte Perkins Gilman found Key's position the antithesis of her own. In a series of
articles published between 1912 and 1914, Key and Gilman sparred, in
the process bringing the term Feminism and the question of its definition to public attention. Key attacked Gilman and Schreiner by name for
their emphasis on women's performance in arenas dominated by men;
she labelled the consequences of mothers' working outside the home
"socially pernicious, racially wasteful and soul-withering" and in contrast
boosted "motherliness" as women's personal and social contribution, the
fount of altruism, unselfish ethics and social cooperation. Gilman responded by perceiving that "what is now so generally called Feminism is
not only a thing quite outside of the Suffrage question, but also a movement in more than one general direction." She called the two schools,

quite divergent in spirit, the Human Feminists (like herself) and the Female Feminists (like Key). "The one holds that sex is a minor department of life; that the main lines of human development have nothing to do with sex, and that what women need most is the development of human characteristics. The other considers sex as paramount, as underlying or covering all phases of life, and that what woman needs is an even fuller exercise, development and recognition of her sex." Gilman concluded her assessment of Key by acknowledging, "whatever it is called and however it expresses itself, the Feminist movement spreads wider, strikes deeper, aims higher, every day."[58]

As Katherine Anthony succinctly described it, Feminism in the 1910s had *two* "dominating ideas": "the emancipation of woman both as a human-being and as a sex-being." Another woman defined the Feminist as someone who "believes in her own sex, is proud of it, and claims for it equal opportunities with men in all walks of life and endeavors."[59] These divergent emphases did not cause real fissures within Feminism at the time. Rather, the simultaneous influence of Gilman and Key represented Feminism's characteristic doubleness, its simultaneous affirmation of women's human rights and women's unique needs and differences. Feminists wanted, soundly enough, to have it both ways—to like men and in some respects to *be* like men, while being loyal politically and ideologically to their own sex; to have an expanded concept of womanhood while proclaiming the variability of individuals within the sex. What distinguished the Feminism of the 1910s was its very multifaceted constitution, the fact that its several strands were all loudly voiced and mutually recognized as part of the same phenomenon of female avant-garde self-assertion. None of its single tenets was brand new, not the claim for full citizenship, nor for equal wages for equal work, nor even for equal *work*, nor for psychic freedom and spiritual autonomy, nor even for sexual liberation, nor for wives' independence. Each of these points had been made at some time, piecemeal, by women before. In the 1910s a significant minority of women elevated these demands to new flamboyance and intensity in combination, naming their constellation Feminism, conceding the revolutionary openendedness and sometime internal contradictions of their project and making that formlessness, that lack of certain boundaries, that potential to encompass opposites, into virtues. Their leaders were secular and educated women used to functioning—though not at the full power they desired—in a world of women and men. They relied on political consciousness and solidarity among women as a group to pursue an even better integrated world of women and men.

The tradition of political action and argumentation laid down by the woman movement was crucial to Feminism's coherence in the 1910s; the contemporary suffrage and labor movements and experiments in radical art and politics supplied the soil in which it grew like an organism. In its genesis Feminism was full of double aims, joining the concept of women's equality with men to the concept of women's sexual difference, joining the aim of antinomian individual release with concerted social action, endorsing the "human sex" while deploying political solidarity among women. Whether these paradoxes would prove fault lines or sources of spiraling growth, time would tell.

2

THE WOMAN'S PARTY

National Woman's Party demonstration outside Democratic National Convention, Chicago, August 1916.

Feminism and "militance" were not the same thing, but common parlance linked them. In 1913, a new national woman suffrage group was founded, and if there was any suffrage organization to which Feminists would likely be drawn, it was this one which identified itself with militant action: the Congressional Union. The brainchild of Alice Paul and Lucy Burns, it produced the Woman's Party in 1916 and shortly afterward the National Woman's Party. This group would take up the term Feminism and become the prime mover in giving it a political and organizational dimension once the ballot was gained.

The seeds for the Congressional Union were planted when Paul and Burns talked their way onto the long-standing but inactive Congressional Committee of the National American Woman Suffrage Association, which was supposed to promote woman suffrage via an amendment to the federal Constitution. Not yet thirty, charismatic, and temperamentally ascetic, Alice Paul had graduated from Swarthmore College (in accord with her Quaker upbringing) in 1905. After spending the next few years in settlement house and charitable work, she enrolled in the London School of Economics in 1908–09. Drawn in by the exploits of the militant suffragettes, she plunged into the movement in England and was arrested and jailed more than once. The following year she returned to the United States to enter a Ph. D. program at the University of Pennsylvania. In Philadelphia she took up with the suffrage movement, cultivating contacts across the board from industrial workers to wealthy sympathizers. In 1912 Paul resumed a friendship with Lucy Burns, forged in 1909 in London. Burns, of Irish-Catholic parentage, was also young, headstrong, and highly educated, a Vassar graduate (1902) who had subsequently studied languages in German universities and then, magnetized by the suffragettes, had traveled as a paid organizer for the Pankhursts' Women's Social and Political Union in Scotland from 1910 to 1912. Paul and Burns initially brought onto the NAWSA Congressional Committee three women whose characteristics predicted the subsequent outreach of the CU: wealthy socialite Dora Lewis (a close coworker with Paul in Philadelphia who became a lifelong ally), experimental Feminist and radical Crystal Eastman, and writer and municipal reformer Mary Ritter Beard. All three had labor movement contacts because they had supported garment strikers in Philadelphia and New York in the preceding few years and all three were, like other serious suffragists, busy with local efforts for state suffrage referenda.[1]

By making connections with the energies of local groups in East Coast cities, the Congressional Committee under Paul's and Burns's leadership in short order engineered an unprecedented march of five thousand suffragists at the Capitol, which took place the day before Woodrow Wilson's inauguration as president in March 1913 and nearly upstaged it. Paul's and Burns's enthusiasms and their intense determination to do things their way diverged so far from the path of NAWSA that in less than a year their Congressional Union was an independent, rival national suffrage organization with its own newspaper, the *Suffragist*. Returning attention to the federal Constitution, on which NAWSA suffragists had not concentrated since 1890, CU strategy harked back to the Civil War era convictions of Elizabeth Cady Stanton and Susan B. Anthony while relying on modern techniques of political organizing and mass media for publicity.

The strategy of the CU to stage grand parades and perpetrate flamboyant incidents in front of lawmakers might have stemmed naturally from native developments, but its decision to "punish the party in power"— its most controversial choice—was patterned after the British suffragettes' experience in a parliamentary system. By 1914 women were enfranchised in nine states. The CU dispatched organizers there to marshal women's votes to defeat Democratic Party candidates because a woman suffrage amendment had not been passed under Woodrow Wilson's administration. In 1916, the group established the Woman's Party, with Nevada historian Anne Martin at its head, in the now twelve states with woman suffrage. It campaigned with even greater vigor against all Democrats, including the incumbent president. "To count in an election," Alice Paul maintained at the time, "you do not have to be the biggest Party, you have to be simply an independent Party that will stand for one object and that cannot be diverted from that object."[2]

To women attracted to the CU this "political" strategy (as contrasted to the NAWSA's traditionally educative approach) symbolized women exercising the power they had, forcing the government to pay attention to them, fighting rather than begging for the ballot. "I believe absolutely in the political way which is the only enlightened way," Mary Beard affirmed, "making the government enfranchise us." The federal emphasis and the personalities and fervor of the CU created strongly positive as well as negative reactions at the grassroots level. Its organizing tactics competed with ongoing state campaigns for suffrage referenda at the same time that its novelty infused the whole suffrage question with new interest. To counter one Massachusetts suffragist's fear that the CU was "planning to duplicate our work (with our one-time workers), carry off our money and leave us in confusion" there was the admiration of a Minnesota leader at the CU's sending "some young women out into the state into places in which there has never been a suffrage meeting. . . . They have gotten up parlor meetings and street meetings in ten counties and over fifteen towns, and they have arranged deputations to three of our Congressmen—all in about two weeks."[3]

The CU made the most of the concurrent expansion of interest in suffrage among women at both ends of the economic spectrum. Like the Pankhursts, Paul and Burns sought to rouse wage-earning women, especially industrial workers, and adopted tactics of labor agitation; they soon gained the adherence of such talented organizers as Margaret Hinchey of the WTUL, Rose Winslow, a Polish-born weaver who had organized for the National Consumers' League, and Chicago trade unionist Josephine Casey. Social activists committed to improving the lives of working women, such as Eastman, Beard, and Lavinia Dock (a public health nurse and leader of the Henry Street settlement), were eagerly drawn in. At the same time, the CU attracted elite adherents. The very imperiousness of its strategy—working at the top, intending to accomplish the feat of woman suffrage for the whole nation by focusing on the small group of federal lawmakers, deploying women's audacious deeds to convince key men—greatly appealed to certain upper-class women. Like the Pankhursts, the CU/NWP was able to turn the elite bias of militance to its advantage, and in more than one way. The more fashionable or renowned the perpetrators of unladylike deeds on behalf of suffrage, the more sensational and newsworthy their behavior appeared; at the same time, wealthy women brought financial resources to their cause, and the connections of those related to or married to men of political influence helped to mitigate punishment by the state.

An immediate CU recruit, who became the financial angel of the group and an important voice, was Alva (Mrs. O. H. P.) Belmont. Paul and Burns and their inner circle, with some trepidation, invited Belmont to join them on the Executive Board in 1914. Over sixty years old, with a reputation for chimerical choices and iron will, Belmont had swept into women's causes just a few years earlier, allowing her fortune to be tapped on behalf of striking garment workers as well as for the suffrage cause. She brought into the CU the membership of the New York suffrage group she had founded, the Political Equity League. Long-festering resentment against her first husband, William Vanderbilt, and memories of the social obloquy she had suffered in divorcing him fueled her ventures. Described by younger women as "hard, flinty, brutal to her 'inferiors,'" Belmont lost little love for women as individuals but saw herself as a leader of the sex. (Doris Stevens once recorded privately, in a spleenful mood, that "even her maid says she is one of only four women in New York who are regarded as blacklisted by domestics in service.") In her resentment of restrictions on women's behavior and her belief that women's "selfness," or expression of self, was a "godly obligation," Belmont was not far from the views of her younger Feminist colleagues, but she differed vastly in her bitter assessments of men and her naked wish for power in the war between the sexes. Belmont's very name evoked the ruling class, a mixed blessing for the CU, realized immediately when the group held its 1914 strategy conference at Belmont's famed Marble House in Newport, Rhode Island, watering place of the robber barons. Mary Ritter Beard, although she encouraged Belmont's alliance, would not attend the meeting for fear it would compromise her credibility in the labor movement. Belmont's presence did warn off some working-class suffrage leaders—Rose Schneiderman, for example—but it drew in donations from rich women.[4]

Although the CU intended to organize a large constituency, it was never a democratically run organization, but a modern, single-issue pressure group. Only a small minority—probably 5 percent—of the crafts on the pro-suffrage sea in the latter 1910s, the CU and NWP made outsize waves because of the devotion and vigor of the organizers and members. Paul's organization charted a course with no contingencies, orienting itself constantly toward a constitutional amendment, its heterogeneous membership accepting direction from above. Paul kept to a narrow course with superb determination. From within her self-perpetuating Executive Committee Paul made autocratic control palatable because of her force of personality and her model devotion to the cause. So long as her object commanded as much fervor as the constitutional route to woman suffrage did, she was highly effective in inspiring and leading what was, in Lenin's term, a "vanguard" party. Although Paul never likened her leadership style to Lenin's, others did.[5]

By virtually all contemporary accounts, Paul was charismatic. "I have seen her very presence in headquarters change in the twinkling of an eye the mood of fifty people," Doris Stevens recounted. "It is not through their affections that she moves them, but through a naked force, a vital force which is indefinable but of which one simply cannot be unaware." Sara Bard Field, esteemed as an orator, appealed to her on one (not untypical) occasion as "dear, wonderful Alice Paul with your great moist violets of eyes that always make me want to be good and with your high, daring soul that makes me want to achieve—not so much for my own sake as for the sake of the race." During the suffrage campaign, according to Inez Haynes Irwin's authorized history of the group, everyone within agreed on Paul's role: "With one accord, they say 'She is the Party.'" A strong sense of her own rectitude and her mission sustained Paul through all travail. Not long after the United States entered World 1917 War I, during some of the NWP's most turbulent days, Paul was rushed to the hospital with Bright's disease, and Sara Bard Field found her there reading the lives of Martin Luther and Prince Kropotkin. To Field's expression of amusement, Paul replied, "Oh their fight—considering their respective eras—was not so dissimilar."[6]

Paul's and Burns' iconoclasm, leading the CU to act boldly even if that caused affront, to reject the predictable decorousness of NAWSA and to affirm that women had political strength (if they would only show it), appealed to women who held the broader agenda of Feminism. Although neither Belmont, nor other wealthy matrons who came to support the CU/NWP, nor Dock, nor Beard for that matter, was especially young, the CU was known as the "younger suffragists." Paul and Burns were much younger than Anna Howard Shaw, who at sixty-seven was the president of NAWSA in 1914, or Carrie Chapman Catt, who was fifty-seven when she took over in 1916. But the temperamental radicalism of the CU was probably as important as chronological age in the way it was seen by both outsiders and insiders as the party of youth.[7] Maverick leaders such as Harriot Stanton Blatch (who was older than Catt), women from disparate locations who preferred to dispense with respectability and get on with the assertion of political demands—such as Maud Younger from California—joined the CU's effort along with "society" and working-class women.

The staff of meagerly paid organizers who traveled around the country for the CU were by and large young women who had entered fully into the Feminist vision and saw themselves as professional stirrers-up; most of them had radical political sympathies. (Newspaperman and friend of labor Frank P. Walsh introduced one, Vivian Pierce of San Francisco, in 1915 as "a radical of radicals," who "might bite a social worker.")[8] Doris Stevens was one, a shrewd and by many accounts beautiful dynamo in her twenties who had graduated from Oberlin College into suffrage campaign work in Montana, Michigan, and Ohio. Attracting the particular interest of Alva Belmont as early as 1913, for years afterward Stevens served as the older woman's ghostwriter and sometime amanuensis, accepting her financial support in calculated fashion in order to persist with her feminist work, even though Belmont's politics and personality often caused her feelings of revulsion. No respecter of the standard proprieties nor of the laws of marriage, Stevens happily considered herself a "firebrand" and carried on love affairs in the 1910s as ardently as she campaigned for suffrage. Her friend Sara Bard Field, ten years older, also exemplified the kind of feminist recruited to the cu/nwp political efforts. Married at eighteen, already a mother, divorced, with a missionary past behind her, an occasional journalist and speaker for radical and labor causes, the lover of a poet and philosophical anarchist twenty years her senior, Field had worked in the Oregon and Nevada suffrage campaigns before joining the Woman's Party campaign in 1916. Convinced that radical redistribution of economic power was necessary, she also spoke for the Industrial Workers of the World, but she gave priority to gaining women "the teeth" to "bite into reforms"; if women did not put their enfranchisement first, she perceived, no one else would.[9]

It "took vision, mentality and political sagacity of an unusual kind to see our principles and to fight for them," Field defended the Woman's Party's 1916 anti-Democratic campaign. "A new sort of woman it took," she insisted, "a militant type, unemotional and logical and yet fired by a desire for justice." In Carrie Chapman Catt's view a "stupendous stupidity" (because of the resentment it would evoke nationwide from Democrats sympathetic to woman suffrage), the effort to "punish the party in power" epitomized the single-issue approach and the particular feminist radicalism of the Woman's Party. They subordinated or sacrificed other political aims in order to make their point about women's enfranchisement. "I do think that you people are doing a ripping stunt and have given suffrage the biggest boost that it has ever had," Helen Marot, a New York trade unionist and *Masses* editor conceded to Field, while having no stomach for it herself: "nothing on God's earth can make me stand for Hughes [the Republican candidate for president]. I know that you do not take him seriously and are only using that as an excuse for your propaganda. But dear Sara, what awful company you have to keep." The political autonomy of Woman's Party adherents in 1916 was symbolized not only in their divergence from most suffragists (conservative or radical) but also in their haranguing the Democratic Party at the same time that many of their husbands or lovers were supporters (and in some cases close allies) of President Wilson. Elizabeth Kent, for example, campaigned for the Woman's Party against Democrats in California, the most populous state where women voted, while her husband, a two-term congressman from the state, headed the league of Independents for Wilson. In years after, although the mass of suffragists remembered it as fundamentally misguided, National Woman's Party stalwarts continued to see their 1916 campaign as what had put woman suffrage on the national agenda.[10]

As 1917 opened, the CU rejoined its western wing to form the National Woman's Party and embarked on a new venture. Following an unsatisfying interview with President Wilson, on January 10, 1917, the NWP sent emissaries to "picket" the White House, carrying banners with the words, "Mr. President, How Long Must Women Wait for Liberty?" Hooted at and even assaulted by roughnecks, the pickets nonetheless persisted daily in their new affront to genteel expectations, making enemies, admirers, and great amounts of newspaper publicity; on Wilson's second inaugural in March 1917, a thousand women marched for hours in an icy rain around the White House—which remained locked. Until June the pickets walked without official intervention, and then arrests for "obstructing traffic," followed by trials in police court, ensued. Like the British suffragettes, NWP pickets never took the option of paying fines, but always went to prison (for its publicity value). By July and August they were receiving sentences of up to sixty days in the Occuquan workhouse, an outdated and ill-maintained facility in Virginia. There, again following the example of the British suffragettes (and, more immediately, of Ethel Byrne, Margaret Sanger's sister, who had been recently imprisoned for distributing birth control devices), they refused to work or eat and had to be force-fed. Alice Paul much later recalled that news of the first imprisonments "led to many resignations from our ranks," but she felt that the party "emerged from all this with, maybe, the sturdier feminists."[11]

The entry of the United States into the Great War, in April 1917, changed the significance of NWP tactics. In convention, the NWP voted to eschew any organizational stance on the war, recognizing its members' varying points of view and reaffirming their common single issue, the ballot. In August, with the country in anti-German furor, NWP banners addressed the President as Kaiser Wilson and accused him of denying to the women of his country the democratic rights he claimed to uphold abroad. When they were mobbed by men on the street, the police stood by, arresting only the pickets. Thousands of NAWSA suffragists (not to mention anti-suffragists), horrified at the picketing, found the NWP's attack on the government during wartime scandalous.

Under Carrie Chapman Catt's leadership, the NAWSA had instituted in 1916 her "winning plan" to orchestrate state-level suffrage campaigns into a drive for the constitutional amendment. (The failure in 1915 of state referenda in Pennsylvania, New York, New Jersey, and Massachusetts had routed more and more suffragists onto the federal path to woman suffrage.) Banking on lawmakers' esteem of women's patriotism, Catt publicly pledged NAWSA to the war effort even before Wilson declared the United States a belligerent. Catt and her lieutenants believed in persuading Wilson in private, not hounding him. Outraged and disgusted with what they saw as absence of political sense as well as decorum in the NWP, they desperately hoped to quarantine their own public image from contamination. That was a difficult feat when the NWP's daring was focusing "the attention of 20,000,000 newspaper readers to the subject of woman suffrage," in the words of the *New York Tribune*. While imprisoned NWP pickets were hunger-striking to protest conditions in the Occuquan workhouse, NAWSA leaders declined to comment on the government's treatment. The NAWSA's failure to sympathize publicly with the pickets' martyrdom brought the NWP some valuable new recruits: the officers of the Connecticut Woman Suffrage Association, for instance, resigned from NAWSA and went to work for the Connecticut NWP, and Sue Shelton White, a Tennessee lawyer and suffrage leader, broke with Catt over this issue.[12]

The NWP's smashing of political and behavioral norms swelled its left wing. At the same time, world-historical events were fatefully redrawing the boundaries between socialism and the progressive left, where a certain amount of fuzziness had been instrumental to the rise of feminism. When the Socialist Party (internationally) opposed participation in the Great War, party members in the United States were internally divided, and prowar progressive reformers found new reason for discriminating socialist from non-socialist allies. Socialist speakers and publications became prime targets for suppression under wartime sedition laws, the more so once the Bolshevik Revolution astounded the world. The unpopularity of the Socialist Party's antiwar stand and new fear of socialism generated by the Bolshevik Revolution necessitated a decision by woman suffrage leaders, who were looking (with more likelihood of success than ever before) for mass appeal yet had been joined and supported for years by socialists. The leadership of NAWSA sloughed off Socialist colleagues, excluding them from speakers' platforms. In the final years of the woman suffrage campaign the NAWSA gave very little credit to Socialist Party contributions. Catt was proud in 1917 to proclaim the NAWSA a "bourgeois movement with nothing radical about it."[13]

In contrast, the NWP kept a neutral stand on socialism as it did on the war, and as a result it became a magnet for socialist suffragists between 1917 and 1919. Pacifists, too, disgusted with NAWSA's jingoism and with Catt's opportunism—for she had a few years earlier played an important role in founding the Woman's Peace Party—gravitated to the NWP. Elinor Byrns, for instance, an insistent pacifist, was in the midst of a speaking and organizing tour in her role as national publicity director for NAWSA when she heard that the officers had pledged the association to the war effort; she resigned immediately by telegram and cancelled all of her speaking engagements. She worked for suffrage thereafter with the NWP. Civil libertarians and labor radicals sympathized with the NWP's identifying the arrested pickets as political prisoners, which turned their banners and picketing into free speech issues in the context of wartime sedition laws. Radical adventurers demonstrating solidarity with militant action for a day joined NWP loyalists on the picket line.[14]

These conjunctions threw fuel on the fire of conservative and anti-suffragist diatribes, which more than ever linked woman suffrage and female emancipation to socialism and like dangers. The journal of the National Association Opposed to Woman Suffrage, the *Woman's Protest*, fulminated, "Pacifist, socialist, feminist, suffragist are all parts of the same movement—a movement which weakens government, corrupts society and threatens the very existence of our great experiment in democracy." The Anti-Suffrage League in Missouri (where state legislators would nonetheless soon grant women the vote) rhetorically queried all 1918 political candidates in St. Louis, "Do you know that there is a close alliance between woman suffrage, Socialism, and Feminism: that Feminism advocates non-motherhood, free love, easy divorce, economic independence for all women, and other demoralising and destructive theories?" and warned that in the six months since women in New York had had the ballot the Socialist vote had increased by half. The national group of anti-suffragists changed the name of its journal to the *Woman Patriot* in mid-1918, adding military preparedness to its concerns, and opened with the salvo, "Antisuffragists to Wage Unceasing War Against Feminism and Socialism."[15] Amid these attacks, Alice Paul's determination to keep the NWP on a one-issue course deepened: only by organizationally supporting the constitutional amendment for woman suffrage, and that alone, could the group keep together its war workers and its pacifists, its rich benefactors and the rest of its heterogeneous adherents.

When the House of Representatives passed a constitutional amendment for woman suffrage on January 10, 1918 (one year to the day after pickets had first appeared at the White House!), the NWP considered it a victory and a vindication. They stopped picketing. After the Senate's failure to pass the amendment (in September) they were back, however, now at Capitol Hill, and they kept up new and shocking demonstrations through the winter of 1918–19, climbing statues, burning "watchfires" in front of the White House while Wilson went to Versailles, setting his "fine words" on democracy aflame as these were announced from the Peace Conference. The Prison Special, a carload of former suffrage prisoners wearing facsimiles of their workhouse garb, toured the country giving speeches. Unemployed munitions workers in Bridgeport, Connecticut, angry at Wilson for ending their union's strike during the war, were recruited by NWP organizers for a watchfire demonstration in January 1919; several of them landed in jail. Louise Bryant, recently returned from witnessing the "ten days that shook the world" with her husband (after all) John Reed, took up residence in NWP headquarters, and was arrested and imprisoned after a watchfire demonstration. When Wilson landed in Boston on his return from Europe in February, and before he embarked again in New York in March, the National Woman's Party mounted large demonstrations which resulted in arrests for "loitering" and similar crimes. The demonstrators were decried as "the I. W. W. of the suffrage movement" by a NAWSA spokeswoman, and the police who restrained them called them Bolsheviks. Nonetheless the wealthy supporters as well as the radical recruits held; in 1919, in an epitome of coalition politics, the NWP mixed Socialists and occupants of the social register, servants and owners of capital, blacks and whites, DARs and new immigrants in common militant purpose.[16]

It took until June 1919 for the United States Senate to pass the suffrage amendment and until August 1920 before the thirty-sixth state ratified it. Both NAWSA and NWP suffragists claimed credit for battling governors' and legislators' indifference or hostility in the final states to ratify.[17] Meanwhile, wartime dislocation and postwar reaction wrenched the political landscape. The federal government's intervention in the national economy during the war, by means of agencies such as the War Industries Board, the Food and Fuel Administration, and the U.S. Employment Service, inspired visions of instituting similar controls for the public welfare in peacetime. As 1919 began, despite curtailment of civil liberties there was eagerness and optimism in the air about the use of the state in creating a new democratic order. From all corners—politicians, professional associations, churches, research agencies—came proposals for new social order, for a "second Reconstruction." The position of labor appeared strong at the culmination of a decade of workers' collective protests. Union membership had shot up under the encouragement of wartime labor demands and the federal government's approval of unionization in war industries. In the setting of wartime emergency, women had gotten jobs in steel and lumber mills, the aircraft industry, and electrical and chemical plants. Almost one-fifth of industrially employed women—though still less than 7 percent of all wage-earning women—belonged to trade unions. The National War Labor Board, pressed by the WTUL, made unprecedented efforts to equalize women's pay. The bastions of the male workplace and the polling place seemed simultaneously to be falling.[18]

In short order, however, the economic disruptions following demobilization and the end of war production pushed women out of most of the "men's" jobs they had entered while it also exacerbated white racism, precipitating a wave of lynchings of blacks in the South and race riots in towns and cities as small as Elaine, Arkansas, and as large as Chicago. The near doubling in the cost of living since 1914 made economic anxiety quick to ignite. And despite progressives' hopes, the federal government dismantled warborn economic controls as soon as possible. Meanwhile, organized labor and organized capital both intended to defend their wartime gains. Strikes of unprecedented numbers, duration, and scope took place in 1919, over thirty-six hundred in all. Industrialists, boosted by wartime profits, were prepared to resist labor demands and instituted an aggressive open shop, anti-union campaign coordinated through employers' associations.

This was 1919. Revolution, famine, vast labor unrest, and reaction echoed through the Western world. The same U.S. newspapers that confirmed in November that Albert Einstein's theory of general relativity had been proved—space was "warped," Newtonian laws overthrown—also announced "World Outbreak Plotted by Reds . . . Lenin's emissaries sought to start rising all over Europe." The Bolshevik Revolution and Communist uprisings in Europe, which lent inspiration to some labor militants, also provoked tremendous backlash in the United States. A majority of the states enforced "criminal anarchy" and sedition laws in order to suppress domestic radicals. Employers' organs denounced unions as "Sovietism in disguise" and in a rising chorus the press lumped sober unionism with labor radicalism and episodic terrorism, linking all to "Red" subversion. Patriotic organizations established during the war, such as the American Protective League, the American Legion, the National Security League, and the American Defense Society, whose leadership crisscrossed with that of employers' associations, found new reasons for being. This "Red Scare," which battered the labor movement and fixed *Bolshevik* and *socialist* as words of defamation, likewise made feminist and suffragist connections to socialism bear all the more negative freight. Public hysteria about "Reds" culminated in the winter of 1919–20, with U.S. Attorney General Mitchell Palmer's brusque deportation of resident aliens who were deemed dangerous radicals, and receded in the spring of 1920.[19]

Then economic difficulties deepened. When the Federal Reserve Board acted to curb inflation, recession and unemployment set in. These were the roiled waters in which the Nineteenth Amendment granting woman suffrage struggled to safe port. As the ratification effort was going on, some NWP feminists joined political company with men envisioning a new liberal–labor coalition. Left-wing unionists and advanced progressives who hoped to mobilize a mass base, including soon-to-be-enfranchised women, founded a National Labor Party in 1919, heedless of the AFL's disapproval. They proposed to stand for the socialization of railroads, communications, major natural resources, and basic industries; and they structured the National Executive Committee of the party to include one man and one woman from each state. Crystal Eastman, who participated in the formation of the party, felt that this structure was "the most revolutionary thing"; "to force women to take an equal share in the actual business of building up the executive machine" meant "more for feminism than a million resolutions."

The contemporaneous Committee of 48—meant to represent the "men and women of the 48 states"—also aimed at a political formation like the British Labor Party and was even more decidedly influenced by the culminating woman suffrage campaign. Among its central leaders were Amos Pinchot, whose wife, Ruth Pickering, was a Heterodoxite and an organizer for birth control as well as a suffragist; J. A. H. Hopkins, former leader of the Progressive Party in New Jersey and personal friend of President Wilson, whose wife, Alison Turnbull Hopkins, had been arrested on an NWP picket line and sentenced to sixty days (but had been pardoned by the president); and Gilson Gardner, a Scripps newspaperman whose wife, Matilda Gardner, had been a member of the NWP National Executive Committee since 1914 and had been jailed in 1917. Other men who had defended the NWP actions on civil libertarian grounds and had protested to Wilson the treatment of the pickets, such as Dudley Field Malone (Doris Stevens's fiancé), also took major parts. The Committee of 48 espoused a democratic rhetoric opposed to economic monopoly and harbored in its ranks a range from socialists to lib-

ertarian individualists. Besides its 1919 platform demands for public
ownership of transportation, public utilities, and principal natural resources and for prohibition of land speculation, the Committee of 48
stood for restoration of First Amendment rights and civil liberties, abolition of labor injunctions, support for collective bargaining, and "equal
economic political and legal rights for all irrespective of sex or color."
Over 90 percent of its supporters polled in 1919 demanded equal legal
and economic rights for women, and between 15 and 20 percent of the
48's General Committee were women, including Mary Ingham, NWP
state chairman for Pennsylvania. In joint convention with the National
Labor Party the group founded the National Farmer-Labor Party in
1920.[20]

Local labor parties provided an outlet for militant feminists' political
ambitions that year. Josephine Bennett, an NWP activist who had had
much to do with the adherence of striking Bridgeport munitions workers
to the NWP picket lines (and whose husband, Toscan Bennett, was one
of the founders of the National Labor Party) ran for the U.S. Senate on
the Farmer-Labor ticket in Connecticut in 1920, joined by Vassar graduate Elsie Hill, daughter of a longterm U.S. congressman and a veteran
organizer for the NWP, who was vying for the office of Connecticut secretary of state. Doris Stevens set up a Woman's Independent Campaign
Committee, including trade unionists and militant suffragists, to forward
the New York state Labor Party campaign of Dudley Field Malone for
governor and Rose Schneiderman for U.S. senator. Harriot Stanton
Blatch and Elinor Byrns ran for local New York City offices as Socialist
Party candidates. Anne Martin ran as an Independent for the U.S. Senate from Nevada in 1920, as she had in 1918, taking from NWP headquarters (to Alice Paul's ire) the valuable organizer Mabel Vernon as her
campaign manager.[21]

In their concern for industrial democracy and platforms of nationali-
zation of railroads and utilities these women could not bring their
wealthy suffragist compeers along with them. Doris Stevens reported to
Martin that Alva Belmont had refused five requests to contribute to Martin's coffers because "she, in her present mood, is so furious against all
movements pointing toward radicalism, she is more class-conscious than
she has ever been before in her life." Although Louisine Havemeyer,
widow of the American Sugar Refining Company "king," had marched in
the picket line, gone to jail, and traveled the Prison Special, she reacted
with "pained horror," finding "dreadful" the ideas for which Anne Martin's campaign stood when Harriot Stanton Blatch explained them. "We

must make up our minds," Blatch consoled Martin, "that altho all sorts and conditions of women were united for suffrage, that political end has been gained, and they are not at one in their attitude towards other questions in life."[22] Indeed, although the suffrage goal had joined women of widely divergent politics in the NWP, it was not simply the victorious close of that campaign that forewarned of the end of coalition. The intensified hostility to radicalism in the wake of the Great War and the Bolshevik Revolution, solidifying the earlier relatively permeable boundaries between socialism and progressivism, also predicted a narrowing of the political spectrum of women able to find a common goal and remain comfortably allied in the party.

Some women were nerved by the challenge of the urgent transition. "Feminism is as broad and definite as we make it," aging activist Alice Park of California felt. "Political freedom—simple permission to vote— is a very tiny part of freedom, and we want all there is." Mary Heaton Vorse believed that newly enfranchised women had the "opportunity . . . to change the course of history"; she was "looking forward to the forming in this country of an historic feminist group, women who will go out to fight the forces of reaction as only they can fight them." Vorse wrote her intents to Florence Brewer Boeckel, editor of the NWP's paper the *Suffragist*, who, while laying plans for an international feminist journal, nonetheless felt that it was "difficult to make the average comfortable woman realize that women have not attained the independence of equality, or complete freedom in any field." Elizabeth Kent, an NWP officer from California, reported, "Many of our women long to drop everything controversial." Another NWP suffragist, afraid to be hopeful in "this balky world," wrote even more pessimistically to Mabel Vernon, "If the Woman's Party dissolves, it will be part of the general scheme—if it goes on, it will be a miracle."[23]

Even before the Nineteenth Amendment was ratified, Belmont had stressed to the inner circle of the NWP the need to continue as an organization to "obtain for women full equality with men in all phases of life and make them a power in the life of the state." Two weeks after ratification, leaders of the party met to discuss whether to disband or continue. Harriot Stanton Blatch stressed the need for a "feminist force" outside the existing political parties, to centralize efforts toward achieving state endowment of motherhood, improvements in education, and the like. Charlotte Perkins Gilman suggested an appeal for unity among women based on mass voting power, on the model of the Nonpartisan League.

It was a "sublime opportunity" to call on all women's consciences, thought Florence Kelley, the director of the National Consumers' League, devoted architect of labor and social welfare legislation, and also a member of the NWP's National Executive Committee. If the moment were not seized, Kelley thought, "there would follow an inestimable loss for women reaching into the centuries." Crystal Eastman advocated an organization which would work toward a multifaceted feminist program: economic independence and free choice of occupation for women, birth control, the endowment of motherhood, and the abolition of all barriers to women's individual development. More seriously committed than ever before to socialist revolution, Eastman understood nonetheless that feminism's goals would not be accomplished by the overthrow of capitalism. Others were more, and less, enthusiastic for going on. Lucy Burns, who assumed that the continuation of the party depended on Alice Paul, foresaw many difficulties herself and rued that the goals mentioned would take "until eternity" to accomplish. Shortly afterward, Burns dropped out of public life altogether. [24]

Although Alice Paul gave her colleagues the impression that she was too exhausted to persist in leading, she was thinking ahead. In July 1920, she publicly enunciated as a worthy goal some form of legislation that would remove all legal discriminations against women. Through the fall, as the leadership planned a grand convention for February 1921 to celebrate the suffrage victory and to settle the future form and goals—if any—of the NWP, Paul was shaping what she called a "purely feminist program." In December, Paul told the National Executive Committee that attorney Sue Shelton White had been surveying sex discriminations in state legal codes and had drawn up a "blanket bill" that "could be introduced in Congress and each legislature to sweep away these discriminations" and "could be offered at the final convention as a possible piece of work for the future." Despite the efforts of some who wished for a broader-ranging statement, the National Executive Committee moved inexorably toward formulating a resolution in line with Paul's intentions, which was to be offered at the February convention. [25]

The convention had both ceremonial and political features. For the first, representatives of more than a hundred women's organizations paraded, carrying wreaths and bearing banners, to the installation of marble sculptures of Elizabeth Cady Stanton, Susan B. Anthony, and Lucretia Mott in the Capitol rotunda. Ironically, the ceremony became political when the NAWSA's alienation from the NWP kept it and its successor, the League of Women Voters, from sending representatives to the rotunda installation. In the political part of the program, speakers for women's organizations were to present their legislative programs as a prelude to NWP delegates' debate about their own future. Organizations vied to have their proposals before the Resolutions Committee and to have the opportunity to address the delegates.[26] Hundreds of women arrived from their state NWP organizations, intending to vent their opinions on the future of the organization. The political debate was only ceremonial, however—at least in the eyes of disaffected delegates—for it rubber-stamped the central leadership's choices.

The machinations surrounding the convention made it clear that the NWP's single-issue politics and top-down control were intentional preferences, not merely artifacts of the intensity of the suffrage battle. Auguring that the party's feminism would be narrower than what the term had included in the 1910s, Paul attempted to prevent the topic of birth control from being introduced at the convention as an item for the party's future agenda. The National Executive Committee struck the speaker for the Voluntary Parenthood League from the preliminary convention program because the issue was "controversial," as Dora Lewis explained on behalf of Paul, and the "most valued members" differed in their opinions on it. After insistent negotiation with NWP headquarters, Margaret Sanger for the American Birth Control League and Mary Ware Dennett for the Voluntary Parenthood League were both allowed to address the Resolutions Committee briefly, and the latter did gain five minutes at the convention rostrum but was never listed on the printed program.[27]

Paul's behind-the-scenes treatment of the issue of black voting rights, forced to her attention by emissaries from the National Association of Colored Women and the National Association for the Advancement of Colored People, further clarified her priorities. Despite links between early woman's rights and anti-slavery reformers, the suffrage movement since the late nineteenth century had caved in to the racism of the surrounding society, sacrificing democratic principle and the dignity of black people if it seemed advantageous to white women's obtaining the vote. Whether the NWP was any more honorable on that score than other groups is debatable. Its insistence on the constitutional route to woman suffrage did seem particularly aimed against the South, where white Democratic legislators stymied woman suffrage attempts at the state level; and the NWP's picketing gained the support of some black women, including two outstanding leaders, Ida B. Wells-Barnett and Mary Church Terrell. Nonetheless, Alice Paul from the start was willing to give way publicly to the race prejudice of whites. On the whole the NWP

probably deserved the bitter assessment leveled by Walter White, director of the NAACP, following a wrangle with Paul in 1919: "if they could
get the Suffrage Amendment through without enfranchising colored
women, they would do it in a moment." Through the year of the ratification campaign, when Southern state legislators were especially exercised lest woman suffrage disrupt their methods of disfranchising blacks,
Paul maintained that the Nineteenth Amendment would not interfere
with states' regulation of voting procedures but would only "see that the
franchise conditions for every state were the same for women as for
men."[28]

Early in 1921 Mary White Ovington, a white founder and officer of the
NAACP, and Addie Hunton, a black field secretary, with Mary Talbert of
the National Association of Colored Women, pressed the NWP leadership for time to present black women's concerns at the upcoming convention. Describing how prospective black voters were being terrorized in
the South and stressing that they would never be able to vote unless
other women took a stand, Ovington asked if Talbert could address the
convention. She also proposed that the NWP appoint a committee to
investigate Southern violations of the Nineteenth Amendment. To Paul's
way of thinking, this was a "racial" and not a "feminist" issue, excludable
from the NWP convention's aim to hammer out a program for women.
The party headquarters encouraged black women to attend as delegates
to speak from the floor and made efforts to facilitate the inclusion of
blacks in state delegations, assuring one inquirer that there would be no
segregation in seating. Paul also conferred with Hallie Brown of the
NACW, Mary Church Terrell, and other black women leaders about representation of the NACW at the ceremony unveiling the sculptures.[29]

Black women's formal presentation of their concerns at the convention
was more significant, however, and there Paul held the line. Talbert confessed to Ovington, "I do not believe that Alice Paul is at all sincere, I
doubt her very much on the color line." Paul was "unquestionably," in
Ovington's judgment, "more influenced by her southern white constituency than by those northerners who believe in working for the colored
woman." After ten days of rapid-fire organization early in February, Addie Hunton led a delegation of sixty black women from fourteen states to
call upon Paul and prod her to make their prime concern part of the
convention program. "Thoroughly hostile" to the group, in Hunton's estimation, Paul gave them only the same opportunity other individuals
had—to speak as delegates from the convention floor.[30] Instead of including black women's disenfranchisement as one of the "remaining

forms of woman's subjection" which the party was to work to eradicate, Paul saw it as a diversionary and divisive issue. The disenfranchisement of black women was an injustice due to race rather than sex, in her view.[31] Paul's disregard of racial injustice in this issue was characteristically callous, but it is likely that her judgment stemmed as much from her commitment to single-issue politics. The battering of radicals in the immediate postwar period seems to have intensified Paul's desire to draw fire on only one point. As in 1917 when the party had not taken a position on the Great War because it refused to commit its membership to anything besides the constitutional amendment, in 1921 Paul ruthlessly pared away what she considered diversions from the central issue.

The largest controversy at the convention was not about black women's voting rights, as it turned out. (Ella Rush Murray, a delegate from New York and a member of the NWP's second-tier National Advisory Council, did present from the floor the resolution urged by the black women, only to see it voted down.)[32] The longest debate surrrounded a proposal, introduced as a minority resolution of the National Advisory Council, to dedicate the party's work to world disarmament. Many participants at the convention believed that the NWP was just the group to organize an international women's peace movement. As Lillian Kerr put it, "we can force war out just as we have forced suffrage in"; world disarmament, she claimed, would "never be done unless women do it!" Belle Case La Follette, wife of Senator Robert La Follette of Wisconsin, encouraged the motion on the ground that "great masses of women do feel that the conservation of life, that the saving of the race from destruction is a feminist movement." Opposition came from Paul's immediate allies and from some left-wingers with pacifist sympathies, including Josephine Bennett, Abby Scott Baker, and Crystal Eastman, who urged delegates to retain the feminist focus of the NWP and to work for pacifism through other organizations. Sara Bard Field—to whom the convention became "a kind of nightmare"—was greatly disappointed when that resolution too was voted down.[33]

Next Crystal Eastman presented her agenda. Predicting that "nobody that has a thread of modern feminism will care a rap" for the NWP if it should adopt an "old-fashioned" legalistic aim, she proposed instead that it stand for birth control, motherhood endowment, and an assault on all customary as well as legal barriers to women's self-realization. Anne Martin favored the proposal for its "splendid educational and propaganda value," and some others agreed that Eastman's forward-looking program was needed to attract younger women, but it was voted down almost two to one. Later, Eastman protested that the five hours left for actual discussion after all the speakers had presented their proposals were insufficient to allow the assembled convention to make up its collective mind. Eastman, in the *Liberator*, and journalist Freda Kirchwey, in the *Nation*, wrote acerbic articles characterizing the NWP leadership as a "steamroller" and a "machine." (Belle La Follette somewhat more gently judged the vote against the disarmament plank "a concession to Alice Paul's leadership.") The majority resolution offered by the National Executive Committee—to regroup immediately under the same name and adopt the program to eliminate women's legal disabilities—was comfortably voted in.[34]

Alice Paul took as evidence of the openness of the convention and as testimony to the NWP's reputation for effectiveness that fifty groups, including pacifists, birth control advocates, and the NAACP, had been there striving for adoption of their causes. More than a little querulously, she wished that women concerned with black voting rights and birth control would address the authorities who repressed them rather than lambasting the NWP. In Paul's view, the convention passed over other questions because its consensus genuinely formed around the goal to eliminate legal disabilities. Paul presumed that equality of legal rights was, like woman suffrage, a "purely feminist" program on which women could unite regardless of their disagreements on other issues. She believed that the attack on legal disabilities provided the kind of "simple, concrete object" required to mobilize people to action. To her credit, Paul asserted the continuing need for an organization dedicated to women's power and to the "removal of all remaining forms of subjection" of the female sex. The single-issue focus of the NWP had been consistent with its heterogeneous membership during the 1910s, and Paul envisioned no difference in the future, as the party moved to define its new purely feminist program. But the way she handled the convention, especially the concerns of black women, forewarned that the party's definition of the purely feminist would this time narrow rather than expand the constituency it sought to unite.[35]

Complaints about the abandonment of black women surfaced from a few. Kelley expressed chagrin that the party had "welshed on the Negro question." Agnes Chase joined the reorganized party with the caustic protest that its circulars ought to have said "for white women" rather than "for women." Ella Rush Murray declined to serve on the party's new National Advisory Council, "in view of certain phases of the recent convention," and ended her subscription to the party newspaper. During the

1920s and afterward, black women leaders looked to their own organizations for agitating and lobbying on issues of concern to them on racial *and* gender grounds, rather than expecting (or finding) that white women's organizations would take up those issues.[36]

Some pacifists continued working with the NWP while also serving peace organizations in the 1920s. Emma Wold, headquarters secretary, founded the Women's Committee for World Disarmament shortly after the convention without severing her NWP ties. Florence Brewer Boeckel became publicity director for the National Council for Prevention of War during the 1920s while remaining on the NWP letterhead. Mary Winsor, Abby Scott Baker, Crystal Eastman, Madeleine Doty, and Alice Park were a few of the pacifists who worked with the NWP as well as in peace organizations in the 1920s. Probably a greater number of others—including Anne Martin, who resigned from the National Advisory Council "with all good wishes"—gave priority to organized work for peace over feminism as the NWP had defined it. "I do not feel the interest in the new Woman's Party which seems to fill the hearts of some of the old group," wrote Jessie Hardy MacKaye, deserting to pacifism.[37]

The stalwarts' stance at that transitional moment was expressed by Elsie Hill, who became temporary chairman of the reorganized party. Replying to a delegate who was displeased with the rebuff to disarmament work, Hill defended the NWP's "unswerving concentration on its aim and the spiritual daring of its tactics" as its "only peculiar merit" and one which the competing resolutions at the convention would have diluted. Although a pacifist (as well as a candidate for political office), Hill had, rather perversely, been persuaded of the need for continuing the Woman's Party by the very eagerness of so many present at the convention to devote themselves to other concerns. In Hill's view, the "natural thing" for women was "always to be drawn hither and thither and give their feeble undominating support to many very appealing issues"; but experience had shown "that women have got to be more powerful in society before they can aid conclusively the real issues which affect them vitally." Therefore "the greatest work" for the NWP was "to stick to the fight to increase the power of women, and their daring to use what power they have in securing immediate results, instead of merely announcing many beliefs."[38]

Two months after the convention the NWP had 151 paid members—as compared to probably 50,000 at its height in 1919. "The old crowd has scattered never to gather in the old way again," a former organizer wrote presciently after visiting the D.C. headquarters. The party's radical reputation from 1919 hung on, breathing a potent disincentive to new members in the decade following the Red Scare. Mabel Raef Putnam reported from Wisconsin that her efforts to recruit were suffering because of the NWP's socialist reputation, although the Socialists who had dominated the state group during the suffrage campaign had all left upon ratification. Katherine Morey similarly reported that NWP organizing in Massachusetts (where anti-suffragists were concentrated) was being undermined by accusations of socialism and radicalism, though she felt that such claims were "certainly grotesque."[39]

Most party members identified with the political left, in fact, like Eastman and Kirchwey, were let down by the convention. Rebecca Hourwich had "wanted the Woman's Party to do something more radical"; Agnes Leach of New York objected that legal disabilities were "felt chiefly by women of property," who could take care of themselves anyway. Sylvie Thygeson of California did not "see how women are to be liberated unless you get at the root of the matter," and she felt that with a "deep-dyed capitalistic regime" in power the NWP's efforts at equalization could only be superficial. Josephine Bennett, though herself "not stirred over the removal of the 'legal disabilities' of women except as a part of a program of much larger scope," generously summarized in a post-convention letter to Paul, "the group gathered there . . . wanted you and no one else to lead them ultimately and under those circumstances it was only right that they should adopt your program." Once a new initiation fee of ten dollars and annual dues of ten dollars were set, more were alienated. Beulah Amidon of North Dakota, a recent Barnard graduate who had been an organizer during the 1910s, refused to recruit members at so high a fee, which she felt identified the party as "a conservative, property-holding, upper-crust group" with whom she was "out of sympathy." Emma Bancroft of Delaware likewise did not want to belong to the new party if it was to be an "aristocratic affair." Elsie Hill remonstrated that both the Socialist Party and the IWW asked their members for a dollar a month, or twelve dollars annually. She emphasized that the organization now had to be self-supporting—the nominal membership fee required by the NWP during the suffrage campaign had made the officers into "beggars" of rich women. "The work must be supported by those who feel the need," she wrote, "and direction of it must be in the hands of those who really care."[40]

As in other reform and women's organizations in the United States, in the NWP the effect of the changed political climate after the Bolshevik Revolution, the World War, the Red Scare, and the announcement of

Harding's "normalcy" was to convert, moderate, or marginalize the left
wing. The party leadership's intentions and left-wing radicals' priorities
in the 1920s were mutually repulsive. In practice, the NWP policy to
eschew any position but equal rights for women tacitly affirmed the status quo in all other respects, making the party anathema to socialists.
The merging and blending of feminist and socialist politics that radical
women had managed in the prewar years became much less possible as
both feminism and socialism became more organizationally and ideologically specific—the former in the NWP, the latter in the Communist
Party. Politically active individuals went one way or the other as the NWP
forswore any goal but equal rights and the Communist Party repudiated
"reformist" tendencies such as women's rights in favor of revolutionary
class consciousness. Many women, of course, took neither of these paths,
but found alternative routes in work for international peace, civil liberties, birth control, or other causes.

Rheta Childe Dorr, for instance, the feminist journalist who had pub-
licized the exploitation of women wage-earners in the first decade of the
century, written for the *Masses,* and joined the Greenwich Village
branch of the Socialist Party as well as Heterodoxy early in the 1910s,
shifted her outlook significantly in the midst of World War I, when she
wholeheartedly supported U.S. entry. Her opinions swung even more
decisively after the Bolshevik Revolution, which she saw as the work of
madmen and autocrats. In the 1920s she continued working with the
NWP for what she saw as its constructive feminist goals, but scorned her
former crowd as Reds motivated by anything from inferiority complexes
to criminal intent. Rose Pastor Stokes, on the other hand, who had been
a member of Heterodoxy and a birth control agitator as well as a socialist
suffragist, became one of the founders of the Communist Party in 1919
and by 1922 asserted her indifference to the "purely feminist" (in what
must have been an allusion to NWP language); she denied the existence
of any "separate woman's problem." A handful of longtime socialist members of the NWP, such as Crystal Eastman (until her premature death in
1927), Mary Winsor, and Alice Park, loyally supported equal rights, but
the party could not recruit new members on the political left by insisting
as it did on purely feminist claims. That was a circular failing, since left-
wing groups gave up on or rejected the feminism that the NWP, with its
unique history and newsworthiness, had appropriated.[41]

Paul leaned toward the well-to-do matrons around her—such as Dora
Lewis, Elizabeth Rogers and Eunice Dana Brannan and Jane Norman
Smith of New York, Florence Bayard Hilles of Wilmington, Delaware,

and Anna Kelton Wiley of Washington, D.C.—in part because of the twelve-thousand-dollar debt remaining from the suffrage campaign. The party paid off its debt in fairly short order, by dunning people for earlier pledges as small as one dollar, by selling whatever was its to sell (and some things that were not) from the old headquarters, by enlisting new "founders" at a thousand dollars apiece and new members at ten dollars, and by receiving a few very large gifts. Edith Houghton Hooker of Baltimore, Maryland, a social hygiene proponent whose views of the party's mandate were always broader than Paul's, remained loyal and became the editor—while her husband served as financial buttress—of the monthly journal the party initiated in 1923, *Equal Rights*. Belmont donated a valuable Washington, D.C., mansion for the party's new headquarters in 1922 (on the condition that no man ever be allowed to join or officer the group) and remained the main source of the party's financial stability. [42] And membership grew, though it probably never reached the party's claim of ten thousand during the 1920s. Assuming that women at work, especially in professional and semiprofessional fields, were eager for equal rights, the NWP recruited members into occupational councils as well as state branches. There were councils for government workers, industrial workers, physicians, and homemakers, and so on, headed whenever possible by famous women such as Ruth Hale (journalists), Zona Gale (authors), Lavinia Dock (nurses), and Ethel Barrymore (actresses). [43]

Alone among women's organizations in unequivocally championing feminism, the NWP was decisive in evolving its meaning. Seizing the term to describe its intent to gain women the same legal rights men had, the party dissipated the emancipatory aura around sexual difference as well as the association of feminism with the socialist left. What remained—an effort of, by, and for women, aimed toward equal rights—epitomized an inevitable paradox. Like 1910s Feminists, the NWP stressed female solidarity. Alice Paul made clear in 1921 that the purpose of articulating the "purely feminist" was to unite diverse women around a shared concern. A 1920s recruit, attorney Burnita Shelton Mathews (later a federal judge), colloquially defined a good feminist as one who "knows a discrimination when she sees one, and is loyal to women as women." More theoretically minded or more caustic spokeswomen of the NWP were even more emphatic. Caroline Spencer declaimed that women who put any other priority above feminism were "followers of men, worms of the dust," failing to see that "the tyranny of half the race over the other half is the first wrong to be righted, and its overthrow, the greatest revolution conceivable." In Doris Stevens's view, the "primary antagonism" was that of man and woman—towering "above the petty quarrels of religious creeds, above the rivalries of classes, above the slaughterings of nations, above the sinister enmity of races."[44] Seeing women as comprising a class from whose commonly held grievances arose their concerted action, nonetheless the party made its goal (and increasingly its only goal) the elimination of legal treatment of women as a class. The intent to be "loyal to women as women" was countered by the intention to erase legal recognition of women as women. The emphasis on equal rights slighted themes of common experience and consciousness among women that would provide an organizing basis for feminism.

At the same time, the NWP's approach denied the possibility that women as such might perceive self-interest in other than "purely" gender terms. By specializing in equal rights, the NWP segregated feminism from other social and political issues that affected women. Although the NWP campaign for equal rights was initiated in a vision of inclusiveness, it devolved into a narrow practice. When, for instance, the U.S. Supreme Court in 1923 used equal rights reasoning akin to the NWP's in order to invalidate the minimum-wage law covering women in the District of Columbia, the party's editorialist approved, and she went on: "It is not within the province of the Woman's Party, as a purely feminist organization, to discuss the constitutional question involved or to discuss the merits of minimum wage legislation as a method of bettering labor conditions. On these points we express no opinion." The question of labor conditions (though for women), like the issue of black voting rights (though for women) thus fell outside the purely feminist. When faced by female opponents, NWP strategy imagined a fictive or abstract unity among women rather than attempting (in any other way than the repeated insistence on equal rights) to encompass women's real diversity. Sustaining their notion of a feminist group dedicated to "the fight to increase the power of women," in Elsie Hill's words, the leadership specialized their view of who, and what issues, belonged to that fight. The NWP's "appeal for conscious sex loyalty," as Edith Houghton Hooker once phrased it, was directed toward members of the sex who could subordinate all other identifications and loyalties—class, ethnic, racial, religious, political—to a "pure" sense of themselves as women differentiated from men. That meant principally those who belonged to and were privileged by the dominant culture in every way except that they were female.[45]

The NWP sustained in the 1920s its peculiar radical elitism, which had been in germ in 1917–19 and was now reinforced by the party's divergence from most other women's organizations on the meaning of equal rights. The insiders took pride in the audacious and heretical quality of their 1917–19 strategy. Even if it had been unpopular, it had succeeded (in their view). They continued in that mold, with its intrinsic elite bias, although it was the opposite of an organizing strategy. The tendency to cultivate the role of a consciously unpopular elite united the party's old guard even when they differed on other issues. It appeared in an early, messianic editorial in *Equal Rights* (probably written by Edith Houghton Hooker) warning that NWP commitment involved "a complete disregard for popularity . . . and an almost ruthless zeal in the prosecution of work," and concluding all too prophetically, "women are born, not made, members of the National Woman's Party." It recurred in a later editorial written by New Yorker Jane Norman Smith, which proudly conceded that women who threw in their lot with the NWP "certainly will not observe an increase in their personal popularity with the outside world, but they will be able to count a milestone or two on the path toward liberty." Although such an approach reinforced the solidarity of insiders, it tended dangerously toward a self-fulfilling prophecy of isolation.[46]

Doris Stevens, who memorialized the pickets' radicalism in *Jailed for Freedom* (and also recounted in its appendix the impressive birth lines and marital affiliations of many of the women arrested), typified the radical/elite role. Stevens embodied a paradox of NWP feminism—that for all of what should have been its magnetic and dramatic appeal to feminist-inclined women, it tended to repel as much as, or more than, to attract. Many testified to Stevens's energy as an organizer and to her spirited beauty—"one of her great assets," recalled Mabel Vernon—though there were also those who said she did not share intimate rapport with the other young women and was a social climber. In the 1910s and early 1920s Stevens found her friends among the left-wing *Masses* crowd in Greenwich Village and Croton, New York. A believer in sexual freedom and independence for wives and husbands, she married Dudley Field Malone after their suffrage-campaign courtship, only to find him a hard-drinking, cavalier, and abusive husband whose practice of "open" marriage served to humiliate her. Despite difficult personal relations in the mid-1920s, as she fought with Malone (from whom she was divorced in 1929) and established a liaison with journalist Jonathan Mitchell (who became her second husband in 1935), she pursued a variety of feminist avenues: she spoke and wrote on birth control, gave a feminist course on "The Problems of Women" at the New York City Labor Temple, wrote

articles and engineered debates on wages for wives, helped found the
Lucy Stone League (in favor of women retaining their own names at
marriage), and envisioned such feminist institutions as a business school
for women. That was in addition to being a principal spokeswoman in
the NWP campaign for the equal rights amendment.

Stevens's high visibility during the 1920s owed not only to her own
considerable talents and commitment but also to the continuing patronage of Alva Belmont. Although Belmont lived in France from 1920 until
her death in 1933, she retained the office of president of the NWP. The
overall extent of her power over policy making is not clear. Her financial
support was so essential, however, that it is reasonable to assume that
her will was not crossed. Alice Paul constantly curried Belmont's favor in
order to keep funds flowing. Belmont propelled the NWP into international work for equal rights, in accord with her own grandiose visions of
an International Parliament of Women. Stevens, back and forth to Europe frequently at Belmont's behest, stood out in all the NWP international efforts, representing the party to the International Woman Suffrage Alliance in 1926 and leading the Pan-American Union's Inter-
American Commission on Women. Belmont's intimacy and support
made Stevens a power for Paul to reckon with, but also threatened Stevens's own autonomy. Giving the principal speech at the party's memorial
ceremony after the old woman's death in 1933, Stevens could not forbear
recalling "the extraordinary intensity of her will and her relentless determination to see her plans carried out; her iron, sometimes ruthless leadership. Her vitality was the marvel of all her friends. Her impatience at
the supineness of women was colossal."[47]

Stevens had close male and female associates, mainly among New York
and international writers, publishers, journalists, and lawyers supportive
of equal rights. From some she evoked warm sympathy and loyalty: "You
are to the highest degree, of the women that I happen to know, an ideal
woman-friend among women and also an ideal woman-friend among
men!" wrote Ruby Darrow, the wife of nationally renowned trial lawyer
Clarence Darrow. Nonetheless, Stevens failed to gain a following not
only because she worked, in NWP style, at the top, but also because she
was seen by those outside her circle (and some inside) as manipulative
and self-interested. Her "faculty for getting in touch with the key men of
a situation," mentioned by Maud Younger in praise, often elicited suspicion and resentment from women. "Anyone who has borne as much disapproval as have the members of our group," Stevens nonetheless believed, "is fairly hardened to . . . disapproval of the way one fights for an

idea." She wrote those particular words in defense of a dramatic act of civil disobedience she perpetrated in 1928, harking back to the flamboyance of 1917: at Rambouillet, France, she led a group of women to confront the representatives of nations assembled to sign the Kellogg–Briand Pact and demanded that a declaration of equal rights for women become part of the treaty. Stevens's boldness in taking actions and the many-sidedness of her analysis of women's economic, legal, and sexual situation manifested the best of NWP potential in the 1920s. The limits of her accomplishments outlined the limits of the NWP's vanguardist strategy.[48]

Stevens's example shows that a few of those in the top leadership of the NWP in the 1920s held to a much more wide-ranging feminist analysis than the party's platform might suggest. The organization's single-issue focus meant, in principle, that its members and sympathizers as individuals could simultaneously pursue other political or reform efforts, and some did, especially in the peace and birth control movements, in women's clubs and professional associations, and in the major political parties; many had busy careers as well. The membership of the NWP was always more diverse, more flexible, and perhaps more imaginative than the top leadership. The party's journal, *Equal Rights*, not only recorded legislative progress but also censured instances of sex discrimination, tracked women's accomplishments around the world, editorialized about the hypocrisies of sex-role conditioning and gender hierarchy, and gave room to autobiographical, historical, and speculative essays on women's condition. The ideas, research, and analyses presented in *Equal Rights* were often outstandingly acute. The party's strong stance against sex discrimination in employment attracted some effective new activists, mainly professionally employed women such as Burnita Mathews. A few renowned artists, including poet Edna St. Vincent Millay, painter Georgia O'Keeffe, and actress Eva LaGallienne, joined, as did aviator Amelia Earhart.[49]

To be central in the party's endeavors, however, one had to accept the conditions of Paul's leadership. Perhaps even more than the radical/elite stance, Paul's unwillingness to allow any leadership inconsistent with her own to flourish counterposed itself against what potential the NWP had to enlarge its constituency. As the convention predicted, in every controversy behind the scenes—and there were many—Paul's silently effective hand could be found, resolving the issue according to her own will, the consequence being a still-coherent party but a narrower, more exclusive one. "In order to work with Miss Paul," Doris Stevens commented dourly (after she became disillusioned), "one has to surrender all." The peerless leadership that seemed an unequivocal asset during the rising campaign for suffrage felt harsher during a long, drawn-out battle with more defeats than victories; it became a liability inside as well as outside the organization. One might truly say that the NWP could not live without Alice Paul and it could not live with her.[50]

As the NWP moved into the 1920s, it carried the marks of its early history into a changed political and economic context. It remained an autocratically run, single-minded and single-issue pressure group, still reliant on getting into the newspapers as a means of publicizing its cause, very insistent on the method of "getting in touch with the key men." During the suffrage campaign the NWP "always worked from the top down," recalled Jeannette Rankin (the first woman elected to Congress, in 1916), and that remained true of both its lobbying and its organizing techniques. In lobbying state legislatures for equal rights bills and state constitutional amendments, and in work toward the federal constitutional amendment for equal rights, NWP lobbyists went straight to legislators, governors, and presidents, not to their constituents. In attempting to garner or to show support for equal rights, Paul's strategy was not to work at the grassroots but to persuade the leadership of large organizations and federations, such as the National Federation of Business and Professional Women's Clubs, the American Association of University Women, or the General Federation of Women's Clubs, to endorse the equal rights amendment. In the largest sense Paul maintained that her project was educative—that her principle was to change people's minds about the relative status of men and women—but she neglected the educative process. Party leaders from the 1920s on skipped over what had been an essential element of the women's rights legacy they saw themselves heir to. Unlike the suffrage movement during most of its history, and unlike the Feminists just preceding, they did not attempt to ignite a grassroots movement toward the transformation of consciousness.[51]

Just as the CU and the Woman's Party had provided organizational outlets for Feminist suffragists in the 1910s, attracting women who envisioned emancipation whole and sought an immediate political expression of that revolt, the NWP created an organizational definition for feminism in the 1920s. Now, however, it stood for specific things: an organization by and for women, working toward the goal of equal rights. By focusing on the law of the land, the NWP assaulted a basic prop to the system of gender hierarchy, one that unavoidably affected women of all sorts and conditions. The equal rights amendment gave succinct legal form to the emphasis Feminists in the 1910s had placed on justice, rights, and equal opportunity. In fact, Henrietta Rodman's Feminist Alliance had even proposed in 1914 a constitutional amendment declaring "that no civil or political right shall be denied to any person on account of sex."[52] That emphasis had been only one side of the Feminism of the 1910s, however, for its assault on gender boundaries, its affirmation of formlessness, its ambiguous ambition of "breaking into human race" had been anything but single in approach. The NWP, focusing organizationally on equal rights, broke Feminism's connections with sex rights and social revolution, and replaced Feminism's attack on gender categories with insistence on legal equality. Since equal rights had not only legal and political but also economic bearing, therein lay a dilemma.

3

VOLUNTARIST POLITICS

Rocky Mountain News

**Enfranchisement Means the Sky's the Limit in
Woman's Sphere**

Drawn by Nina E. Allender

Any good suffragist the morning after ratification.

Political cartoons, September/October 1920

The Nineteenth Amendment is the most obvious benchmark in the history of women in politics in the United States, but it is a perplexing one for the viewer who wants to include more than electoral events in the category of politics. To neglect 1920 as a political watershed would be obtuse and cavalier. Not only was the sex barrier to the ballot eliminated; but also the women's movement to gain the vote was ended. Leaders of the suffrage movement perceived the change in generational experience as well as political status: "Oh, how I do pity the women who have had no share in the exultation and the discipline of our army of workers!" Carrie Chapman Catt exclaimed in 1920. "How I do pity those who have felt none of the grip of the oneness of women struggling, serving, suffering, sacrificing for the righteousness of woman's emancipation."[1] Nonetheless, too great focus on the achievement of the Nineteenth Amendment can obscure surrounding continuities in women's political behavior and the situation of that behavior in broader political and social context.

Striking continuities tend to be overlooked if 1920 is supposed to be the great divide and only electoral politics its sequel. The most important is women's favoring the pursuit of politics through voluntary associations over the electoral arena. Since the early nineteenth century women had influenced what took place in electoral and legislative halls from outside, not only by seeking suffrage but also by inquiring into a wide range of health, safety, moral, and welfare issues. Women had built a tradition of exercising political influence and efficacy—admittedly hard to measure—through voluntary organizations. In 1919, as if predicting the release of such energies long tied up in the suffrage campaign, several new women's organizations were founded, and others blossomed after the suffrage was gained. Inez Haynes Irwin noted in her 1933 history, *Angels and Amazons,* that contemporary women were possibly *over*organized. (Her book ended with a staggering list of associations, from the American Home Economics Association, with 9,000 members, to the United Daughters of the Confederacy, with 12,000 branches and 70,000 members, and the Ukrainian National Women's League of America, with 52 branches and 3,020 members.) In the prevalence of the voluntarist mode (stemming from women's organizations), the use of lobbying to effect political influence, and the kinds of interests pursued (that is, health, safety,

moral and welfare issues), there was much more similarity than difference in women's political participation before and after 1920.[2]

After enfranchisement the National Woman's Party continued under the
same name, but the giant National American Woman Suffrage Association gave birth to the National League of Women Voters. First proposed
by Carrie Chapman Catt in 1919, the League was founded in February
1920 at the NAWSA Victory Convention. At the outset the League took a
scatter-shot approach, reflecting the many interests of its constituent
women. Sixty-four agenda items under the seven headings of citizenship
education, women in industry, child welfare, social hygiene, food supply
and demand, improvement of election laws, and legal status of women
were originally named; these were pared down in 1923 to three basic
areas, (1) efficiency as the basis for public welfare in government; (2)
equal legal status for women; and (3) prevention of war through international cooperation.

The contrast between the membership of the NAWSA at its estimated
height of two million and the small fraction of that total—probably 5
percent—who persisted in the League is often taken to mean that wom-
en's political interest and activism were decimated after suffrage was
won. The two figures are not really comparable, however. The first group
pursued one specific goal for women, made few demands on its local
members, imposed little homogeneity upon affiliates, and used all volunteer labor, but the later organization had many aims (mostly outside
women's rights), made strenuous demands on its local members, attempted to standardize national procedure, and employed professional
staff. Quickly evolving into a "good government" rather than a feminist
organization, its goal being to ready women for political life, the LWV
found itself, ironically, competing with women's partisan activity as much
as preparing women for it.

When in 1920 all women became fair game for party organizations,
Republican and Democratic women's divisions vied with the nonpartisan
LWV for the time and loyalty of women interested in politics. Some leading NAWSA suffragists went directly into party organizations instead of
into the League. In individual practice, activism in the LWV and in the
political parties tended to rival rather than to shore up one another.
Women's divisions in state and national party committees should be seen
as "successor" organizations to the NAWSA as logically as the League was
and is, and women's work through the parties as valid a continuation of
their political activism as League work. Lillian Feickert, for example, a

leading New Jersey suffragist who was named vice-chairman of the Republican state committee in 1920, built the New Jersey Women's Republican Club on the model of the New Jersey Woman Suffrage Association, a grassroots organization with affiliation to county councils. Feickert claimed that three-quarters of the suffragists joined it. By the spring of 1922 the club claimed sixty thousand members.[3]

Generally, where one large or vital pre-1920 women's organization declined or ended, more than one other arose to take its space, if not its exact place. The General Federation of Women's Clubs, which spoke for nearly a million members in its affiliated clubs in 1910 (and even then far underrepresented the number of local clubwomen), rarely gave figures for overall membership in the 1920s; if it had it might have shown a decline. Reporting on those clubs' civic work in the urban planning journal *American City* plummeted from an average of nine or ten articles per year between 1909 and 1920 to an average of less than one per year in the subsequent half decade. In the same period, however, the National Congress of Parents and Teachers Associations—a federation of white women's organizations that had begun as the National Congress of Mothers in 1897, joined with Parent-Teachers Associations in 1908, and neutralized its name (while remaining principally female) in 1924—gathered a massive membership. Almost a hundred thousand strong in 1917, it nearly tripled by 1920 and then more than quintupled during the 1920s, reaching a membership of more than a million and a half. It was organized in every state, in twenty-two thousand local units, by 1931. Its local units took up efforts similar to those of the many unnamed women's clubs of the earlier generation, working to establish playgrounds, libraries, and health clinics, while its national leadership lobbied at the federal level on issues from film standards to international peace. The founding in 1926 of a National Colored Parent-Teachers Association indicated black women's similar concerns for their children's welfare as well as highlighting the racial exclusivity of the original Congress, which cooperated in the founding of the "colored" group. The latter grew rapidly, reaching eighteen thousand members in a thousand local associations in sixteen states before the end of the decade.[4]

The national organizations that had been the most avid advocates for wage-earning women before the Great War did show drastic reductions in membership and resources in the 1920s. These were the National Consumers' League (NCL)—not strictly but for the most part a women's group—and the National Women's Trade Union League. In 1919, under Florence Kelley's direction, the NCL set out a ten-year plan of work, the heart of which was to ensure state regulation of conditions in industry for women. In the same year, the WTUL brought together in Washington, D.C., an International Congress of Working Women, which enunciated labor standards for men and women, called on the League of Nations to enforce these, and established an International Federation of Working Women. Despite such auspicious beginnings neither the NCL nor the WTUL picked up members or momentum during the 1920s, their experience in that respect more akin to that of labor unions than women's associations. More like women's clubs than trade unions, however, both WTUL and NCL had forced their concerns toward public consciousness so far that their issues were absorbed into more formal institutions or taken up by municipalities or states. Pauline Newman much later explained the demise of the WTUL by saying, "the work we did for the unions, the unions did it themselves. They don't need us any more. Education, legislation, organization—they had their own people who did the work we did for them." As pressure from women's voluntary organizations had been instrumental in making local public health and school departments assume some responsibilities for sanitation and for children's safety, in leading states to institute social welfare and protective labor legislation and the federal government to establish pure food and drug laws, likewise it was under pressure from women's voluntary groups, principally the WTUL and NCL, that the Women's Bureau was established in the U.S. Department of Labor to investigate the conditions and protect the interests of wage-earning women. A permanent successor to the Women in Industry Service set up by the Department of Labor during World War I, the Women's Bureau in the 1920s took on the WTUL's set of intentions about educating the public, and, in alliance with the WTUL, staunchly defended sex-based protective legislation.[5]

The WTUL's purpose, to raise the trade union consciousness of industrially employed women as well as to sweeten their lives through association, was increasingly taken up by the Industrial Clubs formed by the Young Women's Christian Association. In 1926 the YWCA stopped requiring that members be Protestant Christians; its membership grew by one-fifth during the 1920s. In 1930 it boasted over six hundred thousand members, fifty-five thousand volunteer advisors, and a professional staff (in local chapters) of almost thirty-five hundred. Among Southern textile workers, especially—where the WTUL also sent organizers—the YWCA Industrial Clubs were important in educating and helping to organize both black and white women workers and in bringing them to testify before legislatures about industrial conditions. The Industrial Clubs served as recruitment grounds for workers' summer schools, which were founded during the 1920s in a sequel to the WTUL's cross-class efforts earlier in the century. College professors and trade unionists were involved, along with the WTUL and the YWCA, in setting up these opportunities for working women to leave their jobs—sometimes at risk to their livelihoods—to participate in short, concentrated periods of education on a college campus. From the first summer school founded at elite Bryn Mawr College in 1921, to the Southern Summer School for Women Workers in Industry established in the mountains of North Carolina at a rented camp, the intent was to provide women workers with new resources with which to understand their situations and to develop leadership skills. They studied politics, economics, and trade union history, instructed by a mainly female faculty from independent colleges. Thus continuing the WTUL's original aim for cross-class cooperation to benefit women wage-earners, the summer schools turned to experts and professionals and college students rather than to matrons for contributions. Also like the WTUL's earlier efforts, the workers' summer schools brought as much to the "allies" as to the workers. One college undergraduate who came to the Bryn Mawr summer school as a tutor recalled, "what made the School so important was the bringing together of two worlds which otherwise might never meet. And although the School provided marvelous learning and training opportunities for the workers, I think it was the college girls whose eyes were most widely opened."[6]

The YWCA was also instrumental in bringing white-collar women workers together. Several score of new professional organizations for women were founded between 1915 and 1930—and the federations of professional women's clubs called Zonta International and Quota International were organized—but most significant was the founding in 1919 of the National Federation of Business and Professional Women's Clubs, as a result of a conference of businesswomen called by the YWCA during the Great War. Lena Madesin Phillips, a Kentucky-born lawyer who was drafted from her wartime YWCA position to become the first executive secretary of the new federation, waxed eloquent on the subject of encouraging business and professional women's teamwork, courage, risk-taking, and self-reliance. Her purpose in the NFBPW was "to bring together . . . women who individually had exercised so great an influence, yet who were as a class non-gregarious. It was to increase their own sense of solidarity, to permit them to function as a whole . . . to secure combined effort by them . . . to increase the value of the group to themselves, their respective communities, and society at large." Phillips thought it "most significant" that the federation should have been founded "at a time when the world is so fluid as to offer the greatest possibilities for the advancement of the interests of women."[7]

The clubs affiliated with the NFBPW were required to have three-quarters of their members actively employed. Nearly half of the women in the clubs during the 1920s and 1930s were clerical workers, who responded to the NFBPW's provision of sorority and the emphasis on career development, new "angles" for women, how to meet sex discrimination in business, professional standards of performance, and so on, that infused its conventions and its monthly publication, the *Independent Woman*. Under Phillips's leadership, the federation in its first three years gathered an affiliation of 368 clubs, in twenty-nine state federations, with a membership of almost thirty thousand. By 1931 state federations existed in forty-six states and included about 1,100 local clubs and fifty-six thousand individuals. The slogan the federation used to develop hundreds of local educational fundraising efforts during the 1920s—"at least a high school education for every business girl"—indicated its orientation toward ordinary white-collar workers, although teachers and other professionals also formed an important part of its membership.[8]

At the local level, urban career women (though not career women only) also gravitated to Women's City Clubs, many of which were distinguished by having clubhouses in which to offer transient or permanent lodgings and a place for women's groups to meet. Women's City Clubs had civic as well as social purposes, undertaking educational work and taking municipal lobbying positions. The New York Women's City Club, for instance, founded in 1915, had a paid executive staff by 1921, hosted debates on elections, and involved its membership in municipal housing, civil liberties, transportation, recreation, and labor issues during the 1920s. The members of the Cincinnati Women's City Club (also founded in 1915) conducted political education through speakers and courses, administered a scholarship fund (for girls starting college), and lobbied on a variety of issues including juvenile detention, traffic regulation, reform of the city charter, and women's health care in local institutions.[9]

The alliance with professionals—social workers, social researchers, college and university professors—so noticeably important in efforts on behalf of women workers and in the YWCA in the 1920s was also apparent in the birth control movement. There, 1919 was also a year of new beginnings. Civil libertarian Mary Ware Dennett, a founder of the short-lived National Birth Control League of the 1910s (and not an ally of Margaret Sanger's) started a new group, the Voluntary Parenthood League. During the 1920s Dennett's organization stood on First Amendment rights and aimed to decriminalize birth control by removing it from federal obscenity statutes. Margaret Sanger, whose leadership was more compelling, in 1919 changed her approach, in the public relations of the American Birth Control League, to reliance on medical doctors and eugenicists. Leaving behind her socialist politics and agitation in working-class communities, and no longer purposely breaking the law to cause publicity and pressure the state, Sanger shifted her emphasis from women's control of their own bodies to eugenic reasoning about better babies. Educating the public and lobbying for the legalization of birth control on the premise of allowing "doctors only" to provide information and methods, Sanger increased her following. In the 1920s, volunteers for birth control who saw the virtues of that approach were mainly middle-class matrons, more socially and politically conservative than the birth control advocates of the 1910s and also more numerous. (One Connecticut volunteer wrote to another, for instance, commending a coworker for having "reached the best type of woman—those active in the Mother's Club and the League of Women Voters. They are women who are deeply interested in the subject of birth control and who will be extremely active and influential in the substantial conservative circles in Norwalk—of course, the more advanced, 'radical' set has always advocated birth control.") The American Birth Control League claimed over thirty-seven thousand members in 1926, almost 90 percent of them female.[10]

What professionals' application of modern science had to offer also fueled the movement for "parent education," a new form for collective study and discussion of childrearing methods, carried on in the past in maternal associations and mothers' clubs. Like the PTA, the movement used the neuter term *parent* although mothers were the principal participants. Flourishing in the 1920s and 1930s, parent education differed from its predecessors by its wedding to science, its reliance on research centers and universities where child study was a developing professional focus, and its behind-the-scenes support from corporate philanthropy. The parent education movement went beyond purely local organization and held national institutes and conferences. The movement had two national magazine outlets, one professional (*Child Study*), one popular (*Parents'*), and two national organizations, the Federation for Child Study (which became in 1924 the Child Study Association of America) and the National Council on Parent Education, incorporated in 1928. Rather than the ministers who had encouraged mothers' clubs in the past, early childhood educators, sociologists, social workers, and psychologists encouraged the local groups and institutes of mothers (and some fathers) who met in the interests of parent education. In this voluntary movement experts as well as amateurs took the initiatives.[11]

One cooperator in the parent education movement was the American Association of University Women, which evolved from the Association of Collegiate Alumnae into a truly national operation in 1921 under its new name, and a decade later had 36,818 members in 551 branches. Its members had to be graduates of accredited collegiate institutions. While its heart was in educational matters pertaining to women as scholars and teachers (at all educational levels, including preschool), the association joined more general women's organizations in lobbying efforts. Black collegiate alumnae, excluded by the spirit if not the letter of the AAUW, founded their own national association in 1924, intending to promote mutual benefit, educational standards, and scholarship among their own race, and also to work toward "better conditions of contact" between white and black college women. In 1932 it had eight branches and almost three hundred members.[12]

Group consciousness among minority-group women gave rise to other new beginnings and generated new energy in women's organizations. The 1920s and 1930s were outstanding decades for the founding of Jewish women's organizations. Both the National Council of Jewish Women and Hadassah had been established by an earlier generation (and both claimed between forty and fifty thousand members by 1930) but in 1921 Junior Hadassah was formed, in 1923 the Conference Group of National Jewish Women's Organizations, in 1924 the Women's Branch of the Union of Orthodox Jewish Congregations of America, in 1925 the Women's Organization of the Pioneer Women of Palestine, and half a dozen more by 1935. The National Council of Catholic Women was formed in 1920, and a decade later there were seventeen hundred local societies of Catholic women, fifty Diocesan organizations, and at least sixteen national societies (for example, the National Catholic Women's Union, the Catholic Daughters of America) affiliated with it.[13]

Black women continued the National Association of Colored Women, the organizational hub which had been central to black suffragist efforts, which related hundreds of clubs through a complex structure of districts and state and regional federations, uniting black clubwomen in communities across the nation in shared goals of social service and racial uplift. Through its biennial meetings and its magazine, *National Notes*, the NACW structured communication, dispensed information, and promoted collective action. Its umbrella covered between 150,000 and 200,000 members—mainly middle-class women, who likely belonged to more than one civic organization—in forty-one states in the mid-1920s. Many of its leaders also pursued their aims through male-dominated black organizations such as the National Association for the Advancement of Colored People, the Urban League, and the Commission on Interracial Cooperation. With disfranchisement and the horror of lynching rife in the South, confronting racial oppression had priority. A writer on black women's "double task" to struggle for both "race and sex emancipation" declared in 1925 that black women's "feminist efforts are directed chiefly toward the realization of the equality of the races, the sex struggle assuming a subordinate place." In 1922, with a federal anti-lynching bill languishing in the Southern-dominated U.S. Senate, Mary Talbert retired as president of the NACW and gathered a small group of female Anti-Lynching Crusaders to spearhead the NAACP's year-long campaign to raise a million dollars and unite a million women in the cause. Ida B. Wells had instigated a one-woman crusade against lynching in the 1890s, but in the 1920s the crusaders delegated hundreds of black women activists to districts, towns, and cities in the South to try to gain financial and moral support—including that of white women—for their campaign. They met with only limited success. All through the 1920s organized black women lobbied for the federal anti-lynching bill, which did not pass, but lynchings in the latter 1920s were reduced to one-third the number that had occurred in the years just after 1919.

Despite—or perhaps because of—the way the NACW had brought women into political activism, its own numbers declined by the end of the decade to about fifty thousand. Civil rights and welfare organizations consisting of men *and* women were conducting the kinds of activities the NACW had begun, and they had the benefit of white financial support. Lacking resources, in 1930 the NACW cut its departments from thirty-eight to two: the home and women in industry. Five years later Mary McLeod Bethune, a former president of the NACW and longtime laborer in the black struggle for freedom, led in establishing a new national clearinghouse, the National Council of Negro Women—moved by her sense that neither male-dominated black organizations nor white women's umbrella groups had encouraged black women to articulate their own voices very clearly.[14]

In response to the Great War, women founded a host of new organizations. One kind were patriotic, security-minded societies such as the American War Mothers (1917), the Service Star Legion (1919), and the more successful American Legion Auxiliary, which (depleting the Service

Star Legion's membership) grew from an initial 131,000 to over 400,000 members a decade later. The American Legion Auxiliary often worked in concert with the longer-established Daughters of the American Revolution (DAR), which more than doubled in size between 1910 and 1932, reaching 2,463 chapters and almost 170,000 members by the latter date. During the 1920s and 1930s these groups advocated military preparedness and were loudly anti-communist, enthusiastically red-baiting, positioning themselves opposite women's peace organizations, for international peace was, arguably, *the* major item of concern among organized women in the 1920s.[15]

In an unprecedented tide of public concern for preventing future wars, voluntary groups from the conservative and nationalistic American Peace Society, through Protestant church agencies, to the left-wing pacifist War Resisters League, formed. Through the 1920s they proposed a range of competing alternatives, including the League of Nations, the World Court, international arbitration conferences, disarmament, and noncooperation with the military. Women could follow a number of avenues instigated and dominated by men, from legalist formulas to rhetorical movements such as Outlawry of War, and they appeared in all the peace societies but clustered in their own. Two women's peace societies were founded in 1919. At a conference in Zurich, women from sixteen countries, both Allied and Central Powers—many of whom had suffered obloquy for opposing their nations' part in the Great War—established the Women's International League for Peace and Freedom. The U.S. section of WILPF, many of its members continuing from the Woman's Peace Party of 1915, included such luminaries of social reform as Jane Addams, Lillian Wald, and Alice Hamilton. A smaller group of women led by the aging Fanny Garrison Villard (daughter of pre–Civil War abolitionist William Lloyd Garrison) established the Women's Peace Society, which took a stance of nonresistance more extreme than the position of the WILPF.

The foundings of the Women's Peace Union of the Western Hemisphere and the Women's Committee for World Disarmament followed these in 1921. In addition, the major women's organizations—LWV, AAUW, WCTU, NFBPW, and PTA—put international peace prominently on their agendas. The fast-growing PTA made peace the first of its lobbying priorities all through the decade and strongly expressed its position that the public schools should educate the next generation to prevent war. In 1925, Carrie Chapman Catt assembled the leadership and memberships of the major women's organizations with peace departments into the National Conference on the Cause and Cure of War. That collectivity, which met annually for many years and formed a basis for peace lobbying, had a cumulative membership over five million at the outset. By 1930 its affiliated memberships claimed to speak for more than one out of every five women in the United States.[16]

The level of organization among American women by 1930 thus appears to compare very favorably to that at the end of the suffrage movement, even considering that membership would have to increase by slightly more than a fifth to keep up with the growth in the adult female population (from under 31 million in 1910 to 37 million in 1930). The number of women in organizations is compelling even though memberships in the various organizations could and often did overlap (which was no less true of the pre-war generation). To take an outstanding example: Jessie Daniel Ames, the founder in 1930 of the (white) Association of Southern Women for the Prevention of Lynching, was during the 1920s the president and then the legislative chair of the LWV in Texas, an executive committee member on her state's Joint Legislative Council (a state lobbying group made up of the League of Women Voters, General Federation of Women's Clubs, National Congress of Mothers and Parent–Teacher Associations, Women's Christian Temperance Union, and Federation of Business and Professional Women's Clubs), political science chair of the Texas State Federation of Business and Professional Women, and founder and president of the Texas chapter of the American Association of University Women.[17]

Repeated foundings and aggregate memberships make it clear that women were joining women's organizations, although with more specialized self-definitions or aims than the previous generation. That these were women's organizations and yet had specialized memberships (professional women, religious women, mothers, women of particular political sympathies) and purposes (birth control, education, peace, opposition to lynching, and so on) suggests at once the increasing diversification among American women and their dual sense of themselves as members of a sex and as individuals possessing singular characteristics and designs. By their very constitutions such organizations were as likely (possibly more likely) to sustain, even to rigidify, the differentiations and diversities among women on racial, ethnic, class, and political grounds as to elide these differences. The more purposive and specialized a women's organization, the more likely it was instrumentally allied with professional expertise and involved with the bureaucratic machinery of government—commissions, bureaus, conferences—that developed rapidly during the 1920s. And the more likely it was to be working in concert with male-dominated organizations pursuing similar purposes. While these were women's organizations, they were not purporting to emanate from or to operate in a separate sphere, as had many of their forebears in the nineteenth century. Consequently, there was an omnipresent potential for the groups working on issues not peculiar to women—peace, for example—to self-destruct by routing their members toward male-dominated organizations that had more funds and thus seemed more effective (as happened with the NACW).

To the extent that much of women's associational life now intersected with government bureaucracy, universities, research institutes, trade unions, hospitals, and so on—much beyond the long-standing pattern for women's groups to be linked to churches—those organizations that were *not* so connected seemed relatively backwater, "merely" women's. That is, in comparison both to more specialized women's groups or activities and to the promise of mixed-sex (male-dominated) organizations, women's clubs of a general nature lost drawing power. They were caught in the middle—too established to rely on their novelty to draw members, as they had in the 1890s, not able to tap into zeal for suffrage as they had in the 1910s, yet not established enough with respect to centers of power to ensure much effectiveness to women. Some of the older generation who had founded these clubs complained, "what new blood has come into your organization this year? What are the ages of the youngest women in the thousands of clubs organized a score or twoscore years ago for one form or another of civic betterment?" while women were in fact founding and joining other women's organizations.

What some of the older generation likely missed in modern women's organizations was the emphasis on womanhood, the proudly sex-defined sentiment that had powered so many earlier associations. "Sex-consciousness," pronounced one of the upcoming generation, was "one of the first things which has to be left behind" by those who were "serious-minded." "Oh, do have done with this eternal talk about women!" was the typical response of the young, according to an older suffragist.[18] The newer women's organizations were so more by habit and expedience than commitment, it might be said: they were "women's," but they submerged the need for a rationale for being so by bringing to the fore other relevant identities of participants, as voters, parents, coreligionists, ideologues, citizens. Where their nineteenth-century predecessors collectively constituted the woman movement and would have recognized themselves as such, the twentieth-century women's voluntary associations did not collectively constitute the feminist movement—nor would most members have recognized themselves as feminists; indeed, they had varying and ambivalent relations to feminism, some opposing it directly. That was as much because *feminism* was a more demanding and ideologically laden concept than *woman movement* as it was because pathways along which twentieth-century women might exert themselves were more various than those traveled by their forebears.

Still bearing the voluntarist legacy of prewar women's groups distinguished by their lack of the ballot, women's organizations in the 1920s and 1930s had the benefit of the new ethos that women were citizens who could and should participate in the public realm. They had the benefit of a much higher rate of high school and college education among women than ever before, and a lower birth rate, which together increased the proportion knowledgeable about social issues and not entirely occupied with childcare, at the same time that three-quarters of all adult women were not gainfully employed. These factors created the pool of women who peopled voluntary associations. Overlapping memberships prevent the recovery of exact numbers for comparison, but it is highly probable that the greatest extent of associational activity in the whole history of American women took place in the era between the two world wars, after women became voters and before a great proportion of them entered the labor force.[19]

Not all of these women's organizations entered politics, but most of them did, and their mode of involvement continued the suffrage organizations' practices of education, publicity, and lobbying legislators more often than running their own candidates. Women's organizations pioneered in, accepted, and polished modern methods of pressure-group politics.[20] The suffrage campaign had brought its leaders, many of whom continued in voluntary associations, a great deal of expertise in the behind-the-scenes operations of government, and they proceeded to apply that expertise in state legislatures and on Capitol Hill. Women's lobbying was now presumably a more powerful engine than ever before, because it drew behind it the train of women's votes. Immediately after the Nineteenth Amendment was ratified, Maud Wood Park, the first president of the LWV, took the lead in forming the Women's Joint Congressional Committee, a Capitol Hill lobbying clearinghouse for ten organizations. The LWV, the GFWC, the WTUL, the WCTU, the NCL, and the NFBPW were all charter members. The WJCC agreed to establish a lobbying committee on behalf of any item that at least five of its constituent members wished to pursue. It started working on two different attempts, federal funds for maternity and infancy health protection (re-alized in 1921 in the Sheppard-Towner Act), and independent citizen-ship for married women (partially realized in the Cable Act of 1922).

The Sheppard-Towner Act, or Maternity and Infancy Act, appeared a clear victory for women's interests as traditionally conceived. Instigated by Julia Lathrop of the Children's Bureau on the basis of findings about high rates of preventable maternal and infant mortality, the act allocated funds to states—on a voluntary basis until 1926—to secure the services of public health and visiting nurses, to mandate childcare conferences, and to devise other public educational methods to improve prenatal care and infant hygiene and nutrition. Social researcher Sophonisba Breckin-ridge later reflected on the act's intent, "it seemed as though the women were just doing on a larger platform what women had been always sup-posed to do—care for women in childbirth, welcome the newborn and nurture the children." But the larger platform had profound significance, for the act was the first allocation of federal funds for welfare purposes. With widespread support from women's groups from the YWCA to the DAR, as well as publicity in mainstream women's magazines, the WJCC lobbied for the bill, its subcommittee on the matter headed by the re-doubtable Florence Kelley. (Kelley's leadership was similarly essential to contemporary efforts to bring federal sanctions against child labor.) The Senate passed the Sheppard-Towner Act by a proportion of nine to one—which differed vastly from the way the Nineteenth Amendment had squeaked through. The House passed it by more than seven to one, despite some political opponents' tirades that it was "inspired by foreign experiments in communism" and some American Medical Association publications' complaints about the erosion of physicians' control over provision of medical services. The bill's passage led a writer in the *Ladies' Home Journal* to call the WJCC "the most powerful lobby in Wash-ington."[21]

The WJCC also took the lead in pressing for the Cable Act. Together the two early accomplishments neatly illustrated the dual legacy of the suffrage campaign, for as profoundly as Sheppard-Towner declared that women, as mothers, differed from men in their relation to the state, the Cable Act declared that women as people required the same relation to the state as men—or almost. The impulse behind the Cable Act was to overturn the patriarchal precedent, codified in American law in 1855 and 1907, that a woman's citizenship followed that of her husband: an Amer-ican woman marrying an alien lost her American citizenship, an immi-grant woman gained citizenship by marrying a male citizen. Those former suffragists and lawyers who pressed for the Cable Act—contending, in Maud Wood Park's words, that "a woman is as much an individual as a man is, and her citizenship should no more be gained or lost by marriage than should a man's"—were mainly concerned with the American who lost her citizenship by marriage and became subject to the disabilities imposed on aliens. The congressmen on the House Immigration and Naturalization Committee who debated the bill were at least as concerned with the issue of immigrant women's facility in gaining citizenship and voting power. Removing the old standard that a married woman's citizenship followed that of her husband, the Cable Act gave American women who married foreigners the status of naturalized citizens, except for those who married foreigners "ineligible by race for naturalization"— that is, Chinese. The 1922 act thus reiterated the racist emphasis of contemporary immigration law and did not accomplish the whole feat of making women's citizenship separate from marital status (as men's was). A subsequent lobbying effort by organized women's groups was required, until the Cable Act was revised in 1930–31 to make wives' citizenship fully independent.[22]

Describing the WJCC in 1924, by which time it included twenty-one organizations, Mary Anderson, director of the U.S. Women's Bureau, asserted with pride that "American women are organized, highly organized, and by the millions. They are organized to carry out programs of social and political action." In Anderson's view, women's organizations operated from motives and resources different from those of men's chambers of commerce, fraternal organizations, manufacturers' associations and so on. Where men's pressure groups relied on economic power in politics and looked for commercial or financial advantage or professional gain, women's organizations were working without self-interest, for the public good, for social welfare, with largely volunteer talent, relying upon their influence on public opinion and "upon their voting strength for their success."[23] Anderson's commentary highlighted how far some women leaders persisted in assumptions, formed in the presuffrage era, about women citizens' salutary disinterestedness. It also unintentionally explained why women's organizations (lobby as they might, and did) commanded only a weak position relative to men's groups. Men had economic clout.

The lobbying efforts of women's organizations were more visible than women's successes in electoral politics right after 1920. Realistic comparisons of women's politics before and after 1920 in the formal electoral arena are, for obvious reasons, scarce. There were women voters before 1920, since twelve states granted woman suffrage before 1917 and eighteen more between 1917 and 1920, but their capacities were inconsistent (since states variously granted local, presidential, and full suffrage) and the years were brief. The limited inroads that women made into party politics after 1920 have usually been compared not against women's actual political performance before the passage of the Nineteenth Amendment but against suffragists' rhetoric—or, more precisely, against subsequent recollections of suffragists' beliefs. Suffragists, however, rarely addressed exactly how or for whom women's votes would be collected, whether electing women to office was a high priority, or whether women's votes were adjuncts or substitutes for the already established practice of lobbying and educational work by women's voluntary associations. They talked about such issues as safeguarding children's health, eliminating political corruption, ending the liquor traffic, and improving the economic leverage of women wage-earners, but they rarely specified by what means the injection of women's votes into the polity was to change things.

Suffragists had to argue tactically and strategically in their campaign and their rhetoric may not have conveyed their deepest beliefs. They typically made either very general or rather modest claims and did not touch the subject of women in political office. There were some overarching—if vague—retorts such as Anna Howard Shaw's to an antisuffragist who objected that voting women would have little time for charity: "Thank God, there will not be so much need of charity and philanthropy!" There was rhetoric—again unspecific—regarding women's inclination against war, such as the Congressional Union's claim that "a government responsible to all women, as well as all men, will be less likely to go to war, without real necessity." There were particular anticipations of women's efficacy, such as Florence Kelley's statement that "the enfranchisement of women is indispensable to the solution of the child labor problem." But typically, suffragists' proposals and predictions in the 1910s were local and to the point, as in the New York Woman Suffrage Party's 1910 convention claims that women's ballots would help to alleviate the evils of inadequate inspection of milk, high prices, overcrowded classrooms, crime, prostitution, and child labor and would enable women to preside as associate justices in children's court and women's night court. Carrie Chapman Catt even warned speakers in the 1915 New York campaign against promising "what women will do with the vote."[24]

The unspoken notion that adding women to the electorate should have transformed politics was nonetheless at the heart of some suffragists' disappointment in the 1920s. They were not the only ones sour on politics, however; both popular journalists and political scientists in the decade expressed a mood of skepticism if not downright cynicism about mass political participation, in contrast to the upbeat idealism frequently voiced by reformers in the 1910s. Social scientists stressed the irrational motivations driving individual political behavior, the inability of the mass public to make objective judgments in popular government, and the likelihood that politicians would manipulate these failings. Observers' discouragement about democratic participation found corroboration in the deepening decline in voter participation, a trend continuous since 1896 and intensifying throughout the 1910s and the 1920s. Mean national voter turnout in the presidential election years 1920, 1924, and 1928 was just over half of the eligible electorate, as compared to an average of almost 80 percent in the late nineteenth century. In the off-year elections between 1922 and 1930, little more than a third of the electorate voted, whereas nearly two-thirds, on the average, had voted in the off years between 1876 and 1896.[25]

The meaning of the trend of declining voter turnout between 1896 and the 1920s is not crystal clear, in great part because the meaning of Progressive reform—that is, whether its intents and/or effects were democratic or elitist—is not transparent either. In light of such reforms of the period as direct election of senators, direct primaries, the initiative, referendum, and recall, it seems ironic or tragic indeed that the Progressive era should have ushered in the decade of lowest voter participation ever. But if reforms intended to keep the reins of the state in the hands of the expert or economically powerful few—as some more than others suggest—then the decline in voter turnout fulfilled rather than undid that aim. "Progressive" voting reforms included the continuing disfranchisement of blacks and whole strata of dissident (Populist or Republican) whites in the South by means of poll taxes, literacy tests, and other bars to registration and balloting. In Northern states, more complicated and rigorous residency and registration requirements limited immigrant voting; and at the municipal level, substitution of at-large for district voting destined minority interest group candidates to failure. Progressive reformers attempted to substitute neutral and informed standards for corrupt influence-peddling, but their emphasis on expert presence and management in the state also diverted control from the populace to an elite of professional and business-managerial experts. The results could be seen institutionalized in the 1920s, in forms including city manager rule of municipal governments, federal and state commissions, and such quasi-governmental institutions as the National Bureau of Economic Research.[26]

"It is a misfortune for the woman's movement," mordantly commented Suzanne La Follette, a feminist and pacifist of anti-statist leanings, in 1926, "that it has succeeded in securing political rights for women at the very period when political rights are worth less than they have been at any time since the eighteenth century." The most persuasive explanations of downsliding voter turnout from 1896 to the 1920s have to do with the entrenchment of the Democratic party in the South and the Republican party's domination of the North and West (and thus of the national government) to the extent that voters' interest in partisan contests, and voters' sense of efficacy, collapsed. The portrait of increasingly dispirited voters does not account for the vigor of third parties during the period, but it does account for the overall trend.[27]

Hull House leader Jane Addams was on the mark in 1924 when to a magazine's question, "Is Woman Suffrage Failing?" she responded that the question ought to be "is suffrage failing?" As she noticed, women's political behavior in the 1920s must be looked at in the context of declining voter participation overall. Because of contemporary awareness that popular political participation was slipping, people were concerned whether women voted; there was more interest, overall, in *whether* than in *how* women voted. Indeed, a rash of attention to the "failure" of women to flock to the polls showed up among journalists and political scientists about 1923–24, significantly shaping views of women's voting behavior for the next half century.[28] Much of the blame for the contemporary drop in turnout was pinned on newly eligible women, although dependable data on actual voting behavior were very scarce, for polls were not counted by sex except in Illinois.

The work of political science probably most influential on views of women's political participation was Charles Merriam's and Harold Gosnell's 1923 study, *Non-Voting*. It was an analysis of six thousand nonvoters, a representative sample of the seven hundred thousand Chicagoans (half of those eligible) who had failed to vote in the recent mayoral election. Filled with earnest suggestions for shorter ballots, longer poll hours, voting by mail, and more vigorous efforts by precinct workers, the study nonetheless likened nonvoters to "slackers who fail their country when needed" and portrayed women—who were two-thirds of the nonvoters—as politically uninformed and unambitious. Half of the women failed to vote because of "inertia," the study concluded—that is, a combination of indifference, ignorance, timidity, and neglect—and more than another tenth did not vote because they did not believe that women *should* vote. Among male nonvoters, "inertia" accounted for only one-third. Men more often missed voting because of "physical or administrative obstacles," such as being absent from the city on voting day, fearing loss of business or employment, or not having met legal residence requirements.

The objectivity of Merriam's and Gosnell's methods for obtaining and coding information from nonvoters was not questioned at the time or later, but perhaps it should have been. Although warned to avoid leading respondents to answers, the interviewers (who were graduate students in political science and so must have been men, with rare exception) may have been led to their own conclusions, particularly in the case of white housewives of foreign parentage who formed the largest proportion of the "indifferent" nonvoters. The coding and designation of the "major" reason for the nonvoter who gave several reasons for her failure left room for interpretation. Some of the categories of major reasons were "indifference," "disgust with politics," and "belief that one vote counts for nothing." Which of these was designated the most important reason for a female nonvoter who expressed a mix of attitudes would have led to differing conclusions about women's political potential. Although Merriam and Gosnell never credited nonvoting as a rational response, even to "disgust with politics," they did see the latter as a more active and politically attuned feeling than indifference or ignorance, as well as one presenting "the hardest problem of political control." A smaller proportion of women than men were reported to be "disgusted," while twice the proportion of women than of men was "indifferent."

Merriam's and Gosnell's emphasis on women's indifference and ignorance overshadowed the perspicacious comments of nonvoters who believed "that one vote counts for nothing." "Mrs. Amanda Miles, a young colored laundress," they reported, "never voted because she saw no difference in her own social economic position whether one candidate or another was in office. She thought there was no need wasting time by voting." "Miss Worth, a young lady who worked with a co-operative exchange, did not vote because she was a member of the Farmer-Labor Party and felt that she would waste her time voting for either a Democrat or a Republican." "An elderly lady in the Hyde Park district thought that the election would be a clean sweep so she did not bother to vote." One West Side woman exclaimed, "what is the use in voting when there are no women candidates?" and said "she did not vote because women did not get the chance they deserve[d]." She was labeled "a rabid Irish feminist" by the interviewer, which suggests that the investigation took an antipathetic approach to women's self-consciously defining their own interests in politics.[29]

Merriam's and Gosnell's work tended to dismiss rather than encourage women as voters; in fact it portrayed women as characteristic nonvoters. Contemporaneous discussions of the national elections similarly stressed "women's ineffective use of the vote"—the title given by two Dartmouth College social scientists, Stuart Rice and Malcolm Willey, to their analysis of the 1920 presidential election, in which less than half (46.5 percent) of the eligible women but three-quarters of the eligible men in Illinois had cast ballots. Attempting to derive national statistics, Rice and Willey reasoned that Illinois women, who had had the vote since 1913, were more likely to use it than those just enfranchised. Although they knew that male voter participation had been declining, they did not know how steeply. They therefore estimated men's participation rate in 1920 (outside the South) at about 75 percent and women's possibly as low as 35 percent. Their highest possible estimate for women's turnout was the Illinois rate. Those estimates—showing women's turnout only half as great as men's—stuck in people's minds, although women's voting actually varied greatly from place to place, group to group, and issue to issue. (Bits of evidence now show, for example, that black women, in the few cities where they were not prevented by violence or by registrars, fulfilled both black suffragists' and white opponents' expectations by registering and voting in greater proportions than did white women—that is, in about the same proportions as black men.) It is now fairly clear that the Illinois rate was not the highest in the nation, and that not simply women's nonvoting but also male voters' sinking interest caused the voter participation trough of the 1920s. Although fewer women than men voted, their voting behavior differed less starkly than 1920s political scientists or popular assessments maintained. Women's use of the ballot also immediately, although not consistently, began to rise.[30]

In 1924, a Presidential election year, magazines bloomed with titles such as "Four Years of Equal Suffrage," "What Women Have Done with the Vote," "Is Woman Suffrage a Failure?" and "Woman Suffrage Declared a Failure," causing journalist Ida Tarbell, famous as a muckraker early in the century and a late convert to woman suffrage, to assert that such lament was "probably the strongest of present deterrents to women's voting," aside from lethargy, and "more serious in its effects than many realize." The title of Ida Clyde Clarke's editorial in *Pictorial Review*—"Why Pick on the Women?"—expressed the aggrievement of many former suffragists about the subject. Thrown on the defensive, the LWV journal, the *Woman Citizen*, ran an extensive symposium of its own in which women from "every walk of life" were queried; they generally responded with annoyance at the need to thrust and parry on the issue. None would call woman suffrage a "failure." In a variety of commonsense ways, they said that it was too soon to make any claims about women as voters. They emphasized that the ballot, aside from its direct political impact, was a symbol of recognition of women's citizenship, a mark of self-respect and public respect, an incentive to self-improvement and civic activity, and an important manifestation of change in modern women's lives. The trade union respondents were the most pessimistic about the potential for gain through electoral politics, although that did not make them any less sure that women should take part. Molly Lifshitz, a Russian immigrant and the secretary of the White Goods Workers Union, thought the question "Is Woman Suffrage Failing?" was an insult to women, who deserved the ballot whether or how they used it. Rose Schneiderman of the WTUL said baldly that women's suffrage had been just as disappointing as men's.[31]

How women voted was another question. In the 1910s, as prospective voters women were often presumed to favor candidates who supported Prohibition and social legislation. When Washington, Oregon, and Arizona each adopted Prohibition shortly after adopting woman suffrage, women's votes were assumed to have turned the tide. There were some claims (mainly from Scandinavian evidence) that women were conservative voters and some claims (from New York City) that women swelled the radical vote. Since the Western states where women gained the ballot early were not the most industrially developed, the question whether women's votes would decisively protect women and child wage-earners was not much tested there; but in New York in 1918, women enfranchised the year before helped to defeat four state legislators who had opposed minimum-wage legislation for women, child labor laws, and other social legislation. Assembly*women* replaced two of the four incumbents.

Elizabeth Tilton, a Massachusetts suffragist and leader in the PTA, was not alone in 1919 in her wish to establish "the tradition now that women go into politics to cleanse"—that is, to throw out corrupt political machines. In Columbus, Ohio, that year, shortly after women obtained municipal suffrage, their organizing and voter registration work through voluntary associations succeeded in dumping the city boss who had been mayor for sixteen years, despite his organization's labeling them a "shrieking sisterhood." Nonetheless, most big-city machine politicians had dropped their opposition to woman suffrage by the late 1910s on the observation and reasoning that enfranchised women had *not* tended to vote together to oppose existing political organizations. Claims about the impact of women's votes were so speculative and contradictory, in fact, that when social scientists William Ogburn and Inez Goltra tried to study scientifically "how women vote" in 1919, they found it equally possible to conclude that there were some sex differences or "that the enfranchisement of women will have no other effect than approximately to double the number of votes previously cast." Similarly, Rice and Willey in 1923, with some more evidence, drew the ambivalent conclusion that women neither "merely vote the same as men" nor "vote with marked independence."[32]

Because of the nature of their past campaign, of course, suffragists had more experience in marshalling men's votes than women's. In 1920, the most notable examples of mobilizing women voters as women occurred not in favor of female candidates but against certain male incumbents who were outstanding enemies of woman suffrage. In Connecticut and New York there were major campaigns to defeat incumbent Republican senators Frank Brandegee and James Wadsworth, both intransigent opponents not only of the Nineteenth Amendment (outdoing their Southern colleagues as exponents of states' rights) but also of Prohibition and child labor laws. Wadsworth's wife headed the National Association Opposed to Woman Suffrage. In both states Republican women teamed with other women rather than with their party to defeat these men. In Connecticut, where the suffrage movement, despite intensive organization, had not succeeded at the state level—nor had it managed to move the Republican-controlled legislature to call a session to ratify the Nineteenth Amendment before Tennessee became the thirty-sixth state to do so—the effort to unseat Brandegee also failed. In a year of Republican landslide he ran more than twenty-five thousand votes behind the rest of the Republican ticket, though. The New York effort had similar results. Although leaders in the new LWV (including known Republicans) formed a nonpartisan committee to urge the Democratic Party to find a suitable candidate to defeat Wadsworth, the senator was nonetheless reelected in the Republican sweep.[33]

The woman's "bloc" action did leave Wadsworth trailing Harding's total in New York by seven hundred thousand votes, and it produced a startling response from Nathan Miller, the Republican who had won the governorship on the same ticket. Invited to address the state LWV convention in January 1921, Governor Miller unleashed a volley against the organization, declaiming, "There is no proper place for a *league of women voters*, precisely as I should say there was no proper place for a *league of men voters.*" The two-party system was so essential to the American form of government, he said, that any alternative political mobilization "is a *menace to our free institutions and to representative government.*" He counseled women to withdraw from the organization. He condemned the League's legislative proposals of federal aid to education, old-age and unemployment insurance, and prohibitions against the employment of women at night. Although Miller tried to cover his tracks when he was challenged by Republican women and taunted by the press, the point had been made. His slander of a woman's bloc as alien to American institutions differed in degree and stridency rather than in kind from most partisan politicians' hostility to methods outside their own control.

Such hostility to women's organizing outside party lines had to impinge on their assessments of whether to continue against the grain or to take the standard partisan route. Jean Burnett Tompkins, who had headed the Women's Non-Partisan Senatorial Committee in New York, recommended in the wake of Wadsworth's victory that women should form "for a time, at least, a woman's party," not to run its own candidates, but to elicit female nominations from existing parties by pledging to vote only for women. Carrie Chapman Catt opposed that approach directly; she made clear in 1919 and 1920 her wish for the LWV to be neither a party nor antagonistic to men, but rather to make its nonpartisanship consistent with its members' entry as individuals into the political parties to change them from the inside. After 1920 the LWV stayed well away from endorsing or opposing particular candidates, concentrating on voter education about political issues, research, publicity, and lobbying.[34]

Tompkins' position was rare, but Anne Martin, former leader of the CU's electoral strategy in the Western states, shared it fully. Martin envisioned a woman's party that would support "qualified women candidates . . . [who] pledge themselves to place the interests of women above the interests of any political party." Not until women in government had thus "caught up" with men, she thought, would "sex, both male and female . . . be out of politics." Having twice lost campaigns for the U.S. Senate, Martin vented in print in the early 1920s her visceral understanding that the nation was still a "sex aristocracy" in which women were "ruled by men." She had little but scorn for the LWV's policy to "train women for citizenship" and "to work with the party of your choice," saying that it handed women over to the Republicans and Democrats "exactly where men political leaders wanted them, bound, gagged, divided, and delivered." Looking at the impediments raised to women's voting and office-holding in some states, at the barring of women from juries in many, at the control of political parties by men despite nominal female representation on national committees, at men's hold on all but a few selective and appointive offices, Martin argued that "women must work as a separate political force to win equality." She hearkened back to the Woman's Party's campaign among women voters in 1916, which she believed had transformed the woman suffrage amendment "from the position of an academic question to that of a national political issue which the President dared no longer ignore." Dissatisfied with the political routes adopted by both the LWV and the NWP, Martin retained the organizer's faith that *were* women's organizations to get together and wholeheartedly campaign among women with a "vital program of feminist issues" and a "lively list of candidates," there would be no problem in "getting out the vote."

Not simply unheard, Martin's voice was, more accurately, repressed. Several women's magazines rejected the article containing her views. When the Western regional journal, *Sunset*, did publish her essay, Martin vented some of her pique at male-controlled women's magazines as well as male-controlled politics. She conceded that a big problem in obtaining equality was what she called women's "inferiority complex"— "the humbleness, the timidity, the fear in the hearts and minds of women themselves, planted there by centuries of teaching that woman is the inferior sex." One of the reasons she rejected the LWV's emphasis on educating women for political life was that she felt it confirmed women's self-depreciation, imbibed from men's standards and interpretations; she insisted that women were already as fit as men for political participation, because of their various backgrounds as mothers, teachers, breadwinners, housewives, suffragists, and reformers. Martin believed that women must forswear their contentedness with indirect influence— as she saw their tradition of lobbying—and head straight toward direct electoral action, winning "woman's share, woman's *half* in man-controlled government." [35]

Martin was not the only one who deplored the voluntarist mode as an evasion of the real stakes in politics. Schneiderman in the *Woman Citizen's* forum expressed chagrin that leaders in the woman suffrage campaign had not, by and large, become candidates for political office. Social hygienist Frances Kellor, who had been prominent in the Progressive Party in 1912, lambasted American women for lack of confidence in themselves, women's organizations for not backing women candidates, and the result, that those women who ran for office neither represented nor were responsible to women. New Jersey Republican organizer Lillian Feickert argued that the indirect method went "back to kindergarten days" rather than taking up the mandate of political leadership.[36] There were two issues here: whether women should wield their political influence indirectly or directly—through the voluntarist, lobbying, and pressure group mode or through candidacies and endorsements in partisan contests—and if the latter, whether they should try for thorough integration into men's parties or hold themselves somewhat separate in a woman's bloc. Neither the experience of the suffrage movement nor the goals of Feminism as articulated in the 1910s gave indisputable guidelines as to which kind of participation offered more for women's interests. Neither the voluntarist nor the partisan mode in and of itself was necessarily the more feminist way to proceed: each had the potential to organize women and to make their presence felt in the state. In both modes, the particular objects sought were as significant as the methods of approach. And both had drawbacks: the voluntarist mode echoed the convention of a separate sphere for women; the partisan method risked cooptation as the alternative to rejection by male-controlled parties.

As far as partisan sympathies went, it had been clear before the Nineteenth Amendment was passed that many politically aware women aligned themselves with male-dominated political parties. (In the final years of the campaign, in fact, Maud Wood Park, head of congressional lobbying for NAWSA, preferred to meet with the members of her Congressional Committee individually, because strong and differing partisan loyalties among the women made them "inclined to be suspicious" of one another and prevented frank discussion when the committee met in full. Though distressed by the division, Park accepted that "party women could not be expected to free themselves from the prevailing currents of thought.")[37] Women had more past experience in the voluntarist mode, and it was known to be a way to gather political momentum; on the other hand, the gain of suffrage had promised that women would be able to break free from that mold. Leaders such as Martin and Feickert felt strongly that women ought to carry their talents and experience at organizing women's political sentiments into partisan efforts, not keep them out.

In entering the partisan arena, however, women were caught in a double bind. Women who aimed for partisan influence or political office were skewered between the two motivations to cultivate male party power-holders and to cultivate women voters. Male party leaders were not going to cede any of their power or place to female newcomers on principle, only on political necessity. What political necessity could women command? Only the voting power to bring candidates to victory or defeat, since women, on the whole, did not control powerful economic interests or have political debts to redeem. How were women voters to be mobilized as such? Doing so was the antithesis of party politicians' modus operandi, as Governor Miller's diatribe against a league of women voters had made clear. Of course, women voters could be mobilized to follow men's established partisan priorities; but if that were to be the case, what was the point of women's entry?

The process of nomination and campaigning for elective office brought women face to face with the same kinds of partisan structures and political chicanery some had faced as suffragists. The pattern appeared immediately after ratification of the Nineteenth Amendment that women could obtain the nomination of the Republican or Democratic party for national office (and most of the time for local office) only when that party was destined to be outvoted. The *Woman Citizen* editorialized: "It is clear that the barriers in the way of women being elected to any political office are almost insurmountable. The dominant political parties do not nominate women for political office if there is a real chance for winning. Political offices are the assets of the political machine. In general, they are too valuable to be given to women. They are used to pay political debts or to strengthen the party, and so far the parties are not greatly in debt to women, and it has not been shown that it strengthens a party to nominate them."[38] The record of women who gained national political office in the 1920s paled before the number who tried and failed, many through third-party candidacies. At the local and state level women did better, especially in nonpartisan contests or in the rare cases when they got the endorsement of the reigning party. The number of women state legislators did rise from 33 in 1921 to 149 in 1929, although that was a tiny fraction of the almost 10,000 men in such offices.[39]

Women's efforts to enter partisan politics were suffused with the irony that the dominant parties were only interested in women who were "loyal," and yet for women to become loyal meant they had to give up any pretense of staking out an independent woman's stance. Loyal partisans of both the Republican and Democratic parties exasperated feminists not only by limiting women's access within the parties but also by elevating to nominal positions a handful of women who paid no attention to organized women, who scorned feminism, who were beholden in one way or another to male patrons and followed their instructions. In the Republican-dominated 1920s, women elected or appointed by the ruling party often showed more loyalty to it than to women as a group. One-term Republican congresswoman Alice Robertson of Oklahoma, for example, was one of the few vocal opponents of the Sheppard-Towner bill in the House of Representatives in 1921, belittling the statistics provided by the Children's Bureau as "sob stuff," claiming that the bill embodied "German paternalism," and joining those who argued that the appropriation would drain the Treasury. In Republican-controlled Connecticut, where the LWV repeatedly and unsuccessfully lobbied the legislature to admit women citizens to juries, female Republican state legislators followed the party line. "Women should be more concerned over the breaking down of homes than over the breaking down of the jury system," testified Republican legislator Alice Coe. When eagerly conferring with the head of the Women's Division of the Republican National Committee on the possibility of departmental appointees in the Coolidge administration, Mary Anderson, director of the U.S. Women's Bureau, had to warn that "the wrong woman is very much worse than the wrong man."

Among the Democrats, too, Sue Shelton White bitterly criticized "the few women who have been artificially reared up as leaders" for being "reared not to lead women but to fool them." Emily Newell Blair, an officer in the Democratic National Committee who became increasingly disenchanted during the 1920s with the possibility that women could assert themselves in party politics, decried such appointments, "cited as proof of women's participation in politics," for being in truth "evidence that women do not participate." Those female appointees, she said, ignored women, and depended "for their power and success . . . upon men." The rub was that party organizations could find (and elevate) such "official" women, the "wrong" women.[40]

Emily Newell Blair began the 1920s believing that women should integrate their political intents with men in the Democratic Party, and she ended the decade convinced that women had to organize separately in order to exert partisan political leverage.[41] Not her presuppositions from the suffrage campaign, in other words, but her experience in party politics led her to the latter conclusion. Suffragists had given few hints overall that they envisioned enfranchised women operating separately from men in politics, even to the extent of forming a voting bloc. In counterpoint to suffragists' references to women's common concerns with the home and children stood evidence of lack of unity—not least, the voices of anti-suffragist women. Even among suffragists, differing and sometimes conflicting or rivalrous tactics caused great acrimony. Suffrage leaders tacitly recognized the diversity among women by purposefully designing appeals to the specific self-interest of diverse subgroups (mothers, wage-earners, black women, white women, professionals). Opinion among suffragists was patently divided over the Great War. Conventionally partisan political differences troubled suffragists' cooperation, too.

The one time that some suffragists *did* attempt to marshal women into a voting bloc, they met with condemnation from the majority of their colleagues and little agreement from women voters. That was the CU's campaign among enfranchised women of the Western states in 1914 and 1916 to defeat all Democrats, an effort to make women's power at the polls count on a single issue. (True to the CU legacy, the NWP was the only women's organization to attempt after 1921 to marshal women's votes on specifically women's issues within the partisan system, and it did so halfheartedly.)[42] Given the peculiarity of the CU strategy, mainstream suffragists may have rejected it as misguided in aim (to defeat all Democrats) rather than in method (forming a women's voting bloc); but further hints appeared, especially as the suffrage campaign neared victory, that politically minded suffragists did not regard women voting in a bloc as possible or desirable, but rather envisioned women's presence flowing through the political system. "I don't believe in women forming separate organizations for any cause; it's always better to work with men," so prominent a suffragist as Mary Garrett Hay (a close friend of Carrie Chapman Catt and the manager of the Woman Suffrage Party's victorious referendum campaign in New York state) was quoted as saying in 1918. The partisan rivalries Maud Wood Park had to deal with among her coworkers predicted a major form of political loyalty that would divide women as voters.[43]

Most politically active women in the 1920s, as well as the LWV as an organization, eschewed the notion of a women's voting bloc in favor of women's diverse individuality. Republican women's leader Harriet Taylor Upton said that women voters did "not want to differ from men on lines of sex distinction"; she predicted that women would never vote for female candidates on sex alone but would choose the most qualified individuals. Grace Abbott, head of the Children's Bureau, declared that women's voting record by 1925 showed they were "trying hard to vote as citizens rather than as women, measuring a party or candidate in terms of their judgment on general community needs." Cornelia Bryce Pinchot, a prominent Pennsylvania Republican, believed that women should enter politics to improve the position of their sex. As a candidate for Congress she felt nonetheless that a unique distinction of women in politics was counterproductive; she wanted to be listened to as an individual, with views on many issues. It would have been hard to find a woman candidate of a major party with a different view on this issue. Freda Kirchwey, influential left-leaning writer for the *Nation*, emphasized that "women are going to vote according to the dictates of class interest and personal interest as well as sex interest." To urge women otherwise, she reasoned, was to "forget they are human beings."[44]

These remarks suggest that feminist reasoning might scuttle the notion of a woman's bloc as well as champion it. Candidates' positions on so-called "women's" issues would not stand alone but would combine with their positions on other questions that concerned women. A woman's bloc, to hold, would have to make a single issue its clear priority. (The 1916 attempt had revealed the thorns of that problem. Even for women who agreed with the NWP strategy in principle, the fact that Democratic incumbent Wilson had promised to "keep us out of war" and Republican Charles Evans Hughes had not was a major stumbling block to voting against the Democrats.) As much as the fiction that women were unified in the political arena laid a foundation for feminist action, it entailed the risk of denying women's diversity and individuality, devolving into prescription of a woman's sphere in politics. Suffragists had stressed women's need to represent themselves—and duty to bring to the state their interests and expertise, which differed from men's—but they had also stressed that women and men were equally and individually citizens. That latter strand of suffragist rationale, renewed in the 1910s, justified and predicted women's integration into political associations with men rather than the formation of a "woman bloc."

There were also defensive reasons why women in partisan politics did not pursue or speak of their goals in terms of mobilizing a woman bloc. The notion of a woman bloc was harshly condemned by mainstream male politicians as well as by right-wing ideologues, described as against the American grain, portrayed as the deployment of destructive "sex antagonism." A *New York Times* editorial in 1918 heard the suffragists' clarion as "women are people—human beings sharing certain fundamental human interests, aspirations, and duties with men." At the same time the editorial censured the women's peace conference that would found the

WILPF because it organized women separately from men. Such separation presumed women were "a class, a group, something apart, with class interests . . . a class which apparently hates and distrusts men," the editorial blustered. The latter was a "socialist" theory, of "a world divided into hostile classes," as well as a "revival of sex-antagonism." Like the outburst of Governor Miller to the New York LWV's anti-Republican action in 1920, such name-calling was supported from the right wing, by the *Woman Patriot's* trumpeting that women's organizations formed an "interlocking lobby dictatorship" on Capitol Hill, bent on "organizing women for class and sex war."[45]

"The woman 'bloc' does not tend to become more and more solidified but tends to become more and more disintegrated," journalist William Hard was not alone in noting in 1923.[46] In retrospect, to imagine that women entering politics in the 1920s should have or could have constituted a bloc of voters similar to the coalition formed on behalf of woman suffrage is to underestimate the meaning of such a proposition and the extent to which it crossed purposes with the existing party system. A woman bloc could not really be expected to exist, given the divisions among women and given the nature of the political system; it could be only an interpretive fiction, involving a willing suspension of disbelief. It was only rarely proposed or explicitly envisioned by women leaders as desirable or likely. Against it there was the real diversity of women's loyalties and politics, and the wish of many ambitious women to get beyond the constraints of sex boundaries. Against it also was the way the major political parties, political commentators, and right-wing pressure groups discouraged feminist influence in political life and ridiculed or incriminated attempts by women to organize apart from or against existing structures of male power. Defenders of politics as usual felt it necessary to slay the specter of a woman's bloc again and again, to denigrate, repress, and ridicule it as fiercely as if it threatened them. The depreciation of women as individual voters in the early 1920s was light compared to the imprecation against a woman bloc. In partisan politics women faced a classic double bind: they were damned outright if they attempted to constitute a woman bloc, and damned by scorn or indifference if they did not form one. For such reasons, voluntarist politics continued as women's principal political mode. Yet under that overarching unity of method were goals in conflict.

4

EQUAL RIGHTS AND ECONOMIC ROLES

"Woman's Work," John Sloan, 1911.

In the 1910s Feminists, like all suffragists, linked political and economic rights. While Crystal Eastman acknowledged that "Feminism means different things to different people," she maintained that economic freedom was its "central fact," its "fundamental aspect." Suffragists connected the vote with economic leverage whether they appealed to industrial workers, career women, or housewives. There was every reason to insist on that link. Women had been historically excluded from the political initiative of the franchise because they were defined as dependent, like children and slaves. According to eighteenth-century natural rights philosophy, women did not possess the independence that warranted individual representation in civil society. While it was more than economic, such "independence" was at base an economic quality. At the very least it denoted self-possession—possession of one's own labor power—comprising the "life, liberty and pursuit of happiness" of which Thomas Jefferson wrote in the Declaration of Independence in only slight alteration of John Locke's phrasing, "life, liberty and property."[1] The link between political and economic capacities in the suffrage movement was, indeed, so much a given that its logic was rarely spelled out. Shortly after Michigan granted woman suffrage in 1918, for instance, the Detroit Women Conductors' Association asserted their aim "to permanently see the right of women to be employed and retained in the service of electric railway companies as conductors," contending that was "sound logic" because "in this state women have been given equal rights with men." A woman lawyer in 1920 had company in her assumption that "suffrage granted, the women have freedom of opportunity. It is now supposed that every woman may use her earning ability, whereas heretofore woman was supposed to be dependent."[2]

Enthusiasm for woman suffrage had gathered momentum during decades of economic and occupational change which brought women's presence in the paid labor force into prominence. Awareness of women's economic participation gained by leaps and bounds during the Great War, when some women were hired into skilled trades and many others entered public service. Wartime labor demand and the new unionism brought almost a fifth of industrially employed women into trade unions by 1920. Although returning veterans unseated most of the women who had held "men's" jobs during the War, the perception persisted that women were fast conquering economic terrain. Public media blazoned outstanding individual success stories. "The scene of contest is now shifted to the economic field," Doris Stevens began in an introduction to the book she was writing in the early 1920s. "The political battle is behind us. The next hill to take is the hill of economic equality for women. . . . Masculinized power in industry is no more desirable than was masculinized power in the state. Wherever we go we have got to go together as human beings of equal importance and equal dignity."[3]

Women's rights advocates in the latter part of the nineteenth century had readily observed the economic aspects of women's political subordination to men. They had claimed woman's "right to labor," by which they meant access to all the rigors and rewards of the market. They had enunciated the principle of "equal wages for equal work." In adopting that staple of the post-Civil War labor movement, the "right to labor for a just wage," women had first to step back and claim that sex should not predetermine one's field of labor. The claim of woman's right to labor really meant the right for women to have their labor recognized and diversified; it emphasized women's right and need, as human individuals no less than men, to serve society and themselves in all the possible ways their talents and energies might allow, and to be adequately compensated for it. An assault on the expectation of women's economic dependence on men, as well as on sex-stereotyping of tasks, reasoning about women's right to labor sometimes emphasized that women, no less than men, deserved the self-possession that resided in economic self-support; consistent with a liberal individualist ideal of women's economic independence, such reasoning was also assimilable to the vision of a cooperative commonwealth.

Women in the latter part of the nineteenth century also justified women's wage-earning by means of what might be called an evolutionary analysis of women's work in a changing economy. The evolutionary view began on the premise that women had always been producers, who carried on their economic functions within the household. Since modern commerce and industry had moved economic production from the household to shops and factories and had replaced home production and barter with wage-earning and cash exchange, it was logical and necessary for women to make the move too. As early as 1869 one Cambridge woman who wished to make housekeeping cooperative observed, "the mighty mechanical powers are rolling, rolling [home production] away from under us. In great part it is already gone, and sewing-machines, washing-machines, machines for every smallest office, are taking from us the little that is left of the old manual labor by which we once fed and clothed the world." Accordingly, women's move to paying jobs outside the home was the inevitable transformation of their traditional economic activity, to be encouraged and facilitated rather than restricted. The evolutionary argument gave weight to economic need, and demand factors in the economy, as much as "rights," bringing women into the labor market.[4]

Influential spokeswomen such as Charlotte Perkins Gilman and Olive Schreiner at the turn of the century strengthened these justifications, stressing the necessity and warrant for economic independence for women and rejecting domesticity as a universal model. Their triumph was to reason simultaneously that social evolution made women's move "from fireside to factory" inevitable and also that women (and men) had to spur that move, by renovating outworn mental custom. (It was a predisposition of reform Darwinists such as Gilman to argue that the inevitable nonetheless had to be shaped.) To Feminists such as Gilman and Schreiner, paying jobs appeared to generate not only money but also the disparities of opportunity, power, and prestige between the sexes. In the United States of the early twentieth century, where occupation was regarded as a cardinal characteristic and money increasingly became the measure of worth, where pride in individuals' achieving their own status pervaded the culture, feminist demands for individual autonomy required an economic basis. Wage-earning offered the prospect of individuation, of self-support as distinct from dependence on family—historically a crucial opportunity for women however great the need to which it was tied.

Feminists in the 1910s, perhaps too unreflectingly, connected women's independence with independent wage-earning; they were also outraged at employers' exploitation of women wage-earners. Their Feminism insisted on women's economic independence in principle and defense of wage-earning women in fact. Since wage-earning women were not necessarily, or mostly, economically independent women—their wages were too low for that—the two commitments were not identical but indeed vibrated with tensions.[5] Because of the tradition of women's unpaid labor at home for the family, validation of women's economic contributions along evolutionary lines did not necessarily accord with belief in women's economic independence. The two might in practice be entirely at odds. The purpose to validate women's economic roles as they were might openly conflict with the purpose to throw open economic horizons for women to declare their own self-definition. These tensions, introduced by the Feminism of the 1910s, flared into controversy over the equal rights amendment in the 1920s. Whether even with votes, women in the economic arena had rights or roles equal with men's was the question.

At the outset, National Woman's Party leaders seemed unaware that equal rights would be much thornier to define and implement than equal suffrage had been. They began surveying state legal codes for sex discriminations, conferring with lawyers, drumming up attendance for a delegation to President Warren G. Harding, and drafting numerous versions of equal rights legislation and amendments at the state and federal levels. In sequel to the suffrage strategy, a constitutional amendment to achieve the purpose of equal rights seemed clearly preferable. Yet the "clean sweep" of such an approach immediately raised a problem: would it invalidate sex-based labor legislation—the laws regulating women's hours, wages, and conditions of work that women trade unionists and reformers had worked to establish over the past thirty years? The doctrine of "liberty of contract" between employer and employed had ruled court interpretations of labor legislation in the early twentieth century, stymieing what attempts there were at state regulation of the wages and hours of male workers. Many leading women in the NWP—Dora Lewis, Maud Younger, Jane Norman Smith, and even Paul herself during her settlement house years—had espoused and furthered the cause of protective labor legislation, accepting reasoning that differentiated female from male wage-earners on the basis of physiology and reproductive functions. Now they had to grapple with the question whether such legislation was sex "discrimination," hampering women workers in the labor market, or a form of necessary "affirmative action." Some members of the NWP most concerned with women wage-earners, including Mary Beard, became alarmed about possible harm to labor legislation when Alice Paul experimentally raised the idea of a constitutional amendment for equal rights in the fall of 1920. Katherine Fisher, a social worker involved in the labor movement in Denver, Colorado—a former imprisoned picketer and loyal believer in Paul's magic—nonetheless protested to her, "no amount of opinions from lawyers would convince me that your amendment was the best thing for women workers, or even that it would not be harmful to their interests." In "these days of the weakness of labor and the control of employers over the government," Fisher felt it was foolish to undermine sex-based laws on the visionary proposition of labor legislation for men and women alike.[6]

But was it possible to affirm equal rights and sex-based labor legislation simultaneously? In Wisconsin, prominent NWP suffragist Mabel

Raef Putnam put together a coalition that successfully lobbied through the first state equal rights bill early in 1921, legislation granting women the same rights and privileges as men *except for* "the special protection and privileges which they now enjoy for the general welfare." That kind of compromise was much in the minds of NWP leaders at the state and national level. Paul advised the head of the Massachusetts NWP in March 1921 to

> be very certain that none of the legislation which you introduce in any way disturbs any protective legislation that may have been passed in your state for the welfare of women. I do not think we want to interfere in any way with the so called welfare legislation that has been passed at the instance of the Consumers League and other organizations for the purpose of protecting women from night work and from too long hours of labor, even though this legislation may not be equal for men and women. That is, it seems to me when there is an inequality in which the position of women is better than that of men, we do not want to bring the standard for women down to that of men, but want, on the contrary, to bring that of men up to the standard existing for women.[7]

However, some within the NWP opposed sex-based labor legislation as a form of sex discrimination, and Paul increasingly heeded their opinions. Harriot Stanton Blatch had long objected to such legislation. Believing that "the next big battle for women is equality with men industrially," she contended to Anne Martin during the latter's Senate campaign in 1918 that although protective legislation should apply "for children to the limit," it should affect either all adult workers or none. "Would you regard it as 'protection' were you when elected to the Senate excluded from debates extending over eight hours, taking place Saturday afternoons or at night?" she argued. "You might advocate curtailment of debate but not for particular Senators on sex lines." Applying the same reasoning to wage-earning women, Blatch was sure that "in many highly paid trades women have been pushed into the lower grades of work, limited in earning capacity, if not shut out of the trade entirely by these so-called protective laws." Devoted NWP worker Dr. Caroline Spencer had opposed the eight-hour law for women workers in her home state of Colorado for similar reasons.

The influence of Gail Laughlin, a contentious lawyer from Maine who was in 1919–20 the first president of the National Federation of Business and Professional Women's Clubs, seems to have been decisive in chang-

ing Paul's convictions. Laughlin chaired the NWP Lawyers' Committee
which in the fall of 1921 drew up drafts of state bills and a constitutional
amendment lacking the kind of "safeguard" exempting clause the Wisconsin Equal Rights Bill had. By late November the handwriting was on
the wall as Paul acknowledged to Jane Norman Smith, "personally, I do
not believe in special protective labor legislation for women. It seems to
me that protective labor legislation should be enacted for women and
men alike in a trade or in a geographical district and not along sex lines.
I think that enacting labor laws along sex lines is erecting another handicap for women in the economic struggle." Some NWP affiliates, however, were still trying to draft an amendment that would preserve special
labor legislation, and they continued to introduce equal rights bills with
safeguards in some states through the following spring.[8]

Meanwhile women leaders in voluntarist politics were becoming nervous and distrustful of the NWP's intentions. When the Women's Joint
Congressional Committee came into operation in 1920, the rectification
of sex discrimination in the law was an item on the League of Women
Voters' agenda, but the defense and advancement of sex-based labor legislation were cardinal intents of at least two of the WJCC's constituents—
the National Consumers' League and the National Women's Trade Union
League—and close to the hearts of the others. Moreover, the LWV, as
the WJCC's prime mover, inherited from its parent, National American
Woman Suffrage Association, a legacy of hostility to Alice Paul's opinions
and methods. Resentment of the NWP had never abated in the NAWSA
leadership, not even during the campaign for ratification of the Nineteenth Amendment. Carrie Chapman Catt continued to judge NWP tactics unscrupulous and its strategies counterproductive, and although she
declined official leadership in the LWV in the 1920s, her influence was
certainly felt. Her close associate Maud Wood Park, who had chaired the
NAWSA's Congressional Committee from 1916 to 1920 and became the
first president of the LWV, was suspicious, a priori, of the new NWP.
(Park never forgot the discomfiture that NWP picketing tactics had
caused her and the harm she believed it had done to the suffrage cause.
Decades later she recounted, "nothing was more exasperating than the
queries [from congressmen] . . . 'Why don't you stop them' or 'Why
don't you women get together? You can't expect us to vote for you if you
can't agree among yourselves.'") Volunteers and attorneys from the LWV
who were surveying state legal codes for sex discrimination early in the
1920s assumed an attitude and practice of noncooperation with NWP lawyers who were doing the same thing.[9]

Leaders in the WTUL were also suspicious of the NWP's intents. Their campaign for woman suffrage had gone hand in hand with concentrating emphasis on labor legislation to protect women workers. As suffragists, WTUL leaders had generally steered clear of the NWP, affiliating with NAWSA or state groups. Ethel M. Smith, secretary of the Legislative Committee of the WTUL, which dealt with equal rights issues in the early 1920s, had been NAWSA's press secretary in 1917 and had teamed with Catt to suppress newspaper publicity about the NWP picketing.

Florence Kelley, director of the NCL, had a different history with respect to the suffrage agitation—she had been part of the inner circle of the NWP and was close to several leaders, including Elsie Hill, the new temporary chairman of the party. On the question of protective labor laws, however, she foresaw her priorities diverging from those of her former colleagues. Having spent thirty years trying to shorten hours and improve conditions for workers by state regulation, she had seen success only with regard to women and minors—on sex-based or age-based reasoning—and she was not about to abandon that entering wedge. At the NWP convention of 1921, Kelley was not only let down by Paul's action "on the Negro question" but was more than a little provoked when Harriot Stanton Blatch's daughter Nora Blatch Barney received applause for ridiculing laws that classed women with children as the "industrial and political wards of the state." Kelley suspected, with reason, that the NWP leadership was more wedded to equal rights than to labor laws.[10]

At Kelley's behest, Paul and three other NWP members met in December 1921 with her and leaders of the LWV, the WTUL, the Woman's Christian Temperance Union, and the General Federation of Women's Clubs to discuss the constitutional amendment formulated by the NWP, which said, "No political, civil or legal disabilities or inequalities on account of sex, or on account of marriage unless applying alike to both sexes, shall exist within the United States or any place subject to their jurisdiction." Kelley asked Paul to hold the amendment back until the safety of the labor laws could be assured and proposed that the words *civil* and *legal* be removed. Paul—refusing Kelley's proposal on the ground that it rendered the amendment worthless—stood on the mandate her organization had given her to pursue equal rights. The NWP had no particular intention to dislodge protective laws, she said, but had been unable, in twenty-six drafts, to devise language to preserve such laws without compromising the amendment's intent. Evading direct questions about her own convictions, Paul conceded that some members of the NWP's National Executive Committee, especially Laughlin, opposed sex-based protection on principle. On the other hand, Dora Lewis and Maud Younger, who were also present as NWP representatives, affirmed their support for laws guaranteeing the eight-hour day and minimum wage for women. Maud Wood Park and Ethel Smith, though not at all inclined themselves to temper their opposition, left the meeting very worried about "a cleavage among women . . . which would be most deplorable and harmful to women's interests." All concerned felt compromise was unlikely. Park told Paul, "You will divide the women's movement."[11]

By mid-1922 Kelley's, Park's and Ethel Smith's organizations had gone on record opposing blanket equal rights bills, as the NWP formulations at both state and federal levels were called. Mary Anderson threw the weight of the Women's Bureau against the NWP's proposals, too. "One really would think," commented Anita Pollitzer, national legislative secretary of the NWP, looking at a New York LWV bulletin that opposed NWP efforts, "that instead of attacking an amendment not yet finally drafted, all women interested in women would endeavor to help in the framing." Already each side thought the other intransigent, though in fact debate was still going on within the NWP. At the February 1922 meeting of the NWP National Council (the ruling body replacing the earlier National Executive Committee), Dr. Spencer introduced for consideration a constitutional amendment worded, "Equality of the sexes shall not be denied or abridged on account of sex or marriage." She argued that the NWP should not be concerned with the fate of special labor legislation. Maud Younger took the opposite side, but the tide was turning. An April letter from Laughlin to the National Council meeting communicated her views, which became definitive: sex-based labor legislation was not a lamented loss but a positive harm to be countered by equal rights legislation. "If women can be segregated as a class for special legislation," she warned, "the same classification can be used for special restrictions along any other line which may, at any time, appeal to the caprice or prejudice of our legislatures." In her opinion, if "protective" laws affecting women were not abolished and prohibited, "the advancement of women in business and industry will be stopped and women relegated to the lowest, worst paid labor."

To the NWP inner circle, Laughlin's point was borne out by a 1923 ruling in Wisconsin, where, despite the Equal Rights Bill, the attorney general declined to strike down a 1905 law which prohibited women from being employed in the state legislature. He likened the prohibition to an hours-limitation law, because legislative service required "very long and often unreasonable hours." Alice Paul read his decision as "an extremely effective argument against" drafting equal rights bills with exemptions for sex-based protective legislation.[12] As NWP lobbyists working at the state level made little headway against the many different codes and legal practices of sex discrimination, the clean sweep of a constitutional amendment appeared all the more appealing—the only effective route to equal rights and the logical sequel to the Nineteenth Amendment. In November 1923, at a grand conference staged in Seneca Falls, New York, to commemorate the seventy-fifth anniversary of Elizabeth Cady Stanton's Declaration of Sentiments, the NWP announced new language: "Men and women shall have equal rights throughout the United States and every place subject to its jurisdiction." The constitutional amendment was introduced into Congress on December 10, 1923.[13]

The time had come for "human legislation," for women to emerge from "leading strings," as M. Carey Thomas, the aging president of Bryn Mawr College, put it: "How much better by one blow to do away with discriminating against women in work, salaries, promotion and opportunities to compete with men in a fair field with no favour on either side!"[14] In its emphasis on the "human" outlook and its aim for women no longer to face discrimination through special treatment, the NWP upheld an essential legacy of Feminism. But as Thomas's language suggested, the NWP position on sex-based labor legislation also sounded suspiciously like a laissez-faire ideology which would overlook industrial exploitation and oppose any state regulation of the employer-employee relation. The NWP took the language of liberal individualism to express its feminism. The party expressed no opposition to labor legislation as such, or to protection of motherhood, only to the law's keeping women "segregated as a class" (in Laughlin's words). Sex-based protective legislation was viewed as an anachronism, an artifact of women's long history of economic dependence, keeping alive in women the self-depreciating "psychology of the unpaid worker" long inculcated by domestic servitude. All such legislation assured was that men would monopolize the most interesting and lucrative jobs. Women workers' real interests lay in obtaining equal access to job opportunities and trade unions. Presenting its opposition to sex-based labor legislation as a positive program of "industrial equality," the party became the champion of working women restricted by protective legislation, such as printers, railroad conductors, and waitresses hampered by the hours limitation and cleaning women fired and replaced by men after the passage of minimum-wage laws. But only a handful of working-class women rose in vociferous support for the ERA. Mary Murray, a Brooklyn Railway employee who had resigned from her union in 1920 to protest its acceptance of laws prohibiting night work for women, was one of the most prominent. So was Josephine Casey, a former International Ladies Garment Workers Union organizer, suffrage activist, and later a bookbinder, who chaired the NWP's Industrial Council and spoke for the ERA from NWP platforms at times in the 1920s and 1930s.[15]

With its program of equal rights by constitutional amendment, the NWP not only diverged from the organizations in the WJCC but also made enemies of the male-dominated labor movement, which supported labor legislation for women. At the first Senate subcommittee hearings on the equal rights amendment, representatives of the American Federation of Labor and several international unions joined a lengthy list of women's groups in voicing opposition. Although women trade unionists in the early twentieth century generally found the AFL unresponsive to their needs—and had turned to state regulation in great part because the AFL offered them so few resources—both AFL leaders and its rank and file agreed with them in endorsing labor legislation for women and children. Male unionists or class-conscious workers in this period did not seek labor legislation for themselves, only for women workers. Assuming that the state was (implicitly if not explicitly) ruled by business interests, they eschewed government action and relied on collective bargaining. A mix of attitudes conditioned male unionists' support for sex-based protective legislation: belief in women's physical weakness, veneration of motherhood and women's place in the home, presumptions about women workers being difficult to organize, and intentions to keep women away from men's jobs. Male unionists viewed women first as women—potential or actual wives and mothers—and secondarily as workers. Women and men in the labor movement converged from different directions in their support of sex-based legislation: women saw special protection necessary to defend their stake, limited as it was, in industry and in union organizations; men wanted to hold at bay women's demands for equal entry into male-controlled union jobs and organizations.[16]

The arguments offered by trade unionists and women's organizations against the equal rights amendment overlapped. They assumed that an ERA would invalidate sex-based labor laws or at least destine them for protracted argument in the courts, where judges had shown hostility to any state regulation of employer prerogatives. They feared that such minimal state welfare legislation as was in place, such as widows' pensions, would also be at risk. They contended that a constitutional amendment was too blunt an instrument: sex discriminations such as those concerning jury duty, inheritance rights, nationality, or child custody would be more efficiently and accurately eliminated by specific bills for specific problems. "Nobody defends such laws today, and practically all thinking women, with the vote now in their hands, are agreed that they should be revised or repealed," wrote Ethel Smith, but she saw no need to throw into legal chaos such provisions as mothers' pensions or the husband's legal duty to support his family. Opponents of the ERA sometimes claimed that it took an unnecessarily federal approach, overriding states' rights, although in this they were hardly consistent, for they also opposed blanket bills at the state level, and at the same time, many of the same spokeswomen were advocating a constitutional amendment to prohibit child labor.

Seeing no trace of activity by the NWP on behalf of labor legislation for *both* sexes, supporters of sex-based labor legislation such as Dr. Alice Hamilton, pioneer of industrial medicine, saw the party as maintaining "a purely negative program . . . holding down in their present condition of industrial slavery hundreds of thousands of women without doing anything to alleviate their lot." Before working hours were legally limited, "we were 'free' and 'equal' to work long hours for starvation wages, or free to leave the job and starve!" WTUL leader Pauline Newman bitterly recalled. Opponents of the ERA cited evidence that wage-earning women wanted and valued sex-based labor legislation and that male workers, too, benefited from limits on women's hours in factories where men and women worked at interdependent tasks.[17]

Spokeswomen from the WTUL and the Women's Bureau attacked the NWP's vision as callously class-biased, rooted in the thoughtless outlook of rich women or at best relevant to the experience of exceptional skilled workers or professionals. Only the elite who did not have to work at all or professionals whose conditions of work were unique could possibly denigrate the benefits of labor legislation for women, thought WTUL officer Elisabeth Christman. A former glovemaker herself, she sputtered in fury to Pauline Newman her wish to "put some of the 'equal righters' in a boiler factory or to work at the conveyor belt in a highly speeded-up mass production industry" so they would know whereof they spoke. Christman and her colleagues argued that the greatest good for the greatest number was served by protective laws; if sex-based legislation hampered some, as the NWP claimed—and it could be shown true, for instance, in the case of women linotypists, who needed to work at night—then the proper tactic was to exempt some occupations, not to eliminate protective laws whole. Christman, Newman, Anderson, and their associates regularly accused the NWP of being the unwitting tool (at best) or the paid servant of rapacious employers, although no proof of the latter was ever brought forward. With Belmont's prominence giving their claims a great deal of credibility, they associated the NWP program with the voice of the ruling class.[18]

While women trade unionists denounced the equal rights amendment as "class" legislation—by and for the bourgeoisie—the NWP protested that sex-based labor laws segregated women "as a class." Labor leaders did justify protection for women workers on the grounds of gender-specific biological and social roles, and they were joined by middle-class women's organizations, social welfare reformers, government officials, and trade union men. "Equality between the strong and the weak when they meet on competitive terms in the industrial struggle . . . too often would be to insure that the physically or strategically handicapped shall be driven to the wall," warned Boston patrician reformer Elizabeth Glendower Evans. "We cannot expect overworked, under-nourished women to have the energy or enthusiasm for joining a union," reasoned Clara Beyer, a capable volunteer in the Children's Bureau and the NCL and later the assistant director of the Bureau of Labor Statistics. "Women who are wage earners, with one job in the factory and another in the home have little time and energy left to carry on the fight to better their economic status. They need the help of other women and they need labor laws," reiterated Mary Anderson. "I must," declared Alice Hamilton, "as a practical person, familiar with the great inarticulate body of working women, reiterate my belief that they are largely helpless, that they have very special needs which unaided they cannot attain, and that it would be a crime for the country to pass legislation which would not only make it impossible to better their lot in the near future but would even deprive them of the small measure of protection they now enjoy."[19]

Such renderings of wage-earning women as weak, dependent, and overburdened swamped the prior Feminist image of women as equal producers of the world's wealth. The civic-minded middle-class women who supported sex-based protective labor legislation were more concerned with working women's motherhood than with economic justice. "The great mass of women," one LWV leader wrote in the *Woman Citizen*, "believe that the most important function of woman in the world is motherhood, that the welfare of the child should be the first consideration, and that because of their maternal functions women should be protected against undue strain."[20] Proponents of protective legislation envisaged wage-earning women as veritable beasts of burden (their double burden lightened, if at all, by the nobility of sacrifice), rather than as a vanguard of independent female personalities. Lavinia Dock criticized that perspective for operating "under the shadow of the caste idea," maintaining wage-earning women's sense of themselves as inferior. Dock supported the equal rights amendment although she was distressed to find herself "separated from old associates in the woman movement, and . . . from trade union friends, when . . . still heart and soul in sympathy with labor." Similarly, Harriot Stanton Blatch was sure that working women were "ready for equality" and thought that "it was the welfare worker who was holding up to them the inferiority complex."[21]

Who were the employed women about whom this controversy raged? The U.S. Census counted approximately a quarter of American women (over the age of fourteen) in the labor force in the early twentieth century. That proportion changed little between 1910 and 1940, but the kinds and the visibility of jobs women held, and the age, class, and marital status of women who held them were changing. The female labor force was becoming an older group under the influence of some state prohibitions of child labor and compulsory schooling laws. In manufacturing, over half (almost 55 percent) of employed women in the 1920s were over twenty-five; in domestic and personal service, where black women were concentrated, three-quarters were. And although movies about the "working girl" virtually always ended with her leaving employment for marriage, the truth did not match the screen image. The proportion of married women who were gainfully employed doubled between 1900 and 1930, rising six times as fast as the proportion of unmarried women. The steepness of the rise stemmed from a very low starting point, of course; even by 1930 less than 12 percent of all married women were in the labor force—but married women composed almost 30 percent of all women employed. These census statistics, moreover, concealed the presence in the labor force of *once*-married women who probably had children to support, by classifying as married only those women whose husbands were present; a single category was made of those who were unmarried, divorced, widowed, or separated from their husbands. In twenty-five state and special studies of industrial and service sites during the 1920s, the Women's Bureau found that single women made up only a little over half of those employed; women who were married (30 percent) and widowed, divorced, or separated from their husbands (17.5 percent) composed close to another half.[22]

At least half of the female labor force worked in taxing, menial jobs that offered long hours, unpleasant and often unhealthful conditions, very low pay, and rare opportunities for advancement. These were the manufacturing operatives (almost a quarter of all women employed) and the even larger number in domestic and personal services (almost half of them servants). In factories women made, on the average, little more than *half* the wages of men; the average woman's plus the average child's wages at the end of the 1920s together equaled less than the average man's wage. In service occupations, women's wages were even lower than in manufacturing. Their wages were so low because women workers were clumped in unskilled jobs (without the opportunity to train for better) and because women were viewed by male employers and by most employees as "secondary" laborers by definition, warranting a fraction of men's pay.

It stood to reason that no one would subject herself to drudgery for a pittance unless the pittance made the difference between bare support and none. To those who investigated, as did the Women's Bureau and its allies in the WTUL, it was clear that women workers in industry and service were there not to earn pin money but to support themselves and their dependents at a minimum level of decency. Whether daughters, single adults, wives, or widows, wage-earning women used their wages to sustain their families, the Women's Bureau showed. Daughters more often and more generously than sons turned their wages over to their parents. More than 90 percent of wage-earning women investigated by the Women's Bureau in twenty-two different case studies from 1888 to 1923 contributed all or part of their earnings to family support.[23]

More than one wage-earner per family was necessary when the wages of an unskilled or semiskilled man employed year-round were barely sufficient to support four, according to contemporary budget studies, and layoffs or ill health were likely to interfere with year-round employment. The "new business civilization" of the 1920s that presidents Harding and Coolidge and managerial executives liked to celebrate looked less than rosy to working-class families. Aggregate statistical increases in gross national product and national income averages masked the fact that wage gains in blue-collar employment were selective and sporadic. In most working-class occupations the war years (1914–20) brought greater gains than the 1920s. The wages of certain groups of workers—notably skilled workers in the building trades, skilled railroad workers, printers, and hosiery and knit goods workers—did grow considerably in the 1920s. But in general, the real wages of unskilled workers (which included most women working in manufacturing) did not increase, and wage differentials widened between skilled and unskilled jobs. Most working-class families lived in economic insecurity. It is unlikely that the half of American families whose incomes were under seventeen hundred dollars a year in the mid-1920s could even obtain a nutritious diet, much less take advantage of the goods of mass consumption which their labor helped to produce.

Although unemployment during the 1920s was not unusually high, it was sufficiently endemic to threaten poverty for probably a third of blue-collar workers on a year-to-year basis. In families such as these, where the men were employed at low wages themselves or were periodically or permanently unemployed, women's wages became an increasingly regular necessity. For decades wives and mothers had turned household labor into cash in ways not necessarily reported to or noticed by census records of the female labor force, taking in laundry or mending, keeping lodgers or boarders. Immigration restriction in the 1920s diminished the number of new arrivals looking for boarding or lodging arrangements, and industrial home work was curtailed through zoning and anti-"sweating" regulations; thus typical opportunities for women in working-class families to contribute to family income without leaving the home shrank, and more wives and mothers had to take factory or outside service jobs in order to bring in any cash. Some of the statistical increase in wives' labor force participation in the 1920s registered that kind of shift. For poor families, legislative restrictions on child labor effected during the early twentieth century meant a corresponding rise in the labor force participation of wives and mothers; when young children were compelled by law to attend school or prohibited from employment—in the Southern tobacco and textile industries, for example—the employment of wives and mothers increased.[24]

In overall pattern, however, women's employment was moving through and gradually out of the manufacturing sector, just as it was leaving behind its nineteenth-century roots in domestic service and agriculture, and swelling in the white-collar areas. Less than 18 percent of employed women worked in clerical, managerial, sales, and professional areas in 1900; two decades later that proportion had more than doubled, and by 1930 it was 44 percent. In the 1910s alone, the proportion of women employed in clerical occupations rose by 140 percent. Because men's work was moving in the same direction but not so rapidly as women's, the pattern of change in women's employment has been called "su-pertypical" of the labor force. The increased demand for women as white-collar workers came from the consolidation, national marketing strategies, and new technologies of American corporations, which re-quired literate and tractable laborers to put to use in record-keeping, personnel, advertising, retail sales, and telecommunications. Employers could rely on the public school system to train the applicants for the general run of clerical hiring. The proportion of teenagers attending high school zoomed up from 10 percent in 1904 to 53 percent in 1920, in conjunction with the changing shape of the economy. Women assumed new jobs, creating new employment patterns, without altering the on-going sex segregation of the work force—the facts that there were men's jobs and women's jobs and they rarely overlapped. As women were hired in new employments—as telephone operators, for example—these rap-idly became defined as women's work, consistent with existing sex seg-regation.

The move of "women's" employment toward the white-collar sector was actually racially specific, established by the numerical predominance of whites. Black women did not share it despite being twice as likely as white women to be in the labor force. White racism enforced by eco-nomic power kept black women in their traditional work in agriculture and domestic service. Virtually barred from jobs in industry until the Great War's increased industrial demand, black women entered factories then (under segregated and inferior conditions); they were kept from clerical or sales work in white establishments until decades later. Outside of agriculture, four-fifths of black women wage-earners in 1920 were maids, cooks, or washerwomen. In the expanding clerical and profes-sional fields, white American-born women took the lion's share—90 per-cent—from 1890 through 1920. In succeeding decades women in these fields were much more likely to be daughters of immigrants than they had been a generation earlier.[25]

Women's white-collar work covered a considerable range, from the very routine to the challenging and near-professional. It had the advan-tage of cleaner and calmer surroundings than the factory and usually shorter hours. The theory that clerical work was an entering wedge was offered to the ambitious by career advice books and by some of the suc-cessful. Because it seemed to lie on a continuum with executive, entre-preneurial, and professional work, it commanded at least nominal pres-tige. Any girl could become a businesswoman, in the parlance of the time, by obtaining white-collar employment, and if the lowly saleswoman or secretary showed the right combination of talents, she might become an executive in her own right.[26]

But despite there being no bar in theory to women's rise via white-collar work, there were limits in fact. The changing character of office work in the 1910s and 1920s—the very changes that made employers seek more female personnel at low pay—made it less likely that an entering position would lead to "a big job." In the office as in the manufacturing plant, the mass production methods of mechanization, specialization, and division of labor accompanied visible increase in scale of operation and were all sought by large-scale employers to maximize efficiency and profit. Scientific management techniques were applied to clerical functions. "Jobs are being analyzed, time and motion studies made, layout and routing studied," observed Grace Coyle, a Barnard College economics lecturer; "piece rates in some places are being set for typing, billing or transcribing." The division of labor was so extensive in larger offices that women hired at entry level positions were likely to be exposed to only a narrow range of tasks, and they were increasingly segregated by job category in the office. The stenographer who in a small office might work near the employer was in larger-scale offices located in the "stenographic bureau." As the number of routine jobs increased, chances for promotion ebbed, especially for women. The likelihood of a personal relationship developing between the manager and the employee, and opportunities for gaining substantive knowledge and skills on-the-job—tacit conditions for seeing clerical work as a route to something better—evaporated under such conditions.[27]

In the mid-1920s a comprehensive study by the National Industrial Conference Board showed that women were clumped in the low-paying areas of typing, stenography, bookkeeping, cashiering, office machine operation, and salesclerking. Men vastly predominated in the higher-paid white-collar categories such as chief clerk, senior cashier, or head bookkeeper. During that decade clerical workers experienced a gain in real wages (as adjusted for inflation), but such a gain was measurable only because clerical wages had dropped so much during the 1910s, when women entered most rapidly into the field. Over the longer period from the late 1890s through the 1920s average earnings in clerical work remained static, registering the multiplication of jobs at the bottom level. The average annual salary of a routine clerical employee in the mid-1920s was $1,200 when the average for all gainfully occupied persons in the United States was $2,010 and the average for those earning under $3,000 (the vast majority) was $1,693. There was real question whether the

woman in ordinary white-collar employment could, any more than the
woman employed in manufacturing or service, realistically consider herself an independent woman.[28]

What was the relation between the meager earnings, in exploitative conditions, of hard-pressed wives and mothers—or the routine jobs of
young women in service and sales—and feminism? A not unsympathetic
critic, a Southern academic, asked rhetorically, "do the feminists see in
the tired and haggard faces of young waitresses, who spend seventy
hours a week of hard work in exchange for a few dollars to pay for food
and clothing, a deceptive mask of the noble spirit within?" and answered
herself, "Surely it is not an increasing army of jaded girls and spent
women that pours every day from factory and shop that the leaders of
the feminist movement seek. But the call for women to make all labor
their province can mean nothing more. They would free women from
the rule of men only to make them greater slaves to the machines of
industry." Indeed, the exploitation of female service and industrial workers at cheap wages cruelly parodied the feminist notion that gainful employment represented an assertion of independence, just as the wifely
duties a secretary had to perform parodied the feminist expectation that
wage-earning would challenge the sexual division of labor and reopen
definitions of femininity.[29]

The controversy over equal rights and women's economic status in the
1920s reverberated with these issues and sharpened the points of contradiction. Women who favored the ERA and those who supported protective legislation alike saw themselves as legatees of feminism intending to
sustain, in law and economic practice, its several impulses: to defend the
value of women's economic roles as they were for what they were, to
prevent economic exploitation of women, and to open the doors to economic opportunity. A struggle over the term *feminism* became part of
the controversy. One advocate of protective legislation fumed that
though a person be "ready to burn at the stake for the Equal Moral Standard, for women's full emancipation in civic and state affairs, in marriage,
in religion, in education, in the professions—let her so much as tempo-
rize in the least on the subject of 'protective legislation for women in
industry'" and she was no longer a Feminist with a "capital F." For "us
even to use the word feminist," contended Ethel Smith, "is to invite from
the extremists a challenge to our authenticity." Detractors in the WTUL
and the Women's Bureau called the NWP "ultra" or "extreme" feminists.
Mary Anderson considered herself "a good feminist" but objected that

"over-articulate theorists were attempting to solve the working women's problems on a purely feministic basis with the working women's own voice far less adequately heard." Her own type of feminist was moderate and practical, Anderson declared; the others, always putting the "woman question" first, were extreme and abstract.[30] Having declared the party the tool of the "ruling class," women allied with labor (and the left), even if their everyday actions challenged male domination, had to separate themselves from the feminism identified with the NWP. These distinctions by anti-ERA spokeswomen forwarded public perceptions of feminism as a sectarian and impracticable doctrine unrelated to real life and blind to injustices other than sex inequality. By the end of the 1920s women outside the NWP rarely made efforts to reclaim the term *feminist* for themselves, and the meaning of the term was depleted.

In the trade of recriminations, there were exaggerations and caricatures. The relation of sex-based legislation to the welfare of women workers was more ambiguous and complicated than either side acknowledged. (By 1925, all but four states limited working women's hours, usually to nine or ten per day, but in nine cases to eight; eighteen states prescribed rest periods and meal hours; sixteen states prohibited night work by women in certain occupations; and thirteen had minimum wage regulations.) By shortening the work week and improving conditions (minimum wage laws, resisted more emphatically by employers, were fewer and not well enforced), protective laws benefited a far larger number of employed women than they hindered; but the laws, both immediately and in the long run, also limited women's economic opportunities. Sex segregation of the labor market was a very significant factor there. In industries monopolizing women, where wages, conditions, and hours were likely to be substandard, protective legislation helped to bring things up to standard. In more desirable crafts and trades more unusual for women, however, where skill levels and pay were likely to be higher—that is, those areas women needed to enter in order to improve their earnings and economic advancement—sex-based protective legislation held women back. There, as a contemporary inquiry into the issue said, "the practice of enacting laws covering women alone appears to discourage their employment, and thereby fosters the prejudice against them." The segregation of women into low-paid, dead-end jobs that made protective laws for women workers necessary was thus abetted by the legislation itself.[31]

Nor was it unambiguously clear that labor legislation principally protected workers', rather than employers', interests. Workers did not unanimously seek the state's protection (indeed, male trade unionists generally did not), nor were employers unanimously hostile. The first major breaks in industry's hard line on freedom of contract came before the Great War in conjunction with scientific management techniques. Employers, especially large corporations, by the 1920s recognized that regulatory legislation could stabilize the labor market and eliminate unscrupulous competition. Although the National Association of Manufacturers, fixed on the individualist-entrepreneurial values of earlier generations, continued to oppose such laws, some employers of women, including white-collar employers, either tolerated sex-based labor legislation on reasoning about "protection of the race," or saw advantages for themselves in it, or both. A vice-president of Filene's, the large department store in Boston, for instance, approved laws regulating the hours, wages, and conditions of women employees because "economies have been effected by the reduction of labor turnover; by reduction of the number of days lost through illness and accidents; and by increase in the efficiency of the working force as well as in the efficiency of management. Legislation tends to stabalize [sic] the labor market by raising or maintaining standards as to hours, wages, and working conditions throughout industry as a *whole,* thus preventing selfish interests from indulging in unfair competition by the exploitation of women."[32]

While the anti-ERA side was right in the utilitarian contention that protective laws meant the greatest good to the greatest number of women workers (at least in the short run), the pro-ERA side was also right that such laws hampered women's scope in the labor market and, perhaps more damagingly, sustained the expectation that women were secondary earners to whom employment advantage was of only secondary concern. Those who advocated sex-based laws were looking at the labor market as it was, trying as best possible to protect women in it, and thereby contributing to the perpetuation of existing inequalities. Those who opposed sex-based "protections" were envisioning the labor market as it might be, trying to ensure women the widest opportunities in that imagined arena, and thereby blinking at existing exploitation. Proponents of protective legislation did not see that their conception of women's needs helped to confirm women's second-class position in the economy. Nor did advocates of the ERA admit to the vulnerabilities that sex-based legislation addressed, while they also overestimated what "equal rights" could do to unchain women from the economic stranglehold of the domestic stereotype.

The one side tacitly positing the independent professional woman as the paradigm, the other presuming the doubly burdened mother in industry or service, neither side distinguished nor addressed directly the situation of the fastest-growing sector of employed women, those in white-collar jobs. In this controversy between women over what feminism meant, the positions were also taken up by, and inevitably were colored by, male "allies" whose principal concerns dealt less with women's economic or legal protection or advancement than with political priorities of their own. At the Women's Bureau Conference on Women in Industry in 1926, the NWP opposition to sex-based labor legislation was echoed by John Edgerton, president of the National Association of Manufacturers. Without ever mentioning equal rights, Edgerton declared that the "handful" of women in industry could take care of themselves and were not served by legislative "poultices." He expended more breath in condemning (in harsh if vague terms) the specter of Bolshevism and other foreign evils stalking America and warning that women's organizations were likely to fall subject to alien influences. At the same conference, Republican Secretary of Labor James Davis defended sex-based protective legislation by proclaiming that "the place fixed for women by God and Nature is a great place," and "wherever we see women at work we must see them in terms of motherhood." Such labor movement careerists as Anderson, Newman, and Christman (whose very life choices represented a wider set of options) thus found in their camp rhetoric befitting the previous century. Woman is "by her very nature . . . the standard of morality . . . the stabilizer of the home," Davis declared. What he saw as the great danger of the age was the "increasing loss of the distinction between manliness and true femininity."[33]

Among the women on the two sides of the controversy, divergent views of women as economic actors—and of womanhood itself—congealed. Deeply differing views of the social significance of gender compounded the bitterness of the conflict of personalities and tactics that had dragged on from the suffrage years. Opponents of the ERA who resented finding themselves opposed to something called equal rights maligned the NWP as "pernicious" and described its members as women who "discard[ed] all ethics and fair play," an "insane crowd" who espoused "a kind of hysterical feminism with a slogan for a program." "If I had not seen them with my own eyes and heard them with my own ears," a friend of Mary Anderson's wrote her after the Women's Bureau's conference on Women in Industry in 1926, "no one could ever have made me believe there could be such a diabolical group of women. The agitation has united our groups of women much closer against such fanatical reproach to womankind."[34]

The advocates of the ERA in the NWP had before their eyes an image

of women who were eager and robust; supporters of protective legislation saw women overburdened and vulnerable. The former claimed that
protective laws penalized the strong; the latter claimed that the ERA
would sacrifice the weak. The supporters of the NWP looked at women
as individuals and wanted to dislodge gender differentiation from the
labor market. Their opponents looked at women as members of families—daughters, wives, mothers, and widows with family responsibilities—and believed that the premise of "mere equality" was "not enough"
to take those relationships into account. Forced into theorizing by this
controversy, not prepared as philosophers or legal theorists, spokeswomen on either side in the 1920s were grappling with definitions of
women's rights as compared to men's that neither the legal nor the economic system was designed to accommodate. The evaluation whether
"equality" required that women have the "same" rights as men or "different" rights could not be made without delving into definitions of equality
and difference themselves. Did equality pertain to opportunity, treatment, or outcome? Should difference be construed to mean separation,
discrimination, protection, privilege, and/or assault on the very standard
that the male was the human norm?[35]

Both sides had implicit conceptions of women's distinct "difference" as
a social group; their conceptions came into conflict especially around the
issue of the sexual division of labor. Women such as Smith, Kelley, Park,
Newman, and Anderson believed that sex-based legislation was necessary because of women's biological and social roles as mothers. They
claimed that "the inherent differences are permanent. Women will always need many laws different from those needed by men." "Women as
such, whether or not they are mothers present or prospective, will always need protective legislation." "The working mother is handicapped
by her own nature." Florence Kelley broke decisively with her former
NWP colleagues on those issues. "So long as men cannot be mothers,"
she believed, "so long legislation adequate for them can never be adequate for wage-earning women; and the cry Equality, Equality, where
Nature has created Inequality, is as stupid and as deadly as the cry Peace,
Peace, where there is no Peace."[36] Their approach stressed maternal nature and inclination as well as conditioning and implied that the sexual
division of labor was eternal.

The approach of the NWP, on the other hand, presupposed that wom-
en's differentiation from men in the law and the labor market was a particular, sociohistorical construction, not necessary or inevitable. The sexual division of labor arose from archaic social custom, was enshrined in

employer and employee attitudes, and reified in the law. The approach of the NWP assumed that wives and mothers as well as unencumbered women would want and should have open access to jobs and professions. Party proponents projected that the sexual division of labor (in the family and the marketplace) could and should be altered, if women could secure the same rights as men and have free access, regardless of family role, to wage-earning. That view made a fragile potential into a necessary fact; it merged two feminist promises—that women's wage-earning would challenge the sexual division of labor and that it would provide the means for women's economic independence—and went further to posit that these tenets were necessarily in the process of being realized as women entered gainful employment.

Wage-earning women's experience in the 1910s and 1920s, however, as investigated by the Women's Bureau and other proponents of sex-based legislation, showed that the inchoate potential for women's gainful employment to challenge the sexual division of labor was only very selectively and marginally realized. The majority of women's wages were not sufficient to bring them economic independence; women earned as part of a plan for family support (as men did, though that was rarely stressed). Contrary to the NWP's feminist visions, those places in the nation where wives and mothers of young children were most intensively engaged in gainful employment were also where the sexual division of labor was most oppressively in place. To every child growing up in the region of Southern textile and tobacco mills, where wives and mothers worked more jobs at home and in the factory than any other age or status group, and for less pay, the sexual division of labor appeared no less prescriptive and burdensome than it had before women earned wages.[37]

Critiques of the NWP and its ERA as "abstract" or "extreme" or "fanatical," frequently voiced by proponents of protective labor legislation, represented the gap between feminist tenets and harsh social reality—between the potential for women's wage-earning to challenge the sexual division of labor and the social facts of gender and class hierarchy that clamped down on that challenge—as an oversight of the NWP, a failure to adjust their sights. By such opponents the ERA was casually called "naive" or more acidly denounced as purveying "a doctrine which asks no questions, a doctrine capable of development and theoretical application off in a world apart where one need make no compromise with biology, psychology, politics, history, industry." Anne Martin, who kept her distance from the NWP in the 1920s, related to Sara Bard Field the private opinion of Hull House leader Jane Addams that the ERA was "'legalistic'—opposed to life and opposed to history." "Miss A.[ddams] said if Miss. P.[aul] overcame her ignorance of society and life by reading and living more, she would never be in the barren position today of fighting for such an amendment," Martin recounted; Addams thought that "protective legislation for women and children is necessary to overcome nature's handicap, has always preceded better legislation for men, and equalizes for all in the end." Even Harriet Stanton Blatch conceded that "a law not meeting the demands of abstract justice may still come nearer to serving humanity than no law at all."[38]

Such criticisms of the NWP's "abstraction" were attempting to sustain the double-barreled message of early Feminism, what Katherine Anthony had looked for as "the emancipation of woman both as a human-being and a sex-being." They manifested the impulse to incorporate women's unique reproductive endowments and social obligations in provisions for equal opportunity. As much as defenders of sex-based protective legislation were grappling with these difficult problems—problems that would still be present more than half a century later—their immediate resolution was to portray the "difference" that the legal system needed to accommodate in terms of merely customary notions of women's place and purpose. "Average American women prefer to make a home for husbands and children to anything else," Mary Anderson asserted in defense of her position. "They would rather fulfill this normal function than go into the business world."[39] The language used, labeling proponents of the ERA "barren" and defenders of protective legislation "normal," reeked of the derisive means always used to circumscribe women's aims within the patriarchal household. That even such women as Jane Addams and Mary Anderson adopted such language, although they themselves had purposefully not married in order to devote their lives to causes larger than the individual family, measured how tightly grasping were the tentacles of that worldview in which wife- and motherhood were women's all.

Spokeswomen defending protective labor legislation kept alive a critique of the class division of wealth, but they lost sight of the need to challenge the sexual division of labor, in the labor market and at home, that was the root of women's "handicap" or "helplessness." In contrast to the NWP's emphasis on the historical and social construction of gender roles, advocates of sex-based protective legislation echoed customary public opinion in proposing that motherhood and wage-earning should be mutually exclusive. They easily found allies among such social conservatives as the National Council of Catholic Women, whose representatives testified against the ERA because it "seriously menaced . . . the unity of the home and family life" and contravened the "essential differences in rights and duties" of the two sexes which were the "result of natural law." Edging into plain disapproval of mothers of young children who earned, protective legislation supporters became more prescriptive, less flexible, than wage-earning mothers themselves, for whom cash recognition of their labor was a welcome benchmark. ("Why should not a married woman work [for pay], if a single one does?" demanded one, a mill worker who came to the Southern Summer School for Women Workers and who protested that taking in boarders or washing was "as hard work as women can do." "What would men think if they were told that a married man should not work? If we women would not be so submissive and take everything for granted, if we would awake and stand up for our rights, this world would be a better place to live in, at least it would be better for the women. . . . why would it not be all right for them to go to a factory and receive pay for what they do?")[40]

Wage-earning women en masse probably found the views of protective legislation advocates more palatable, however, than the equal rights challenge to the sexual division of labor. Although schooling and citizenship taught women to claim their individual rights—and the campaign for suffrage had emphasized women's rights as well as their obligations—myriad cultural lessons also taught women to disqualify themselves from the model of individualist striving. The NWP's approach to equal rights presupposed a view of self and social relations in which atomistic individuals, male and female, were joined in society by competition and contract. Wage-earning women more likely had experienced upbringing in which interdependent male and female roles appeared organically linked and justified by religion and tradition. Working-class women raised in immigrant communities were predisposed to understand gender roles as building blocks of family mutuality and interdependence, of neighborhood and kin cooperation and survival.[41] The equal rights promised by the NWP—especially as negatively presented by trade unionists and other defenders of sex-based legislation—appeared to subvert those roles without providing secure alternatives.

The onset of the Depression in many ways worsened the ERA controversy, for the one side thought sex-based protective legislation all the more crucial in such hard times, when need drove women to take whatever jobs they could get, and the other side argued that protective legislation prevented women from competing for what jobs there were. The 1930s showed, too, that opposition to the equal rights amendment in the

labor movement and in the LWV ran deeper than the issue of labor legislation alone. When the Fair Labor Standards Act of 1938 mandated
regulation for all workers, and the U.S. Supreme Court made it the law
of the land in 1941, the labor movement and the LWV still opposed the
ERA. By 1944, however, the NWP elicited support from major women's
organizations, most importantly the NFBPW and the GFWC, as well as
from the national platforms of both the Republican and the Democratic
parties.[42]

The controversy over the ERA testified to the difficulty of translating
1910s Feminist conceptions, multifaceted and even internally contradictory as they were, into law and social policy and practice. The crosscutting aims to protect women in the economic arena and to open opportunities to them there were most obviously at issue. But those aims led
directly into considerations of women's equality with as against their difference from men and of women's solidarity with or likeness to each
other as against their heterogeneous individuality and their potentially
conflicting identifications besides gender. The policy of the NWP displayed the feminist paradox of women mobilizing as a class to defeat
discrimination against them as a class, but more important, the controversy it generated brought into question the NWP's basic premise. What
kind of a "class" were women when their occupational, social, and other
loyalties were varied; when not all women viewed "women's" interests,
or what constituted sex discrimination, in the same way? The problem in
its ideological dimensions cut across both class consciousness and gender
identity. At its heart was not only the question whether in law and social
policy each woman should be treated as an individual or as part of a social
group, but also what social group was the most relevant categorization.
The battle over the ERA of the 1920s seared into memory the fact of
warring outlooks among women while it illustrated the inevitable interdependence of women's legal and political rights with their economic
situations. Its intensity indicated how fundamental was the re-vision
needed, if policies and practices of economic and civic life deriving from
a male norm were to give full scope to women—and to women of all
sorts.

5

MODERN TIMES

When lovely women vote

To thousands of women of this type— charming, educated, well-to-do, prominent in the social and civic life of her city, we put this question: What tooth paste do you use?

To our delight, the majority answered Listerine Tooth Paste. Certainly to women of means, the price of 25¢ could not possibly have been a factor in deciding upon a tooth paste. Obviously, the quality of the dentifrice itself and the brilliant results

it accomplished were responsible for their choice.

Won't you try Listerine Tooth Paste? See how thoroughly it cleans. How swiftly it erases blemishes and discolorations. How gleaming white it leaves the teeth. How it refreshes the mouth and sweetens the breath. Bear in mind, incidentally, that it costs you but half of what you would ordinarily pay for tooth paste of equal quality. Lambert Pharmacal Co., St. Louis, Mo.

LISTERINE TOOTH PASTE the quality dentifrice at 25¢

Advertisement in *American Magazine*, October 1932.

"The women of yesterday probably could not have done it at all," advertisements for the Piggly-Wiggly food markets, innovators in self-service, praised 1920s housewives. The modern woman, choosing her own groceries off the shelf with "no clerk to persuade her," had "astonished her husband . . . and the world." "Her new, wide knowledge of values, her new ability to decide for herself, is one of the wonders of the world we live in."[1] The modern woman and her world described by the ad were part of an urban industrial economy of mass production, individual wage-earning, and money purchases—the enlarging norm. In 1920, for the first time, America's population was more than half urban. The bulk of rural residence and agricultural production in the national economy had sharply diminished. Americans were not only more concentrated in cities than ever before, they were clustering in and near the largest cities, in part because of the newly popular automobile. In 1910 there was 1 automobile per 265 persons in the United States; in 1928, the ratio was 1 to 6. Automobile transportation stimulated the building of suburbs, where population growth outdistanced that of central cities. Large metropolitan areas grew the fastest, accounting for almost three-quarters of the expansion of the U.S. population in the 1920s. The New York metropolitan area grew faster than twenty-eight states combined.

Urban households could take advantage of municipal services such as water and sewers, gas, electricity, and garbage disposal. The great majority of urban families at all economic levels had indoor plumbing and gas or electric lighting by the mid-1920s. Rural electrification was proceeding, although not evenly. Inside and outside the cities, income as well as location dictated families' ability to partake in the modernization of the household. Still fewer than three-fifths of white tobacco workers' households around Durham, North Carolina, for instance, used electricity even by 1935, and fewer than two-fifths of the black workers' households were so equipped—or had indoor toilets. Black wives and mothers who were tobacco workers washed their families' clothes in pots in the yard and cooked on wood or oil-burning stoves, while glossy magazines were displaying housewives freed from drudgery by "electric servants."

Households were smaller, because married couples were having fewer children and because nonfamily residents were less likely to be present. Demographic changes in age structure and marital patterns, as well as new legislative restriction of immigration, meant that boarders and lodgers were less common. Live-in servants became increasingly rare: white women turned their backs on domestic service as soon as they could switch to jobs in factories or stores or offices, and black women, who had little alternative to domestic work, asserted the importance of their own families by doing day work instead of agreeing to live at their employers'. Because of the concentration of urban apartments, less than half of American families owned their homes (and among those in large cities the proportion of homeowners was much smaller). The suburban boom set in motion by the automobile began to reverse that trend, however. Between 1922 and 1929 more than three-quarters of a million new housing starts occurred per year, an average which more than doubled that of any previous seven-year period.

The nation's economic growth, as measured by manufacturing productivity, per capita income, and the ratio of consumer outlay to net national product—much heralded in the 1920s despite how unevenly realized it was across income groups—fueled the forward drive of the newly labeled "mass consumption" era. Manufacturers believed that industrial progress relied on high-volume, mass-market purchasing, and they went about stimulating demand with market research, advertising, and new retailing techniques. With mail-order merchandising, rural as well as metropolitan households contributed to large and sustained growth in purchases such as irons, stoves, vacuum cleaners, washing machines, and refrigerators. The institution of the "installment plan" of payment was an important specific factor in U.S. economic growth in the 1920s: it encouraged people to stretch their consumption habits beyond what they could afford, changing attitudes that had focused on saving to focus on spending. In 1925, consumers used installment credit to purchase more than two-thirds of the household furniture and gas stoves sold, and at least three-quarters of passenger cars, pianos, washing machines, sewing machines, mechanical refrigerators, phonographs, vacuum cleaners, and radios. Manufacturers and advertisers made the concept of a family's "standard of living," introduced by family budget investigators, tantalizingly measurable in the form of the gas stove and the electric iron as well as the automobile. Consumer goods such as canned and packaged food and ready-to-wear clothes also surged in availability. Food factories' production doubled between 1914 and 1926, while the population grew by less than 15 percent. Canned soups, vegetables, and fruits, packaged cereals and crackers were used by all income groups in the 1920s, their use rising consistently with income.[2]

New national "chain" stores, the innovation of national brand names, and mail-order catalogues marketing mass-produced items all portended a new level of standardization and uniformity of life. In the 1920s an American mass culture became possible, as the conjunction of mass production and marketing techniques with new technology added the radio and the movies to print media already crossing the nation. New forms of communication forged common information and values with an unprecedented immediacy. During the 1920s, 40 percent of all homes in the United States acquired radios, and weekly attendance at movies doubled—reaching 100 to 115 million by the end of the decade. Surveys reported that movie stars had replaced leaders in politics, business, or the arts as those most admired by the young. Modern habits of production, consumption, and recreation moved to homogenize long-standing differences between South and North, country and city. Because of the mechanization and standardization of household equipment, the rapid decline after 1900 in availability of domestic servants, and the reach of mass media, regional and even income-related differences in household standards and procedures among housewives narrowed in the 1920s and 1930s. More culturally diverse than ever before because of the waves of immigration between 1880 and 1920, the American population was exposed to unprecedented pressures toward cultural uniformity.[3]

The mass consumption era announced changes in women's patterns of work, and yet it was far from clear whether such visible signs as machines and industrially produced goods inside the home (and women outside it working for wages) gave evidence of the economic evolution feminists wanted. Although the rising rate of divorce evoked more commentary, marriage was more popular than ever in the 1920s. People were marrying younger, and more of them were marrying. Contrary to alarmists' complaints, women's wage-earning seems to have encouraged younger and more frequent marriage, since both members of an affianced couple could contribute to savings toward a household. Of the men and women born in the twenty years after the Civil War, almost 10 percent never married. The median age at first marriage for the 90 percent who did marry was about twenty-six for men and near twenty-four for women. In the generation born thirty years later (from 1895 to the outbreak of the Great War), who came of age from the late 1910s through the Depression, the proportion who never married dropped to near 6 percent, and the median age at first marriage declined to about twenty-five for men and even further for women, to twenty-two and a half.[4]

The same cohorts of women who were flowing into secondary and higher education and into the job market in the 1920s, in other words, were those who were marrying younger and making more certain to marry. Increasingly, a young wife stayed at her paying job at least until she became a mother. Wives' labor force participation rose six times faster than single women's did, between 1900 and 1930, reflecting the willingness of more single working women to marry (without discontinuing work) as well as the decisions of married women to enter the labor force. "The girls nowadays think about nothing but getting married," one head of an employment bureau complained at a vocational conference of 1924, but a representative of the National Federation of Business and Professional Women's Clubs calmly responded that marriage did not prevent good office work.[5]

The trend was especially apparent among college graduates, who presumably had the most potential for higher-paying jobs. The nineteenth-century women who pioneered in collegiate education had more often than their age-peers remained single; those who married did so later in life. At the select women's colleges, graduates' rates of marriage appeared as low as 50 percent at the turn of the century. After 1910, however, in conjunction with the expanding reach of the collegiate experience, more college women married and at younger ages. Between 1890 and 1930 the proportion of Americans aged eighteen to twenty-two in college full-time more than quadrupled. By 1930 nearly 20 percent of that age group was enrolled full-time in college or graduate school, and more were in junior colleges and normal schools. Women's attendance had advanced faster than men's. Only 35 percent of college students in 1890, women composed almost half of the larger college population of the 1920s. The less rarefied an experience college attendance became, the more likely that women students' marital patterns would assimilate to the middle-class norm. So they did.[6]

Perhaps women, including employed women and college students, were more eager to marry because heterosexual expression and enjoyment were more recognized aspects of their lives. Hull House leader and pacifist Jane Addams, who saw her own kinds of social concerns superseded in the 1920s by young people's emphasis on personal freedoms and "self-development," sagely observed that that new trend was "always associated in some way with the breaking down of sex taboos and with the establishment of new standards of marriage." In fact heterosexual behavior among young women had changed. The generation who came of age in the 1920s reaped a harvest of changes in sexual ideology and practice that had been planted before the turn of the century and had begun to bear fruit in the 1910s. On indices of heterosexual freedom investigated by Alfred Kinsey during the 1950s, the young women of the 1920s differed from their predecessors more than any of their successors in subsequent decades differed from them. That is, while the incidence of "petting," premarital sexual intercourse, extramarital intercourse, and achievement of orgasm in marital intercourse all moved consistently upward for women born between the 1890s and the 1920s, the greatest jump occurred between the group born before 1900 and those born in the first decade of the twentieth century. The widest differences of all appeared in premarital petting and premarital intercourse, the exploits of the young. (Extramarital sexual experience did not increase so dramatically as premarital sex did.) The younger generation began petting at younger ages, and the proportion of those born between 1900 and 1909 who had petted to the point of orgasm before the age of thirty-five was almost double that among women born before 1900. The change in incidence of premarital sexual intercourse was even greater. Only 14 percent of the women born before 1900, in Kinsey's sample, admitted to having had premarital sexual intercourse before the age of twenty-five, compared to 36 percent (more than two and a half times as many) of those born in the first decade of the twentieth century. Once they married, increasing proportions of women were reaching orgasm in marital sex, the difference being most pronounced between young wives born before and after 1900.

Among women with college education the pendulum swung the widest arc. College-educated women born before 1900 were less likely than their less well-educated age-mates to have premarital sex, Kinsey showed, but those born later were *more* likely.[7] That stratum of young women who were most expected to "do something" with their lives, who had in earlier generations stood out for their high-minded ideals, stood out in the 1920s for their confrontations with taboos about smoking, drinking, petting, and staying out at night. The select women's colleges showed the greatest contrast in social life between the prewar and postwar generations. No longer so happily "all girls," students in the 1920s and after expected their recreation to include men—and sex. A physician at Stanford University who had been studying women's sexual hygiene since the late nineteenth century, Dr. Clelia Mosher, confided to her diary her shock at the extent and frankness of her female students' questions about sex in the 1920s. She kept her scientific decorum but suspected that "when there is so much smoke there must be some fire."[8]

Women such as Addams or Mosher were as much taken aback by the generalized emphasis on sex—the fact that sex was seen as what was most interesting—as they were chagrined at young women's energies being diverted into such channels. Charlotte Perkins Gilman, for instance, condemned women's new "licentiousness" as an imitation of the vices of men "precisely in the manner of that of any servile class suddenly set free." Jane Addams and her friend Emily Greene Balch agreed that the 1920s trend was especially curious to the "two generations of professionally trained women" who lived "completely celibate lives" without thinking it difficult, and who did not give evidence of "Freudian" abnormality.[9] They were aware that accepting female sexuality was for the young in the 1920s almost a matter of conformity. From popular, intellectual, and social scientific writers swelled a tide of scorn for "Victorian" sexual morality, monochromatically conceived as repressive and hypocritical. Movies, pulp magazines, and advertising copy made the "thrill" of sex their overt or hidden agenda. The moviegoer in a typical Midwestern town in the mid-1920s, for instance, could choose one week from among *The Daring Years, Sinners in Silk, Women Who Give,* and *The Price She Paid;* the next week offered *Name the Man, Rouged Lips,* and *The Queen of Sin. Flaming Youth* promised "neckers, petters, white kisses, red kisses, pleasure-mad daughters, sensation-craving mothers, by an author who didn't dare sign his name." A new cultural apparatus formed around the revelation that sexual expression was a source of vitality and personality (not a drain on energy as nineteenth-century moralists had warned) and that female sexual desire was there to be exploited and satisfied.[10]

To most young women of the 1920s, the unleashing of female passion seemed their own invention. "We do all the things that our mothers, fathers, aunts and uncles do not sanction, and we do them knowingly," a student preened in the *Ohio State Lantern* in 1922. "We are 'playing the game' . . .—smoking, dancing like Voodoo devotees, dressing decollété, 'petting' and drinking. We do these things because we honestly enjoy the attendant physical sensations." The college girl "is armed with sexual knowledge," she declared; "She kisses the boys, she smokes with them, drinks with them, and why? because the feeling of comradeship is running rampant. . . . The girl does not stand aloof—she and the man meet on common ground."[11] It was ironic indeed that young women delighting in heterosexual camaraderie gave no credit to feminism, which they associated with "sex antagonism." Yet the restless Feminists of the 1910s had led the way for the heterosexual claims and behavior of the postwar generation. Their assertion of female eros went with their intent to widen women's scope to the infinite—to make the female self equal to

that of the male—to eliminate sexual hierarchy in the most intimate domain as in every other. They intended heterosexual fulfillment to join
with individuality and chosen work. As Feminists had in the 1910s,
young women in the 1920s connected female heterosexual expression
with bravado, pleasure, and knowledge, with a modern, and realistic
approach to life—perhaps even with a more egalitarian ideal of relations
between the sexes—but they did not (by and large) connect it with feminism. The younger generation looked across the generational divide and
saw Victorian sensibilities, as though the venturesome Feminists of the
1910s had never existed.

Feminists of the 1910s had not particularly acknowledged their forebears on sex questions either—the free lovers, radicals, and sex hygienists of the late nineteenth century and even that minority squarely within
the woman's rights tradition (such as Elizabeth Cady Stanton) who had
despised "prating" about women's "purity." Several phases and generations of thought on sexuality had overlapped in the woman movement as
a whole, and in the suffrage movement in the 1910s. The majority
strand, enshrined in public as characteristic of the woman movement,
championed the spiritual over the carnal in female motivations, often to
the extent of claiming female moral superiority. It presupposed that both
the erotic and reproductive connotations of women—their very bodies—had figured largely in men's exclusion of them from male scenes of
power and privilege; by such logic, women had to keep close self-control
over their own sexuality in order to gain parity with men.[12] That approach was attacked by Feminists in the 1910s and by many more voices
in the 1920s.

Feminists of the 1910s overtly rejected that stance, although they
derived much of their own ideological grounding from the critique of
traditional marriage and the insistence on women's self-protection and
control of male sexual access that such an "anti-[hetero]sexual" view af-
forded. For Feminists, sexuality was a frontier for expression of freedom—a zone to invade rather than to evade. The older view seemed to
them an empty assertion of women's moral power through proprieties, a
discouragement rather than an encouragement to women to enter men's
world; it did not speak to young women of the early twentieth century.
Recalling the 1910s from the vantage point of 1929, Lillian Symes put it
succinctly: "my own generation of feminists in the pre-war days had as
little in common with the flat-heeled, unpowdered, pioneer suffragette
generation which preceded it by a decade or two as it has with the postwar, spike-heeled, over-rouged flapper of to-day." Far from "prigs,"

Symes insisted, her generation were "idealists." "Political freedom and
the right to enter the professions and arts had been almost gained by a
braver, grimmer, and more fanatical generation of feminists behind us.
These were the women who had had to make the famous choice between
'marriage and a career.' We were determined to have both, to try for
everything life would offer of love, happiness, and freedom—just like
men."[13]

That the endorsement of heterosexual passion and pleasure was a
double-edged sword for Feminists in the 1910s was suggested by the
dissension over Ellen Key; by the next decade, 1910s feminists saw such
experimentation as a boomerang, because of the continuing disparity in
men's and women's social and economic prerogatives. "I was the poor
apostle of freedom," Doris Stevens remonstrated to Dudley Field Malone in 1927, justifying her suit for divorce on the basis of his cruelties
and infidelities, "you were the communicant who profited by my doctrine." There was no impulse among early Feminists now nearing or in
middle age to go back on the claim to women's heterosexual entitle-
ments. (Indeed, Doris Stevens, while complaining of Malone's behavior,
had been carrying on an extramarital love affair for several years with the
man who would become her second husband.) What was cast into question was the relation of forays on the sexual frontier to the balance of
social and economic power between the sexes. The generation of the
1910s saw their own banner of freedom transformed, as Lillian Symes
wrote, into "the promiscuous pawing and petting permitted by so many
technically virtuous young women to-day."[14] Advertising and mass media
took up women's heterosexuality as their own agent, blunting the Feminist point that heterosexual liberation for women intended to subvert
gender hierarchy rather than to confirm it.

Likewise, social science, aggressively describing and defining marital
and sexual roles in the 1920s and pushing aside folk wisdom or religion
or medicine, assimilated the news of women's heterosexual passions.
With more to say about women's roles and marriage than ever before,
social science also had new authority in the 1920s. Its promise to explain
the nature and sources of human behavior through objective empirical
observation and methodologically rigorous analysis had enormous popular as well as academic appeal. After half a century of development, by
the 1920s the separate disciplines of sociology, economics, political science, psychology, and anthropology were marked out and established in
institutions with the large-scale support of corporate philanthropy. Thousands of social scientists carried on research and taught in hundreds of

American colleges and universities; their work was popularized in print and audiovisual media; it pervaded the content and tone of personnel management and marketing strategies in business and industry, government procedure, and investigation and journalism of all sorts, and it was drawn on (not least) by advertisers eager to determine the motives and weaknesses of potential consumers.[15]

Psychology in particular was seen as a tool to enable prediction and control of "the human element"—perhaps even to realize vague concepts of social engineering that had surfaced in the previous decade. Although Freudian ideas had been bruited about by "advanced" thinkers since the first decade of the century, and some Freudian terms were used with superficial familiarity, it was not psychoanalysis but mental hygiene and behaviorist psychologies that dominated during the 1920s. All these shared, however, a focus on irrational sources of human behavior and the revelation that people were motivated by sources in their own psyches of which they were consciously unaware, as well as the assumption that deeply buried sexual motivations underlay actions in public. Typical popular absorption and reproduction of psychology were exhibited by a female journalist pondering the comparatively low proportion of college-educated women who married and became mothers: she not only posited that "the greatest cause of individual failure is psychic maladjustment, the conflicts, inhibitions, anxieties, fears and other emotional disturbances which may cause serious mental disease, and which certainly are responsible for warped and distorted lives" but also put the question whether the college-educated woman's pursuit of a career was "a sublimation for other desires."[16] The most influential male psychologists, such as John B. Watson and Floyd Allport, took an instrumental approach, believing that psychology's outstanding promise lay in its potential to bring about individuals' "adjustment" to salutary social norms.

Eclectic and varied as they were, practitioners of psychology in the 1920s found common ground opposing Feminism's pronounced aims, trivializing or anathematizing women's desires for self-definition and protests against male domination. Superseding the iconoclastic women social scientists of the previous generation who had undertaken empirical research to unseat Victorian shibboleths and had found no significant differences between the sexes in mental functioning, psychologists in the 1920s conceptualized sex differences in mental functioning anew. They located sex differences in the realm of temperament or "adjustment" to life rather than in the narrow realm of cognition. Lewis Terman and his associates led in constructing quantifiable measures of "masculinity" and "femininity," which, they claimed, were real and scientifically verifiable qualities that illustrated a range from normality to "deviancy." (Their method of measurement persisted as a diagnostic tool through the 1960s.) In this model of well-being, biological sex was clearly matched by psychological correlates; but the so-called empirical data out of which the categories of masculinity and femininity were constructed were purely social conventions. (For example, one gained masculinity points by answering "no" to the question "do you like to have people tell you their troubles?" and by indicating dislike of foreigners, religious men, and women cleverer than you. Femininity points were gained by answering in the negative such questions as "were you ever fond of playing with snakes?" and by disliking sideshow freaks, bald-headed men, and riding bicycles.)[17]

Psychologists' reinvention of femininity had clear repercussions as it spilled over into social-scientific assessments of the pros and cons of women's careers. The arena of paid work was considered conventionally masculine; a man's ability to provide financially for his wife and children was an important component of male self-image and satisfaction, of masculinity as conventionally understood. Even the male sociologists seemingly most sympathetic to feminist intents, such as Ernest Groves, who saw women's domestic role as a social construction and understood that women gained satisfaction similar to men's from work outside the home, also warned that the woman who was "coarsened or hard-boiled" by business life would "repel men." As did many people at the time (with more and less dire interpretations), Groves warned in the late 1920s that women's opportunities for gainful employment would reduce the marriage rate, both because women would become too independent and choosy to be satisfied with the mates available and because men would not be attracted to "hardened" women.[18]

Although social science was not monolithic but rather comprised a series of contesting views, the field in the 1920s did present a united front on the point that its expertise was crucial to establishing modern, realistic, effective, and democratic social order. Social science practitioners conveyed their sense that their disciplines could both explain feminism itself as a phenomenon and could lead in solving the problems feminism addressed, especially the problem of reconciling women's demands for love, work, and individuality. It was a measure of the looming explanatory presence of social science that *Nation* writer Freda Kirchwey included three psychologists' commentaries when she ran a series of seventeen self-reflective autobiographical sketches by feminists in 1926–27.

The series, called "These Modern Women," included (under cover of anonymity) the very exemplars of Feminism—Crystal Eastman, Inez Haynes Irwin, Sue Shelton White, Genevieve Taggard, Ruth Pickering, and others—and was intended to reveal "the origins of their modern point of view toward men, marriage, children, and jobs."

The woman psychologist whom Kirchwey enlisted, Beatrice Hinkle, a Heterodoxy member and Jungian analyst, assayed the attitudes expressed in the seventeen essays as "a normal protest against external collective restrictions." She saw "a definite analogy between their attitude of revolt and that of subject peoples and exploited workers of the male sex" and believed that "behind their stridency and revolt lies the great inner meaning of woman's struggle with the forces of convention and inertia." The response of neurologist Joseph Collins, on the other hand, sank to the ludicrous level of personal speculation: "which one of these women should I have liked to companion? There were two. . . . One had strong lusty desires. . . . Another . . . seems to have neither ambition nor determination to administer the world . . . and her only reason for being a feminist is dictated not by effect but by intellect." The third commentator was leading behaviorist John Broadus Watson, probably the most influential psychologist of the decade, whose empyrean arrogance belied his claim to method: "I can read women only after making careful observations of their behavior over long periods of time. Then I put two and two together like any other scientist. When a woman is a militant suffragist the chances are, shall we say, a hundred to one that her sex life is not well adjusted?" His biases bristled from his "scientific" declaration, "most of the terrible women one must meet, women with the blatant views and voices, women who have to be noticed, who shoulder one about, who can't take life quietly, belong to this large percentage of women who have never made a sex adjustment." (In Watson's imagination of a "behaviorists' utopia," outlined at this time, no women left home for industry: all were kept "busy and happy from morning till night" with the special tasks of keeping themselves desirable and attractive to men and mastering the "technique of sex.")[19]

Such commentary revealed not only how far psychology had incorporated female sexuality into prescriptions for "adjustment" but also how it had—despite boasts of empiricism—incorporated long-standing biases that women's "adjustment" consisted in serving men's needs and pleasures. Rejecting the moral positions and value judgments of their predecessors, social scientists of many sorts in the 1920s often operated on the assumption that appropriate values would emerge from the science itself while failing to acknowledge how prevailing values had constructed scientific guideposts and practice. "As a naturalist I cannot express an opinion," stated the psychologist C. Judson Herrick in exemplary decorum. Since the first propositions in the mid-nineteenth century that a science of society was possible, the desire to use social science in pursuit of a variety of social goals had warred with its claims to reportorial neutrality. Both motivations were visible among women who took up social science as a means toward education and wider opportunities. For them, the environmentalist presuppositions of social science were a welcome alternative to restrictive beliefs about women's innate nature. As the social sciences expanded, many more women made careers for themselves there than in medicine, natural science, or other comparable professional fields. If feminism tried to speak through the voice of modern social science, however, it was necessarily muted, especially in the 1920s, for the contemporary social scientific insistence on eschewing metaphysical or philosophical claims and sticking to experimental and empirical findings left room for no acknowledged critical standpoint. Insofar as it was based on the observable—and it claimed to be based entirely on the observable—social science tended to limit its vision to what was already present, to confirm that, and to inhibit vision of alternatives.[20]

Women in social science contributed in the 1920s to the articulation of a new marital ideal, "companionate marriage." In fact social scientists of varying intentions converged upon that model, much as reformers of varying stripes—social hygienists and sex rebels among them—had converged upon more open public discussion of sexual behavior in the previous decade.[21] The label, companionate marriage, was set into the literature in the title of a book by Judge Ben Lindsay of Colorado, whose work with juveniles had persuaded him that young people ought to be friends and perhaps lovers before embarking on the serious matter of marrying. While conservatives lambasted Lindsay and lamented the crumbling of the economic and ideological bonds of the large patriarchal family, a rising chorus of social scientists, social workers, journalists, and even jurists championed the direction in which family life was moving, becoming a specialized site for emotional intimacy, personal and sexual expression, and nurture among husband, wife, and a small number of children. That view of the family's evolution resembled the heterosexual pattern Feminists had envisioned. Where Feminists' stand on sexuality in the 1910s had indicted bourgeois marriage, however, the sexual pattern advanced in social science (and popular culture) of the 1920s confirmed bourgeois marriage as women's destination.

Like Feminist critics of the 1910s, marital advice-givers in the 1920s
and 1930s looked back and saw Victorian marriage as hierarchical and
emotionally barren, based on dominance and submission. They sought
to substitute an ideal of intimate sexual partnership, in which female
sexuality was presumed and marriage was valued for eliciting the partners' individuality as well as for uniting them. Marriage advice books
now made sex the centerpiece of marriage; they portrayed the sexual
adjustment and satisfaction of both partners as principal measures of
marital harmony and even as instrumental means toward social order.
Incorporating sex and marital camaraderie, and yet leaving intact the
sexual division of labor, the companionate marriage model was broadcast
far afield of the Feminist camp by a range of spokesmen and women.
What was thrown overboard in the transformation of Feminist critiques
into social scientists' proposition of companionate marriage was the bal-
last anchoring harmony between the sexes to sexual parity in the public
world as well as the bedroom.[22]

Although some theorists of companionate marriage explicitly proclaimed loyalty to the "man on top" (as in one marriage text's declaration,
"the act of sex is appropriately the central fact in the psychological situation of marriage, for in the act a complete system of domestic behavior,
both active and passive, can be anticipated"), the ideal boosted marriage
as more appealing than ever to women. Some female social scientists
believed the model furthered their reformist intentions. Phyllis Blanchard, convinced that the "objectivity" of social science had helped her
resolve her own conflicting desires for personal autonomy and heterosexual love, surveyed hundreds of young women on these issues and concluded that "girls are today demanding positive values of marriage"
rather than merely looking to escape their parent's authority or find economic security. Usually skeptical anthropologist Elsie Clews Parsons
similarly maintained that "in the talk of women . . . desire for integral
satisfaction in marriage is more consciously or realistically expressed than
ever before. Emotional and sexual appeasements are considered as well
as social or economic advantage." Blanchard stressed the new importance
of the "sex side of marriage": "The husband is no longer satisfied with
good natured acquiescence; he must have a passionate response to his
own desires. And the wife expects to find in him the perfect lover who
will arouse ecstasies of sensual pleasure." Her conclusions illustrated the
tendency of so-called objective observation to present prescriptive ideals
as established facts: "marriage has now become the entrance into a fuller
and richer life; an opportunity for sharing joys and sorrows with a mate
who will not be merely a protector or a provider but an all-around com-

panion. . . . Girls are setting higher ideals than ever before and will probably not be content unless they realize them. . . . The modern union of man and woman is visioned as a perfect consummation of both personalities that will involve every phase of mutual living."[23]

Insofar as it turned prescription into generalization and portrayed marriage as indeed symmetrical, the companionate marriage model left feminists (as well as any other women) little rationale for avoiding marriage; it removed the ground underneath the objection, made by prior generations, that marriage was a system of domination that imprisoned women's individuality. When psychologist Leta Hollingworth, at a meeting of Heterodoxy in 1927, included in her definition of the "perfect" feminist a woman in a happy marriage with children, she was refuted by no one— although a visitor observed that the remark shattered the calm of life-long member Helen Hull (who remained unmarried and was probably lesbian).[24] Just when individual wage-earning made it more possible than ever before for women to escape the economic necessity to marry, the model of companionate marriage with its emphasis on female heterosexual desires made marriage a sexual necessity, for "normal" satisfaction.

Once female sexual drives were acknowledged, the woman who did not marry was looked at in a new light, and relationships between women were inevitably reassessed. Nineteenth-century ideology of women's moral influence and glorious maternity, by veiling female eroticism, had made same-sex intimacies innocent. Madeline Doty, for instance, went through high school and college unaware of either heterosexual relations or "the impure relation that can exist between women." When in law school (just after 1900) her innocence ended, knowledge of the latter made her "appalled and upset," perhaps because she had been devoted to a female teacher through high school and college. The same scrutiny by physicians, sex reformers, and ethicists that had rolled back Victorian reticence about sex placed new labels of normality and abnormality on the spectrum of human behavior from heterosexual to homosexual. Rising high school attendance and commercialized forms of urban recreation promoted heterosocial mixing, and intimacy among women appeared suspect even—or especially—among the young in schools and colleges, where same-sex peer and student–teacher relationships in earlier generations had carried important emotional freight. By the same yardstick that sexual "spheres" were measured archaic, women's exclusive intimacy with each other appeared a deviation. Floyd Dell continued to use feminist language in the 1920s to sum up the change with deceptive ease: "the intensity of friendships between people of the same

sex . . . we now regard as an artificial product, the result of the segregation of the sexes and the low social position of women. As women become free and equal with men such romantic intensity of emotion finds
a more biologically appropriate expression."[25]

As Dell's language suggests, there were strong prescriptions for biological and psychological "appropriateness" in the new emphasis on sexuality. Not only clinicians and social science writers but all the popular media that drew on them paired attention to women's erotic nature and
warrant for heterosexual fulfillment with recognition and incrimination
of homosexuality in women. The recognition of lesbianism and its categorization as deviant brought science to the enforcement of heterosexual
norms. The woman who stepped out of line in the nineteenth century
had often been sexually slurred as promiscuous, but in the twentieth
century she would increasingly be condemned as lesbian. On the relationship between these phenomena, the language of some male sexolo-
gists and psychologists (like Watson) was utterly plain: appropriate "sex
adjustment" would remove the cause for, and mean the end of, women's
demands for rights and independence. As one doctor baldly put it, "the
driving force in many agitators and militant women who are always after
their rights, is often an unsatisfied sex impulse, with a homosexual aim.
Married women with a completely satisfied libido rarely take an active
interest in militant movements."[26] That virulent reductionism was typical
perhaps only of some obsessed intellects, but the contamination of wom-
en's causes by association with "maladjustment," especially meaning insufficient heterosexual inclination, was a general theme in popular and
scientific culture in the 1920s.

Both in the concern of professionals and in a wide range of popular
media stalked a huge cultural anxiety about the potentiality as much as
the reality of women's escape from men's erotic and economic control.
When erotic drives were admitted to be as constitutive of women's nature as of men's and valued apart from reproduction, same-sex relationships came to be suspected as alternatives to women's relationships with
men, and therefore threats to existing sexual and social order. The specter of women on their own, satisfied with and by each other, gained
credibility from newsworthy evidence of unmarried women's earning
power—in the arts, entertainment, sports, and professions—as well as
from the public leadership in civic, social welfare, and suffrage organizations of women who had no evident male partners or guides. The facts
that most women agitating for their rights in the suffrage movement had
been married, and that the originators of Feminism were erotic adven-

turers who wished to combine independence and heterosexual love, faded beside the fears that connected women's rights and feminism with lesbianism. The shift of concern within both professional and popular literature and fiction, which now portrayed the woman who failed to mate heterosexually as a social danger—irrational, unwholesome, mannish, or frigid—and explained relationships between women as immature (at best) or psychologically sick, constituted an emphatic backlash against the idea and practice of independent women.

How social scientific, medical, and popular classification and denigration of same-sex relationships actually affected feminists and lesbians is very difficult to assess. Feminists in the prewar years had also been accused of being "man-haters," but the link between a woman's independence and suspicion about her sexuality was more immediate and direct in the 1920s. Certainly the use of epithets to condemn and control the unruly behavior of women had a long history; and it was more usual than not for the condemnation to be sexual in character. Nineteenth-century women who were "strong-minded" were typically condemned as "unsexed" or a "third sex"—if they were not read out from the rolls of the respectable entirely by being branded "godless." Nonetheless, there is reason to see the condemnation of women's rights by association with "abnormality" and specifically with homosexuality in the early twentieth century as unprecedentedly effective. Science was no more (and perhaps less) authoritative than religion as a keeper of social norms, but many feminists themselves had embraced science as a means to their end of liberation; when science spoke of their own motivations, could they help but listen? ("Our greatest hope for an increase in happiness in the relations between men and women depends on the continuation of scientific research and further applications of science," Phyllis Blanchard declared.) If nothing else, the new emphasis forced a woman to examine her sexual motives if she was dissatisfied with her situation, and especially if she complained of sex discrimination or looked more to women than to men for her intimate relationships or supportive community. Overt critique of marriage all but disappeared among women who were organizationally, politically, or professionally working to advance women's rights in the 1920s. Were all these women persuaded that companionate marriage would eliminate remaining inequities in women's and men's private relationships, or were they nudged into defensive silence by the insistence on heterosexual adjustment? In the NFBPW—three-quarters of whose members were unmarried—some women were certainly thrown on the defensive, for early in 1927 they proposed to the national convention to alter the name of the federation's journal, the *Independent Woman*. They "detected in it a slight militancy which antagonizes men—employers, prospective advertisers, and others."[27] Although the motion did not pass the convention, the willingness of its proposers to concede (at least outwardly) to the pressure of norms of femininity suggested that they were anxious about the equation of single professional women's independence from men with lesbianism.

The label of sexual maladjustment pinned to feminism exercised a kind of social control different from past deprecations because it stigmatized an identifiable group—that is, lesbians. Whether lesbian sexual behavior was more suppressed or expressed as a result of changing sexual norms is probably impossible to measure. The Kinsey study did not document any increase in homosexual behavior, in contrast to the increases it found in all sorts of heterosexual behavior. One might speculate, however, that that contrast, rather than measuring different trajectories over time in heterosexual and homosexual *behavior*, actually reflected differential willingness over time to *admit* to heterosexual or homosexual eroticism. It is reasonable to hypothesize that women acted in multivalent ways upon the new acceptance of the legitimacy of female sexuality. As heterosexuals did, women drawn to homosexual behavior might appropriate the greater leeway for female sexual assertiveness in the modern era, when there was greater opportunity as well as greater necessity to develop a sense of themselves as lesbians. Not all social scientists or physicians condemned homosexual behavior or assumed it should be "cured," and medical and social scientific investigations confirmed that women found sexual and emotional satisfaction with one another even while they portrayed that choice as aberrant. Among a small group of writers and artists, certainly, lesbianism was more overt and acknowledged in the 1920s than ever before, and the lives of some outstanding women achievers of that generation reveal sustaining sexual relationships with individuals of both sexes. The boosting of heterosexuality that characterized the new emphasis on sexual identity could, at its most destructive, lead lesbians or women uncertain about their sexuality to self-condemnation and self-hatred, but that was not its necessary result. Evidence from a group of twenty-five lesbians in Utah in the 1920s and 1930s, middle-class and almost all employed in white-collar and service occupations, shows their awareness of the medical and scientific stigmatization of homosexuality, their need for complete cover, their sensitivity to being characterized as masculine or feminine, but withal their resistance to incorporating negative analyses in their own self-assessments. They rejected the label of psychopathology and led successful occupational and social lives.[28]

No less than sexual and marital relations, the household became fair game for social science in the 1920s. Although public discussion of "wages for wives" surfaced occasionally, the women who paid the most substantial and influential attention to upgrading the status and conditions of housework were professional home economists.[29] Comparative studies of time spent doing housework, begun by home economists in the decade under the influence of ideas of scientific management, showed that for urban no less than rural wives, housekeeping was full-time work. Despite modern advantages, only 10 percent of urban housewives spent less than thirty-five hours per week on their tasks, and the bulk of them had work weeks comparable to those of rural wives, over fifty hours. "It is the routine housework—the provision of meals, the care of the house, the laundering and mending that still requires the bulk of the homemaker's time," reported the innovator of time-budget studies of two thousand rural and urban housewives in 1929. This only confirmed what most women well knew: more than two-thirds of a large and varied pool of women polled by the Young Women's Christian Association in 1926 believed that "homemaking, if well done, is a full-time job." Although advertisements said new technology reduced both the exhaustion and the working hours of the housewife, "labor-saving" household appliances were more effective in raising standards of cleanliness and order—and encouraging housewives to meet them—than in shortening hours of domestic labor.[30]

Home economists agreed that a principal result of technological advance applied to the home was a rising standard of household care. The items in commonest use in the 1920s—the gas stove and electric lighting and irons—arguably improved the comfort and effectiveness of women's domestic labor but did not make it less of a full-time job. If housewives saved time by using appliances or packaged commodities, they reallocated it to child care, shopping, or matters of household management in order to improve their working environment or their result. As home economists and advertisers of household durables and consumables proclaimed the cleanliness, comfort, adjustment, and efficiency that a woman's proper care of household and family could bring, housewives took seriously the opportunity they had to improve their families' health and security. Expectations of material health and welfare had leapt beyond those of earlier generations. Manufacturers, advertisers, and the federal government's agencies and bureaus located the "American standard of living" in the 1920s in the intact private home. Their efforts swamped the small movement that innovative women in the prewar years had made toward cooperative solutions to the problem of women's domestic labor. Aggressive marketing of some household appliances—washing machines were the prime case—returned to the home labor that the previous generation of urban families had paid to have done outside, if they could afford it. The upper-middle-class housewife with an array of electric "servants" that she had to operate herself, since she lacked the domestic help her mother had had, found the modern household more rather than less demanding.[31]

The new government agency status of the Bureau of Home Economics in the U.S. Department of Agriculture (the largest employer of women scientists in the 1920s and 1930s) symbolized the extent to which women's traditional concerns had been bureaucratized and professionalized, on the premise that the modern home had technological and scientific content. The bureau's leaders became public spokeswomen on the central feminist question whether women could successfully combine outside employment with management of a household. Here they were in an anomalous position. In their public words the ghost of Charlotte Perkins Gilman echoed. Defining the new homemaking in the 1920s, these women made it a scientific study on the Gilmanite premise that housekeeping was not the province of "instinct." Chase Going Woodhouse, the social scientist and expert on women's vocations who headed the Division of Economics at the bureau in the mid-1920s (on leave from her faculty position at Smith College), argued that the homemaker must see herself as a professional and "force public opinion into a revaluation of the work of women in the home . . . clearing away the tradition that women are 'born homemakers.'" Lillian Gilbreth, an engineer specializing in the household (and the mother of the twelve children whose family life inspired the book *Cheaper by the Dozen*), treated the homemaker first and foremost as a worker. She analyzed housework tasks for greatest efficiency according to the principles of scientific management, and she insisted that sex differences, if they existed at all, were irrelevant to the efficiency of work in the household. Hildegarde Kneeland, who conducted the time-budget studies, protested that not every woman should have to adopt the occupation of housewife simply because she got married. Amey Watson, a specialist in domestic employer–employee issues, asked rhetorically, "is it not rather a social ideal that every woman shall look forward to her own self-support after marriage, . . . that she shall wish to have her own chosen work?" Home economists approved—by their own example, if nothing else—women's, even wives' and mothers', employment outside the home. Woodhouse, for instance, kept up an active professional life while married and the mother of two children born in the early 1920s. "The woman who prefers an occupation outside the home," she declared, "could have no better friend than the professional homemaker who, standing for training and scientific procedure, can insist that here is a profession into which people are graduated through hard work and not merely through the accident of being born a woman."[32]

At the same time, all of these women avidly built up and explicated the complex significance of what went on in the home, in order both to counter the devaluation of the housewife (of which they were well aware) and to justify their own field of work. As professionals, they took feminist ideas intended to break the link between female gender and the predetermined role of wife/mother/housekeeper, and turned them to support fields of research and employment where ordinary housewives' occupation had been. In corollary, housewives' attention to professional standards and guidance became a necessity. Woodhouse saw the "new profession of homemaking" as something "much greater" than "simply staying at home, 'doing the housework' and 'devoting oneself to husband and children.'" She proposed the homemaker's work as a "task of synthesis, of drawing upon all the natural and social sciences in an effort to solve the problems of the home." The components of that task included supervising and caring for the household, directing family purchasing, caring for children, arbitrating the interests of different family members, formulating a philosophy of life for the family (to guard ethical, cultural, and moral standards), and establishing relations between the family and the community. Amey Watson's analysis of the "minimum essentials in operating a household" consisted of four categories—planning the family's standard of living, taking care of physical needs of family members, taking care of the emotional and educational needs of family members, and dealing with social problems. These categories accumulated thirty-nine subcategories of "invariable" tasks. How a homemaker could accomplish those adequately and still undertake "her own chosen work," Watson did not specify.[33]

If these spokeswomen showed little of Gilman's contempt for the value of women's day-to-day domestic ministrations, they more wholly lacked her radical imagination of the archaic home undone and transformed to the benefit of women's freedom. They valiantly compared homemaking to nondomestic work, analyzed it with reference to its managerial and worker functions or its business and spiritual elements, and assimilated it to a professional model. At the same time, they assumed that women were and would continue to be responsible for that work, the care and feeding of men and children in private households. The more they expounded the variety and value of homemaking properly understood, the wider the door was opened to blaming women who failed to appreciate its merits. Anna Richardson of the American Home Economics Association, for example, conceded that isolation and lack of adequate recognition contributed to an "inferiority complex" in the homemaker. She nonetheless insisted that women had only to discern how really vital homemaking responsibilities were, in order to find the "professional demands" of the work clearly evident and satisfying. Their "product" was the most important one: "happy, healthy, useful human beings." Besides inadequate knowledge or poverty, according to her, the most serious source for women's dissatisfaction with the homemaking occupation must be "personal maladjustment."[34]

Like the responsibilities of housekeeping, the duties involved in child-rearing had never been so multifariously defined. New storehouses of medical and social scientific expertise increased the resources and directives available to parents who wanted to raise healthy and happy children—and who didn't? For hundreds of years the Protestant republican tradition in America had likened parents' opportunity to rear virtuous children to the seedbed from which social order would flower. The proposition that parents had more than religious or moral influence—that is, that they had the resources of modern science at their fingertips to help them direct their children's fates—was a much more recent development.

Not only the new kinds of concern lavished on children, but also the extraordinarily large proportion of women maturing in the 1920s who remained childless, point to the high tension surrounding modern motherhood. More than a quarter of all the American women born in the first decade of the twentieth century, those who came of age in the 1920s, never bore children, despite the waxing marriage rate. That proportion was far larger than the proportion who remained childless among women born in any other decade from the 1880s to the 1950s. Not all of the sources and motivations of the demographic pattern can be accounted for, but it does suggest that parenthood at this time seemed fraught with responsibilities or stress that a lot of women wanted to avoid. People were marrying younger and more uniformly and wives were testifying to more sexual satisfaction, but fewer of them were producing children. That disparity highlighted in a unique way both the value that was being placed on marital sex apart from reproduction, and the positive volitional element in modern motherhood.[35]

The trend toward smaller families was, of course, a long-term one: the birth rate had been declining for more than a hundred years by the time the twentieth century opened. Without any significant advance in contraceptive technology, the average number of children born to a white woman who lived until menopause had been halved between 1800 and 1900, from 7 to 3.5. Abstinence or infrequency of coitus, the withdrawal method (coitus interruptus), abortion, spermicidal douching, and (late in the century) the condom or the rhythm method, together with sufficient motivation, effected that reduction in overall fertility, although none of those methods—except abstinence—reliably enabled people to plan their families. Margaret Sanger promoted the female-controlled method of the diaphragm, a significant advance in birth control technique early in the twentieth century. The birth control clinics set up by Sanger and some of her allies operated within a narrow legal margin, however, only in some states and only under medical license; they could meet only a fraction of the demand. Not until 1936 did the Second Circuit Court of Appeals, in *U.S. v. One Package,* remove birth control devices from the reach of the federal anti-obscenity law. The American Medical Association withheld its approval of dispensing birth control devices until the following year. In the 1920s and 1930s the principal users of diaphragms were educated and well-to-do married women whose physicians would privately provide prescriptions and instructions. Social scientists Robert and Helen Lynd found striking differences between "business-class" and working-class women's knowledge and use of birth control in their study in Muncie, Indiana, in the mid-1920s. The former—twenty-seven women whose husbands had entrepreneurial, managerial, and upper white-collar occupations—all used modern contraception and took it for granted. In contrast, less than half of seventy-seven working-class wives used any form of birth control, and only slightly more than a quarter used even "moderately scientific" means. Women's desires for contraception were generalized far beyond the business class, however. In the space of five years in the early 1920s, Sanger received a million letters from mothers asking for methods of birth control. Her clinic in lower Manhattan served a clientele—evenly divided among Catholics, Protestants, and Jews—whose average family income was twenty-one dollars per week. The clinic could not accommodate all comers. By whatever combination of will and traditional and new methods, the birth rate dropped especially rapidly in the 1920s and 1930s, owing less to significant changes in fertility among those most likely to use the diaphragm than to falling fertility among foreign-born women (who were marrying later and less uniformly than immigrants of earlier decades had) and to falling rural fertility rates, probably linked to the farm depression. Although contraceptive means were still highly controversial, limiting fertility within marriage was clearly an accepted idea.[36]

If childbearing was voluntary and could be planned—and increasingly, women at least of the business class assumed that it was—the decision to have children became a more strenuous one, the responsibilities thus entered upon more willfully accepted. And now science offered not only new expertise about nutrition, sanitation, and childrearing practice, but also new measures of parents' success or failure in raising their children to psychological well-being. Where nineteenth-century doctors located "nervous" disorders in neurology and biology, early twentieth-century social science shifted the burden to social and environmental factors. The early twentieth-century field of mental hygiene introduced and familiarized the public with the concept of a normality believed to be measurable by standardized tests. Parents were put on guard for "abnormality," that is, for "infantile" or "neurotic" behavior in their growing children. Mental hygienists urged on the social science consensus that the prime duty of the family in modern industrial society was no longer economic production but provision of the right environment for children's healthy and normal adjustment. By focusing tremendous attention on childbearing, practitioners in the field of mental hygiene paved the way for competing psychological and psychoanalytic theories of early childhood to drive into the minds of parents in the 1920s. (Acceptance of the new rhetoric rang out in Lorine Pruette's wry adaptation of it to feminist purposes: "every discontented housewife is a menace to the mental hygiene of the child.")[37]

Social scientific attention to childrearing converged with the woman's rights tradition in severing motherhood from instinct. By the 1920s behavioral social scientists looking for causation in the external environment rather than in innate drives stampeded over the "instinct psychology" that had enjoyed brief prominence, showing that the concept of instinct was too vague and malleable, its sources in nurture or nature too unclear, to be scientifically useful or measureable. Woman's rights advocates had a more direct interest in destroying the notion of maternal instinct. Both to elevate the maternal role and to enable women to exercise choice in their adult lives, motherhood had to be lifted above the level of the animal. At least since the time of Mary Wollstonecraft, some aspiring women had contended that female reproductive capacity did not automatically qualify women for adequate performance of motherhood, which required will and training. "You may observe mother instinct at its height in a fond hen sitting on china eggs," Charlotte Perkins Gilman riposted to turn-of-the-century sentimentalists: "instinct, but no brains." Gilman sharpened to a fine point a line of argument that had preceded her. The reasoning that adequate performance in motherhood required education had a double edge, however. The principle that maternal expertise was achieved, not inborn, easily produced the corollary that mothers should study for it and nothing else. Advocating training for motherhood also put control in the hands of the trainers, who in the 1920s were increasingly not older and wiser mothers, but experts with professional training in medicine, psychology, mental health, sociology, education, or social work.[38]

Mothers of all regions and classes eloquently testified to their concern for their children's health and welfare, and their eagerness to learn what science could provide, in hundreds of thousands of requests and inquiries that poured into the U.S. Children's Bureau (established in 1912). In Muncie, the Lynds found both working-class and business-class mothers more concerned for their children's well-being and privileges than they recalled their own mothers being. Lorine Pruette observed the middle-class mother, "shaken out of her old complacency," anxiously shepherding her children to specialists. Scientifically oriented directives, emanating from public health and social work agencies, schools, women's clubs, magazines, pulpits, newspapers, and the federal government, swarmed to meet mothers' readiness. (Half of the babies born in 1929 were touched by government-issued childrearing advice, according to the Children's Bureau's estimate.) Gwendolyn Berry, who was studying gainfully employed working-class mothers, duly recorded that "the greater emphasis on child health, education and child psychology in comparatively recent years is increasing the number of agencies outside the home assisting the mother in meeting her responsibility for child culture," but she concluded that these agencies were "increasing the work of the mother somewhat by imposing higher standards upon her."[39]

Mothers' manifest desire to gain from the findings of modern science fueled the parent education movement, a new name and a new attitude in adults' collective study and preparation for the best childrearing. The term *parent*, used from the start in the 1920s, both welcomed fathers and neutered the participation of mothers. The new child study, as it was also called, was an arena where social science practitioners of various sorts converged in the mid-1920s, dissociating their aims from what they saw as the moralism, sentimentalism, and sloppy biological thinking of the past. In some respects a folk movement, parent education seeped into secondary and higher education curricula, in departments of sociology and psychology as well as in home economics, social work, and mental hygiene, as Rockefeller Foundation funding for child development research fostered the credibility of the field.

No specific regimen for child training distinguished the parent education movement. Indeed, the reading lists published by the national organization listed hundreds of educators, ethicists, and psychologists of various stripes, from John Dewey to John Watson to Sigmund Freud. The only orthodoxy for which the movement as a whole could be said to stand was the redefinition of the parent–child relation as a *problem*, one that required science and controlled research on the part of professionals and study as well as affection on the part of the parent. Parent education encouraged mothers to seize their destiny with grips provided by scientific researchers. Trumpeting that science was the only avenue to understanding, it placed that understanding on an infinitely receding horizon. Experts had to admit that the state of knowledge was imperfect—that was their reason for continuing research. But mother herself was more imperfect. While the parent education movement proposed to bridge the gap between parents and modern scientific knowledge, parents were on the receiving end; the weight of authority was clearly with the professionals. If in the early 1920s, the parent education movement was a fluid arena in which amateurs and professionals met and an occasional woman was catapulted into professional child study, professionals' authority was institutionalized in the government-sponsored social work agencies, child guidance centers, and nursery schools which multiplied during the Depression.[40]

Both the new child study and the new homemaking took as a premise that female gender did not in itself qualify or suit women for those practices: not every woman was born to be a parent or housekeeper. In both fields some spokeswomen advocated professional standards, and directives derived from social science, with the explicit intent to to liberate women from time-worn constraints. By claiming that child training and housekeeping required the intervention of modern science and professional standards, they theoretically offered women a hand and a break in the continuity of traditional duties. "In this complex age, it takes more than any one human being can know to take charge of a child's full development. Every mother should avail herself of all the assistance obtainable," affirmed Sidonie Gruenberg, a prime mover in parent education. Herself a mother who had risen from volunteer to career status, Gruenberg saw no inconsistency between the aims of parent education and the aims of mothers to have careers. She reasoned that the child of an employed mother could have the benefit of the most "up-to-date and scientific principles" and the companionship of other children in a progressive nursery school while escaping haphazard ministrations at home; moreover, the child would benefit from the mother's satisfaction with her own work and would respect her as an individual because of it. She envisioned, however, only a privileged home supported by two parents' substantial incomes. Even then, Gruenberg warned that the employed mother must discriminate as to which tasks could be delegated and which could not and must schedule herself so as to retain enough time and energy to create a good home. If the principles of parent education or the new homemaking justified professional supplements to the wife/ mother's presence, in reality only the exceptional woman could take advantage of that approval. Such supplements were out of the financial reach of most people; and the underlying current in both the new child study and the new homemaking always towed back to the wife and mother herself. For most of the more than twenty-two million women working at home as unpaid housekeepers, the practitioners of the new standards for their homes and children were no one but themselves.[41]

Both the new child study and the new housekeeping aroused anxieties about performance that knowing standards alone could not allay. Into the breach came advertising, borne by new media such as *Parents' Magazine*, indicating how to deal with problems by purchasing commodities. Established in 1926 to take advantage of interest aroused in parent education, the purpose of *Parents'* was stated to be "translating the valuable but often technical material of experts into workaday language." "Many of us cringe at the revelation of our inadequacies," an early promotional announcement led mothers to agree, as "educators, psychiatrists, writers and social workers are turning their searchlights on Parents . . . [who] realize that instinct and tradition are not sufficient equipment for their highly important job." The magazine's circulation boomed, reaching two hundred thousand just five years after its founding, in the trough of the Depression. "The business of parenthood survived the Depression in surprisingly good shape," indicated the trade journal *Sales Management*.

Parents' was the only magazine sufficiently "Depression-proof" to show a gain in advertising revenues every year from 1927 through 1934.[42]

Through advertising, manufacturers and retailers of household and child-related products explicated modern femininity. The homemaker was linked to the new housekeeping, and the parent to modern child-rearing, through purchasing. Advertisers drew arms and ammunition of scientific credibility from the stockpiles provided by the social sciences, and the conflicted definition of the modern woman provided ample terrain for psychological battle. In the 1920s the modern advertising industry came into its own. Manufacturers and retailers themselves had carried on small-scale, local advertising in the nineteenth century, usually in printed text intended to give information (sometimes false information!) about the product. By the turn of the century the specialized advertising agency had begun to appear, and pictorial representation entered the field. Large companies aiming at a national market saw the advantage of superseding reliance on the local retailer, moving instead to appeal directly to the consumer through "name brands" nationally advertised. The acknowledged role of national propaganda in World War I hastened advertising professionals' self-consciousness about their field's potential and businessmen's estimation of it. The business deduction allowed for advertising under wartime taxation of excess profits also caused the scale of advertising to balloon.

Twentieth-century advertising adopted science as the standard of industry's advance and the consumer's advantage, as the modern authority from which advertising gained its edge of expertise. Turning to sales purposes the social science norms of efficiency and "adjustment," advertisers presented themselves to consumers as educators and to their clients as especially informed manipulators of human behavior. It was well accepted by practitioners in the 1920s that advertising had advanced beyond supplying information to creating "needs," as symbolized in the name of one of the earliest nationally advertised brands, "Uneeda Biscuit." Increasingly, advertising technique exploited psychological revelations of the irrational motivations lurking under civilized behavior and employed symbolism and mental association pictorially, to set the emotions of the consumer to work to make the sale. It was an "open question," wrote sociologist Robert Lynd in a piercing commentary published in 1930, "whether factors making for consumer confusion in our rapidly changing culture are not actually outstripping the forces making for more effective consumption. . . . The business of selling commercial products as substitutive reactions for more subtle forms of adjustment to job security, social insecurity, monotony, loneliness, failure to marry, and other situations of tension has advanced to an effective fine art."[43]

Whatever the multifarious and variable result of advertising on perception and behavior—a matter that resists exact measurement (to say the least)—it is worth noticing that most ads were beamed toward women, who presumably absorbed a larger dose of what it served than men. As one ad in the industry journal put it, "The proper study of mankind is *man* . . . but the proper study of markets is *woman.*" Countless publications of the 1920s cited the statistic that women made 80 percent of consumer purchases. Advertising and marketing people habitually referred to the consumer as *she*, and home economists provided open invitation to do so by heralding consumption as the queen of the homemaker's tasks. "Her most important work," announced Woodhouse, "is that of director of family relations and family consumption." Not a new theme—reformers and suffragists at the turn of the century had already portrayed the home as the hub of a radiating network of economic factors, in order to show the most home-bound woman her connection to a wider world—the emphasis on women's consumer roles reached new heights in the 1920s. Purchasing was in fact more frequent and complex in an era of mass production and merchandising, and dominant social theory defined the economic role of the family as consumption, rather than production as in former days.[44]

Advertisements themselves worked and reworked a contention that home economists favored, that purchasing was an arena for choice and control in which women could exert rationality and express values. "Too frequently . . . monopolistic factors really determine what goes on in the market, and advertising and sales organization beat down individual judgment," one might object, as did a writer in the *Journal of the American Association of University Women;* "such control" over production as demand theory would predict "the homemaker does not, of course, exert." But even she urged homemakers to understand the importance of their position and "its potentiality for the general welfare." Modern merchandising translated the feminist proposal that women take control over their own lives into the consumerist notion of choice. In a staggering conjunction, an ad in the *Chicago Tribune* boasted, "Today's woman gets what she wants. The vote. Slim sheaths of silk to replace voluminous petticoats. Glassware in sapphire blue or glowing amber. The right to a career. Soap to match her bathroom's color scheme." General Electric linked "the suffrage and the switch." Advertisers hastened to package individuality and modernity for women in commodity form. New graphic

and photographic techniques enabled advertising to become a visual me-
dium with subliminal influence as never before, intentionally selling
women not only sales pitches for products but also images of themselves.
(Visual advertisements enmesh us, as a recent critic has said: "they invite
us 'freely' to create ourselves in accordance with the way in which they
have already created us.") Of course, the economic power behind such
purveying of images of the modern woman was many times greater than
that behind any competing model. [45]

A few outraged individuals cried out that women were being sold a
streamlined and glamorized version of their traditional place vis-á-vis
men. "When will women, patient creatures," Anne Martin demanded
early in the 1920s, "see clearly enough to protest against . . . the pictures
of themselves as wives and mothers appropriately arrayed in housewives' uniforms, working oil, gas, and electric stoves, furnaces, carpet-
sweepers, washing machines and clothes-wringers, or cooking and serving various foods—all the wares of the advertisers—with sweet, seraphic
smiles on their faces? As if they never had, or wanted, another thought!"
Martin contended that the magazines devoted to "women's interests" in
particular broadcast policies and images antithetical to women's economic equality. "Against the incubus of these so-called 'women's' or
'home' magazines, edited chiefly by men," she protested, "how can our
sex be roused to feel that they have not yet even the poor measure of
'freedom' that men have?" She quoted one senior editor of a women's
magazine as saying, "our advertisers are afraid of women getting too progressive and spending less time on housework, thus cutting down their
purchases of the things listed in our guaranteed advertising." (Indeed,
the dollar volume of advertising devoted to household soap and similar
consumables swelled almost ten times over between 1915 and 1929, rising from twelfth to sixth place among the various commodities advertised
in thirty major magazines.) Martin fumed that women were "lulled into
forgetfulness of their contemptible economic status and into complacency over their 'new freedom,'" by women's magazines administering
"raw narcotics" on their editorial pages and "subtly blended doses of
soothing syrup" on the fiction pages. A male critic later in the decade
similarly argued that manufacturers and advertisers who sold home
products formed a conspiracy to regiment the thinking of readers of
women's magazines. In sarcasm he rendered their outlook: "the ladies,
bless 'em, are progressing in seven-league boots; their place is with the
pots and pans." [46]

Advertisers succeeded in uniting modern emblems with woman's traditional priorities, promoting an ideal of the vigorous, gregarious woman who was scientifically aware of the best methods for caring for her husband, home, and children and capably responsible for their welfare. No longer the demure, diffident, "delicate," or submissive housewife, the modern woman liked to have fun, knew what she liked, and was attractive to men. In such prescriptions of women's relations to men, sex appeal took the place that submission had held in the nineteenth century, and sex appeal was big business. Robert Lynd reported that in 1929 the billion-dollar toiletry industry of "beauty items" was spending more on advertising than the seventeen-billion-dollar food industry and the six-and-a-half-billion-dollar auto industry. Even love and romance were mass-produced commodities, in the eyes of one sardonic female observer. She saw "hundreds of press agents" for romance in the mass media, instructing women in the two schools of "glamour" and "the little woman"—the one showing how to be a sparklingly appealing "pal" to men, the other "concentrating almost entirely upon the romantic aspects of the home, the lighted hearth, the savory pot, the sacrosanct bedroom . . . the tete-a-tete next to the radio."[47]

Gaining ground and credibility from reference to science, and acting as agents of profit-making enterprise, popular media and advertising took the upper hand in prescribing models for fulfillment of womanhood. Not duty imposed by church or state but personal "adjustment" and "fulfillment," demanded from within, called women to the performance. What was unprecedented here was less the didacticism, or sense of knowing best (which traditional sources had shared), than the way in which women's household status and heterosexual service were now defended—even aggressively marketed—in terms of women's choice, freedom, and rationality. The purposive agents of modernity had to take women's desires for and emblems of emancipation into account. As one evidence of the new era, Feminism supplied a resource drawn on by many takers. The culture of modernity and urbanity absorbed the messages of Feminism and re-presented them. Feminist intents and rhetoric were not ignored but appropriated. Advertising collapsed the emphasis on women's range and choice to individual consumerism; the social-psychological professions domesticated Feminists' assertion of sexual entitlement to the arena of marriage. Feminists' defiance of the sexual division of labor was swept under the rug. Establishing new formalism, these adaptations disarmed Feminism's challenges in the guise of enacting them.

6

THE ENEMY OF SOCIETY

JANE SMITH

Linoleum Cuts by Margaret Schloemann

Out in the World:

Graduated from the state university, 1917
Worked on the local paper, 1917-18
Got an humble job on a city paper, 1918-19
Married Richard Roe, rising young journalist, 1919
Got a raise. So did Richard. 1920
Took a staff position on a weekly magazine.
 Richard got another raise, 1921.
Daughter arrived. Jane took four months off, two
 before and two after, and then worked part
 time two months. 1922
Jane got a raise. So did Richard. 1924
Son arrived. Four months off again, and two
 months part time. 1925

Present status:

Jane is earning $250 a month, Richard $350.
They have a sunny six-room apartment in an un-
fashionable neighborhood with the use of the
back yard. Their daughter is in nursery school,
8.30 to 5, daily, under the best modern care,
physical and intellectual. Cost, $50 a month.
A housekeeper who has had two years hospital
training cares for the baby and does the general
housework at a salary of $80 a month with board
and room. Laundry and heavy cleaning are done
by Mandy, one day a week, $4 and carfare.

Left column schedule:

7—7:30
Rise, bathe, dress, help four-year-old with buttons.

7:30—8
Breakfast.

8—8:15
Confer with housekeeper.

8:15—8:30
Richard and Jane walk to nursery school with daughter.

8:30—9
Jane to her office, reading morning paper en route.

9—9:20
Morning mail.

9:20-9:30
Brief chat with friend and fellow-worker, back from month on the Coast.

9:30—11
Dictate letters and give directions to secretary.

11—12
Informal staff conference—a stimulating gathering of friends, engaged in an absorbing joint enterprise.

Bottom schedule:

12—1:30
Lunch with national authority in her field, discussing mss. for forthcoming book.

1:30—3
Cut and edit promising mss. Outline her department for next issue.

3:30—4
Read over and sign letters. Glance through and part her second class mail.

4—4:15
Gentle conversation with shy, aspiring author.

Right column schedule:

11:30
Home and to bed.

8:30—11
New play.

6:45—8
Dinner. Two friends in. Good talk.

6:30—6:45
Freshen up for dinner.

6—6:30
Undress baby and give him supper.

5:30—6
Help four-year-old undress. Read her a good night story. Richard home.

5—5:30
Ride home, continuing book en route. Find four-year-old finishing supper.

4:15—5
Read first chapters of book she is to review for next issue.

From the *Survey* magazine, December 1, 1926.

ANN BROWN

By Beulah Amidon

Safe in Woman's Place

Graduated from the state university, 1917
Taught in local schools, 1917-18
Promoted. "One of our best young teachers — I'm afraid the city schools will soon take her." 1918-19
Married John Doe, rising young journalist. Gave up teaching job, moved to the city with John and undertook housekeeping job, 1919
Housekeeping, bridge, clubs, etc., 1919-21
Daughter arrived; John got a raise, 1922
Son arrived, 1925

Present status:

John's salary $250 a month. They live in a four-room bungalow on a tiny lot in an unfashionable suburb, so far out that theatres, concerts, lectures and old friends are beyond reach. Ann "does all her own work," except the washing and sometimes part of the ironing for which she has a woman who "comes in," half a day a week, cost $2 and carfare. Daughter is unhappy, whining, bad-mannered, a nuisance rather than a joy. Ann worries about her cruelly, realizing that to have a happy, joyous child one must spend more time and money and patience and thought than she can give her little girl. The baby is "delicate." Ann had to work full time to the day of his birth, and resume her job when he was three weeks old. John begins to feel tired and discouraged. There never seems to be money enough. Ann doesn't have time or buoyancy for "play." His office complains that he is "losing his punch." His is not a conquering mood.

5:30—6
Rise, bathe, dress, heat bottle.

6—6:30
Change and feed baby and re-make his bed. Put blankets to air.

6:30—7
Prepare breakfast.

7—7:30
Help four-year-old dress and prepare food formula for day

7:30—8
Breakfast.

8—8:15
Swift glance at front page of paper, speed the parting husband, shut front gate and send four-year-old out to her sand-pile.

8:15—8:30
Clear breakfast table, make grocery list, receive ice man and mop up after him.

8:30—8:45
Spank daughter who climbed over fence. Answer telephone. Dismiss peddler. Put baby's wash to soak.

8:45—9:30
Wash dishes, make beds, slick up living room, rescue four-year-old from (1) bumped head; (2) flower bed (John's tulips beyond rescue) (3) a caterpillar.

9:30—9:50
Accumulate baby's bath and bathe baby.

9:50—10
Put vegetables through sieve. Heat milk.

10—10:20
Feed baby and locate him in carriage asleep.

10:20—10:30
Slip on clean smock, superficially wash four-year-old, start to grocery store.

10:30—11:30
Buy meat and groceries at cash and carry, saving twenty-one cents. Speak to plumber about sink, got ten beyond first aid. Exchange news with two neighbors. Slap daughter's hands for meddling with fruit display. Buy her all-day sucker "to get

some peace."
Walk home.

11:30—12
Locate baby in pen. Prepare lunch. Answer telephone as lunch is on table.

12—12:10
Re-heat vegetables and milk.

12:10—12:45
Give four-year-old's lunch, eating hasty meal herself.

12:45—1
Give baby orange juice. Settle both children for naps.

1—1:15
Clear away lunch.

1:15—2
Baby's washing.

2—2:30
Change baby, give him two o'clock bottle, put him in pen out of doors.

10 p.m.
Bed.

9:45—10
Change baby and administer last bottle.

9:30—9:45
"Pick up" living room, put out milk bottles, heat baby's bottle.

8:15—9:30
Sew creepers. John dozes and reads on the lounge.

7:30—8:15
Clear table, wash dinner dishes. John potters around yard.

6:45—7:30
Dinner. Potatoes somewhat scorched. Ann tired, mussy and impatient. There seems to be nothing to talk about except daughter's behavior and son's stomach.

6:30—6:45
Put dinner on table.

6—6:30
Undress four-year-old. Husband arrives. Get children to bed, both protesting vigorously.

5:45—6
Give baby cereal and undress him.

5:30—5:45
Set table, put meat and vegetables to cook.

5—5:30
Give four-year-old her supper.

4:30—5
Prepare vegetables for dinner. Make dessert. Fix daughter's supper.

4:15—4:30
Change baby—all his clothes this time.

3:30—4:15
Chat with neighbor who drops in. Make buttonholes, scold four-year-old who doesn't want to play in yard, pay garbage collector, write down recipe for Fruit Fluff, dispose of sewing machine salesman.

3—3:30
Cut out baby's new creepers.

2:30—3
Bathe and dress four-year-old. Send her out to play in yard.

"Has Modern Woman Disrupted the Home?" asked the journal of the National Federation of Business and Professional Women's Clubs at the end of the 1920s. "No," journalist Ruth Hale blithely responded. Wife of newspaperman Heywood Broun (until she sought a divorce), mother of a young son, and founder of the Lucy Stone League—in support of married women keeping their "maiden" names—as well as a member of the National Woman's Party, Hale continued, "I believe that every woman should be a money-producing unit. Needing the money has nothing at all to do with it. But just being able to tell anyone that you have three cents of your own and won't they please mind their own business; to know that you are free and independent and can call your soul your own—that is what economic independence is. We need not worry at all about the home, for what one may consider neglect of the home today, may, in fifty years from now, be considered intelligent care of the home." Neither Hale nor the male respondent—debonair theater critic, magazine founder, and editorial wit George Jean Nathan—appeared vexed by the substance behind the question. Nathan answered "yes"—modern woman, with her tendency to leave the fireside and take a job, had disrupted the home—but he saw little harm and less to condemn in that, for the home had not been very interesting anyway, and men were to blame for its disruption too.[1]

Few public commentators on wives' gainful employment outside the home in the 1920s had the superficial complacence of Hale or Nathan. Public sensitivity around the issue testified to the impact on common consciousness made by Feminism and by the exceptional women attempting to realize its tenets. Both the feminist critique of women's "sexuo-economic" dependency and the necessity of earning money pressed on by modern industrial capitalism had raised profound questions about the gender assignment of economic roles. Despite predominant sociological theory of the time, which conveyed the view that the family was no longer an economically productive unit, such questions did not find easy answers but rather revealed the lack of consensus on the value and meaning of women's work outside and inside the household. The high level of attention given to women who intended to combine career and marriage attested to how extraordinarily iconoclastic that combination was. In theory, and even more in practice, it had the potential both to redefine marriage on the new basis of the wife's economic autonomy and to redefine women's stake in the labor market.

The "great woman question of to-day," and "the very essence of feminism," Crystal Eastman wrote in 1927, is "how to reconcile a woman's natural desire for love and home and children with her equally natural desire for work of her own for which she is paid."[2] Where the battle for women's access to equal work had historically been fought on one front, the battle for egalitarian marriage on another, overlapping trends of the 1910s and 1920s joined the two. Nineteenth-century advocates of women's right to equal work had, by and large, seen paid employment as alternatives to marriage. Aside from claiming on individual grounds woman's right to enter the market, they contended that women were forced to marry as a means of economic survival, a state of affairs good neither for women nor for the ideal of marriage. Expanding economic opportunity would assure more secure and fully intentional marriages (at least on the part of women), they reasoned, by giving women freedom of choice to marry or not. Although a few white and black club women at the close of the nineteenth century explicitly addressed married women's right and need to continue occupations outside the home, discussion usually concerned the abstract "woman's" right to labor (without reference to marital status) or dealt specifically with women who, by choice or not, lacked economic support from any man.[3]

Charlotte Perkins Gilman's *Women and Economics* (1898) represented a turning point on the question. Gilman stingingly denounced the sexuo-economic relation of wives to their husbands, at the same time celebrating the potential for marital intimacy between self-supporting women and men. In the 1910s, Feminists moved the focus of the economic question more pointedly to the wife and mother. Taking "all labor for their province," as Schreiner declared, they grounded their rationales both on the "right" to labor and on the historic evolutionary forces that were bringing women's productivity out of the home. The most acute analysts pointed out that the overall progress of women workers would remain marginal so long as the majority of adult women—that is, wives with husbands present—were working at home unpaid. "The economic independence of the unmarried woman is constantly hampered and impeded by the economic dependence of the married woman," Katharine Anthony recognized: women's work outside the home was poorly paid *because* women's work at home for the family was unpaid. Furthermore, unpaid domestic employment accustomed women to the undervaluing of their work. Gilman put it succinctly in her newsletter the *Forerunner* in 1916: "until 'mothers' earn their livings, 'women' will not." By 1920, with women's presence in the labor force an inescapable reality, age at marriage declining, and marriage becoming more universal than in previous generations, the issues of employment and marriage for women were inevitably joined.[4]

College women frequently named this their own, the "modern" problem. An editorial in the *Smith College Weekly* late in 1919 announced, "we cannot believe it is fixed in the nature of things that a woman must choose between a home and her work, when a man may have both. There must be a way out and it is the problem of our generation to find the way." The time had passed, observed Phyllis Blanchard, since "there was a fairly clear cut division between the life of wife and mother and that of the professional or business woman who was assumed to be as sexless as the worker bee." When attorney Elizabeth Read planned a session on women's "civil disabilities" for the American Academy of Political and Social Science convention in 1925, she included a segment on "work and careers after marriage," intending "to get as much plain talk as possible about how possible it is for married women to have children and do something else at the same time—and we must indicate how widespread the determination is of many of the younger generation that marriage shall not swamp their entire existence." The issue resonated in scores of articles and inquiries with titles such as "Can a Woman Run a Home and a Job, Too?"; "The Wife, the Home and the Job"; "College Wives Who Work"; "From Pram to Office"; "Why Do Married Women Work?"; "The Home-Plus-Job Woman"; "Babies Plus Jobs"; "The Two-Job Wife"; or—for a change—*The Delicatessen Husband*.[5]

It was rare to find a year in the 1920s in which any magazine with a wide middle-class readership, whether high-brow or middle-brow, did not contain an article on this question. Dorothy Dix, the most widely read newspaper advice columnist in the country—who herself believed that "economic independence is the only independence in the world. As long as you must look to another for your food and clothes you are a slave to that person"—said that the question most frequently asked of her was, "should a woman work outside home after marriage?" Here was an area where more than one generation could presumably find common cause. M. Carey Thomas, under whose presidency at the turn of the century less than half of Bryn Mawr's graduates married, acknowledged the new generation's priorities. Not giving up hope for a favorite niece who married, Thomas hoped she would contribute to "the all important burning

question of whether a married woman can hold down a job as successfully as an unmarried woman. This must be proved over and over again
before the woman question can get much further and I have set my heart
on your making a success of it and so bringing great help to the 'cause.'"[6]

Women's organizations responded to the interest. The Woman's Press
of the Young Women's Christian Association, in conjunction with a request from the National Federation of Business and Professional Women,
published a debater's manual, entitled, "Shall I Go on with My Job after
Marriage?" The American Association of University Women set its Committee on the Economic and Legal Status of Women to study the combination of work, marriage, and children by college graduates. The
Bureau of Vocational Information, and vocational bureaus at individual
colleges, turned their attention to the combination of marriage and career. By 1929, when the Institute of Women's Professional Relations was
founded as a successor to the BVI, one of its stated concerns was "adjustment between the home and women's professional interests." At that
point the Barnard economist Emilie Hutchinson spoke unequivocally
her belief that "the gainful employment of women after they are married
. . . is the heart of the economic problems of employed women today. So
long as marriage is regarded as an alternative to gainful employment, so
long must women find their economic opportunity restricted and subordinated to what is regarded as their real 'vocation.'"[7]

It was one thing for an economist to make a statement, another for
women to carry the statement into practice. Gainful employment outside
the home was a fact for only a small proportion of married women. In
1930, after a decade in which the proportion doubled, still less than 12
percent of the married women in the United States worked for pay outside the home, according to the U.S. Census. Even a smaller proportion
were pursuing "careers," which received the lion's share of attention. At
least two-thirds of employed wives, by the best estimates, worked in
domestic or personal service, agriculture, and manufacturing; these were
the doubly burdened workers whose plight worried the Women's Bureau. Wives' employment in the white-collar sector, however, especially
in clerical work, was rising fastest. In 1910, less than one-tenth of female
clerical workers were married, a proportion much lower than among
manufacturing operatives or professionals. By 1930 clerical work (and
salesclerking too) included a higher proportion of wives than the other
occupational areas—about one-third. If all the white-collar (including
professional) fields are taken as a proxy for careers—certainly an over-
generous estimate—that meant that still less than 4 percent of all the

Table 6.1: Percentage of Wives Who Are in the Labor Force[a]

	1890	1900	1910	1920	1930	1940	1950
Black	23.	26.	n.a.	33.	33.	32.	36.
White	2.	3.	n.a.	7.	10.	14.	17.
All	5.	6.	n.a.	9.	12.	17.	25.

Table 6.2: Marital Status of Women in the Labor Force[b]

	1890	1900	1910	1920	1930	1940	1950
Married (husband present)	13.9%	15.4	24.7	23.	28.9	29.6	
Divorced, widowed, separated	17.9	18.4	15.	n.a.	17.2	21.	
Single	68.2	66.2	60.2	n.a.	53.9	49.4	

Table 6.3: Percentage of White-Collar Women Who Are Married (Husbands Present)

	1890	1900	1910	1920	1930	1940	1950
Professional[c]	n.a.	n.a.	12.2	19.3	24.7	n.a.	n.a.
Clerical[c]	n.a.	n.a.	9.	18.3	32.1	n.a.	n.a.
Saleswomen[b]	n.a.	n.a.	n.a.	21.1	33.5	42.7	n.a.
Schoolteachers[d]	n.a.	n.a.	n.a.	9.7	17.9	22.	n.a.

[a]Lynn Weiner, *From Working Girl to Working Mother* (Chapel Hill, UNC P., 1985), 89.
[b]Winifred D. Wandersee, *Women's Work and Family Values, 1920–1940* (Cambridge, Harvard U.P., 1981), 68, 100.
[c]Elizabeth K. Nottingham, "Toward an Analysis of the Effects of Two World Wars on the Role and Status of Middle-Class Women in the English-Speaking World," *American Sociological Review* 12 (Dec. 1947), 670n.
[d]Lois Scharf, *To Work and to Wed: Female Employment, Feminism, and the Great Depression* (Westport, Conn. Greenwood, 1980), 76, 85.

married women in the country were experimenting (as Emilie Hutchinson put it) with the combination of marriage and career (see tables 6.1–6.3).[8]

Surveys of female opinion, especially youthful opinion, showed that new convictions about the importance of continuity in women's employment warred with received knowledge about the importance of women's domestic roles. A poll of about 350 middle-class high school girls (median age 16.5) elicited their ambivalence about the future. When home and career were posed as alternative life choices, two-thirds of the girls said they preferred the domestic role. But in response to an open-ended question about what they would like to be, two-thirds made a career choice. Phyllis Blanchard's survey of fifteen- to twenty-six-year-olds, mainly college students and white-collar workers, revealed greater commitment to domesticity but still conflicting sentiments. Asked "do you prefer a career to marriage?" 82 percent said no; but when they were asked what they desired for satisfaction in life, 32 percent gave first place to success in various creative and professional fields, reducing the proportion who most favored "making a home for husband and children" to 58 percent. Only 6 percent approved of mothers of young children working outside the home, however. Among 500 women of a wider age range sampled by the YMCA, almost three-quarters believed that "a woman will find her truest self-expression through her husband and children," but 40 percent also thought "every woman wants a career as well as a family."[9]

There were certainly reasons other than feminist ones that wives took on jobs and professions, and women social scientists were among the clearest in acknowledging them. "In an age where the emphasis is on consumption," observed Lorine Pruette, a trained social scientist by the mid-1920s, "women need wages, want wages, to keep themselves afloat on the tide. . . . As our pleasure philosophy takes deeper hold, as the demand for luxuries, artificially stimulated by advertising, mounts giddily higher, there is no help for it—the women have to go to work." Just as obviously, she pointed out, "the manufacturers need the women as consumers, need the two-wage family and its demands to keep the factories going. . . . It is a vicious, or engaging circle, as you like." Emilie Hutchinson distinguished three levels of motivation among wives: those "under obvious economic pressure who must work whether they want to or not"; those "adding to the family income to maintain or raise their standard of living"; and those impelled "by a clear conviction of economic independence as the foundation of responsible adult life." In retrospect, it is impossible really to dissect which were more important, what might be called "intrinsic" changes in understanding of woman's place or the "extrinsic" pulls, as sociologists Robert and Helen Lynd put it, of a "skyrocketing psychological standard of living." More realistically, these two kinds of motivations should not be seen as entirely separable or mutually exclusive.[10]

Economist Grace Coyle wryly observed that social disapproval of and employer resistance to hiring married women had brought about "what Lucy Stone could never have accomplished so extensively by exhortation," that is, "the continuing use of maiden names after marriage" by wives at work.[11] As Coyle's comment suggested, married women's gainful employment more surely took the form of feminist vision than it guaranteed the content. As much as there were other than feminist reasons impelling married women into the labor market, however, public discussion of wives' paid employment always related, implicitly or explicitly—in resistance, defense, critique, refutation, or confirmation—to the feminist connection between gainful employment and economic independence for wives. This was a measure of how fundamentally the proposition of wives' independent earning subverted the traditional conception of marriage.

For wives, the proposal of economic independence in the 1920s was as radical as the proposal of political citizenship for all women had been three-quarters of a century before, when woman suffrage was first seriously entertained.[12] Under Anglo-American common law, husbands owned their wives' labor power as well as their property, and in return had the obligation of support. The marriage contract in its economic aspect resembled an indenture between master and servant. Both parties had rights and obligations: the husband owed the price of his independent, superordinate role, which was to support his wife; and the wife owed service (her labor) and obedience. Because of statutory revisions of common law that began in the mid-nineteenth century and spread from state to state, by the early twentieth century wives had won considerably more rule over their own property and earnings than they had had a century before. Their release from the economic dictates of the common-law tradition of marriage was far from complete, however.

In fact, the legal underpinnings for wives' economic independence were a jumble of contradictory elements. So far as case law was concerned, husbands still owned their wives' domestic labor to such an extent that married women's obtaining the vote in 1920 should be judged a conceptual anomaly. The right of suffrage based on the concept of individual independence—meaning individual ownership of one's labor power—was still, in 1920, self-contradictory for wives. Reversing the sequence of liberal theory that predicated the vote on having an independent stake in society, wives gained political independence—if the ballot can be so called—while yet lacking the clear legal right to economic independence. That perhaps measured how far the meaning of the ballot in the twentieth century had diverged from its eighteenth-century origins, but it certainly signaled the unresolved competition, in public and legal terms, between women's personae as economic producers and women's personae as wives.

Feminists in the early twentieth century (and public opinion in general) usually considered the possibility for wives' economic independence as though the state laws referred to as "married women's property acts" and "married women's earnings statutes" had entirely overridden common-law tradition. In fact, by that time, married women had statutory rights to make contracts (except, in some states, contracts with their husbands), to sue and be sued, to own and convey property, and to keep their own earnings, as though they were not married. Judicial construction of the statutes was as important as the laws, however. Despite statutory language which in most cases assimilated the economic freedom of the wife to that of the unmarried woman, as late as the mid-twentieth century the husband's common-law right to his wife's services in the home had not been abrogated. Nor had its correlate, the husband's requirement to support his wife. Judges' interpretations of the married women's earnings statutes (when cases based on them came to court) barely recanted on the common-law tradition that the essence of marriage was the wife's domestic service for her husband. A 1925 summary by a legal scholar concluded that "courts have taken the narrow view" that the wife owned her own services and earnings "only when engaged in an employment by third persons; and that her husband is still entitled to her labor in the home and perhaps in his business." Even this development came about through a doctrine centered on the husband's consent, the doctrine that the husband could "relinquish" his right to his wife's services or (in post–Civil War language) "emancipate" her from the common-law obligation to labor for him, so she could be employed by third parties. But the principle that the husband might relinquish his right to his wife's services *in* the home was by 1925 "nowhere recognized."[13]

The truth was that the language of statutes granting married women the right to their own labor directly contravened the economic concept of marriage, and judges went with marriage—as a matter of public policy—rather than against it. As late as the 1920s and 1930s, courts in some states interpreted even wives' work for third parties, if it was undertaken at home, or in some cases if it was "like" domestic work, as belonging to the husband. (He, not she, had the right to collect for the services she performed.) The husband's right to his wife's domestic services wrested any legal foundation from under the concept of wages for wives to be paid by the husband; since she owed him her services (by definition), any contract for such services would be, in legal language, "without consideration" and thereby invalid.[14]

Wives' "labor, beyond the domestic duties required by the marital relation, belongs to themselves," one woman inquiring into the situation summarized at the end of the 1920s. Like her, most commentators emphasized how much the law had changed regarding married women's economic capacities, rather than how much it remained the same. In practice, of course, the legal limitations did not become apparent to every wife. A married woman might receive payment from a third party for domestic labor that legally belonged to her husband, so long as he raised no objection; a wife might even receive wages from her husband for her domestic services, so long as the matter never came to court. (Similarly, women with complaisant husbands who gave them generous allowances never felt the sting of economic dependence.) Neither statutory law nor judicial interpretation perfectly mirrored nor absolutely shaped social experience. The law was, however, a repository of long-standing ideology about the marriage relation, and it continued to influence and structure what was possible in that relation. It made clear that still, in the 1920s and 1930s, marriage was a labor contract. It was still a labor contract like indenture, in which the worker could not without great sacrifice exercise the time-honored alternative to acquiescence or protest—that is, leave the job and find another. "In all states the husband owns the wife's labor so far as she lives the traditional married life," declared attorney Blanche Crozier, with deceptive equanimity, in the mid-1930s. The stable common-law concept of what the wife owed her husband, as well as the real content of domestic duties, amounted to no small restriction on the wife's exercise of her productive capacities. The concept operated most powerfully, although most invisibly so long as untested, for those women who were not employed outside the home.[15]

Blanche Crozier summarized: "Everywhere and without exception the husband owns the wife's labor performed at home and of the general nature of housework. It is therefore true that for the great majority of people the husband owns the wife's labor; and any case in which he does not is the result of a considerable departure from the traditional and still typical situation of marriage."[16] Without using her legal phrasing, probably many married women intuitively agreed. A series of articles in *Women's Home Companion* in 1923 soliciting the attention of the "homemaking, housekeeping woman," and proposing to address her needs to regularize and minimize her domestic labors, provoked an inrush of two thousand letters from women eager to share their everyday problems. The housewives and homemakers who wrote in, from farm and city, with grade school to college educational backgrounds, showed that they understood the economic bargain of marriage and its limits in a cash-based society.

Although discomfited by being left out of the system of cash reward, and aware that their labor was thereby devalued, the homemakers writing in knew what they owed and felt committed to the nurturing and childrearing role of the wife and mother; that spurred their toleration of the situation. "I have an inferiority complex. I know it, and am ashamed that I tolerate it; but I know equally well that it comes about through my lack of financial independence. I can figure it out *ad infinitum*, that my services are worth such and such an amount . . . and yet, because I don't get an actual cash return for certain definite services rendered, I feel dependent, which brings a lot of mental and spiritual ills that I don't need to enumerate to you, who are all probably familiar with them," admitted one middle-aged woman with a college education behind her. The Irish wife of a carpenter wrote, "don't you think I'm not a-wanting to do my share. But I want an eight-hour day, too, like the men, and the rest of the time with my children." "My children are bright and normal in every way and I love them dearly, but I know there isn't a woman who will read this letter who doesn't understand me when I say that I have no personal life. I am only a piece of machinery that nobody realizes the value of, unless I should stop," the wife of a teacher contributed. Another mother said, "any woman who keeps her own house, does her own cooking, and cares for her children, has a harder job than the average worker. But it isn't a paying job. . . . We pay a terrible price for acknowledging we are 'provided for'—our self-respect. And when you have no self-respect you cannot command respect."

"I suppose my problem is the same as that of thousands of other mothers who do their own work—three meals a day to prepare and the time between filled with endless washings, ironings, mendings, cookings, and cleanings," chimed in a mother of two children who desperately wanted less housework only so she could have time and strength for more babies. Another wrote, "I would not change my life if I could. I mean I had rather be married than not be; I adore my baby and love all children; and home to me is the most wonderful place this side of heaven. . . . But . . . I hate 'being provided for.' And not for one minute do I consider myself provided for. But everybody else does, except other mothers and housekeepers. There's the rub, and it isn't a square deal."[17] That cluster of attitudes had been presaged in a Carnegie Lyceum audience's response, in 1909, to a debate between Charlotte Perkins Gilman and Anna Howard Shaw on the question, "is the wife supported by her husband?" From a large and mainly female audience attracted by the sponsoring Women's Trade Union League, Shaw received warm endorsement when she argued that the wife more than earned her support in her household labors. Gilman, taking the other side, persuaded only a few voices to vote yes, but she received enthusiastic applause (according to a newspaper report) "when she said that women could not have a financial standing in the family because they were not rewarded in proportion to their work."[18] The 1920s wives and mothers writing to the *Women's Home Companion* likewise knew that their domestic labor had real (if unpaid) economic value, and although not necessarily satisfied with the situation they understood the marriage contract as requiring labor that precluded gainful employment outside the home.

Very likely the bulk of *un*married employed women at the time shared that view of wives' obligations. Although nearly a quarter of women professional workers and a third of women white-collar workers were married by 1930, that meant the great majority remained unmarried, and those included "career women" who saw their own aims at odds with marriage. (One example, attorney Mabel Walker Willebrandt, declined to marry a man of whom she was very fond, explicitly because her memories of an earlier marriage made her see marriage and economic independence as mutually exclusive alternatives. To her parents she admitted her "sort of inferiority complex . . . over making money." "For the sense of victory it would give me, I want to make it myself," she wrote, "especially since there's no such thing as getting it out of a clear sky with no donor attached!")[19] Perhaps many single career women resented the new notion that marriage and career were *not* either/or propositions. When the BVI asked a sample of women lawyers, early in the 1920s, "how, in your judgment, should women solve the seeming paradox between vocation and marriage?" the answers revealed more opposition than optimism. Some of the older lawyers were most adamant that, as one wrote, "marriage is a vocation in itself. The institution of marriage is for the purpose of establishing homes and raising children. . . . When women learn that marriage is a business and not a pastime there will be less business for the lawyer in the divorce courts." Another agreed, "it has been well said that law is a jealous mistress, and as society is still ordered, the moral, religious, domestic and social claims upon a married woman are prohibitive of her devoting herself to the practice of law successfully after marriage." Only a third of the nearly one hundred queried, three-quarters of whom were single, thought the "paradox" could be solved; and some of them belied themselves, like the young voice declaring, "there is no paradox to my mind. They should go hand in hand. No woman's life is complete without love and marriage, but there should be a thorough understanding before marriage that she may continue work, if she so desires." She concluded, "many women, in my experience, do not desire to continue."[20]

In a larger survey, of secretaries, the BVI's question "what are the advantages and disadvantages of secretarial work for a married woman?" gave many single respondents the opening to grumble about married women in the field. The sex segregation of jobs and male domination at the top levels in most offices exacerbated competition between women—single or married—while also doubling the message that it was women's destiny to succeed in relation to powerful men. The very limited and unpredictable advancement possibilities in white-collar occupations meant that in order to look for promotion women had to compete with each other in a kind of parody of the stereotypical rivalry among women to land an eligible male. In most office work, women could advance in their careers only by retreating, in effect, to the professional performance of the wifely adjunct role. The power that a female white-collar worker could realistically hope to gain was the power *behind* the throne; the privilege realizable was that of being adjunct and indispensable to an important man. The analogies to wifehood in subordinate office work exacerbated tensions between single and married women. In the BVI study, single clerical workers emphasized the disadvantages suffered by their married office-mates more than the married respondents themselves did, and the indictment was similar to bigamy: the major point was the divided loyalties of secretaries who also had husbands and homes.[21]

The common-law concept of marriage, enshrined in public policy and reflected in popular preconceptions about wives' and mothers' most defining roles being homemaking and childrearing, also informed the labor market. "The gainfully employed married woman continues to be regarded by no small group of persons as an 'enemy' of society," a researcher on overt discriminations against wives had to admit. More than 60 percent of school boards in 1,532 cities polled by the National Education Association in the mid-1920s discriminated against married women in new hiring. In half of the school systems a single woman teacher was forced to resign—either immediately or at the end of the year—if she married. Since teaching was the principal occupation of college-educated women at the time, such policy amounted to a class-based proscription against gainful employment for middle-class wives. Private employers also frequently opposed the hiring of married women in white-collar work, thus causing the expedient Lucy-Stone-ism on which Grace Coyle commented. Whether through formal policy or informal means, employers hearkened either to the claim that married women were insufficiently devoted to their work or to the ideal that, for social order, they belonged at home. The fact that public and private employers articulated policies of restriction announced, ironically, that married women were seeking jobs, at the same time that it perpetuated the either/or choice for women (between marriage and career) and upheld the work ethic for the married man, the normative equation of masculinity with the provider role.[22]

Women who would advocate or attempt to put into practice the combination of marriage and career thus looked out at a very unfavorable environment, to say the least. They faced an unwelcoming labor market in which their own devaluation was an important bastion against equal pay for women. They had to swim against a deep tide of conventional estimations of their real "vocation"—including their own internalized sense of responsibility for the health and welfare of their families—and take into account newly articulated assessments of their femininity as well as old and new requirements of homemaking and childrearing adumbrated by professionals and product-makers. Even in progressive circles, the belief that women could and should combine family life with outside employment was very distinctly a minority viewpoint. When the social work journal *Survey*, a rallying point for social reformers and an outlet for progressive opinion, ran a feature in 1926 entitled, "How Should the Family Be Supported?" only one of the four opinions presented recommended "parents' wages," in other words, employment for both husband and wife. Opposing views were given by William Green, president of the American Federation of Labor, who declared for the husband's wage and argued that wives' and mothers' entry into the labor force degraded family life; by social researcher Agnes Peterson of the Women's Bureau, who advocated mother's pensions, by which she meant state assistance to mothers with children in the absence of a male breadwinner; and by economist Paul Douglas, who touted the family wage, men's pay adjusted to reflect the number of their dependents.[23]

The one who spoke for both parents' wages was Alice Beal Parsons, a feminist and pacifist who the same year published a book, *Woman's Di-*

lemma, in the Gilman tradition. Parsons decried continuing restrictions on women's scope and argued forcefully the inevitability and the need for women's full integration into the world of paid employments. She carefully examined (only to lay to rest) counterclaims based on putative differences between the sexes or on the preservation of the home. Unlike some of her contemporaries, such as Lorine Pruette and Ethel Puffer Howes, Parsons (who was the mother of a young child at the time) did not embrace the alternative of part-time work for wives and mothers, viewing it as insufficiently attuned to the twentieth-century reality of specialized work outside of the home. Rather like Gilman, she offered a battery of suggestions for socialized and professionalized housework, nursery schools, and daycare centers to make mothers' outside employment feasible. Beyond Gilman, she stressed that husbands and fathers would have to do their share in or around the modern household—she refused to see housekeeping as "naturally" a woman's task. Another major feminist text of the same year, Suzanne La Follette's *Concerning Women,* took a similarly equalitarian approach to the household, acerbically noting that investigations of the exhaustion of employed married women never made it an argument "for expecting the husband to share in the wife's traditional burden as she has been forced to share his." An anti-monopolist and anti-statist, La Follette was unique among her contemporaries in recognizing how far marriage customs and laws, especially in their economic impact, carried on the traditional chattel status of wives. Taking a position close to that of the late nineteenth-century free lovers, she contended that all state sanctions regarding marriage should be abolished.[24]

If Parsons and La Follette tended to slight the extent to which women's labor remained a mainstay of the household and of family life, they both took an equalitarian approach to the household that was unusual among rationales for married women's employment. From a wider range of women's voices, two separable and, in fact, competing rationales for wives' gainful employment took shape in the 1920s. The two were basically class-differentiated, one addressing the prosperous and educated woman who might combine marriage and career, the other dealing with the working-class wife under economic duress, the "home-plus-job" woman or "two-job wife." Between these two understandings, there were important differences, even cross-purposes, but they also shared important similarities in their concessions to companionate marriage ideology and to conventional opinion—in other words, in the priority they gave family life.

Those who spoke up for the married career woman in the 1920s were concerned by definition not with factory or service workers but with professionals, upper-echelon white-collar workers, managers, entrepreneurs, or creative artists. In such outlets as middle-class and intellectual magazines, publications of women's organizations, and empirical social science research, they offered a positive view of the combination that attempted to deal with explicit and implicit objections.[25] The genre of career–marriage advocacy began with the tacit premise that marriage was entirely volitional—not a necessary means of livelihood as in the past—since women could earn their own livings. It also assumed that marriage was desirable for normal women, just as careers were desirable. In Crystal Eastman's words, "love and home and children" and "work of her own for which she is paid" were "equally natural desires" for a woman. It was her expectation that women's true fulfillment consisted in having both economic autonomy and heterosexual intimacy. There was an ominous side here. If desiring love and home and children was natural, then not desiring them must be unnatural or abnormal. Women who did not have men or children in their lives by choice or chance—women who chose to make their homes with women—were stigmatized not only by the increasing valorization of heterosexual eroticism in the culture at large but also by the career–marriage adaptation of it. Just as the career—marriage model posited that sexual fulfillment through marriage (and motherhood) was a woman's natural right, it diminished the nobility and even the acceptability of a woman's preferring another priority to marriage.

On the premise that marriage and motherhood should be available to every woman, career–marriage advocates went on to say that these should not circumscribe her exercise of the full human range of her talents or training. Many women were unsuited by temperament or education to full-time domestic occupation; women as individuals deserved the right to continue extradomestic pursuits, and society benefited from their doing so, the reasoning went. The wife and mother who was also a career woman could afford to hire help to take on the day-to-day requirements of housework and childcare, and, moreover, happier family life would result since she was gaining satisfaction from her own work. Advocates contrasted the frazzled and frustrated housewife, pestered by petty details, unable to enjoy her children or command their respect, unable to communicate with her husband about anything but domestic tedium, to the woman who had outside interests and a salary of her own who was eager to come home to her children and husband at the end of the business day. Some advocates stressed that, far from being deprived, children gained from their mother's occupation since they had more varied exposure and economic advantages and escaped the risks of too much parental doting.

Career–marriage advocates took for granted that marriage was companionate, not hierarchical, although every rarefied discussion of housekeepers, baby nurses, play groups, nursery schools, and maids—every focus on the managing of home, husband, and children that the career woman herself had to account for—showed a lack of parity between husband and wife in the marriage. Englishwoman Vera Brittain roseately judged, on a visit in 1926, that America had "succeeded in abolishing the sacred immunity of the male from all forms of housework," but a handwriting analyst who claimed to have heard from ten thousand women employed outside their homes pronounced on the contrary that this was "THE ONE ANGLE ON WHICH NO ONE EVER TOUCHES. . . . that the man expects and demands of the woman the same work in the home that he does when he is the sole provider"—even if he was out of work. "Some of the women who have written me about this have raged," she related, "and some have been grieved and some have a grim sense of humor which allows them the grin but most of them are astonished, when they have gone out and got a good job, to discover that by not so much as one pudding a month, are they expected to do less than they have before." She claimed, too, to have been repeatedly unable to place an article about the problem in any magazine, because of male editors' or owners' opposition.[26] Evidence surfaced willy-nilly that the husband's authority or failure to adjust his own traditional expectations could cause problems. Most clear-cut were situations where a geographical move determined by the husband destroyed the wife's career designs. The gender injustices in the labor market, as much as husbands' legal rights or whimsical preferences, structured that problem; so long as men commanded much larger incomes than women, the location of the husband's job would take precedence. A wife who found herself unemployable because of her husband's location had to demand, "can it be in the divine order of things that one Ph.D. should wash dishes a whole lifetime for another Ph.D. just because one is a woman and the other a man?"[27]

The career–marriage genre contained no critique of husbands' power over wives or, indeed, of the institution of marriage.[28] Since its advocates adopted the heterosexual premises of companionate marriage ideology, they stepped off the path of critique of marriage that the nineteenth-century woman's rights tradition had traveled in its insistence on woman's right to labor and professional advancement. Although career–marriage advocacy avoided discussing intramarital authority, the frequent litany about the "cooperative husband" was a warning sign. It was no joke that women said, "marry the right man" in answer to their balancing question. The "right" man was one whose ego would not be jarred by his wife's having her own identity and income, perhaps the man whose field of work could give his wife an "in," the man who earned substantial income or—more necessary if the combination was ever to spread beyond the most privileged—who would help with the housework and children. Not that husbands were any more disposed than the generality of wives to contravene the common-law concept of marriage. In the mid-1920s, when Lorine Pruette had sampled opinions of over three hundred men applying for work through a commercial employment bureau, she found that only 4 percent held the "radical" view that wives should be expected to contribute earnings to the family; 31 percent believed that wives might work outside the home unless there were young children demanding attention; but 65 percent held that married women should devote themselves to the home, period. One investigator of "gainfully employed married women homemakers" concluded her study with a deadly serious 250-word prescription of "Characteristics of a Husband Who Will Assume Responsibility as a Homemaker in the Home in Which the Wife Is To Be Gainfully Employed."[29]

Some women social scientists during the 1920s aimed to answer further with facts the questions that swarmed around the marriage–career proposition from both sympathetic and antipathetic sides. Were wives and mothers able to perform on the job? What careers did they follow? Was the married career woman endangering her husband's and children's welfare? Who did the housework? What were the conditions—if any—that enabled successful combination of career and marriage? Given the controversial nature of the subject, such studies were always at least subtly—and often more than subtly—tendentious; although they were empirical they could not be neutral. For instance, two different studies of the career–marriage attempts of college-educated women both showed that only a small proportion (12–13 percent) were employed wives. Beyond that the studies diverged: one showed married alumnae (and especially those who were mothers) more frequently working part-time, and earning considerably less than their single counterparts, whereas the other found the married workers more often full-time and earning the same as the single women—and the mothers among them earning more than the childless. The contrast between the two, both of which claimed

to show run-of-the-mill college graduates, underscored how every presentation on the subject, regardless of claims to empiricism, bore a message. It also suggested that continuing employment after marriage was
exceptional enough even among the small stratum of white college alumnae, that there was no typical or predictable experience. Because a married woman's principal obligation was presumed to be (and most likely
she presumed it to be) direct care for her family rather than producing
income, contingent factors besides her preparation and willingness to
work bore on her employment and earnings more than on a man's or a
single woman's—her geographical location (which her husband had legal
right to decide), the health and demands of her children, employers'
willingness to hire her, her family's economic resources, and her husband's attitude.[30]

Virginia Collier's book, *Marriages and Careers: A Study of One Hundred Women Who Are Wives, Mothers, Homemakers and Professional
Workers*, undertaken under the aegis of the BVI in the mid-1920s, made
perhaps the most ideal statement of the career–marriage position. Collier put "sympathetic cooperation from husband" at the top of her list of
the four most important requirements for a woman's happy management
of career, marriage, and motherhood; the others were good health, vocational training and experience before marriage, and short or flexible
hours of work. Collier's study group was an unusual bunch, not a random
or representative sample, but women selected because each one was
known to be managing all the roles named in the title. Not all were
literally professionals—quite a number were in the arts and some in real
estate, sales, publicity and so on—and it is a measure of the privilege
and authority that the word *professional* conveyed that Collier used it to
denote the women's employment status. The one hundred women were
very highly educated, concentrated in large cities (indeed, three-
quarters of them lived either in Boston or New York) and very well-off.
Two-fifths of them had financial backing in starting their careers. Their
median annual earnings were between two thousand and three thousand
dollars, although one-third worked only part-time. Almost one-fifth of
them earned over five thousand a year. Nearly two-fifths of the full-time
workers and two-thirds of the part-time workers were fortunate enough
to have flexible hours.

The extraordinary advantages of Collier's group are clear. They were
not representative even of female professional workers, most of whom
were low-paid teachers. Ninety of Collier's one hundred subjects employed domestic servants, at a time when only 5 percent of American

households did, and almost half of the ninety had two or more in help. Slightly over half of the husbands were reported to help with the home and children, though a number of women seemed dubious whether even a very willing husband could "take an even share of responsibility." Husbands were not well enough acquainted with domestic detail, they reported; and female servants were used to being accountable to the woman of the house. In contrast to Collier's findings, a contemporaneous study of "college wives who work" showed that only two-thirds of them employed any domestic help at all, and only half of those had full-time help. An investigation of 652 "gainfully employed married women homemakers," three-quarters of whom were professionals, under Depression conditions found only one-fifth with domestic servants, and another fifth with some part-time help; three-fifths employed only an occasional window-washer or dressmaker and otherwise no help at all. Most of the husbands in this group were reported to be helping with household matters, most frequently along managerial or decision-making lines, however; only a quarter helped with general housework.[31]

Collier's group was also unusual in that they all were mothers. More than four-fifths of them had continued their occupations while their children were of preschool age, and only one-third said that childbirth or childrearing created undue breaks in their careers. Studies of gainfully employed wives more representative than Collier's found that from one-third to two-thirds of them had borne no children.[32] Collier's intentional focus on mothers highlighted how significant concern for the care and rearing of children was in negative attitudes toward wives' careers. Virtually all women entering discussion of these issues separated the proposition of marriage and career from the proposition of marriage, *motherhood*, and career. Career–marriage advocates, who did not pretend that the path was clear or the travel easy, admitted that childrearing put up the most worrisome roadblocks. "We all know only too well the complicating factors and mixed motives," wrote a journalist pursuing the question whether the college woman must choose between marriage and career, "the new responsibilities and demands of child training and the advance in psychology and pedagogy which have been superimposed upon all the cares and duties of motherhood; the dwindling supply of domestic servants; the glamour and interest in professional work; the need for money so that greater opportunities can be provided for the family; and the conflict caused by emotional ties which for centuries have bound women to their homes." Similarly, another weighed the issues for the professionally trained woman: "on the one hand, a keen interest in

her professional work, a real need of income, the fear of mental stagna-
tion, and the restlessness that comes from filling all her day with petty
things; on the other hand, new demands in child care that were unknown
even a decade ago; a supply of domestic helpers that is fast diminishing
both in quality and quantity; and, like a cloud over all her activities, her
own emotional conflict that is rooted deep in her maternity." (How many,
one wonders, had the equanimity of economist Elizabeth Brandeis
Raushenbush at the University of Wisconsin, who, while confessing to a
friend that "this parent business is quite a job and I clearly don't shine,"
could nonetheless conclude about her nursery-school-age son, "I trust I
shan't ruin him entirely. Fortunately, I have faith that a good many children survive their parents' defects!")[33]

Some career–marriage advocates dealt with this problem by recom-
mending building a career for six to ten years before having children,
then letting vocational interests lie while children were young, and gear-
ing up again once children were of school age. That was the position of
Eva Von Baur Hansl, an early proponent of and organizer for the BVI,
who wrote on the question in the 1920s when she was a mother of two.
"I am an ardent feminist," she claimed, "who regards it as axiomatic that
a woman has every right to pursue any career she may elect. But to this
I would add the corollary that when she chooses to bring children into
the world, they have a prior claim upon her attention." If a mother could
attend properly to her children while continuing her career full steam,
Hansl had no objection, but from her own experience she doubted
that was possible; there was no adequate substitute for mother's "being
there."

Hansl's approach presupposed not only that childbearing was entirely
under a woman's control and prediction but also that if she undertook it
she had, as it were, assumed the risk it brought to her profession and her
salary. Hansl did not consider the sacrifice of seniority and cumulative
career advancement that her proposition required, nor did she discuss
the difficulties a career woman might have readjusting to domesticity.
Hansl's model was feasible, perhaps, for the woman who had both the
financial resources to give up earning money and the talents, energy,
connections, and line of work to resume a career after ten or more fallow
years, but how many fit that description? Occupied with parent education herself, Hansl believed that the "new science of child study" would
offer women professional occupations consistent with their family responsibilities.[34] Hansl's position potentially subverted the peace of mind
of women such as those in Collier's group (who took no break from their

careers), but she did little better than Collier at sounding realistic or
appealing to the great mass of women who understood their continuing
labor at home as crucial to their families' welfare. Generally, career–marriage advocates underrated (as, indeed, Charlotte Perkins Gilman and
Olive Schreiner had) the material value and symbolic meaning of wom-
en's domestic presence, when that value and meaning were still central
to most adult women's identity.

In a subgenre of individual tales by "ex-feminists," the difficulties of
managing and the realities of husbands' resentment and resistance rose
to counter the views of career–marriage advocates. These writers pic-
tured themselves not as reactionaries but as realists who might like the
combination of career and marriage in theory but found it impossible in
practice. One ex-feminist, the mother of a four-year-old, explained that
her independence had foundered because her husband refused to share
in the housework and their income did not suffice to hire competent help
with the child and house. Like her own, the husbands of all the women
she knew, including those who persisted with careers, "complacently
take it for granted that, while their wives have work in the outside world
as strenuous as their own, it is still up to them, being women, to see that
this other job, the domestic one, runs smoothly." Male and female roles
had so far been only superficially altered, she felt, leaving intact male
egotism on the one side and on the other women's "maternal instinct"
which prevented women from "being ruthless, as men are, at realizing
our individual ambitions and personal satisfactions." Another woman described how her success in establishing a writing career while raising
three daughters threw her husband into psychosomatic illness which
only abated when her income dropped. "Perhaps these lost men are necessary casualties along the way to women's freedom," she rhetorically
allowed, but did not herself agree: "freedom is not won by mere transfer
of power." A third ex-feminist illustrated from her own experience how
irreplaceable were the presence and thoughtfulness of the wife and
mother. After stop-and-go attempts to sustain her career, interrupted by
what she saw as her children's needs, she decided that "in a successful
marriage, as in all other smoothly running combines, one person must
be subordinate to the other, and in ninety-nine cases out of a hundred it
is more expedient for the woman to be." She was willing to affirm that
"there is no bigger job, no better job, for woman as she is designed than
the complex one of wife and mother."[35]

The common values shared by career–marriage advocates and ex-
feminists were as marked as their differences; that is, both groups justi-

fied their views on the basis of marital harmony and beneficial family life. Certainly, career–marriage advocates took women's professions much more seriously than ex-feminists did and saw the accommodation of paid work to marriage and motherhood as a permanent feature of modern life. The ex-feminists were more pessimistic, and more inclined to accept husbands' authority, than were the career–marriage advocates. Yet career–marriage advocates conceded the entire ground of contemporary beliefs about the mother's role in childrearing except the expectation that mother had to be physically present all the time. Collier approached this issue from several directions, not only by illustrating how well children of professionally employed women could be cared for, but also by dwelling on the reciprocal benefits marriage, motherhood, and career could bring to the woman who undertook all. Perhaps to fend off the notion that the woman serious about her career had to forego motherhood, she prompted her respondents to speak of the ways in which marriage and motherhood had fostered their careers. Overall, three-quarters of Collier's sample believed that wife-and-motherhood enhanced the value of their paid work. Half—not the lawyer, hat designer, geologist, or dancing teacher, but women in teaching, writing, painting, real estate, medicine and social work—perceived that their experience as wives and mothers contributed to the content and performance of their employment. One artist (reflecting psychological biases of the day) believed that "a woman who does not have babies has almost as great an interference with her creative work in trying to find adequate substitutes for her normal sexual outlet, as the woman with the actual babies themselves." A writer believed that her experience of having six children was all grist for her mill. A graphic artist, who had ended her employment after marriage but was compelled by her husband's illness to resume earning after she became a mother, had now—as the mother of two—reached an annual income of eighteen thousand dollars! She believed that the conditions of her marriage and motherhood had motivated her vocational struggle and success as nothing else could have.

Collier (like Hansl) found especially promising those women whose outside employment stemmed from or aimed to improve family life. At least three women, displeased with the schools available for their children, became school founders and directors themselves. One educator directed a national association for child study; another, who was the mother of four, founded and directed a bureau of educational experimentation for young children. (These two were undoubtedly Sidonie Gruenberg and Lucy Sprague Mitchell, although no one was named.) Another mother of four had begun as a leader in women's clubs and been tapped by the Commonwealth of Massachusetts to head the Mother's Aid Board. One sociologist was the author of a textbook on the family; another worked for an employment bureau dealing with part-time jobs for women. Among the researchers in Collier's group, one was investigating nursing mothers and infants; another, fear reactions among children under three.[36] For women who worked successfully in those veins, the putative conflict between their public vocations and private maternal duties could be minimized.

A constructive way that women dealt with the tension between career aims and raising a family was by devising occupations concerned with child development, which seemed to them relevant in more than one way and more conventionally justifiable. Clara Savage Littledale exemplified success and some of its ironies along these lines. A world-traveling journalist and fiction writer when she was single, she married the managing editor of the New York Times in 1920, bore a child in 1923, and settled into a domestic life, continuing some writing at home. When the publishers of a new magazine asked her in 1926 to become its editor, however, she accepted—for it was to be Parents' magazine, the bible of child-study and parent-teacher groups. Although Parents' appealed to mothers who were devoted to home duties alone, Littledale preferred maintaining a professional career. She took only six months' leave when she bore a second child in 1927. Her household cares were managed by a cook, a maid, and a housekeeper, and she could content herself and her public with the knowledge that her "editorial contacts with outstanding authorities" enabled her to be a better mother. She publicly insisted that the feasibility of a woman's combining career, marriage, and motherhood was an individual matter, dependent on each woman's wants and talents and on her husband's attitude.[37]

Like Littledale, the women whom Collier studied felt psychologically and economically secure while combining marriage, motherhood, and career—but their extensive psychological and economic resources were preconditions for, rather than results of, combining the three without stress. Collier was as observant of the individual solution as Littledale: "so long as husbands are individual, so long as children are individual, woman will find an individual solution to her individual situation," she maintained. The more that was said, the more it became a self-fulfilling prophecy that acknowledged a lack of collective or institutional support but did not look to create any. Consistent as it was with the impulse of Feminism to characterize women as heterogeneous individuals rather than as one type, that approach dropped Feminism's corollary insistence on the need for solidarity among women to counter gender restrictions that affected them as a class. The emphasis on individual resolutions chiming through the career–marriage genre offered little encouragement and no mode of resistance to the woman whose individual situation was not propitious.[38]

Ethel Puffer Howes's Institute for the Coordination of Women's Interests was the most ambitious attempt in the 1920s to get beyond an individual approach to the career–marriage combination and to give credence and value to women's domestic labor without allowing it to usurp all else. Howes had an unusual personal history. Identified as brilliant at a young age, she obtained advanced degrees at Radcliffe and at German universities and made a distinguished career for herself in academic psychology and philosophy. From 1899 to 1908 she taught (at the rank of instructor, of course) in the same Harvard department that included William James and George Santayana. She married late and in her midforties bore two children. In the 1910s—now teaching at women's colleges—she became an active suffragist. Once suffrage was gained, Howes turned her attention to what she called "continuity" in the lives of educated women.

Howes first looked to collaboration among women to address the "inexorable routine of housework." Through magazine articles and organizing efforts, she directed women's attention to the potential in cooperative nurseries, kitchens, and laundries. She made clear her abhorrence for the "crude antithesis" embodied in the phrases "home-making versus career" or "marriage versus achievement," which she felt harbored "implications which no normal woman of spirit and intelligence will accept for a moment." Both women's intellectual *and* their affectional capacities deserved nourishment and room to grow, she insisted. In 1925, welcomed by Smith College and awarded a grant by the Laura Spelman Rockefeller Memorial Fund, Howes set up the Institute for the Coordination of Women's Interests to experiment with means by which women might combine professional interests with marriage and motherhood. Her own ten-year-old son and eight-year-old daughter stayed in Scarsdale, New York, with her husband while she spent half the week at the Institute in Northampton, Massachusetts.

Howes believed that "it is far from a small matter of special devices or personal adjustments by which women may participate in both professional and family life; it is a matter of transforming the whole social setting and the inner attitudes of men and women to accept the twofold need of women as fundamental." The Institute pioneered a cooperative daycare facility to serve the preschool children of employed mothers, a cooked-food service to enable women to buy nourishing meals for their families rather than prepare all at home, and a training school for "home assistants," whose jobs were to be treated as reputable work. To design and implement the Institute's programs, Howes enlisted trained nutritionists and home economists (all women), believing that such professionals should be allies of, not models for, every woman. In fact, she deplored the move on some college campuses to make homemaking woman's "profession." Homemaking in her view was something universal, a "potential part of life for every woman," to be prepared for the way health and hygiene were, not to displace training for a vocation.

The second prong of Howes's approach was to promote career lines suitable for part-time and freelance work for mothers who wished to work from a home base. In its pilot programs, the Institute focused on freelance writing and residential and landscape architecture. A woman needed thorough training and two years' "footloose" experience before trying "to operate . . . in the wilds of domesticity, so to speak!" Howes recommended. Conceding that part-time work would likely prevent women from "penetrating to the innermost circles of a profession," Howes boosted the intellectual and spiritual value of working on the "fringes." She was not above advising "careful selection of a husband"— that is, marrying a man for whom one could contentedly become an assistant or researcher—for a woman who wanted to persist in intellectual work.[39]

The Institute tried to steer a course between the Scylla of a male model for women's professional life and the Charybdis of a romantic and sex-specific model for women's fulfillment, acknowledging the attractions and dangers each held. That was the best wisdom career–marriage feminism offered. Although the Institute's pilot cooperative programs marked out an alternative to prevalent resignation to individual solutions, it did not address the needs of women who lacked a college education or financial security in their marriages. Only intellectual scope, not economic independence or support of dependents, figured in Howes's pronouncements about continuity and integration in women's lives. Nonetheless, her insistence on redefining both careers and domestic life made the Smith College faculty and the Laura Spelman Rockefeller Memorial Fund leery. Founded when the elite women's colleges were adjusting to the fact that most of their graduates would become not scholars but wives and mothers, the institute was a casualty of the dissension aroused in that transition. Howes's accurate distinction of her aims from those of home economists or "professionalizers" of the home did not prevent Smith College from ejecting the institute, six years after its founding, on the same reasoning that led it to reject home economics: for being vocationally oriented and sex-typed, for having "unintellectual and unacademic concerns." Upholding the tradition of liberal arts inherited from men's colleges, the Smith College faculty repulsed Howes's intent to make conscious "the hidden unconscious conflict in educated women's lives between their two main interests." Like Hansl, they left the way clear for students as individuals to choose and to assume the risk.[40]

Career–marriage advocacy stood for individual choice, self-fulfillment, intellectual continuity, and social contribution. It steered clear of threatening the citadel of the male provider role. Its prosperous middle-class or professional spokeswomen, not wishing to rouse male resistance, left the economic factor in abeyance: they did not challenge male domination in the family head-on; they announced neither the Feminist standard of individual economic independence nor the expedient standard of family economic need. To the labor reformers and social investigators who were prime advocates of sex-based protective labor legislation, career–marriage advocacy was more of a problem than a solution. Those spokeswomen offered a different explanation for married women's employment, along the lines of feminist evolutionary thinking about the movement of women's work "from fireside to factory."

Understanding women's wage-earning as the modern equivalent of women's historical economic productivity, representatives of the Women's Bureau and its allies in the Children's Bureau, the Women's Trade Union League, and National Consumers' League tirelessly researched and demonstrated that economic necessity was what brought women into the labor force and kept them there in increasing proportions past marriage and motherhood. They insisted on the permanence of women in the labor force. They criticized the failures of vocational education to expand women's vocational opportunities. They demanded equal pay for equal work. On the rising trend for married women to take paid employment, however, they felt compelled to quash any incipient notion that the woman with home plus job was an avatar of feminist progress. On the contrary, they saw married women workers' aims rooted solidly in family loyalty and economic need. They saw mothers in long-suffering and self-sacrificing hours devoting themselves to eking out family budgets, even at the risk of haphazard childcare arrangements. Continually forced to weed out the hardy notion that women entered the labor market selfishly, frivolously, or to earn pin money, the Women's Bureau and its allies showed how essential not simply to self-support but to family support were wives' and daughters' earnings. As the sources of most of the useful information about industrially employed women, these reformers incorporated an interpretation of employed working-class women's economic roles along with the facts.

Well able to prove that women's cash earnings were essential to family support, Women's Bureau publications assumed that was the sole reason women entered or desired to enter the labor market. That view, that wage-earning wives' and mothers' employment was ipso facto a form of devotion to family maintenance, obviated the question whether the women themselves wished to earn money or follow an occupation outside the home. To Mary Anderson, director of the Women's Bureau, such considerations were luxuries only a few could afford. Yet not all working-class wives saw the issue so simply. In the politically left, trade union–strong Seattle of 1919, thirty-one out of fifty-two female correspondents to an advice column in the labor newspaper unequivocally supported married women's right to work outside the home, and more than a third of them were employed wives themselves. They attacked the customary sexual division of labor, defended married women's employment as both individually and socially desirable, and used words such as justice, democracy, individuality, freedom, equal opportunity, and equal development to explain their position.[41]

The Women's Bureau, intending to make the specific economic pressure on most wives and mothers in the labor force understandable and their employment unquestionable, disparaged other motivations women might have for working. Since Women's Bureau personnel were operating in a government bureaucracy and trade union milieu composed of men who were indifferent if not hostile to their concerns, they may have consciously or unconsciously assumed a defensive posture, trying to deflect criticism by stressing wage-earning as a form of women's traditional roles (integral to family life) rather than as a new departure. Although they were most sympathetic to the pressures on the wife who needed to earn, the Women's Bureau and other female labor reformers in the protective legislation camp opened no door to the possibility that a wife's or mother's earning gave her a sense of personal accomplishment or autonomy; rarely did they even note the importance of cash recognition of her labor as compared to her unpaid services at home. They left little room for her nondomestic interests or aspirations or for the conceptions of economic freedom or justice for the wife envisioned by the Seattle respondents.[42]

This understanding of the "two-job wife" shied away (although in a different direction) from the feminist tenet of wives' economic independence as much as or more than the career–marriage advocates did. The Women's Bureau always linked its explanation of married women's presence in the labor market to the insufficiency or instability of the male breadwinner. In a study of women's work in laundries in twenty-three cities, for instance, bureau investigators found that 40 percent of both black and white workers were married, and one-third had children under fourteen. For both the black worker and the white, the bureau cited "failure on the part of the husband"; "the need of support for herself or herself and family was the principal reason for her working." As much as the bureau's approach likened the wife and mother's motivation in the labor market to that of the husband and father—both derived from economic need, both likely continuing—it nonetheless implied that wives (and mothers more especially) were *properly* economically dependent on their husbands' wages. In opposing the equal rights amendment, the bureau and its allies sometimes warned that "blanket equal rights" would endanger the legal requirement for a husband to support his wife; they approached that requirement as an unequivocal good, giving no critical attention to the fact that its necessary corollary was the wife's duty to render unpaid services in the home.[43]

When the Women's Bureau found that a substantial proportion of women in service and industry were mothers of children under the age of six, that was unequivocally interpreted as working-class desperation and crisis. From sobering evidence of working-class poverty, such as the Children's Bureau's correlation of the highest infant death rates with mothers who earned wages outside the home, female labor bureaucrats and reformers not only judged that mothers' wage-earning was detrimental to their children and to society, but also saw the best remedy in increasing *men's* wages so that wives and mothers could stay at home. Julia Lathrop, director of the U.S. Children's Bureau, put this view succinctly with respect to child welfare. "The power to maintain a decent family living standard is the primary essential. . . . This means a living wage and a wholesome working life for the man, a good and skillful mother at home to keep the house and comfort all within it. Society can afford no less and can afford no exception."[44] That approach doublecrossed not only the assertion of women's permanence in the labor market but also the Women's Bureau's plentiful evidence that mothers in industry were widowed, divorced, or separated from husbands—they simply had no male support.

As much as their investigations pointed out how underpaid and exploited women workers were, the prescriptive view of working-class family health held by Women's Bureau and Children's Bureau personnel and their allies confirmed the economic hierarchy that made the male breadwinner principal, the woman secondary and undervalued. The female labor reformers' own emphasis on women's continuity in the labor market, and on the necessity for vocational training and equal pay for equal work, warred with their ideological commitment to the concept of the family wage. The Women's Bureau's attempts to make way for women in the labor market were undercut and overwhelmed by its endorsement, in effect, of that concept. Widely supported by male trade unionists, the concept of the family wage embraced the common-law meaning of marriage: the husband's duty to support and the wife's duty to render services. As much as the claim for the family wage had arisen as a working-class demand to wrest a decent standard of living from employers, it was also an invidious form of gender distinction in the labor market, making women's economic dependence, and the devaluation of their labor, conditions for the privileging of male workers as providers.[45]

Rather than attacking marriage itself, both of the rationales for married women's employment in the 1920s sidled in on its conditioning of women's economic behavior. Career–marriage advocates argued as if individuals, through individual arrangement, could make the economic constraints of marriage invisible, and indeed, some individuals could. They deflected attention from economic issues and concentrated instead on women's outlets for talent or energy, ignoring for the most part how far class privilege underlay their assumptions. The labor reformers' tactic, in contrast, made the economic bargain of marriage visible but accepted it. Focusing more rather than less attention on the economic aspects of women's employment, they legitimated wives' and mothers' presence in the labor force not as an alternative to the economic bargain of marriage but as a consequence of its deformation or nonfulfillment.

The more the Women's Bureau stressed that insufficiency of men's wages was the reason for wives' employment, the more career–marriage advocates had to placate bourgeois husbands' male pride and show that wives' employment had other motives besides dire financial need or male unreliability. The more career–marriage advocates ignored the importance of economic arguments, however, the less they understood the case of working-class women. The two lines of reasoning used in tandem in the past to justify women's right to labor—the liberal individualist argument against sex-typing of one's scope and social contribution and the evolutionary argument about women's constant historical economic contribution—had devolved in the 1920s into contradictory readings of women's economic motivations, applied discretely to bourgeois and working-class women. Although both acknowledged that employed wives were riding the tides of historical change, and both jealously guarded the terrain of family loyalty, the two rationales operated at cross-purposes, making need and preference mutually exclusive rather than mutually supportive explanations for married women's employment.

Empirical studies of the 1920s investigating married women's motivations to take employment made the ideological bifurcation between need and preference a staple of social scientific treatment of the issue. But even these studies, however tendentiously constructed, revealed that the separation was not complete in fact. For instance, when Eleanor Coit and Elsie Harper investigated motivation for employment among 519 women from nineteen states who were domestic servants, manufacturing operatives, telephone operators, and lower-level clerical and sales help, they reported that more than a quarter of the women lacked husbands' support; most of the reasons the women cited for seeking employment were financial. Virginia Collier, on the other hand, stressed that 87 of her 100 respondents named their principal motivation to be finding an outlet for talent or energy; 48 of them named no other. However, one-third of Coit and Harper's group also expressed interest in their work for its own sake, and more than a third of Collier's sample listed financial motivations as a first, second, or third reason for employment. A third of each group, in other words, admitted overlapping self-expressive and familial-economic motivations. As farsighted as both Women's Bureau spokeswomen and career–marriage advocates were in identifying married women's employment as the twentieth-century issue, their discussion in the 1920s rarely focused on that overlap.[46]

The Women's Bureau would not endorse married women's preference for employment, but the career–marriage advocates were compelled by hostility to their project to adopt the signpost of need. "The day has not come," one college-educated woman wrote in 1928, in a model of understatement, "when the married woman who works for any cause other than direct economic necessity may escape the criticism of her friends, her community and often of her own family."[47] Chase Going Woodhouse heralded a new, more economically expedient approach to career–marriage advocacy in the late 1920s when she reported on the work patterns of AAUW members. She stressed how unexceptional were college-educated wives and mothers who worked for pay, how "much like any other group of educated women in business and the professions," how far exemplifying "the trained woman who works as a matter of course." Woodhouse made the economic motive central to these employed married women even though they were clearly middle-class. Shadowboxing with her assumed opposition, Woodhouse pronounced that her respondents did not hate housework, and moreover did not make militant feminist statements about their individuality, but simply aimed to assist their husbands in bearing the heavy economic burdens of maintaining their standard of living.[48]

As the Depression descended, inciting outcry against employed married women for taking jobs away from men and single women, no rationale other than an economic one could make any headway. In Viva Boothe's report on gainfully employed women in the family in the *Annals of the American Academy of Political and Social Science* in 1932, justifications for all women's presence in the labor force had converged. Neither the entry of women into industry nor their entry into the professions was "the result of conscious and deliberate revolt on the part of women against prevailing social attitudes," Boothe wrote to summarize various studies of women's motivations; both were "due primarily to new experiences forced upon them in the process of living in the present order." Boothe took pains to point out that even married women who expressed preference for employment intended it "for the purpose of affording a more adequate life in the home rather than to provide an escape." The evolutionary view quashed those who would return to the good old days: "it is impossible to change the trend and find women back in the home under conditions that formerly prevailed," Boothe declared. At the same time, her emphasis on inevitability masked women's deliberate actions and refuted the impact of feminism. Virginia Gildersleeve, the dean of Barnard College, deflated pretensions even more flatly: "The modern woman's decision to work outside the home is not a momentous one on the woman's part as so many would have us imagine. It was forced on her by the man-made industrial system."[49] In short, the "new woman" in her role of gainfully employed wife and mother was not a conqueror of new terrain but a creature of circumstance.

The Depression magnified existing hostility to married women's employment; prohibitions and discriminations multiplied. By 1938 a National Education Association survey of 291 cities revealed that more than three-quarters of them would not hire married women as teachers. The

following year a National Industrial Conference Board study reported
that 84 percent of insurance companies, 65 percent of banks, and 65
percent of public utilities had restrictions against hiring married women.
When the Social Security Act was passed, the regional director in New
York City received more than a thousand anxious phone calls from married women who had been using their maiden names and were afraid
they would have to reveal their marital status to their employers in order
to register for Social Security! (They did not have to.) Yet, just as malev-
olent rhetoric and administrative bars rose, so did the employment of
married women. Even the proportion of female teachers who were married increased from under 18 percent in 1930 to 22 percent by 1940.
Overall, the numbers of employed married women increased by almost
half in the Depression decade; the proportion of employed women who
were married rose from under 30 percent to almost 36 percent. In 1940,
15 percent of the wives in the United States were in the labor force, as
compared to under 12 percent ten years earlier. The principal expansion
was not in professional and upper white-collar jobs, where male prerog-
ative gathered force in the economic stringency, but at the lower levels—
in domestic and personal service, for example. Marital status was rarely
an issue for employers hiring women as chambermaids, factory operatives, office cleaners, or part-time saleswomen at lower wages than male
factory operatives or unskilled laborers commanded.[50] The economic
function of hostility and discrimination against married women's employment, especially visible during the Depression but present also both earlier and later, was not to prevent women from entering the labor market
entirely but to keep them in its least lucrative or desirable sectors, conscious of marginal propriety, relieved to have work at all.

If, as newspaperwoman and NWP feminist Ruby Black recognized,
"women and men will not be equal in the economic world unless marriage and parenthood constitute no more a bar to a woman's employment
than to a man's," that was patent reason for women workers to continue
to be identified by marriage and parenthood. Private employers discriminating against married women typically reasoned that wives, by definition, did not need to work because their husbands were legally bound to
support them.[51] That understanding of need came less from social scientists' or labor bureaucrats' emphasis on the material necessity propelling
women into the labor market than from the longstanding economic concept of marriage itself—enshrined in common law and in custom—requiring the husband's support and the wife's service to him. Having to
confront such deeply ingrained beliefs, and not free of them themselves,

career–marriage advocates and investigators of the two-job wife more obviously confronted each other. The alternatives they marked out for dealing with women's unpaid labor in the home were to underrate it or to succumb to it. Hardly more than their critics had feminists solved the problem of how to regard women's labor in the home when they focused on women's labor outside it.

7

PROFESSIONALISM AND FEMINISM

America's Women Diving Champions

There is one sport in which our women are supreme—the sport of diving. Whether from the high diving board or the low, American women have made a clean sweep of the world's championships. In the center of this page we see Helen Wainwright, of New York, our national low-board champion who, in about a year, will make her great attempt to swim the English Channel. Flying around the page are Aileen Riggin, of New York, former Olympic Champion; Helen Meany, of New York, National Champion; and Betty Becker, of California, the present Olympic Champion. The photographs show the girls in the exact positions in which they were snapped by Albert P. Schlafke, a Brooklyn photographer

From *Vanity Fair*, June 1925.

Women's unprecedented feats of a "masculine" character captured popular imagination in the 1920s. By swimming the English Channel in 1926 in less time than any of the male swimmers preceding her, nineteen-year-old Gertrude Ederle became a symbol of women's new athletic accomplishments. Amelia Earhart, the logkeeper with a male pilot and mechanic, crossed the Atlantic by air in 1928—one year after Charles Lindbergh had made his solo flight—and became an American heroine, the female equivalent of "Lindy." Film actress Mary Pickford's meteoric rise to partnership in United Artists with Douglas Fairbanks, Charlie Chaplin, and D. W. Griffith in 1920 at a salary of one million dollars a year riveted popular attention. Repeatedly voted "the most popular girl in the world," Pickford reinforced her own role as a model, announcing that she liked to see her own sex achieve and was "proud to be one of . . . the girls who earn their own living." There was a carnivalesque fascination with such anecdotes of women on top, evidence of women's physical endurance, bravery, and (not least) money-making which seemed to deny the old wisdom of men's leadership and announce the blurring of gender lines. To the casual observer, the new exploits of women achievers implicitly answered feminists' objections that women's activities were predetermined by sex.[1]

In the feminist intent to "take all labor for our province," however, the more gradual and numerous entry of women into the male-dominated professions had always commanded more importance. Since the mid-nineteenth century, women's rights activists had made access to the professions part and parcel of their demands for balancing the sexual power in society. The "learned" areas of the law, medicine, the ministry, and so on, were arbiters of custom and convention as well as forms of livelihood, and women's exclusion from them rankled not only as a reflection but as a positive shaper of sexual hierarchy. Olive Schreiner herself, while sympathizing "with all the women of the earth, in whatever direction they are working, who are helping to do away with artificial distinctions of sex," thought women's advancement in the professions more significant than the vote: in 1912 she induced her own niece to give up the time-consuming work of being secretary of the Women's Enfranchisement League in Cape Town in order to study law, maintaining, "if she passes her law exams well and gets admitted to the bar here, and still more if she becomes a great lawyer and one day, perhaps, a judge, she will be doing far more to raise the standing of women in South Africa than if she had led the franchise clubs."[2]

Feminist reasons for women's entry into the professions multiplied in the early twentieth century because the professions themselves, expanded and reformed by the credo of science, bulked larger as sources of power and prestige. If women lacked power in the social world, the professions embodied the notion that organized knowledge *is* power. They were therefore obvious citadels to conquer as part of women's attainment to education and citizenship. Moreover, as roads to social and economic power in modern America the professions were more likely than business or politics to be open to women's travel. Without capital, entrepreneurial success was a freak; without even the vote, politics was impossible; but the "career open to talent" was epitomized in professional ideology. Theoretically, brains and commitment were the only prerequisites for the training that would lead to expertise. Unlike business or politics, careers in the professions were not easily reducible to the profit motive or the naked drive for power; the hallmarks of the professions were training and service, open to idealization by aspiring women.

Professional ideology and practice in the late nineteenth and early twentieth century accelerated stress on rationalism, scientific standards, and objectivity. Although those tenets counterposed certain longstanding stereotypes of women (who were presumed to be emotional, subjective, irrational, and personal), they nonetheless chimed in with an important chord in women's rights ideology. Again in contrast to business or politics, where personal factors such as wealth, contacts, and personality admittedly figured, the very impersonality of professional expertise invited women to enter that arena. Neutral scientific standards, based on knowledge rationally and objectively apprehended, constituted an alternative to subjectively determined sex constraints and an avenue to democratization of the power of knowledge. Because of the close relation of the professions to education and service (where women's contributions were acknowledged, to an extent); and because the professions promised neutral standards of judgment of both sexes, collegial autonomy, and horizons for growth, they became a magnet among the potential areas of paid employment for women.

The structure and ideology of the professions were also forms of occupational regulation. The training, credentialing, licensing, and employment standards established within professional groups (not without internal struggle) from the nineteenth through the early twentieth century were intended to establish and maintain their privileged positions. Professionalization took place during the latter part of the nineteenth century in old and new areas that were based on book learning and on the premise of offering a trained mind—not a product as such—in the service of others: law, medicine, the ministry, engineering, architecture, education, and so on. By self-definition professionals were experts who gave the benefits of their education, authority, and service to society in return for pay, recognition, and influence. Their training and ethics were sanctioned by their own autonomous group. Also by self-definition, professionals were male, except in areas peopled by women before the era of professionalization, namely primary school teaching and nursing, and in some (similarly low-paid) fields aspiring to professional recognition, such as social work. In the early twentieth century, diffuse "professional standards" were being adopted in many occupational areas—even in business and politics—indicating both the growing culture of professionalism and the persuasiveness of this rendering of any occupational group's self-definition and justification for existence.[3]

Growth in women's professional qualifications and employment was very rapid from the late nineteenth century through the 1920s. Among all employed women, those classified as in professional service grew steadily from 8.2 percent in 1900 to 14.2 percent in 1930. The group of "professional and kindred" workers classified by the Census was more than 40 percent female in the early twentieth century when the labor force was little more than 20 percent so; women thus composed a much larger segment of professionals than of the overall labor force. These aggregate figures sidestep questions of women's access and power in the male-dominated professions, however, for female monopolization of teaching and nursing accounted for most of women's share in professional service. Three-quarters of the rise in female professionals before 1920 was attributable to expansion in teaching and nursing, neither of which had the professional autonomy or the high pay of the male-dominated professions.[4]

The proportion of women entering the male-dominated professions (and achieving the college and higher degrees requisite for professional work) did increase from the late nineteenth through the early twentieth century, but unlike women's participation in the labor force overall, it did not continue to ascend steadily through the twentieth century. There are significant differences among professions; it matters whether one looks at lawyers, doctors, college professors, teachers, scientists, screenwriters, social workers, or some other professional group. In some male-dominated professions in which women made token access but very little headway, their gains were continuously incremental in a miniscule way through the first half of the century. That was true of lawyers and practicing scientists. The field of medicine looked different. There was a surge in female practitioners of medicine in the late nineteenth century, owing principally to the founding and operation of women's medical schools and hospitals by and for women. Women doctors were most concentrated and visible in a few large cities, such as Boston, Chicago, Minneapolis, Los Angeles, and San Francisco, where their proportion in the profession rose to peaks between 14 and 19 percent. In the first decade of the twentieth century, at its height, the proportion of women among physicians and surgeons nationally reached 6 percent, but it slipped thereafter.

A setback similar to that in medicine occurred somewhat later in academia. Of the learned professions, college and university teaching had by far the highest proportion of women. As women's colleges and normal schools were founded and coeducation expanded in the late nineteenth century, women increasingly won faculty positions. In the 1910s the proportion of women among faculty members rose especially sharply, increasing by about one-third to almost 30 percent of the whole. But after the late 1920s all the numerical indices of women's progress in academia leveled or dropped off, including the proportion of college students who were female, the proportion of Ph.D.s, and the proportion of faculty members (table 7.1). In awards of Ph.D.s—some index to potential professional life by the early twentieth century—the rise and fall were marked. In the early 1920s, after decades of steady gain, women received over 15 percent of Ph.D.'s awarded, but their proportion slipped down slowly thereafter, plummeting abruptly in the early 1950s to a proportion close to that of 1900 (about 9 percent).

Women's hold on the field of schoolteaching began a decline in the 1920s, too, which continued through the 1930s. That was due in the first instance to the expansion of high schools, where teaching jobs offered more pay and prestige than primary education and drew more male competitors, and in the second instance to the Depression, when jobs even in female-dominated professional fields looked much more desirable to men. By 1940 women still held three-quarters of the teaching jobs, but that was noticeably less than the 86 percent of the field they had held in 1920. The Depression also reversed the feminization of the social work profession. Female social workers composed half the field in 1910 and increased to 80 percent by 1930, but their hold was cut to 65 percent during the Depression decade by men's incursion.[5]

Table 7.1: Women as a Percentage of Total Students, Graduates, and Professionals

	1890	1900	1910	1920	1930	1940	1950	1960	1970
Undergraduates[a]	35.0	35.0	39.0	47.0	43.0	40.0	31.0	36.0	41.0
B.A.s or first professional degrees awarded[a]	17.0	19.0	25.0	34.0	40.0	41.0	24.0	35.0	41.0
Ph.Ds awarded[a]	1.0	6.0	11.0	15.0	18.0	13.0	10.0	10.0	13.0
Ph.Ds awarded[b]	n.a.	8.8	11.3	15.1	14.7	13.5	9.4	10.8	n.a.
College/ university faculty[a]	20.0	20.0	20.0	26.0	27.0	28.0	25.0	22.0	25.0
College/ university faculty[b]	n.a.	17.6– 26.2	23.2– 24.4	22.4– 24.6	28.2	27.9	28.1	n.a.	n.a.
Schoolteachers[c]	65.5	n.a.	n.a.	86.0	81.0	75.7	n.a.	n.a.	n.a.
Social workers[c]	n.a.	n.a.	56.0	66.0	80.0	65.0	n.a.	n.a.	n.a.
Lawyers[d]	n.a.	n.a.	1.1	1.4	2.1	2.4	3.5	3.3	4.7
Screenwriters[e]	n.a.	n.a.	n.a.	n.a.	33–50		15.0	8.2	8.2
Scientists[f]	n.a.	n.a.	n.a.	4.7	5.8	7.0	n.a.	n.a.	n.a.
Physicians[g]	4.4	5.6	6.0	5.0	4.4	4.6	6.1	6.0	7.2

[a]Patricia Albjerg Graham, "Expansion and Exclusion: A History of Women in American Higher Education," *Signs* 3 (1978), 764–65.

[b]Susan B. Carter, "Academic Women Revisited: An Empirical Study of Changing Patterns of Women's Employment as College and University Faculty, 1890–1963," *Journal of Social History* 14:4 (Summer 1981), 679–87. Carter's figures for Ph.D.s represent an average of those awarded during the first four years of each decade. Her figures for proportions of women faculty for 1890, 1900, and 1910 are expressed as ranges because of differing ways to figure existing data. See chap. 7, n. 5 (p. 350) on disparities between Graham's and Carter's figures.

[c]Lois Scharf, *To Work and to Wed: Female Employment, Feminism, and the Great Depression* (Westport, Conn., Greenwood, 1980), 6, 9, 66, 85, 91.

[d]Cynthia Fuchs Epstein, *Women in Law* (N.Y., Basic, 1981), 5.

[e]Lary May, *Screening Out the Past* (N.Y., Oxford U.P., 1980), 188–89, 291 n. 38.

[f]Margaret Rossiter, *Women Scientists in America: Struggles and Strategies to 1940* (Baltimore, Johns Hopkins U.P., 1982), 133. Figures are actually for 1921, 1927 and 1938, rather than 1920, 1930, and 1940.

[g]Mary Roth Walsh, *Doctors Wanted: No Women Need Apply* (New Haven, Yale U.P., 1977), 185–86. Walsh shows greater ranges in single cities, which are hidden by aggregate national data: e.g., in Boston, from a high of 18.2 percent in 1900 to 8.7 percent in 1930; in Minneapolis, from a high of 19.3 percent in 1900 to 7 percent in 1930; in Chicago, from a high of 13 percent in 1900 to 7.5 percent in 1930.

Combining the demographic changes in female-dominated and male-dominated professions, one can generalize to the extent of saying that the high point in women's share of professional employment (and attainment of advanced degrees) overall occurred by the late 1920s and was followed by stasis and/or decline not reversed to any extent until the 1960s and 1970s. That generalization does not exhaust the subject, however, and may even be misleading in several respects. Definitions and practices within professions, and in the bulk and prestige of professions in relation to each other and to other employments, have shifted and changed from decade to decade. Also, rates of increase of any group within a profession depend so much upon the base point that comparison from decade to decade can be problematic, especially when small numbers are involved. (The rate of increase in women lawyers, for instance, from 1869, when the first woman passed the bar, to 1880, when there were 75 women lawyers, was mathematically much higher than the rate between 1910 and 1920, when the number of women lawyers grew from 824 to 1738, yet to perceive a falling-off seems misguided.)

Most significant, the measure of women's presence in any professional field as a percentage of the total is responsive to changes in male participation in ways that may not be immediately obvious. In an enlarging profession, if women are making gains but men are making even greater gains, the change in women's participation will appear as a proportional loss. To assess women's ambitions and achievements, it is as important to know the change in numbers of women professionals relative to population, in other words, to know the rise or decline of women professionals among all women as well as among all (male and female) professionals. A declining proportion of women in a profession may or may not mean a declining proportion of women professionals of that sort among all women: it depends on the overall growth in the profession and on men's entry. In medicine, for example, the declining proportion of women among all physicians and surgeons between 1910 and 1930 reflected an actual drop in the number of women in the profession, from 9,015 to 8,388. In academia, on the other hand, although the proportion women took of all doctorates declined between 1930 and 1940, the number of women earning doctorates increased by 32 percent (from 311 to 419), far outdistancing the decade's growth rate for the adult female population.[6]

Still, the data regarding women's overall share of professional employment (or prerequisites) are very important, indicating within any profession how large or small women's participation bulked vis-á-vis men, laying a framework for evaluating how negligible or significant a counter to male professional authority women's presence appeared or how relatively deprived or advantaged women might feel. By the 1930s professionally employed women were a declining proportion of all employed women, as well as a declining proportion of all professional workers.[7]

The expectation of the nineteenth-century women who pioneered women's entry into professions—that the more women entered, the easier it would be for their successors—thus was not fulfilled. The example of medicine is the most striking. In the period of women doctors' surging numerical strength at the turn of the century, more opportunities than ever before were opened to them in formerly all-male medical colleges and hospitals, and the necessity for and relative appeal of all-women medical schools and hospitals declined. After admitting some women, however, the coeducational schools and hospitals rapidly established quotas for female students (usually 5 percent) and in no way furthered women's progress. The all-women's medical institutions for the most part lacked the resources to make a comeback in a period when the American Medical Association, the voice of the profession, was establishing ever more rigorous and exclusive standards.

Beside medical school quotas, the principal bar to women's becoming physicians after World War I was that they were not admitted to internships, which were increasingly a requisite to medical practice. In the nineteenth century, interning had not been a significant part of medical training. In 1904, the American Medical Association estimated that half of medical school graduates continued on to hospital training; but by 1913 it was three-quarters, and up to 90 percent among the graduates of prestigious schools such as Harvard and Johns Hopkins. That trend continued in the 1920s. Women medical school graduates had to search for and travel to the few scattered internships open to them. Statistics collected by the AMA in 1921 indicated that 40 of 482 general hospitals permitted women to intern, though not all of these 40 had ever had a woman intern in fact. Medical boards in seventeen states required internship for medical licensing by 1932. In the 1930s, about 250 women medical school graduates each year had to compete for 185 internships open to women, while less than 5,000 male graduates found more than 6,000 openings available. Deepening the disadvantage, medical schools often cited female graduates' difficulty in obtaining internships as a reason not to admit more women students.[8]

Women in the professoriat, even at their greatest numerical strength, also experienced frustrating restrictions. With few exceptions, they were confined to the lower ranks, regardless of their training or teaching experience. One researcher, Marion Hawthorne, discovered a distressingly low correlation between faculty women's rank and either the degrees they held or their years of teaching experience, in her survey of 844 women employed at 122 accredited colleges and universities in the late 1920s. Faculty women's low rank, in addition to meaning low pay, meant that they could have little influence on whether new appointments of women were made. Structures and patterns of sex discrimination that dogged the paths of women scientists and social scientists in academia have recently been documented in detail, and there is no reason to suppose that women in other departments fared substantially differently. Women's presence was severely limited by quotas and by administrative regulations such as anti-nepotism rules, which prevented a husband and wife from being employed within the same department or university. Since advancement took place through personally conducted mentor relationships between leading men and their protégés, women who made it into faculty's lower ranks but were without supportive male mentors usually stayed there or were channeled into areas unofficially deemed women's work, such as nutrition or home economics. Except in such areas, even women who carried on major research rarely reached the rank to have graduate students or protégées of their own.[9]

As important as each profession's protection of its prestige was the assumption (palpable in the labor market) that women did not have warrant for economic gain as men did. The overall tendency to regard women's economic demands as less worthy than men's breathed force into professional exclusivity. Suffrage activist and feminist Inez Milholland, a lawyer by training, saw women professionals' difficulties in the 1910s as a result of the long tradition "that woman is an inferior being whose work is to be treated and paid for as such." She thought that the "distrust of woman's work bred of her inferior status is the chief difficulty of professional women."[10] The experience of women in professional work was intrinsically tied to the general position of women in the labor market: if women professionals habitually gained fewer opportunities or promotions and lower pay, and found themselves segregated into areas designated as women's work, that was also true of women in the labor force generally.

A full assessment of the patterns of women's progress in various professional fields would take into account not only structural developments in each profession but also its relative economic advantage. The salary a profession might command was always a factor in women's professional entry. Women found entry into the field of medicine, for instance, in the mid-nineteenth century when neither the pay nor the prestige of medical practitioners was consistently high. Women made the most rapid gains in college teaching during the 1910s when academic salaries were particularly depressed. In contrast, when academic salaries were booming in the 1950s, the proportion of women on college faculties was at its nadir. In anthropology, the one science that welcomed women into training in the 1920s and 1930s, jobs were virtually nonexistent.[11]

For the scientific professions in particular, detailed historical research has revealed that male practitioners' deep-lying and perhaps unacknowledged convictions of female inferiority meant that they rarely accepted women as serious and deserving contenders for leadership, promotion, or reward; male academics protective of the reputation of their fields seldom welcomed female colleagues as equals. Male professionals' fending off of female interlopers suggested that they considered the presence of women colleagues above a certain point incompatible with their own vision of professional excellence, a threat to professional esteem. Unambiguous male predominance became an implicit and essential condition of continued professional identity and distinction. Male leaders in the American Psychological Association, the professional body in the science with the largest female representation (except nutrition), engineered a bureaucratic route to subtle but effective defeminization in the mid-1920s. Women comprised 18 percent of the American Psychological Association's membership in 1923, reached a peak of 34 percent in 1928, and still comprised 30 percent in 1932. In 1926 the association introduced a two-tiered membership system, naming all current members "fellows" but dictating that future fellows, a level above ordinary members, would be elected by the Council (a virtually all-male group). Women remained only 18 percent of the fellows through the 1930s.[12]

Perhaps it was where women had gained the *most* headway and made the most substantial numerical impact that professional backlash against feminization was most visible—that is, in medicine and in the professoriat. Congruent but not contemporaneous patterns show up: an earliest period of women's advance through their own institutions of higher learning and their own institutions for practice; opening of opportunities in formerly all-male institutions; growing assumptions of female acceptance and integration in the mainstream (formerly all-male, now coeducational) institutions; relative weakening of the appeal and vigor of the all-female institutions; and then, after superficial integration, backlash—through explicit barriers (e.g., quotas), segregation, and marginalizing of female influence, emphatic equation of professional prestige with male leadership and colleagueship—taking place when women's pioneering solidarity had weakened. In medicine, the downturn occurred before 1910; in academia, not until the late 1920s. In male-dominated professions in which women had made smaller inroads, such as law, the pattern of advance and retreat does not appear, although prejudice against women as worthy representatives of the profession was endemic.

The plateau and relative decline in women's numerical proportions in the male-dominated professions has been linked by some historians to the weakness of organized feminism in the 1920s, and yet under examination that link begs the underlying questions.[13] Several things throw doubt on the causal priority of feminist organization in explaining patterns of women's professional progress. First, women *were* highly organized in women's (although not declaredly feminist) voluntary associations all through the interwar years. Second, it was during the very peak of mass mobilization of women for suffrage and feminism that women's hold on the medical profession fell into decline. Third, the patterns of rise and decline in medicine and academia, although congruent, differed by two decades in timing; and no pattern of peak and decline (until the 1950s) appeared in women's proportion in the powerful male-dominated profession of law. It seems unlikely that the one explanation of weakness in organized feminism in the post-suffrage decade could explain these several different patterns.

Data from the Great Depression, on the other hand, show much more persuasive evidence of congruence *and* contemporaneity in deflation of women's professional employment of virtually all types, owing to the economic squeeze. The Depression years made clear that, once past initial entry, women's advance or retreat in professional attainment was closely linked to the economic worth of professional jobs in comparison to other employment. The Depression pushed women down in the labor force, not out of it. While the proportion of women at work increased, the proportion in professional pursuits declined, and for the first time in decades the proportion of employed women who were domestic servants increased. With the exception of medicine, where the previously declining proportion of women rose slightly, the 1930s much more consistently than the 1920s forced change in the same (downward) direction in women's proportional hold on professional employment, visible either in a slower rate of improved entry or in absolute decline. Although the proportion of lawyers who were women continued to rise, it was at a slower rate than in the 1920s or 1940s.

In even the feminized professions women lost ground. Employment reliant on public money, such as teaching and social work (to a greater extent than ever before, because of New Deal programs), appeared newly appealing in contrast to the insecurity of private enterprise. Men saw jobs in schoolteaching, social work, librarianship, and even in the almost entirely female field of nursing in a more favorable light, and employers took the opportunity to hire male applicants where possible. Male librarians had over 15 percent of the field at the end of the 1930s, as compared to under 9 percent ten years before; and men moved on from one-fifth of the social work field to one-third.[14] The striking pattern of women's slippage in professional fields in the 1930s underlines how far women worked under a systematic disadvantage in economic competition with men.

Together these sorts of evidence make the case that particular patterns of rise and fall in women's share of professional work relative to men's in the first half of the twentieth century can more reasonably be attributed to large-scale economic and labor market conditions and to factors within each profession (including prejudicial and structural barriers and fluctuations of economic advantage) than to the state of organized feminism. Still, the question of the feminist motivations or consciousness of women in the professions is at least as interesting—and is not the same—as the questions if or why proportions of women in the professions changed. Although entry to the professions was a goal shaped in the women's rights tradition, it is not unambiguously clear that the most favorable index for feminism in the early twentieth century would have been increasing proportions of women integrated among formerly all-male practitioners. That would presuppose women's smooth accommodation to the structure and ambience of existing professions. Perhaps evidence of women's solidarity, women's protests against sex discrimination, women's efforts to turn occupations more to suit their own needs and predilections—all contradicting the assumption of accommodation—would be as good or better indices. What were the motivations and attitudes of women in the professions? Were professional women's outlook and practice themselves perhaps forms of feminist organization?

The career woman in the 1920s was the exception rather than the rule, but only the woman in a very unusual field of work was actually a "first." Women maturing in the 1920s had been accustomed during their whole youthful lives to hearing news of women's advance in the labor force and in the public arena. The beneficiaries of substantial change in the structure and content of women's paid and unpaid occupations in the thirty preceding years, aspiring professional women in the 1920s might reasonably have agreed with Doris Fleischman (a pioneer, along with her husband Edward Bernays, in the public relations field), in her *Outline of Careers for Women*, that "it is not so long since the feminist movement broke down the barriers that kept women from occupational fields which men had regarded as exclusively their own. Today there are few pursuits which women do not follow with more or less success. The opportunities are almost unlimited." They might reasonably have assumed that men's remaining discriminatory attitudes would pass away rapidly as women proved their mettle, as did Judge Jean Hortense Norris, a New York City magistrate who had begun her career in private legal practice in the 1910s. Admitting that sex was still a handicap to women lawyers, Norris prophesied that in twenty-five years it would be unnecessary even to ask about sex prejudice: "the woman lawyer of 1950 will be regarded solely in her professional capacity." [15]

To accentuate the positive seemed the order of the day. Perhaps women in highly male-dominated professions where tiny but incremental advance was continuing, such as law, or women in newly invented fields where gender stereotypes of practitioners were not so embedded, such as public relations, were more optimistic than those experiencing a sense of enforced limitations. Of the women lawyers queried by the Bureau of Vocational Information in 1920, only half of 123 respondents conceded that men had the great advantage in the profession, and only 12 of those said there really was no comparison since men *had* the field. Of 79 answering a question about limitations or disadvantages in the work, less than a third mentioned the conservatism of the profession in its continuing prejudice against women. Newspaperwomen queried by the bureau during 1918 were even less willing to perceive or admit to sex discrimination. The more insistently the bureau's questionnaire thrust the issue of sex discrimination—especially impalpable sex discrimination—before the newspaperwomen's eyes, the more they shied away from answering the questions. Thus, of the 51 who returned questionnaires, 47 answered a question about their duties on the job, 36 replied as to the salary range; 27 responded to a question whether they experienced discrimination from male colleagues, but only 23 to the same question regarding their male superiors; and only 12 were willing to compare men's and women's chances to get "the big story." The responses that were given weighed toward the positive side. One editorial writer for the *Boston Record* replied to the question whether newspapermen discriminated against their female colleagues, "certainly not. Newspaper men are usually over the average of intelligence. Nowadays that sort of question is absurd." [16]

Some women were a lot more willing to complain, especially in academia, where sex discrimination was also better researched. The ladder ranking system made women's progress or lack of progress more immediately visible and quantifiable in college and university teaching than in some other professions. A study by the American Association of University Professors' Committee W in 1920 showed that only 4 percent of the full professorships in coeducational institutions were held by women, and, if the field of home economics were excluded, women held less than 3 percent. Ella Lonn, a historian at Goucher College, undertook a more refined study shortly after. She looked at seventy AAUP-approved universities—the research universities that were the vanguard of the academic profession in the 1920s—and within their faculties focused strictly on the "academic" lines, excluding home economics, physical education, performing arts, education, agriculture, and professional schools. She found that women comprised 9 percent of the academic faculty thus defined, and held only 1.3 percent of the full professorships (a proportion very like women's stake in the legal profession at the time). According to a study by the American Association of University Women of its members' occupational progress, the limited promotion and salary range available to women in college and university teaching did not justify obtaining the Ph.D. The maximum salary achieved by those thirty-two college teachers in the survey who had fifteen or more years of teaching experience and the B.A., was the same as the maximum achieved among the forty-five who had the same experience and the Ph.D. Women's academic salaries averaged lower than men's both because women were less likely to be promoted to higher ranks and because the principle of equal pay did not operate at any rank. The justification that men (and not women) had to support families was called into play regardless of its applicability to a particular situation and regardless of its irrelevance to standards for promotion and pay among men as a group.[17]

A survey undertaken by Barnard economist Emilie Hutchinson, of 1,025 women who had obtained Ph.D.s between 1877 and 1924, let loose a torrent of complaint about sex bias in appointments, fellowships, research assistantships, promotions, and pay in colleges and universities. One associate professor of English wrote, "When every agency in the country tells you that in English particularly, every president and head of department insists on having only men in higher positions, it seems to me idiotic to encourage young women to take the higher degrees with the thought of getting anything like a fair deal. I could write a volume on the effects of this situation on one's whole viewpoint." More than three-quarters of those surveyed were willing to encourage other women to gain the degree; those on teaching faculties were most solidly for it. The unemployed in the group (who comprised more than 15 percent) were understandably much less sanguine, half of them advising against young women's pursuing doctorates. Even the favorable testimony dwelled lukewarmly on the intrinsic gratification in intellectual challenge rather than the reward of promotion, renown, or salary. Many comments echoed a college professor of French who said, "unless a woman wants to meet with untold discouragement, I certainly would not advise her working for a Ph.D. She cannot hold a very good position in the teaching profession without one, but I feel that women as a whole are treated so unfairly, that I would advise a woman to seek another field of labor— unless she has family connections or influential friends who will see that she can get as good a position as a man with similar training." Marion Hawthorne reported similarly from her survey of 844 academics that only women "of exceptional ability" felt they were able to match the position of male colleagues, and that "the rank and file of the respondents seem to have developed a defensive attitude bordering on martyrdom, and complained, waxed bitter, and voiced resentment toward the conditions of which they were victims."[18]

Even those professional women who admitted or protested that sex discrimination was rife, however, tended to accept the burden of proof on themselves, maintaining that by redoubling their efforts, working hard, and downplaying rather than emphasizing the fact that they were female, their professional achievements might outshine their sex. Women had "to offer more than men in the same fields" to secure positions or opportunities, two university deans conceded to Emilie Hutchinson, and women did try to offer more. In a strategy of overqualification in preparation for academic employment, almost 72 percent of women scientists in 1921 obtained doctorates, as compared to 58 percent of the men. So did 83 percent of women scientists in 1938 as compared to 70 percent of the men. Deliberately stoic in the face of male scientists' hostility, these women accepted as inevitable the double standard that they had to outperform men in order to be credited at all. Any mistake by a woman confirmed female inferiority in male colleagues' eyes, but the logical converse did not hold: the outstanding woman scientist was viewed by men as an *exception* to her sex. Women in a variety of fields recognized this syndrome. Helen Hamilton Gardener, the first woman to serve on the U.S. Civil Service Commission (1920–25), commented with regard to women in government that "any woman's failure is held against all women, but a man's failure is his individual weakness." Therefore, "every time a woman fails it hurts not only herself but it hurts all) other women."[19]

Formulations such as Gardener's led women professionals to severe self-policing, through self-criticism and enforcement of standards of merit even more rigorous than the professional norm. Ella Lonn, for example, after surveying the professoriat and finding distressing evidence of male prejudice against women in university positions, made one of her major recommendations that women instructors encourage only exceptional female students to go on for the Ph.D. The Association to Aid Women in Science, a group formed among pioneer women scientists in 1898, provided a telling example of women's upholding standards of merit to their own self-blame. The group had established in 1901 a one-thousand-dollar prize for the best experimental work submitted by a woman, in order to encourage others to follow in their footsteps. A quarter-century later, assessing why it had seen fit to award the prize only six times in fourteen competitions (despite 184 applicants overall), the association took the occasion to condemn the applicant group for mediocre work, when it might as well have championed its own rigorous standards or raised the question of the hindrances to young women scientists' accomplishments.[20]

Women professionals blamed themselves in more than one way. When the Professional Pan-Hellenic Association, a group uniting professional "fraternities" formed by female college graduates, undertook a study of the problems of professional women in 1928, it revealed a common awareness that women had not achieved equality of opportunity, advancement, or pay. Many respondents noted a lack of self-confidence which prevented women professionals from performing up to their full capacities. The representative of the physical education "fraternity" attributed that handicap to the fact that women did not receive fair recognition for what they did and were surrounded by prejudice, which made them bitter and therefore less efficient. The law "fraternity's" judgment was harsher. "Women's chief problem is within themselves," their representative wrote:

They may possess the training and ability to make decisions in connection with their work, whether professional or business, and yet they will not, as a general rule, take the responsibility of making such decisions, and instead of acting on these questions or problems independently and receiving proper recognition, they take their suggestions to their superiors for approval. Women deliberately raise the question of prejudice, often unconsciously, it is true. If they will only ignore that prejudice, discuss their work and hopes of progress in it with their masculine associates on the assumption that no possible prejudice exists in their particular line of work, they frequently will discover that their masculine associates forget it, too. Women are too prone to blame all failures on their part to the sex prejudice whereas it is probably responsible for only a small part.[21]

Even recognizing the inequalities of opportunity they faced, women in professions saw "development of a more professional attitude among women"—in the words of the Research Committee of the Professional Pan-Hellenic Association—as the number one method to resolve their problems. Elizabeth Kemper Adams set a tone for the decade in her 1921 study, *Women Professional Workers*, which maintained that women would disprove reductive generalizations about themselves "by displaying professional competence and tenacity of a high order and by refusing to accept either privileges or disabilities on the ground of sex. . . . In the long run, they will succeed in proportion to the extent to which they meet professional standards as workers and citizens and not as women." In corollary, Adams thought that separate organizations for women professionals might be valuable to help them gain confidence and experience, but she saw such organizations as representing "merely a stage in the professional evolution of women," valuable as "a means of education in managing affairs" and not as "manifestations of a separatist and feminist spirit." Although she recognized that women in current male-dominated professional societies were members only on paper, usually voiceless, she imagined organizations in which women and men would share responsibility.[22]

The numbers of women's professional organizations that were founded between 1910 and 1930, in lines of work from architecture to x-ray, in fact provided their members with the companionship of their peers, recreation, and moral support; many encouraged present or future women colleagues by offering fellowships or prizes. Some announced policy stands on relevant political questions such as the equal rights amendment. But the organizations, which had to speak uniquely for women in order to attract members and yet were created to uphold the professional ethos, which discouraged women from any sex-based loyalty, had a problematic identity and an ambiguous mandate. Encouraging professionalism among women was their purpose; yet how could they act collectively for women while sustaining the standard "neuter" definition of professional? Collective activity by women, for women, appeared to gainsay that definition. Women professionals may have shunned joining such organizations on the same grounds of neutral professionalism for which those organizations presumably stood. The membership of the American Medical Women's Association, for example, never exceeded one-third of the women physicians in the country. (It was founded, ironically, in 1915, the same year that the American Medical Association first admitted female members.) It became an accomplished lobbying group, but women physicians did not flock to it and some even condemned it as counterproductive to women's advancement in the medical mainstream.[23]

There were, by the latter 1920s, a few voices calling for concerted solidarity by professional women on their common ground as women. Ruby Black, a journalist and member of the National Woman's Party, was one; after chairing the Professional Pan-Hellenic Association's Research Committee she concluded that cooperation and solidarity were crucial. Another was Lena Madesin Phillips (leader in the National Federation of Business and Professional Women's Clubs), who advocated "patronage of women by women" and "promotion of women by women" in recognition of the fact that discrimination against women existed and had to be countered. These voices were few and far between, however, in contrast to the general view that the individualist meritocratic principles of the professions were to be believed in and doubly adhered to.[24]

Professional women on the whole seemed to assume that any connection with feminism would prove detrimental to their professional progress. Although rejecting some male respondents' judgments after her survey of universities, Ella Lonn took to heart male professors' objections that female colleagues were "almost sure to develop grievances and to air them constantly"; the men remarked that women were "too inclined to look at things from a controversial feminist point of view" and complained, "instead of becoming an integral part of the university, they show a tendency to become a foreign, irritating body within the university." Lonn inclined to accept blame on these points. As a result of her findings she recommended that the AAUW establish a standing committee "not to conduct an active campaign for the advancement of women in university positions—I trust we would not be so guilty of such folly— but to watch the situation closely, to save us from the indiscretions of the impatient, and to offer suggestions."[25]

Women aspiring to the upper reaches of professions and the business world (where "professional" procedure was becoming a desideratum) took a similar lesson from the bias they felt. In public relations, Doris

Fleischman reasoned that the "definite amount of prejudice that remains in many men's minds against the effectiveness of women" was "purely psychological" and therefore best handled "by convincing men through intelligent handling of problems, and not by slaying the dragon of anti-feminism." Ruth Hahn, an executive, advised, "I am not pleading for any such naive and futile cause as 'We women must hang together.' Not for a moment. That would be foolish and absurd, as though men and women had pitched two opposing camps and were out for battle." Instead, she recommended, "it is up to us not only to meet men on their ground but to exercise the kind of initiative which will go them one better." Elizabeth Kemper Adams admonished professional women to avoid "any spirit of jealousy or antagonism towards professional men," assuming that "the rabid feminist or anti-feminist, whether man or woman, will not be a useful member of a professional group, and will come to seem more than a little archaic."[26]

The tension between feminism and professional identity was not new in the 1920s. Although the first women to enter male professions saw their attempts as part of "the cause of woman," by the latter part of the nineteenth century professional ideology itself was increasingly magnetic. There was lively debate among the few women lawyers in the 1880s whether a woman should pursue her profession *because* of her sex (to vindicate woman's capacities or to help her sisters) or must *forget* her sex in order to pursue her profession. For one lawyer of the 1880s who assumed that "every woman in the Legal profession must . . . long for . . . assurances of that close empathy born of mutuality of interests, which women alone can extend to a woman," and argued for the particular service of "Lady lawyers" since the "Laws are in many instances inimical to the well being and interests of women," another stressed, "*do not take sex* into the practice. . . . Don't be 'lady lawyers.' Simply be lawyers, and recognize no distinction—no existence of any distinction between yourselves and the other members of the bar. This will be your surest way to that forgetfulness of self which will give your mind freedom to achieve success." A third urged women lawyers to offer each other moral support so as to "reach a plane where we will be as calmly confident of the propriety of following the bent of our own natures as any man is." "The time will come," she predicted, "when no 'double consciousness' will disturb a *woman* who wishes to be a *lawyer.*" Young women doctors, too, by the 1890s were eager to define their objectives according to the rationalist, empiricist canons of the new medical science and to integrate themselves into the community of male physicians; they were inclined to distance themselves from the more moralistic, wholistic, empathic approach of the first generation of women doctors, which meant leaving behind institutions for women only.[27]

The double consciousness of oneself as a woman and a professional was the legacy of nineteenth-century presuppositions about the different temperaments and social roles of men and women. Operating from a firm—sometimes oppressively firm—set of assumptions about the domestic socialization that white middle-class women shared, female aspirants to male-controlled professional arenas around the turn of the century often sought to legitimize their pursuits by emphasizing their identification as rational and neutral professionals. The tension between the two poles of identification was stressful, but generally productive, especially in the culminating dozen or so years of the suffrage campaign.[28] At that time, the efforts of some women to gain professional training, competence, and rewards were contemporaneous with the larger suffrage movement's attempt to assert women's full citizenship. As diverse as the suffrage movement was, and as various the arguments used in it, it had the overarching theme that women were united in social definition by their common disfranchisement. Whatever professional women envisioned for themselves, disfranchisement necessarily classed them, in civic and public life, with all other women. As much as women entering professional careers at that time may have wished for "forgetfulness of self," they were forced both by disfranchisement and by the spirited, multifaceted movement of women to gain the vote to think of themselves as women and to see their own professional struggles as akin to the struggles of women as a group for just recognition and opportunities.

The height of the suffrage movement diverted or temporarily masked the ongoing trend for women in professions to dissociate their vocational aims from aims of women as a group. The gain of woman suffrage therefore marked a turning point in women professionals' conceptions of themselves. No major formal barrier to women's professional accomplishments now remained, and no palpable form of social or civic identification classed all women together. A woman lawyer queried by the BVI about the impact of woman suffrage on women's careers in law pronounced, "she has the attention of the court as a voter—she has gained in self-respect herself and the change in herself reflects the respect of others. She feels she has a right to be a lawyer."[29] The professional ethos, with its own promise of freedom from sex-defined constraints, was released to flourish in aspiring women's minds. Women professionals in the

1920s did not deny the instrumentality of feminism in breaking down barriers to women's first entry to the professions, but they assumed that since women had been admitted to professional ground and no formal bar remained, the professions' supposedly neutral and meritocratic ideology was not only their best armor but their only hope. As the scientific areas (and all areas increasingly wanted to call themselves scientific) led the way, emphasizing that the professions' hallmarks were objectivity, empiricism, rationality, impersonality, and collegially determined standards, feminism seemed more openly to conflict with those hallmarks. The intensification of the perceived conflict between feminism and professionalism was part and parcel of a larger process of purging politics, advocacy, or reform from within professional definition.[30]

In theory, of course, the setting of empirical, rational, and objective standards for access to and advancement within the professions (or any employment) was of great benefit to women, whose exclusion from lucrative and influential positions resulted from customary, nonrational, and subjective limitations. If there were ascertainable standards rather than subjective criteria for training, achievement, and so on, then women could strive to meet those standards and proceed as if they were to be judged as individuals, rather than being judged a priori inferior on account of sex. In the nineteenth century, before "credentialing" of professions was fully systematized, the great bulk of women had no professional job access at all, while a few benefited from nonrational criteria (mainly family advantages). Women who entered the legal profession by apprenticing themselves to fathers, brothers, or husbands provided the foremost examples. A formal, objective credentialing system was the only hope for access for a wide spectrum of women—provided that arbitrary discrimination against women was not a premise of the whole system.[31]

The professional credo, that individual merit would be judged according to objective and verifiable standards, made a promise so potent to women professionals that they upheld the ideal even when they saw it travestied in practice. The report of a committee set up by the AAUW in 1925 to look into universities' standards for promotion and tenure reasoned especially lucidly about the value of objective professional standards.[32] "The way to avoid any danger of prejudice in the appointments and promotion of women was to formulate objectively and definitely the standards for promotion and to establish the procedure most likely to result in the objective application of those standards in decisions regarding individuals," the committee concluded. "If this objectivity in appointments and promotions were established in colleges and universities it would go a long way toward abolishing any conscious or unconscious prejudices against the promotion of women." The committee also pointed out that such objective formulation was a way to assure academic freedom, protecting the person with unpopular ideas from being judged on that ground. Just as the resort to objective standards was seen by the politically heterodox as a way to safeguard their opportunities—by separating politics from professional competence and expecting to be judged on the latter alone—so was it seen by women.[33]

In deceptively bland language, the AAUW committee went almost so far as to say that the academic profession was not professional because it was not objective—but it stopped short. Proposing questions to be pursued by the American Council on Education and by colleges on a "self-study" basis—such questions as "how is teaching ability objectively tested?" and "what are the best evidences of productive scholarship?"—the committee did not concede that the sex prejudice and discrimination they wished to fight might shape colleges' answers to such questions or affect the application and enforcement of objective standards. For them, adherence to the professional ethos was not only ideologically appealing but strategically necessary because of the marginal position women professionals held. Without the meritocratic pretensions of the professions women had no warrant for advancement or power within them at all. There was no authority outside the professional apparatus to which they could resort to enforce fairness within, except possibly public opinion—the clientele. (But women professionals did not find other women a ready constituency to enforce their claim on professional service; they complained that women were even less likely than men to seek or trust their services.) Women's lack of power and leverage in the male-dominated professions meant that, had they criticized the application of "objectivity" as male practice, they could easily have been dismissed entirely. An essential component of professional definition was the claim to self-regulation, an essential practice was the closing of ranks against outsiders, and had women poised their strategy against rather than with the professions' objectivity they would have marked themselves as outsiders.[34]

In many respects the difficulties of women professionals in combining feminism with professionalism were the same as those of women in other male-dominated arenas, such as electoral politics and trade unions, where they also had to struggle to be accepted as insiders. As in the professions, loyalty to the predominant ethos—to male partisan priorities in the case of politics—was a necessary although not a sufficient requisite for women's acceptability. In politics, to show loyalty to partisan priorities meant, for the most part, abandoning feminist rhetoric and giving up any visibly independent stance on behalf of women.[35] In trade union practice, too, the very possibility of leadership on the part of women required compromises with traditions and preferences already established by men, which (needless to say) did not encompass self-assertion by women on behalf of women.

The trade union career of Dorothy Jacobs Bellanca in the 1920s provides a poignant and instructive example. An insurgent from the age of fifteen, when she organized Baltimore women buttonhole sewers into a local of the United Garment Workers and led in their strike of 1909, she was one of a handful of women delegates at the founding convention of the Amalgamated Clothing Workers of America in 1914 and subsequently a lifelong organizer and educational worker for that union. Bellanca's acute sensitivity to sex discrimination throughout her career, and her commitment to articulating the interests of women workers, warred with her conviction that the union was the best vehicle for achieving justice and power for working-class women and men. Well aware that sex discrimination characterized the union as well as the employer, she advocated that women clothing workers develop strong locals, become committed trade unionists, and thus gain the respect of male unionists. Owing in large part to her efforts, the ACW's membership in the 1920s was half women, and so were a quarter of the organizers hired during the decade—a much larger proportion than in other unions (although still not parallel to women's numbers in the clothing industry). Bellanca had long had it in mind to set up a Women's Department in the union to attract more women workers and to encourage their participation. When the department was established in 1924 with her at its head, she stressed that it not only served women's interests but also benefited the entire trade union movement by recruiting more women members. Some of the men in the ACW nonetheless objected to the department's exclusive meetings, entertainments, and procedures for women trade unionists, contending that these divided the working class. Under such pressure, Bellanca gave it up the next year despite its being her pet project. "Very often one has to do things against one's self for the benefit of the organization," she conceded, not sacrificing her interest in organizing women but not wishing to be considered an irritant to her male colleagues or an outsider to their aims.[36]

Women who would be leaders in trade unions (as in politics) found that compromises with—or even echoes of—the male-established structure were prime requisites for continuing. Ann Washington Craton, after leaving her position as an organizer for the ACW, wrote in the *Nation* in 1927 that women participants in the trade union movement had, in order to keep even minor leadership positions, "discreetly learned to play the union game as men play it. . . . On the theory than a poor union is better than no union, they steadily refused to embarrass labor officials by a vigorous protest at the discriminations and inequalities to which women have been subjected in the unions." That meant that "they have been unable to achieve any outstanding leadership among the rank and file of trade-union women." As in politics, if it was men's priorities that ruled anyway, there was little inducement for women to want women leaders: a male representative would likely carry more weight. If dissident women leaders and their potential followers made a special case for women, on the other hand, they faced the likelihood of men's accusations of disloyalty, in unions as in politics and in the professions.[37]

These were some significant parallels between the situation of women professionals and that of women attempting to gain footing in other male-dominated structures. In all, women followed a necessary strategy of proving loyalty and shoring up the guild in order to shore up their own positions as participants. But only the professions made intrinsic to their ideology the tenet of sex neutrality. The claim to judge practitioners on individual merit as persons (not as men or women) in the dispassionate search for truth and usefulness was essential to the professions' self-definition; that claim made the question of the relative power of male and female practitioners unspeakable. In bald contrast, the editor of the *Advance*, the journal of the ACW, admitted during the controversy over the Women's Department that "leaders of unions are not likely to leave their positions of vantage in favor of women, any more than women would in favor of men. The battle for mastery is a human trait, a very human trait too."[38]

Professional ideology also encouraged professional women to see a community of interest between themselves and professional men and a gulf between themselves and nonprofessional women. That angle of vision was counterproductive to feminist practice, perhaps most noticeably in the professions which women dominated numerically, such as social work or education. In initiative, education, and drive, members of the feminized professions were potential leaders among women, but the professional ethos encouraged them to see other women as clients or amateurs rather than colleagues in common cause. It encouraged them to see a different scope and destiny for themselves than for women in general. This distinction of the elite from the mass was apparent if not acknowledged in the work of female government appointees (in the Women's Bureau and Children's Bureau, for instance) who dealt with the problems of women and children. With respect to the professional community as a whole, leaders of the woman-dominated professions were in much the same position as female aspirants within each male-dominated profession: struggling for professional credibility and having to outperform men in their rigor and standards.[39]

Chase Going Woodhouse, whose work in women's career development traveled much beyond home economics—she headed the clearinghouse Institute of Women's Professional Relations by the end of the 1920s— used to amuse audiences by saying she wished to have engraved on her headstone: "Born a woman. Died a person."[40] Woodhouse's anecdote encapsulated the ambiguous promise of professional identity, and indeed of all women's struggles to gain place in male-dominated fields. To "break into the human race" as professionals (in the words 1910s Feminists had used) meant to leave behind the sex loyalty that was a prerequisite for feminism. Very few women with professional ambitions in the 1920s and 1930s were able to distance themselves sufficiently from the culture of professionalism to see the element of self-diminution and denigration of women in Woodhouse's throwaway line. What women professionals intended was to amplify the woman into the person, to leave behind only the ascription of inferiority or frivolousness associated with their sex. They were not able to acknowledge that the male-informed professional ethos had enforced their sense of that inferiority.

Although declared feminists often were women pursuing professions (as, for instance, many NWP members were), that did not mean that professional women generally were feminists. The time demands of professional life coincided with its ideology more often than not to remove professional women from feminist political activity. Dr. Caroline Spencer complained that she could not find younger women in Denver, Colorado, to take up NWP work in the mid-1920s because "they are all so immersed in business or some other pursuit that they cannot give the time or the thought necessary." Mary Gertrude Fendall wrote in pique along the same lines to Jane Norman Smith when the latter was national chairman of the NWP, "why do women think they should give up every interest in the world when they start out with a business or profession? They are just the sort who should serve on boards, etc., like men do."[41]

Professionalism and feminism might stem from the same motivation: the motivation 1910s spokeswomen had eloquently expressed not to be limited a priori by womanhood. As the number of career women increased, however, so did the likelihood that they could not be identified as feminists in any other respect than that they pursued professional careers. The sketches of women prominent from the latter nineteenth through the mid-twentieth century in the biographical dictionary *Notable American Women: The Modern Period* collectively make that point. When the biographical subjects are grouped by their decades of birth, it becomes clear that women born in the 1860s and maturing in the 1880s included the highest proportion involved in woman's rights or feminist activity (34 percent). Each subsequent decade's group showed a smaller proportion of women thus involved, down to 15 percent for women born in the 1910s. Others in addition became notable for service, enterprise, or other activities organized with or for women although not clearly woman's rights endeavors, and that proportion too peaked early, among women born in the 1870s (at 39 percent), and then persistently fell, to 10 percent for women born in the 1910s. Three-quarters of the women born in the 1900s and 1910s, who came of age in the 1920s and 1930s, became notable for some reason *other* than woman's rights or woman-oriented pursuits.[42]

In contrast to nineteenth-century women's small likelihood of distinction except in woman's rights or woman-oriented activities, twentieth-century women stood out as individuals, for pursuits not obviously determined by sex nor undertaken for the advancement of their sex. The trend toward individual accomplishments unrelated to womanhood as such or to gender identity might be read to measure the success of feminism's aims—or the exhaustion of its spirit. Each reading has its truth. That was a dilemma of twentieth-century feminism, to require gender consciousness for its basis while intending to explode gender prescriptions.

8

IN VOLUNTARY CONFLICT

The Socialist-Pacifist Movement in America Is an Absolutely Fundamental and Integral Part of International Socialism (Lusk Report Page 11.)

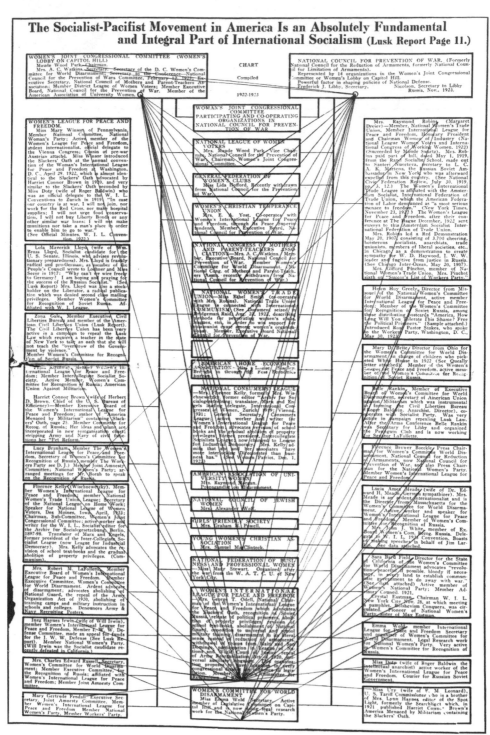

The Spider-Web Chart, 1924.

"The time will come when the human race will become so human that we shall not need separate women's organizations," aging California feminist and pacifist Alice Park hoped in the mid-1920s. Still at present, she observed, "women are lost in a man's organization. . . . They do not yet dare to take an equal part. And until the time comes when they can and will, I feel that they get more benefit out of an organization that is entirely their own." A multiform activist—pacifist, advocate of simplified spelling, vegetarian, loyal National Woman's Party organizer in Palo Alto, and founder of a small Housewives Union there—Park made these statements with reference to the Women's International League for Peace and Freedom. "My first object is always feminism," Park usually mentioned in her speeches for the WILPF. She thought it incumbent upon feminists to work for peace because "war hurts women"; but she also devoted herself to WILPF in the belief that as a women's organization it "will be able to do things to forward world peace that perhaps could not be done in any other way."[1]

Of the women in organizations of probably greater number and kind in the 1920s than ever before, few were as clear as Park in articulating feminism as their motivation. On the whole, women's organizations finessed the question of what it meant to speak politically for women. They laid claim to the form of separate women's organizations more surely than they justified the content; for the feminism of the NWP was anathema to most, while the ongoing tendency to see women as mothers threatened to hobble the impact such organizations might have on public policy. Just as Alice Park easily linked her pacifism with her feminism, however (as though there were little need to explain the connection), on the whole women's organizations took up international peace as an area especially needing and suiting the political influence of enfranchised women. Park was not untypical, in the wake of world war, in merging her political concerns for the freedom of women and the protection of peace. The movement for disarmament was a place where the Feminist legacy of the 1910s sought to express itself. In a more generalized way, the peace departments in large-scale women's organizations accepted an undergirding assumption of the liberal peace movement, that vital domestic policies—or, in their version, expectations for women's advancement and security—could not be accomplished under the threat of modern, total war.

In the 1920s, women's claim for a peacemaking role focused less on celebration of maternity and nurturance than on the belief that exclusion so far from nation-states' warmaking councils gave women a head start and a clearer and more objective view toward devising methods for maintaining peace. If men had, through history, resorted to war and vengeance, women might bring into international affairs an alternative unstained tradition of temperate behavior. That analysis led women to demand not only mechanisms to preserve peace but also female representation in national and international decision-making bodies.[2] An arena of mass voluntary participation, and one in which continuity with Feminist efforts of the 1910s and justification for women's participation were more explicit than in many others, the peace movement opens a window for observation of voluntarist politics in the 1920s. Its problems were those more generally found in defining the collective interests of women as a political group, its triumphs and founderings generally instructive of the milieu in which contests for women's political force were waged.

The tumult over the disarmament resolution at the NWP convention in February of 1921 was one indication of the crossover between women's declared interests and pacifism. Another was Carrie Chapman Catt's throwing away her prepared speech on "Psychologies of Political Progress" at the League of Women Voters convention shortly afterward, and instead delivering a crackling impromptu appeal to "compel action in Washington" on disarmament. In the winter of 1920–21 there was already considerable public aggrievement at postwar increases in the U.S. military budget. Senator William Borah of Idaho, an "irreconcilable" opponent of American entry into the League of Nations, built on that sentiment in proposing, late in 1920, that a "naval holiday" be undertaken by the United States, England, and Japan. Borah's resolution for limitation of naval construction crystallized a popular demand for limitation of armaments that had been heard from many sectors of public opinion. Incoming President Harding, however, was known as a "big-navy" enthusiast, and his preference for preparedness over disarmament was supported by the Navy Department. The outlook for realizing Borah's proposal or anything like it seemed dim.

Shortly after the NWP convention, some of its participants took the lead in founding a Women's Committee for World Disarmament, which proved to be the match that ignited public sentiment to shift the Harding administration's stance. Its work mobilized other existing groups. The committee was small, very zealous, and organized in a fashion familiar to the NWP, with a small group of officers, an executive committee, and state chairmen. Four of the six officers—Emma Wold, Sue S. White, Julia Emory, and Florence Brewer Boeckel—were NWP notables. The executive committee and state chairmen included both NWP suffragists who were sticking with the reorganized party like stalwart Florence Bayard Hilles, and women who were on their way out like radical Mary Gertrude Fendall, as well as women who linked the group to other peace and women's organizations, like Belle LaFollette and Lucia Ames Mead of the WILPF. The WCWD aimed both to prevail on the president to call an international conference on world disarmament and to demand of Congress a reduction in arms expenditures.

Its first splash was to make March 27, Easter Sunday—only two weeks after its formation—Disarmament Day. Using women's organizational networks, the group succeeded in instigating mass meetings in sixteen states. The biggest was in Washington, D.C., where Borah addressed the crowd. Within short order the WCWD sent a large delegation of women to speak to Harding, expanded its operations to thirty-two states, and began planning a Disarmament Week for the latter part of May, working through the Women's Christian Temperence Union, the National Federation of Business and Professional Women's Clubs, and church and college groups. Thus began the momentum of publicity and educational campaigns that resulted in waves of speeches and meetings of various voluntary groups and a flood of petitions, telegrams, and resolutions to the president and Congress. Although the fact that Great Britain was interested in a multilateral conference on sea power was certainly significant, without the arousal of public opinion in the United States it is unlikely that the Harding administration would have taken the step, as it did in midsummer, to call the Washington Disarmament Conference. The newspapers of that year reflected how far organized female opinion was understood as the impetus. As peace workers raised hopes for actual disarmament in the months preceding the conference, President Harding attempted to quell rising expectations. In a letter to Ella Fried of the Brooklyn Citizen's Committee for Universal Disarmament, reprinted in papers all over the nation, Harding emphasized that no universal disarmament was contemplated, only a "reasonable limitation," only "something practicable." Mrs. Fried, not satisfied, rejoined by urging the president to propose a reduction by *half* of all nations' armaments. "When that has been done," she added, "the women of the world will furnish you further suggestions as to what is reasonable and practicable." (Harding did not respond.)[3]

Although the demands of WCWD and LWV leaders that women be selected as delegates to the conference were not met, four women were appointed to the Advisory Committee to the United States delegation—none of them the hotheads of the WCWD, but prominent club women.[4] The Washington Conference created a 5–5–3 ratio of ships between the United States, Great Britain, and Japan, a significant limitation of warmaking power. After the conference, the WCWD considered its work done and disbanded, but women pushed forward under other aegises. One was the National Council on Limitation of Armaments, formed in 1921 as a result of the WCWD's momentum, an umbrella group covering more than two dozen women's, church, labor, and farm organizations. Many of the prime movers in the WCWD continued on with the National Council on Limitations of Armaments (by 1922 called the National Council for Prevention of War). Florence Brewer Boeckel, for instance, remained its educational director all through the decade. The most important women's peace organization, however, was the Women's International League for Peace and Freedom. An international organization formed in an era of nationalist revolutions, WILPF did not commit itself to pacifism—that is, to the principle of nonresistance—although a plurality of the delegates attending its Third Congress in Vienna in 1921 were inclined that way. The United States section of WILPF opposed the covenant of the League of Nations because of its defense provisions, advocated U.S. recognition of Russia, worked for noncoercive international agreements, and led in the effort to reduce military expenditures (which was a central campaign of the National Council for Prevention of War coalition as well). Members of WILPF considered the Washington Disarmament Conference only a start, since "the only effective disarmament was total and universal."

Both the National Council for Prevention of War and WILPF principally used publicity, education, and lobbying, but at least one WILPF activist, Harriet Connor Brown, advocated that women organize nonpartisan groups of voting women pledged to elect to Congress candidates who would halt military expenditures. Women controlled the "balance of power" to decide elections "by holding ourselves a mobile mass . . . outside of political parties," she argued.[5] Even before the Washington Conference, WILPF advocates had begun to testify for reduction of military appropriations at hearings of the House Military Affairs Committee. Harriet Connor Brown became an expert on the military proportions of the national budget. Testimony such as hers reinforced congressional reluctance to expand military appropriations in an era of postwar exhaustion and drive for federal economy. An attempt by the U.S. Department of the Army to gain momentum for peacetime military conscription was quashed in 1920, and congress cut appropriations for army personnel in both 1920 and 1922.

After the Washington Conference, the House Naval Affairs Committee attempted to cut the personnel recommended by the navy from 120,000 to 67,000 men, stirring a debate in Congress and in the nation on the meaning of the new naval treaty. Should the United States build a naval force up to the maximum allowed, and what number of personnel (not regulated by the agreement) should be provided to equip it? With women's groups around the country passing resolutions on reduction of armaments, and WILPF testifying before the Senate Appropriations Committee (and talking about election strategies for November 1922), big-navy advocates fought back. They instigated a propaganda campaign counter to the anti-militarists, involving not only navy men themselves but also chambers of commerce, American Legions, and the International Association of Machinists (whose shipworkers feared for their jobs). Now warning of "perilous" measures of economy and pointing the finger at pacifists for "scuttling the fleet," that campaign culminated in the creation of Navy Day, a celebratory burst of national patriotism in late October 1922 advertised on radio and newsreels as well as in speech and print.[6]

The women's campaign for peace had quickly aroused some formidable opponents. At that very time Harding's secretary of war, John D. Weeks, undertook to boost the public image of the army. A former senator from Massachusetts and a conservative anti-suffragist, Weeks had been defeated in his bid for reelection in 1918 by a vigorous campaign led by the Massachusetts Woman Suffrage Association. Lucia Ames Mead, who had presided over the Massachusetts suffragists, was in 1922 the head of WILPF-U.S. Weeks's War Department began sponsoring army officers on speaking tours to patriotic organizations, espousing preparedness, and lambasting the disarmament talk of "silly pacifists"—especially those caught up "in the enthusiasm of newly conferred suffrage." Friction between the army and women's peace organizations generated heat by the end of the year, after Mead released to the press a letter from Weeks in which he insisted on the army's potential role in quelling domestic threats to social order, including strikes.[7]

Army officers began denouncing WILPF by name. Brigadier-General Amos A. Fries of the Chemical Warfare Service, who was by political predilection closely tied to the division of military intelligence that kept

watch for domestic subversion, accused the WILPF of circulating among
its members an oath of wartime noncooperation "nothing short of trea-
son." Fries, whose area had consistently been under attack by women
pacifists lobbying against chemical war, may have been confusing WILPF
with the much smaller, radically and uncompromisingly pacifist Women's
Peace Union of the Western Hemisphere. The WPU stood for nonresistance, was affiliated with the War Resisters' International, and *did* require
of its members the affirmation "that it is my intention never to aid in or
sanction war, offensive or defensive, international or civil, in any way,
whether by making or handling munitions, subscribing to war loans,
using my labor for the purpose of setting others free for war service,
helping by money or work any relief organization which supports or con-
dones war." Its prime movers were NWP-affiliated feminists Caroline
Lexow Babcock, Elinor Byrns, Alice Beal Parsons, Mary Gertrude Fendall, and Mary Winsor. In the WILPF there were members who sympathized with such an oath, but there was no consensus within the United
States section to adopt one. Officers of the WILPF-U.S. called for correc-
tion of Fries's accusation while continuing to issue press releases criticizing the War Department.[8]

Fries also attacked the coalition National Council for Prevention of
War. He found support from civilians such as Frederick Wile, a Philadelphia journalist, who deplored the "systematic, sinister and sleepless pacifist bloc," noticed darkly its 1922 political campaign efforts, and forewarned—with clear reference to upset gender roles—that "Uncle Sam
will wake up one morning to discover that long-haired men and short-
haired women have enthroned themselves in the place where patriotic
intelligence once prevailed." In December 1922 Fries announced that
the purpose of the NCPW was "to establish communism in America." He
chose as a particular target Florence Watkins, executive secretary of the
National Congress of Parents and Teachers and a member of the executive board of the NCPW. Why the peace agenda of a seemingly benign
organization that dealt with children's education would have so alarmed
the military was implied in an intelligence officer's private comment, "all
the work of industrial and physical preparation for defense will have
been wasted if the younger generation are going to turn out to be pacifists and internationalists." Feeling the heat of slanders on the NCPW for
its treasonous intents, the General Federation of Women's Clubs and the
PTA (the two largest women's organizations in the coalition) took the cautious road and withdrew their affiliations in December 1922.[9]

Florence Watkins did not abandon either of her positions, however, and the manipulation taking place deceived neither her nor Elizabeth Tilton (legislative secretary of the PTA). Tilton, an ardent advocate of peace and Prohibition, dismissed the "Communist" accusations as nonsense, judging "that a group of ambitious men are trying to railroad the Peace Movement out of the way." She perceived a divide and conquer technique: "They are trying to capture certain sentimental groups of women who are flattered by their approach and get them to open up the women's organizations for use." The PTA continued its emphasis on peace, but Tilton was suspicious of the military's inroads in the GFWC. "I think there is a real drive to throw out from the women's organizations women who are liberal," she wrote to Watkins. "I note how Mrs. George Minot Baker, who has always worked with the reactionary party here in Massachusetts, was made Chairman of the Programme Committee of the General Federation, and now the General Federation announces that its Convention will be devoted purely to the spiritual values of women. I fear that it has been captured by military groups who do not want the women to be active in the coming political campaign."[10]

From Fries' Chemical Warfare Department came the infamous Spider-Web Chart. Allegedly compiled not by Fries but by the librarian in the department, Lucia Maxwell, the chart described twenty-nine women leaders and fifteen women's organizations and showed graphically how they interlinked through the NCPW and the Women's Joint Congressional Committee. It announced at the top "the Socialist-Pacifist movement in America is an Absolutely Fundamental and Integral Part of International Socialism," in a quotation from the Lusk report (an earlier alarmist investigation of domestic "subversion" in New York state). The chart named the Women's Committee for World Disarmament, and the WILPF and all the major and less than major women's organizations with components designated for international peace efforts, even including the Girls' Friendly Society and the American Home Economics Association. Of the twenty-nine individuals named, eleven were NWP feminists. The Spider-Web Chart seems to have been framed principally to defame pacifists, but the links drawn to the WJCC also tied the lobby for social and welfare legislation (such as the Sheppard-Towner Act, sex-based protective labor laws, and the proposed constitutional amendment to prohibit child labor) to "international Communism." As long-time activist Anna Garlin Spencer wrote to WILPF leader Emily Greene Balch, "*all* women's organizations have been slandered."

Between mid-1923 and mid-1924 the chart began to circulate among such interested parties as the American Defense Society and J. Edgar

Hoover of the FBI. Henry Ford gave it a boost in March 1924 by publication in his reactionary newspaper, the *Dearborn Independent,* which (at five cents a copy) commanded a large audience nationwide. Leaders of the WJCC, discovering the source of the chart, angrily descended on Secretary Weeks. Charging the Chemical Warfare Service with a "contemptible attack on the women's organizations of the country," and brandishing before him the voting power of the WJCC's membership, they demanded that he get rid of the document. Weeks tried to exculpate the War Department (by blaming Maxwell in her capacity as chair of the Patriotic Committee of the League of American Penwomen) and ordered the chart destroyed and removed from circulation. But the damage was already done. One Spider-Web spawned another (perhaps many others). A later version circulated by a retired Cambridge businessman included three times as many men's names as women's (all but two of which differed from those on the first chart) and color-coded the incriminated organizations: red—radical; pink—progressive; yellow—pacifist.[11]

The hyperpatriotic groups keeping the chart in circulation were products of World War I which had spurted into anti-radical activity in 1919 and which now took the offensive again to repair the anti-militarism of 1921. Critic Norman Hapgood labeled these groups "professional patriots," willing to ride roughshod over all civil liberties but their own. At least twenty-five and perhaps as many as twice that number of ultrapatriotic societies operated in the 1920s, acting as a vanguard of reaction, making stand-pattism look liberal, often catering to the basest aspects of American chauvinism and isolationism. Their presence tended both to polarize political opinion and to shift the whole spectrum to the right. Formerly anti-suffrage groups among them, hanging on to battle the paired evils (as they saw them) of feminism and socialism, kept attention focused on women's politics. The right-wing groups had a higher estimation of the coherence and power of the woman bloc than anyone else. ("I think nobody in the world seems to appreciate our talents so much as the antisuffragists," Dora Lewis sarcastically commented on the report of the 1921 NWP Convention published in the *Woman Patriot.*) Mary Kilbreth, former president of the National Association Opposed to Woman Suffrage, wrote personally to Harding to oppose the Sheppard-Towner bill as an evil product of the feminist bloc. The *Woman Patriot* accused women's organizations of "organizing women for class and sex war."

Right-wing pressure groups had stepped up their scrutiny of women's peace organizations in 1923, spurred by a crudely sensationalized pamphlet by one R. M. Whitney, "Peace at Any Old Price," which claimed that the WILPF was under the control of the Soviet government. The military slander of liberal women's organizations in 1923–24 may have stemmed from perception of spreading support for pacifism among church and student groups that winter. It may also have been timed, as Elizabeth Tilton suspected, to reduce women's impact on the 1924 elections, to divide women's ranks, and especially to prevent women from mobilizing in support of Independents and progressive Republicans. ("This word Communism frightens the women," Tilton observed in a confidential memo to Watkins.) At the same time, magazines were bleating about the "failure" and "ineffectiveness" of women's votes.[12]

Not to be daunted, that spring, some active anti-militarists and other women who had been involved in progressive politics since the Committee of 48 in 1919 formed a Woman's Committee for Political Action in Washington and called a conference "to rally to progressive standards all women who put principles before parties or candidates." Present and former NWP members (Anne Martin, Harriot Stanton Blatch, Isabelle Kendig), associates of the Committee of 48 (Ruth Pickering, Eleanor Taylor Marsh), and left-liberal journalists (Freda Kirchwey, Ruth Hale) stood out in the initial grouping. The committee's first letterhead placed Carrie Chapman Catt at the top of the advisory group—along with Charlotte Perkins Gilman; *Pictorial Review* editor and NWP member Ida Clyde Clarke; and Wisconsin NWP suffragist, author, and intimate of the La Follette family Zona Gale—but between April and May 1924 Catt's name disappeared. This committee's initial statement of principles emphasized the need to take public utilities, natural resources, and the financial system out of the "hands of the few," to achieve peaceful economic development, and to abolish war.[13]

The formation of the group was related to the Conference on Progressive Political Action, a consortium called into being by leaders of the sixteen railway brotherhoods in order to mobilize farmers' and workers' votes "in the interests of the producers" for the 1922 elections. Though the CPPA did have nominal female representation—Agnes Nestor of the Women's Trade Union League was on its national committee, for example—it looked for a male constituency. It addressed its calls "Dear Sir and Brother"; it demanded the nomination and election of "*men* who can be trusted." It looked on women as wives rather than a significant portion, themselves, of the nation's wage-earners and farmers, grouping women with children as both "effective campaigners when they put their hearts to it." The CPPA had its sights on a third-party candidacy in the 1924 campaign, and a cardinal motivation in the Woman's Committee for

Political Action was to organize coherent representation of women's political interests at the convention the CPPA had set for July 4, 1924.[14]

At the conference held by the WCPA early in May, fifty to one hundred people heard speakers wax eloquent on such issues in its platform as civil liberties, labor defenses, and public control of railroads, natural resources, and money and credit. Emma Wold and Florence Brewer Boeckel gave speeches on the issue of international peace. Harriet Connor Brown delivered a carefully prepared paper on means to raise government revenue without raising tariffs. Owing perhaps to some overflow from an international congress of the WILPF, which had been held in the same city just days earlier, the WCPA conference strengthened the peace plank in its statement of principles, changing "progressive reduction of armament by international agreement" to "the abolition by international agreement of war as a means of settling disputes between nations." Under the guidance of Meta Berger (a prominent Socialist from Wisconsin), conference participants decided to work up state branches of "progressive" women in order to send formal representation, as invited, to the CPPA convention. At the concluding mass meeting, Harriot Stanton Blatch summoned the women "Forward—to Direct Political Action," calling on them to abandon the two old corrupt parties and to work for a new liberal party. Ruth Hale closed the meeting "with a strong demand for the election of a substantial woman's bloc in Congress." Within a few months the NWP had launched its 1924 campaign for "Women for Congress."[15]

The Woman's Committee for Political Action, like the anti-militarist sentiment so strong within it, united women who were split over the question of the equal rights amendment. As the Woman's Committee's links to the CPPA (which was grounded in the labor movement) became more salient, women on both sides of the debate on protective labor legislation still worked together on the political organizing of common interest to both. By June 1924 the WCPA could name members in forty-two states, had branches operating or organized at work in twenty-five states, and was sufficiently established to send thirty-six accredited delegates representing seventeen states to the July 4th convention. There, NWP member and WCPA executive secretary Isabelle Kendig shared the spotlight with Mabel Costigan, an officer in the LWV who introduced that organization's welfare recommendations (which had been given short shrift by the Democratic and Republican conventions). The convention named Wisconsin Senator Robert La Follette as a candidate for president of the United States. The economic views and opposition to World War I which damned La Follette in mainstream Republican halls endeared him to pacifists and to many women reformers. Where the Republican and Democrats had declined, La Follette's platform endorsed the constitutional amendment prohibiting child labor that had just passed both houses of Congress. La Follette's platform also included a plank on women's rights similar to the Wisconsin Equal Rights Bill: it advocated "removal of legal discriminations against women by measures not prejudicial to legislation necessary for the protection of women and for the advancement of social welfare."[16]

Once La Follette declared for the presidency, the WCPA collapsed itself into the Women's Division of the La Follette–Wheeler campaign, for which it may have been a stalking horse all along. Isabelle Kendig maintained, "we intend to keep our identity separate because when a woman's organization joins a man's, the men always are elected to the outstanding posts and given the real jobs." Whether in fact the Progressive Party apparatus was much different from that of the Republicans or Democrats, with respect to giving women opportunities, can be doubted. Anne Martin was infuriated by the La Follette–Wheeler Committee's bypassing her to head the campaign in Nevada and choosing instead the man who had been her Socialist rival for the Senate in 1920 but had received only 494 votes to her 4,981. The Women's Division's recommendation that the National Campaign Committee be enlarged to give equal representation to women received a pocket veto. Although some women got Progressive Party endorsement in state campaigns—four out of the five women supported for Congress from Pennsylvania by the NWP ran on the Progressive ticket—all of them lost.

La Follette marshalled the largest third-party vote ever in U.S. history except for Theodore Roosevelt, whose Progressive Party was really a sector of the Republican Party, with state and local machinery to support it, unlike La Follette's. In the nation as a whole one out of six voters (and in the nine major cities, more than one of five) chose La Follette, though he was not even on the ballot in all states.[17] After La Follette's defeat, Kendig conceded that women had not found the opportunities they should have in the Progressive Party—they had been pushed off to the side or expected to fulfill purely social functions. She proposed that a fully independent group, a National League for Progressive Women, was needed. The Woman's Committee sent out a call for such an independent organization, but once the railway brotherhoods stashed the CPPA in January 1925, the Woman's Committee slipped from sight too. Anne Martin's harsh judgment that the third-party effort had diverted women from organizing themselves, and had swallowed "progressive women of the near-feminist type" to no advantage of their own, may, in retrospect, have been warranted.[18]

Nonetheless, the enthusiasm of pacifist, feminist, and Progressive women for La Follette was more reason for the military and right-wing groups to raise the alarm about where women's energies were heading. The direction of those energies in 1924 appeared to conservatives to be consistently hazardous, from the Sheppard-Towner legislation in force to congressional passage (in June) of the child labor amendment—from the Cable Act to the recent introduction into Congress of a constitutional amendment for equal rights—from the Washington Disarmament Conference to the making of a viable presidential candidate of a man who had opposed World War I and was running on an antimonopoly platform. Pacifist feminists were demonstrating new boldness at this time, too. The WPU began in the spring of 1924 its lobbying and publicity campaign for "the complete abolition of the war machine and of all legal sanction for war, offensive or defensive, international or civil." True to the NWP tradition, in which its main proponents had been schooled, they held a parade in Washington with banners demanding, "Make War Illegal. Abolish the Army and Navy," interviewed almost the entire Senate, and took their resolution to all the party conventions, though only the Farmer-Labor group endorsed it. The WPU gained the support of Senator Lynn Frazier of North Dakota, who introduced into Congress in 1926, and every session thereafter until 1937, a constitutional amendment written by the WPU which would make war illegal, deprive Congress of the power to declare war, and abolish the armed forces in the United States.[19]

In May, the international congress of the WILPF in Washington, D.C., created headlines, bringing to the United States women eminent in peace work from twenty-two countries. Preceded by a mass rally and addressed by Senator Borah, the congress discussed proposals ranging from a new international organization without the military sanctions of the League of Nations to a United States of Europe. The delegates urged democratic control of foreign policy, outlawry of war, and abolition of conscription; they issued a special condemnation of chemical warfare; and they advocated bringing the influence of women and men into equilibrium in international order. These proceedings brought hyperpatriots into bristling array. They not only rehearsed their claims against pacifists as "slackers" and subversives, they also accused the WILPF delegates of being Russian and German agents, thus throwing into panic the local

U.S. committees who had been set to welcome the women as they traveled from Washington to Chicago aboard a designated train, the Pax Special. Martha Trimble, WILPF coordinator for the Pax Special, was told by press friends that the War Department had "determined to do everything possible to hinder our peace work" and had pressed newspapers to "give [the WILPF] hell" in their coverage."[20] It was reportedly in horrified reaction to the WILPF congress—which even antagonists could attend and observe—that Fries and his like sought the cooperation of women's patriotic societies and found aid readily forthcoming. In June 1924 the Daughters of the War of 1812, the American War Mothers, and the American Legion Auxiliary joined with the Daughters of the American Revolution and several other like-minded societies in a Patriotic Council to oppose pacifism and subversion. From that point, right-wing women, in coalition with military and reactionary men's groups, played a much clearer role.

Though founded with patriotic purpose, the DAR had not been much distinguishable from other women's clubs before the Great War. But during the war and even more so after it, the society turned its attention to preparedness and to defense against external and internal enemies. In 1919 it identified the major enemy as Bolshevism, endorsed the American Legion's plea for universal military training, and subsequently chimed in with the right-wing subversive-hunting men's groups. The numerous and growing membership of the DAR (it was larger than the LWV) was mainly inactive. A small group at the head called the shots. After 1924 those leaders spearheaded attacks on pacifism in liberal women's organizations, speaking for a network of male and female zealots who were also roused against the child labor amendment. At its Continental Congress in 1925, the DAR established a new arm called the National Defense Committee to respond to the spread of pacifism and coordinate "a definite, intensive campaign" to combat "the plan for destructive revolution in the U.S. by Red Internationals." The same resolution noted that "Moscow International Communist Organizations are increasing at a tremendous rate and sweeping thousands of unsuspecting pacifists into cooperation with the Communists' programs, camoflaged [sic] as measures for peace for the purpose of appeal but in reality paving the way for Red revolution."[21]

A fracas in the National Council of Women revealed some of the repercussions of patriotic women's organizations' countermobilization against pacifism and feminism. In 1888 both the National Council of Women in the U.S. and the International Council of Women had been founded as umbrella groups by suffragists and temperance workers. By the 1920s the NCW, to which the DAR and almost every other women's organization belonged, had little independent function but as the U.S. representative to the International Council of Women. The latter, as a supra-supra-women's club, was of necessity limited to symbolic politics. In 1924, leaders of the NCW were looking ahead to hosting the quinquennial meeting of the International Council of Women the following year in Washington, D.C., when several super-patriot organizations among its constituents threatened to secede unless the WILPF were forced out. Driven by its urgent concerns to hire the DAR's mansion and to obtain some public funding for the upcoming quinquennial, the NCW put pressure on the WILPF to withdraw. (At about this time, too, the Women's Joint Congressional Committee, wounded by the Spider-Web Chart, made clear that WILPF was not among its constituent members, and although that was and had been true, the explicit dissociation was unprecedented.) The leaders of WILPF initially balked at the unwarranted request from the NCW, but fairly soon decided that continuing membership was not worth the fight. The leadership of the DAR agreed to let their hall to the quinquennial meeting on the condition that no "radical" or "pacifist" addresses take place there. The NCW had taken steps to assure such before-the-fact censoring when the DAR abruptly reneged on the arrangement anyway, forcing the NCW, at great inconvenience, to make alternative arrangements.[22]

When the meeting of the International Council of Women did convene, with over two hundred distinguished delegates from thirty-six countries in attendance, its keynote was international peace. Unlike the WILPF meeting a year earlier, however, all radical approaches to ending war were purposefully excluded from this group. Two convention pageants paid honor to the military and to the war dead. The *Christian Science Monitor* noted that WILPF had left the NCW "not quite voluntarily" the year before, and that the NCW's president, Mrs. Philip North Moore of St. Louis, was a "conservative of conservatives." Not all was bound to go smoothly at the conference, however. In one incident, the choir of black women singers supposed to entertain, discovering that delegates' seating arrangements in the hall were racially segregated, refused to perform and were joined in a walk-out by blacks in attendance. (Mary Church Terrell remembered it as the worst encounter but one between black and white club women.) Lucia Ames Mead, WILPF leader, found her conception of the NCW—"that people of every race, creed and political belief are welcome to remain once accredited and having paid their dues and behaved courteously to other members"—rapidly being superseded.[23]

Members of the American War Mothers and DAR in attendance saw the pacifist menace everywhere, rending the atmosphere, so newspapers reported, with "bickerings, insinuations, and trouble of all sorts." Then the bogey materialized. In an exhibition booth in the convention hall, officers of the NCW were "astounded" to discover literature describing war as legalized murder, urging a constitutional amendment to outlaw war by eliminating military appropriations, and advocating immediate total disarmament—all written and published by members of the Women's Peace Society and the WPU. The officers immediately created a bonfire of the offending pamphlets. "We are not willing that this council shall be used as the vehicle for violent [sic] pacifist propaganda," said one, although she affirmed the rights of affiliated individuals to have and discuss their individual opinions.

Meanwhile, the plenary sessions of the International Council, after impassioned debate stirred by English feminist pacifists, rejected extremes of both left and right and endorsed partial, gradual, controlled, multilateral disarmament. Resolutions also passed binding member councils to make efforts to bring all nations into the League of Nations and the World Court. On all of these risky questions, however, the Americans abstained. Their President Moore publicly vented her annoyance at "censorship" attempted by "ultra-patriots," but she did so by capturing their own ground, venturing that women attached to the International Council and their families had "the more enviable records for gallantry and service in wartime, compared woman for woman with many of their critics." Just as the International Council's quinquennial convention concluded, the National Patriotic Council formed by right-wing women's groups was holding a meeting of its own, inside the U.S. Department of the Interior building, with General Fries as an honored speaker. There, the head of the American War Mothers denounced the International Council of Women for meddling in U.S. affairs and warned, "the American War Mothers refuse to be asphyxiated into silence. . . . They know their voices will be heard by the country."[24]

The NCW episode showed that moderation—even capitulation—did not insulate women's peace efforts from attack from the right. So did Carrie Chapman Catt's taking up the mantle of leadership in the mid-1920s. As right-wing pressure groups tabooed pacifist and anti-militaristic efforts by women, Catt emerged as the leader down an alternate route, devised by heads of women's organizations in the WJCC who were still interested in work for peace but wary of the WILPF. Impelled by friends in the LWV, the American Association of University Women, and liberal internationalist groups like the Foreign Policy Association, Catt called a coalition meeting of women concerned with peace, which took place in January 1925 as the first National Conference on the Cause and Cure of War. Catt's effort united the LWV, the AAUW, the GFWC, the YWCA, and the WCTU with national women's religious bodies under an umbrella National Committee. The WILPF was carefully left out, though individuals involved in WILPF, if they belonged to other organizations as well, could take part. Mary Anderson of the Women's Bureau described the first conference as "almost like a reunion of womanhood," bringing together women "from all over the United States—club women who have not formerly associated themselves with any movement for peace and many of the old suffrage crowd."

By its very size and scope the NCCCW occupied a very broad middle of the road. Catt intended it to be an educational rather than a political group. Although its founding was reportedly motivated by women leaders' chagrin that their own work became invisible when they joined with men in church and secular peace groups, the format created for the NCCCW was hardly designed to enhance women's sense of their own political leverage. Typically, dozens of male "experts" on military and diplomatic issues addressed an audience of listening women. Catt made it clear that neither in programs nor pronouncements was the organization going to "attack the government" or the military. She found, however, that her constituents dragged her even further from criticism of warmaking than she would have liked. Agreement on publication of the "Findings" from the first Conference was stalled by the GFWC's refusal to endorse the statement, which in its view "did not sufficiently emphasize the need of preparation for security." The GFWC remained the most "ticklish," uncomfortable with any statement that even mentioned "reduction of armaments," but the head of the YWCA was also disinclined to take a "political" stand and the WCTU was balky, Catt's private notes revealed.[25]

Catt, who thought she had made it clear that she was not a pacifist but rather a pursuer of international peace by practical methods, was shocked when she was tarred with the same brush that had blackened disarmament advocates. Even before the first NCCCW conference ended, the American Legion Auxiliary was denouncing the participants for taking part in a plot to destroy the United States. In 1927 the DAR sprang into headlines again by prominently including Catt, Jane Addams, and many other distinguished social workers, journalists, lawyers, and ministers on a "doubtful speakers" list circulated among its clubs. On the blacklisted women and men the DAR pinned such labels as "communist," "internationalist," "pro-Soviet," "feminist" (women only), and "revolutionary feminist" (Alice Paul and Alva Belmont only!). Some dissident DAR members' objections elevated the episode into a national controversy, contemporaneous with the height of agitation to save Sacco and Vanzetti from the electric chair. It was in effect a replay of the Spider-Web Chart, again the year before a presidential election. (Nor was the Spider-Web Chart out of circulation. Catharine Waugh McCulloch, Chicago lawyer, former suffrage leader, and LWV officer, complained in 1927 of having to contend with a Lieutenant-Colonel Lee Alexander Stone, who spoke before the Illinois Democratic Women's Club to condemn the child labor amendment. He called Florence Kelley a "Leninist" and then "warmed up" to the Evanston DAR about the Spider-Web, "classing pacifists with Russian Reds." McCulloch was frustrated by the impossibility of replying "to his misstatements and insinuations, sneers and slurs as they ought to be.") Catt came into the fray in print to refute "Lies at Large." The *Woman Patriot* rejoiced that Catt had had to admit she was opposed by other women, thus cracking the "woman bloc" and piercing the illusion that her ideas about international peace and women's rights were the ideas of all women. Catt had no such illusion, writing at the time to an old friend, "I do not think women can be joined together for any one purpose because the difference between the reactionary and the progressive is too great to be bridged."[26]

Extremist pronouncements from super-patriotic women's groups found answering echoes in wider sectors of American opinion primed to be hostile to whatever smacked of sympathy to Bolshevism—as feminism, internationalism, and federal regulations on employers' freedoms were said to. Right-wing women's groups contributed avidly after 1925 to the publicity and lobbying campaigns against ratifying the child labor amendment and against further funding for the Sheppard-Towner bill, which resulted in the demise of both of these "women's" measures.[27] The effects on women's organizations were palpable. Mass women's organizations like the GFWC and the PTA, whose members spanned the political spectrum, shied away from taking stands on controversial or potentially controversial issues. The LWV and the NFBPW instituted more cumbersome, time-consuming, localized decision-making on issues, to protect the national office from attack, and hailed it as a virtue (which in certain respects it was). President Maud Wood Park "developed and refined the healing and unifying technique of holding items at the study level until a broad measure of agreement was reached," the LWV's chron-icler recorded. The WILPF shifted the weight of its attention from direct attacks on the military budget to new methods of international arbitra-tion and agreement. But the women's patriotic societies did not let up: for instance, when WILPF executive secretary Dorothy Detzer testified in Congress early in 1928 against a proposed bill to build naval cruisers, Mrs. Noble Newport Potts, president of the National Patriotic Council, was there to warn the House Naval Affairs Committee chairman, "that's a dangerous woman you've been talking to." [28]

The super-patriotic attacks not only beat the drum to the right and revealed that women spanned the spectrum from the reactionary to the progressive. Their agitations about Bolshevism and subversion affected the meaning and practice of feminism, by association and by analogy. They inculpated the very notion of women as a political group or class as un-American, a "Bolshevik" notion. The New York Times had forecast that approach in 1918 when its editorialist linked the WILPF's exclusive organizing of women to "a socialist theory." Right-wing zealots were more polemical than the New York Times, more direct even than Governor Nathan Miller had been in denouncing a league of women voters as a "menace." The idea that women might perceive and mobilize for com-mon political interests was denounced as sex antagonism and class war-fare, in a claim close enough to prejudices shared by mainstream politi-cians to cause political resonance. [29]

The censorious atmosphere, tingeing the idea of sex solidarity with the blush of "Sovietism," hindered women's organizations from developing a political rationale for or analysis of their constitution by sex. After the attack by Governor Miller, the LWV omitted references to a woman bloc and became a good-government organization. "Four years after the League's inception, members had ceased to think of themselves primar-ily as women, and had begun to think of themselves as citizens," a sym-pathetic historian of its efforts wrote. In the later 1920s, WILPF activists downplayed former justifications for peace advocacy as natural to women; they increasingly worked in concert with men who shared their politics rather than seeking an antiwar crusade among their own sex. The WPU remained unequivocally pacifist and feminist, but tiny in numbers and slight in influence. [30]

Though ill conceived, the right wing's purposeful contamination of the notion of sexual politics with the radioactive quality of class warfare was well targeted. Feminism required at least an incipient understanding of women as a political class defined by the social construction of gender.

The NWP recognized that, and it was the one women's group that the *Woman Patriot* specifically likened to the Workers' (Communist) Party. The *Woman Patriot* named the NWP "the extreme left wing of the feminist movement," called its occupational councils "soviets," and declared that "like the Communists, the Woman's Party seeks first equality, and then dictatorship—and largely by similar tactics and organization!" It asserted that the NWP was as unrepresentative of American women as the Communists were of American labor.[31] (The fact that U.S. Communists also denounced the NWP as bourgeois and called the ERA harmful to the working class made no difference, for logic was not the stock-in-trade of this political discourse; guilt by analogy was no less handily insidious than guilt by association.)

It is difficult to judge how far the reinvigoration of Red-baiting in women's organizations in the mid-1920s affected the NWP, for what seem to have been its results took the direction the party had headed anyway since 1920. From the DAR's blacklisting of Carrie Chapman Catt, Doris Stevens drew only the "lesson to all feminists to keep their skirts clear of all other movements." Before the blacklisting controversy had died down, the District of Columbia organization for the NWP nonetheless cordially invited the president-general of the DAR, Mrs. Alfred J. Brosseau, to call at NWP headquarters when she was visiting the city.[32] Alice Paul's leaning toward decorous, wealthy, and Republican women was consolidated, moreover, when the NWP took the unprecedented step in 1928 of formally endorsing the Republican presidential ticket. The party had never before endorsed a national candidate, and it was a greater innovation not to blame but to reward the party in power—for the Republicans had held the White House since 1920—when the equal rights amendment was not secured. The stated reason for the endorsement was that Charles Curtis, Herbert Hoover's vice-presidential running mate, had introduced the ERA into the Senate. But the Republican platform did not embrace the ERA; it only nodded in the direction of equality for women.

Certainly NWP leaders had come to see an enemy in Alfred Smith, the Democratic presidential candidate who had been governor of New York since 1922. New York leaders of the NWP were also its national leaders, and they had for years carried on state-level work for equal rights in direct confrontation with a network of women's organizations, welfare workers, and trade union supporters honeycombed within Al Smith's administration. Jane Norman Smith, a long-time Republican, director of NWP "industrial equality" work in New York, and veteran of many battles over sex-based protective labor legislation, was national chairman of the NWP in 1928. It was under her leadership that the decision to endorse the Hoover-Curtis ticket was made.[33] A more explicit Republican than Paul, Smith trusted entirely in Paul's vanguardist approach. "The only reason the Woman's Party has been able to get anywhere is because it hasn't been hampered by an organization along the lines of the League of Women Voters, and hasn't been confronted with an endless amount of red tape when action was necessary," she believed.

Spokeswomen for the NWP denied Republican partisanship, but the endorsement aroused immediate and in some cases fatal objections from several members. Lavinia Dock, one of the party's remaining socialists, most picturesquely remonstrated, "I could no more cast a vote for the Republican Party than I could swallow a large, smooth, green caterpillar." Sue Shelton White, a Tennessee Democrat, disavowed the party's choice and never came back to the fold. Emma C. Johnson, who had enlisted as a "founder" six or seven years earlier, saw the decision as "a fair piece of 'railroading,'" judged that the organization had "grossly betrayed women," and tendered her resignation. Most objectors made the point that Curtis himself would not be president and that Hoover, whose campaign among industrial working women was headed by WTUL leader Margaret Dreier Robins, promised no brighter prospects for the amendment than did Governor Smith. The basis for the endorsement seemed even flimsier when on October 26, 1928, Hoover made a statement opposing any change in protective labor laws applying to women. Newspaperwoman Ruby Black protested that the NWP would be a laughing-stock if it continued to support Hoover. Not as a Democrat, but as "a Feminist first of all . . . not greatly interested in any other issue," she implored a change, but a special meeting of seven members of the National Council, led by Jane Norman Smith, affirmed the endorsement a few days later.[34]

Although Paul was not present for the endorsement, the action had her hallmarks. Paul saw 1928 as a repeat of the strategy of 1916.[35] Although in both cases the strategy came from the top and its partisan impact would have been the same—adding to the votes of the Republican Party—in other respects the new policy inverted more than repeated the earlier one. It illustrated the different relation of the NWP to political context in 1928 as compared to a dozen years earlier. Support for the dominant Republican Party could not be interpreted as an attack from the left, as the 1916 strategy could despite the de facto help given to Republicans. The 1928 policy was not an organizing campaign among voting women but a pronouncement from headquarters. Since it supported, rather than opposed, an incumbent president, it intended to sustain rather than unsettle the political status quo, indicating the distance of the NWP's orientation in the 1920s from its disruptive image in the 1910s.

The endorsement of the Hoover–Curtis ticket, while hardly inconsistent with Paul's earlier leanings, may have also been motivated by the intent to gather unassailable political cover around the party's feminism—which it did not give up. The political climate, in other words, fed the party leadership's willingness to narrow and specialize its constituency and goal. For being avowedly feminist and viewing women as a political class, the NWP came under attack. Indeed, attacked by both right (as Communist) and left (as an enemy to the working class) the NWP leadership deepened its commitment to single-issue politics. By 1930 several NWP women who also had other causes sloughed off, perhaps made unwelcome and in any case rejecting the conditions of Paul's leadership, although not the intent for equal rights. Mary Gertrude Fendall and Vivian Pierce went to civil liberties causes, Mary Winsor to birth control and pacifism. Emma Wold, Mabel Vernon, Florence Brewer Boeckel, and Rebecca Hourwich Reyher left to concentrate their work on international peace. Reyher, whose departure stemmed from her disaffection with Paul (as well as from the practice of the New York branch to meet on weekday afternoons when Reyher, who worked nine to five, could not attend), recalled that "as time went on, there is no question but that the Woman's Party had a hard core of very conservative, very conventional women, and there is no doubt in my mind that Miss Paul was more comfortable with such women." By 1933 Doris Stevens too became alienated, for she discovered that the bequest she had long been counting on had been removed by codicil from Alva Belmont's will— owing to Alice Paul's machinations, Stevens was sure.[36]

As much as right-wing political pressure incriminated feminism, crippled the cohesion of women's organizations, and made cautious their goals, women's political efforts had their own centrifugal tendencies. By the late 1920s the crevasse visibly widening on the question of Prohibition— as much or more than any other issue—sounded the death knell of illusions that women were joined in political consensus. Hearing Ella Boole of the WCTU proclaim before Congress in 1928, "I represent the women of America!" Pauline Morton Sabin felt, "well, lady, here's one woman you don't represent!" and went on to found the Women's Organization for National Prohibition Reform, which worked for repeal of the Eighteenth Amendment. Sabin was a New Yorker born to wealth, social position, and Republican politics. Her political activities refuted the shibboleth that women followed their husbands' votes: she was president of the Women's National Republican Club and an active fundraiser and director of Eastern women's activities for the Coolidge and Hoover presidential campaigns; her husband was a Democrat. The couple shared opposition to Prohibition. Chairman of the board of the Guaranty Trust Company, Charles Sabin served on the executive committee of the Association Against the Prohibition Amendment (a virtually all-male group founded early in the 1920s). The WONPR was an entirely independent organization which sought no help from the men's association and rather quickly exceeded it in membership.

Sabin first organized women of her class and station—Mrs. Coffin Van Rensselaer of New York, Mrs. R. Stuyvesant Pierrepont of New Jersey, Mrs. Pierre S. du Pont of Delaware. After the organization was formally launched in Chicago, with a national advisory council of 125 women from twenty-six states, it gathered middle-class women of a much broader range, including political activists, employed women, and housewives and mothers. Its approach built on substratum convictions that the state should not intervene in private life. Sustaining the ideal of temperance, its publicity stressed that the Eighteenth Amendment had perversely stimulated alcohol consumption and at the same time had escalated political corruption and sponsored an atmosphere of lawlessness that endangered the nation's youth. The membership rose to three hundred thousand by mid-1931 and twice that a year later—which was probably three times the size of the Association Against the Prohibition Amendment and also more than the WCTU. The WONPR actively challenged the stereotype that women supported Prohibition. It disputed the WCTU's declaration that three million women under the aegis of the GFWC endorsed the Eighteenth Amendment. After WONPR leaders pointed out that their own members also belonged to GFWC clubs and asked for a poll of the GFWC membership on Prohibition, the WCTU stopped making that claim.[37]

Many struggles of the 1920s found women on opposite sides. The impact that women activists of one stripe or another could and did make—for Prohibition or against, for or against the military—ironically proved the absence rather than the substance of gender solidarity. The 1920s shattered any confidence that women should or would act predictably together on candidates of either sex, on legislative protection of working women or children, on peace, or on Prohibition. If in 1929 Ella Boole testified that she and her organization represented the women of America, Pauline Sabin and her organization were there to undermine her assertion. The 1920s showed that women leaders disagreed on issues just as men did, and even as men did not, and that on no particular issue could a prominent woman count on the generality of women following her without others opposing. Yet those revelations did not mean that women were not organized in "women's" groups—quite the contrary.

Just how organized American women were was demonstrated in the latter half of 1928, after U.S. Secretary of State Frank Kellogg and Foreign Minister Aristide Briand of France signed the Pact of Paris, a multilateral treaty by which all signatories renounced war as an instrument of national policy. Despite the controversy wreaked by the DAR, the networking function of the NCCCW set up channels of communication from national to local women's organizations so effectively that under its auspices thousands of local meetings were held all around the nation to discuss and adopt resolutions in favor of ratifying the Kellogg-Briand Pact. In January 1929, when the NCCCW held its annual meeting in Washington, members from all the forty-eight states presented 12,553 resolutions, the result of as many meetings, to their senators. In some localities, patriotic women's organizations took part and American Legion representatives spoke. But pacifists were not elated by ratification of the treaty when the Hoover administration and the Senate at the same time were moving ahead on a greatly expanded naval building program. The mass orchestration of opinion was possible because it took place at the same level of moral sentiment as the treaty—a rhetorical substitute for, rather than a material step toward, disarmament and the ending of war.[38]

From the 1920s, women's presence in politics more likely portended conflict than consensus. Gains on one side or another of a political question (like some individual women's political careers) might contribute to a subgroup's aims while giving the lie to sex solidarity. Yet coalition on substantive women's issues was not impossible. Women's organizations lined up to lobby for revisions of the Cable Act in 1930, for instance, to support the principle that a woman, whether married or not, should have the same right as a man to determine her own citizenship. The LWV testified and organized representatives from the NFBPW, AAUW, American Home Economics Association, National Council of Jewish Women, YWCA, GFWC, and WCTU to appear before the House Committee on Immigration and Naturalization; endorsements also came in from the WTUL and NWP. In the 1930s women's organizations en masse opposed state and federal sanctions against the married woman wage-earner.[39]

Ironically—in light of continuing opposition to the ERA from women's groups—when such coalitions formed it was to support efforts to enable women to act and to be treated "just like men." Toward that direction converged the effects of partisan politicians' depreciation of the woman bloc and the right-wing incrimination of feminism as sovietism, as well as the centrifugal tendencies among women themselves. Some of the basic impulses of Feminism converged there too. Hadn't feminism celebrated women's diverse individuality, encouraged women to run the whole range of human peculiarity—like men—rather than keeping to a single mold? "Women are, in Alice Duer Miller's famous phrase, people," Walter Lippmann approvingly recalled a suffragist humorist's line, when in 1928 he pointed out that public revelations of a few women's partisan manipulations had availed to "destroy the illusion that women have a special mission to redeem politics." By that point women's behavior (or misbehavior) like men's in politics could be seen as an alternative to rather than a goal of feminism. By the late 1920s the observation that women acted politically like men served less to describe a range of freedom than to prescribe women's lack of power as a group. The activity without unity among women's organizations could be perceived as no "women's" activity at all.

"Don't Worry About the Women," commentator Frank Kent titled the relevant chapter in his sardonic popular book, *Political Behavior.* "The fact is there is no such thing as sex solidarity in politics," he declared: women were not all alike, did not vote together, and would rather follow a man than a woman every time. Women's continued economic dependence on men made them "just as credulous, just as undiscriminating and unintelligent in political action" as their male "meal tickets" and meant that women's voting served only a "multiplier" function. His denial of the relevance of gender in politics and others like it—bearing prescriptive as much as descriptive intent—had the ring of inevitability. To similar effect, a political journalist reviewed the performance of women legislators in the U.S. House of Representatives during the decade. "Experience so far has proved the fallacy," he judged, "of the expectation that women can or should be elected members of Congress for the purpose of advancing any special interests of women, children or anybody or anything else." Those congresswomen who served "most acceptably and most successfully" did so when they had "eliminated the matter of sex so far as possible," and based their work "upon exactly the same premises as the work of other members of Congress."[40] His admonition to eliminate the matter of sex was also a formula for no sex solidarity, no visible political role for women as such, no feminist appeal to a female constituency. There was no clear ground on which to make it as a woman and make it in a man's world. That was an unwelcome outcome for the intent to create the human sex.

CONCLUSION

Cover of special issue of the *Survey* magazine, December 1, 1926.

No question, feminism came under heavy scrutiny—and fire— by the end of the 1920s. From one point of view, feminism appeared archaic, a polemical stance perhaps needed to storm bastions of male privilege early in the century when women had been confined to their own sphere, but now superseded by the reality that women and men worked and played together every day. In the eyes of other critics, feminism looked too fearsomely futuristic, projecting a world in which women's self-seeking destroyed gender assignment, family unity, kinship bonds, social cohesion, and human happiness.[1] Feminism was condemned on the one hand for harping on definition by sex, and on the other for dangerously (although futilely) trying to obliterate sex distinctions. Feminists constantly had to shadowbox with two opposing yet coexistent caricatures: the one, that feminism tried to make women over into men, the other, that feminism set women against men in deadly sex antagonism.

Indeed, within little more than a generation drastic alterations had occurred in women's character and opportunities as citizens and workers, in women's freedom of social behavior, ideals and practices in marriage, and self-esteem. Women who had been suffragists and feminists in the 1910s, if they assessed things in the latter 1920s, never failed to acknowledge the distance already traveled toward women's freedom from sex-defined restrictions. Not only complacent spokeswomen but also the dissatisfied credited what seemed to them enormous salutary changes, even if they went on to protest against still-constraining stereotypes or to deplore economic or political inequities. Alice Beal Parsons' *Woman's Dilemma* and Suzanne La Follette's *Concerning Women*, the two most sustained feminist critiques written in the 1920s, both started with appreciation for gains already made.[2] But their views were joined by opponents in the discourse about women's roles vis-à-vis men's, masculinity and femininity, the future of marriage, home, and family. The status of women became not only a symbol for all that had changed in that respect but also a touchstone for grievances in the rumblings of acculturation to increasing institutional scale, bureaucratic rationalization, specialization, and mass commercialization. A cacophony of voices cast on the modern woman blame and praise, naive and cynical interpretations, and snide asides ranging from the vituperative to the merely inferential or whining. The editors of *Current History* found "no aspect of present day social history more controversial in character or more delicate in its implications than that of the new status of Woman," when in 1927 they assembled a special issue on the topic. There Carrie Chapman Catt's essay, "Woman Suffrage Only an Episode in Age-Old Movement," Leta Hollingworth's "The New Woman in the Making," and Charlotte Perkins Gilman's "Woman's Achievements Since the Franchise" could be read side by side with neurologist Joseph Collins's warning "Women's Morality in Transition," self-stated conservative Anthony Ludovici's "Women's Encroachment on Man's Domain," and Catholic rector Hugh L. Mc-Menamin's "Evils of Woman's Revolt Against the Old Standards."[3]

Celebratory comments on the emancipation of women thrived in advertising and popular media, there coopting and diluting feminist pretensions. Complaints, on the other hand, spanned two poles which might labeled with the titles of female commentator Gina Lombroso Ferrero's essay, "Feminism Destructive of Women's Happiness," and male journalist Creighton Peet's "What More Do Women Want?" At one side were disquisitions on the point that women's "imitation" of male modes—the shifting of the rock of secure gender roles—threatened not only social order and the upbringing of the next generation but also men's virtues and women's authentic satisfaction. Theorizing about women's "real" happiness and its relation to societal health became an essential theme in social analysis and in anti-feminism of the twentieth century. On the other side were male accusations that both the culture and the economy had become disgracefully feminized by pandering to women's demands and tastes. Never mind that these lines of criticism crossed each other, the one steeped in anxiety to secure the protean masculine and feminine in a fixed and known hierarchy, the other sure what the feminine was and finding its baneful influence rampant. The increased likelihood that women would think and act for themselves—perceived to be manifest in wage-earning outside the home, a climbing divorce rate, and the waning of patriarchal familial authority—was at the center, drawing fierce onslaught.[4]

Toward the end of the decade eddies of reaction were perceptible in middle-class cultural vehicles and so were assertions of more conservative social values, especially as those had to do with experimental change in the family roles of men and women. The same magazines that had five years earlier published women's serious discussions of the combination of marriage and career were full of male aggrievement at women's failure to be satisfied and female dissection of pressure to go "back to the home." If a woman analyzed a creature called "Feminist—New Style" in print, she was parried by a man's caustic proposal of a "Virist—New Style." One left-wing 1910s Feminist felt it necessary to expose "The New Masculinism" by the late 1920s, and she titled her backward glances "Still a Man's Game: Reflections of a Slightly Tired Feminist."[5]

To defend and explain what change had been wrought, many women began to put feminism in the broader context of world-historical changes in living patterns induced by industrialization and modern times. Beatrice Forbes-Robertson Hale attributed the "change in the status, opportunities and interests of women amounting to a revolution" over the previous several decades to "the inevitable effect of two forces: the theory of democracy and the fact of industrialism." To Gina Lombroso Ferrero's denunciation of feminism as "the demand for woman of all the rights possessed by man, the determined effort to bring woman to the enjoyment of all privileges enjoyed by man," an American writer and reformer, Martha Bensley Bruere, riposted that feminism was simply women's recovery from the "jarring crash" of industrialization, which had shunted manufacturing out of the home. Feminism, Bruere said, "is the hunt for a new resting place, for a new job; the adjustment to the new conditions it imposes; the new training it requires; the different physical demands that new work makes . . . the necessary change of mind toward work, oneself, men, marriage, children, government, money, morals, and the life everlasting." By the end of the 1920s and early 1930s such analyses had a strongly defensive and self-justifying tone and stood mainly on the economic plane. "The machine age has taken away from the home much that occupied the bodies and brains of women and substitute activities must be found to stimulate woman's interest and effort, otherwise instead of being an economical asset she will become a heavy liability in the lives and work of men," one writer typically summarized.[6] Such assessments dealt less with the march of democracy, perhaps not only because of the economic crisis and not only because woman suffrage had not had world-shaking effects, but also because the rise of European fascism cast doubt on the expectation that democratization was irreversible.

Certainly it was plausible that modern women's wage-earning had been propelled by factors other than their own motivation: for instance, by businesses' desire for tractable workers in factories and offices; by demands of war production; by sex-typing excluding men from certain "womanly" tasks; by families' needs for cash. This emphasis on historical forces had feminist tradition behind it, since Charlotte Perkins Gilman had argued that woman's path out of the home was mandated by modern social and economic specialization. It had the advantage of accommodating in its sweep masses of women who had never explicitly ventured any feminist intentions. It was a feminist version, so to speak, of "cultural lag" theory, which was a preoccupation of contemporary social theorists with the gap between the speed of industrial and technological change and human cultural adjustment and adaptation.[7] At its most helpful, the view of feminism as the adjustment or reconditioning (another word Bruere used) of women to modern industrial society confirmed the correctness of women's struggles to escape definition by biology and domesticity and aligned feminist intents with the forces of progress. At worst, however, it obliterated women's agency in making their lives, hingeing women's emergence from traditional sex-determinants on "forces"— which usually meant men's doings—outside women's control. Rather than confirming feminism as a standpoint or a struggle, the emphasis on historical forces blanketed the need for feminism and the possible utility of it. Such an emphasis left women ideologically helpless in the face of state reversals such as were on view in Hitler's Germany.

More, it altered the past, chiming in with the more widespread "disremembering" process by which Feminism was selectively absorbed and repressed. In one example, a 1926 symposium in the *Survey* called "Where Are the Pre-War Radicals?" the respondents—themselves insurgents of various sorts before the Great War—barely recalled women's militance. They looked back mainly on prewar efforts to extend democratic control through the initiative, referendum, and recall, to harness great wealth, and organize the working class. Only Morris Hillquit, the Socialist lawyer who had in 1917 been a credible candidate for mayor of New York City, mentioned feminists (in the same breath as pacifists and anti-vaccinationists) as part of the "motley" crew of prewar radicals. Charlotte Perkins Gilman specified that Prohibitionists and "Equal Suffragists" had attained their prewar goals. Of the twenty-three respondents the only woman besides Gilman was Ida Tarbell, the nonfeminist and even anti-suffragist journalist whose 1906 exposé of Standard Oil epitomized the muckraking genre. In Tarbell's recollection, "the pre-War radical was often not a wise man—an experienced or patient man." But he was, her pronouns indicated, a man. There was a sharp irony to the *Survey's* thus consigning Feminism to oblivion, for its symposium was stimulated by the publication of memoirs by Frederic C. Howe, husband of the founder of Heterodoxy.[8]

The view of feminism as adjustment to historical forces also made the larger feminist past hard to recapture. It made the new status of women seem right and inevitable, but it threw a veil over women's own purposive efforts to defy limitations dictated by sex, to establish their full right to labor, and in other ways to alter gender hierarchy. By hiding the instrumentality of feminist ideology or collective action in forging the new woman from the old, it projected little necessity for ideology or action in the present and future. It urged on the presumption that American women's emancipation came about through a "revolution without ideology."[9] The basis for continuing feminist advocacy was missing. Instead of an either/or view, a more interactive understanding of the relation between feminist intentions and the changes in women's economic lives (hence their whole lives) forced by modern industrial capitalism might have provided such a basis.

"The modern feminist does not assert her equality with men, she assumes it, and proceeds accordingly," declared Ida Clyde Clarke, a well-known journalist, National Woman's Party member, and editor of the *Pictorial Review*. The "1929 model" feminist was a "well rounded, perfectly balanced, thoroughly informed and highly intelligent person . . . who manages her home, holds her job, and so on, in the normal way." Yet, looking around them in the late 1920s, women who imagined a world without invidious gender distinctions had to notice the limits of feminist accomplishment. "Women have freedom of education, but restricted opportunities to use it," Carrie Chapman Catt admitted. "Women have the vote, but the old prejudices still rise to forbid freedom of action within the political parties." "The best that can be said is that certain women have advanced themselves," observed a political commentator in the nation's capital.[10] A few critics, such as Anne Martin, spoke even more harshly, protesting that men overwhelmingly dominated political, legal, and economic power while the great mass of adult women continued to be absorbed in the affairs of individual households, family relationships, and children, and sources as disparate as political party caucuses and marital advice tracts ridiculed or calumniated women's purposeful sex solidarity.

One approach on which women of several sorts converged was to affirm equality of opportunity regardless of sex. "Certainly the time ought to have come where the question of *man* and *woman* does not enter in, where the place of sex is disregarded and the work and the individual are considered," expostulated Susan Kingsbury, director of the Bryn Mawr College Department of Social Economy, in reaction to Depression-related instances of economic injustice to women. That was a compromise area of feminism where opponents and proponents of the equal rights amendment, women trying to integrate themselves into men's institutions and professions and those working through women's institutions and organizations, women of different partisan and political persuasions, even women of different generations could find a common denominator. Catt, for instance, summed up women's ages-long struggle for freedom and independence as "a demand for equality of opportunity between the sexes. It means that when and if a woman is as well qualified as a man to fill a position, she shall have an equal and unprejudiced chance to secure it."[11] Such sympathetic generalizing about feminism as there was in the late 1920s leaned toward egalitarian and economic emphases like Catt's. Equality of opportunity was the most unexceptionable goal by which feminism could be justified in the American context. It was essential to professional women's toehold on their fields. During the Depression, an emphasis on equal economic opportunity became a necessary rallying point among women seeking to combat government and private regulations restricting married women's employment.

The problem with equality of opportunity as a feminist clarion was that it urged women to disregard sex, as Kingsbury's language revealed. Since it did not address the paradoxical realities of women's situation, equality of opportunity had little power to mobilize women as a sex. Such evenhanded advocacy did not stir the numerous young women, guided by "ex-feminists," who judged equality of opportunity to be as absurd as more daring feminist intents so long as women had the babies. Professional women, on the other hand, might enthusiastically support equality of opportunity and yet frown on feminism. Among ambitious young careerists who intended to seize the main chance and relied on advancing by their individual talents, feminism was a "term of opprobrium," journalist Dorothy Dunbar Bromley found in 1927.[12]

Equality of opportunity was embraced, nonetheless, as a way out of a conceptual problem that dogged would-be feminists and women leaders through mid-century, whether they admitted it or not. That problem resounded in all attempts to organize women to change the sexual structure of political and economic power. How were women to be understood as a gender group vis-à-vis men without suppressing women's differences from one another and without fixing women into a definitional straitjacket of sex-typing? What would generate the subjective attitude—the "we"-consciousness which Simone de Beauvoir later accused women of lacking? The belief and partial reality behind the singular nomenclature of the *woman* movement had dissipated; yet operable concepts of the social construction of gender, ongoing convictions of what women shared as social and political actors, had not been surely identified. "The

essential fact about the New Women is that they differ among themselves, as men do, in work, in play, in virtues, in aspirations and in rewards achieved. They are women, not woman," wrote Leta Hollingworth.[13] The new woman's refusal to be specialized to sex militated
against a new unifying and political conceptualization of womanhood.
The observable heterogeneity among women in modern political life
presented the spectacle of more women working politically, economically, organizationally—locally and nationally—than ever before, together constituting the disappearance of the woman movement. Literally
millions of women were organized into groups, competing with and opposing one another rather than gathering into one denomination. Advocates of sex-based legislation combatted equal rights amendment supporters. Women lined up on the political spectrum from left to right.
Women were pro- and anti-Prohibitionists. Women professionals differentiated themselves from women volunteers and clients. Women had
different ideological predispositions on questions of marriage and employment tangled up with their education and wealth, their class and
race and ethnicity.

In the twentieth century, unlike in the nineteenth, not every woman
who ventured beyond home joined the woman movement. Some women
had navigated over or around sex barriers, making all perceptions and
claims regarding sex and sex discrimination equivocal as compared to
generations earlier. The wider spectrum of behavior achieved bred an
elite stratum, women who were able to take advantage of new opportunities—women who were still marginal (although not marginal in the
sense of dispensable), on the borders of given categories, edgy. They
were not fully at home in male houses of power, though seeking to live
there, nor resting content outside.[14] The very resources that powered
exceptional women to stand out made them less likely to understand the
position of ordinary women, and sometimes to rue the failure of the mass
of women to wake up and see things their way. That was as true of the
declared feminist elite (that is, the NWP) as it was of professional elites
among women. (Doris Stevens recalled—in tribute—that Alva Belmont's "impatience at the supineness of women was colossal.")[15] If wom-
en's activities in the public arena in the late 1920s and 1930s looked like
elites contending with each other more than galvanizing the mass, that
distinction of elite from mass was a result of women's success in pushing
aside the bars to the public arena—or, more correctly, a result of the
limits to that success. Women had achieved entry to the same arenas
men occupied, but not welcome or integration or parity.

The growing presence of such marginal women was the surest accomplishment if not the best promise of feminism. They included individuals of outstanding accomplishment and variety. Even if (or because) the advancement of women was a dearly held goal among such individuals, even if (or because) they worked through female networks, by and large they muted the promptings of sex solidarity and the name of feminism. In part that stemmed from a desire to be effective with men—which is to say, to be to some extent conciliatory. Thus Molly Dewson, head of the Women's Division of the Democratic Party in the 1930s, who probably accomplished more than any single person besides Eleanor Roosevelt to increase women's role in national politics under FDR, wrote to a presidential aide, "Mac, I am not a feminist. I am a practical politician out to build up the Democratic Party where it sorely needs it." In part that attitude stemmed from a desire not to limit women to being "only" women. Thus Sara Fredgant, an Amalgamated Clothing Workers officer in workers' education, reflected that her work in the 1930s had not been aggressively feminist because "I had so many more concerns. I was concerned about women. That's true. I wanted women in a position of leadership. I worked with women. I wanted them to assume more leadership. But I also worked in a field where there were other important parts which I wanted them to be active in and to participate in and to make their contribution as *human beings* and as *workers,* and not only as women."[16]

There was the Feminist legacy and the feminist paradox: how to be human beings and women too. Women in the interwar period were uncomfortably aware of the liabilities of making reductive generalizations about women as a group. Eleanor Roosevelt described the problem concisely when she wrote in 1940, "women must become more conscious of themselves as women and of their ability to function as a group. At the same time they must try to wipe from men's consciousness the need to consider them as a group or as women in their everyday activities, especially as workers in industry or the professions."[17] If heterogeneity among women was a fact that posed new difficulties for feminism, the opposing conventional roster of stereotypes and preconceptions about women as a sex and how they differed from men posed old ones. Centuries-long tradition equating women's differences from men with inferiority meant that an articulation of sexual differences always risked reconfirming rather than subverting gender hierarchy. As proponents of sex-based protective legislation inadvertently revealed, emphasis on how women's needs and predilections differed from men's could easily slide into conformity with conventional stereotypes or, worse, with eternal prescriptions. In the attempt to talk about women's likeness or solidarity in political and social life, all the sex prejudices that feminists had for decades been trying to unseat—the very prejudicial assumptions that had required a counteremphasis on equality—inevitably got in the way. In the modern era both social science and popular media were rife with characterizations of women's temperamental, psychological, and somatic differences from men. More than matters of popular gossip, femininity and masculinity were matters for scientific judgment as never before. Gender themes pervaded twentieth-century language, usually without acknowledgment. The more that science, religion, or politics baroquely specified how women still did differ from men, the more that women leaders, with few exceptions, emphasized equality of opportunity and "disregard" of sex. They joined in a pervasively duplicitous discourse in which profound sex differences were presumed to motivate men and women in private (where women were women) and yet to be absent— disregarded—in the public arena where women as individuals were to have the same access as men.

A third reason that persuasive rendition of women's solidarity or con- sciousness as a political class escaped beyond reach was that incipient attempts at it were quashed and tabooed, or translated from political to sexual categories. Where equality of opportunity was a widely acceptable reasoning, a woman bloc was not. Once women gained the vote and nominal entry to normal political channels, political solidarity on the ba- sis of sex was seen by male politicians as an ideological as well as practical threat and was magnified into sex war. Women's desire to team with women was labeled lesbianism. If the divisions of opinion among women themselves did not dissuade potential adherents from feminist thought and action, they were warned off on the one side by risks of the con- straints of sex stereotyping, and on the other by accusations of sex antag- onism. Little wonder that the self-titled "serious young" declared that the first thing for women in the modern world to leave behind was "sex- consciousness."[18]

There was a little groundswell of opposing opinion in the early 1930s that recognized and responded to the monotone in the feminist chorus on equality of opportunity (or disregard of sex). A few women began to stress from a feminist point of view that women had to "regard" sex. They criticized women's adherence to male norms in the economic and politi- cal world, arguing that by so assimilating, women were devaluing them- selves. These voices stressed that women had to be loyal to and respect women if they were to share full humanity with men both individually and collectively. Emily Newell Blair, who had taken a leading role among Democrats during the 1920s on the assumption that integration of women into the political parties was the route to shared political power, came to advocate the formation of women's blocs in the parties by 1930 and envisioned women gaining economic power by taking over certain industries in which they had some foothold. Historian Mary Beard developed a powerful critique of the way higher education on the male model had "deepened the intellectual cowardice" of women, making them into spokeswomen for institutional and cultural priorities defined by men, with the result that the "best"-educated women reduced to a whisper the influence of women in society.[19]

Two psychiatrists, Beatrice Hinkle and Olga Knopf, beginning from different psychological perspectives, arrived at similar analyses stressing the extent to which women had accepted the domination of "masculine methods and attitudes." Women active outside the home had become, in Hinkle's words, "almost wholly identified with masculine psychology," thus ironically remaining in a state of "psychic dependence" on men and failing to trust their own strengths. "Women have lived so long in the belief that they are the inferior part of mankind that it is still hard for them to accept their equality, no matter how firmly they seem to demand recognition as equals," Knopf similarly observed. She was guided by the "the most thoroughgoing identification" and "feeling of solidarity with women" as she aimed to set women on a constructive course, neither self-belittling nor overly aggressive. Perhaps women such as Hinkle and Knopf, Blair and Beard spoke up because they recognized that the younger generation were not moved by equality of opportunity as a feminist agenda; perhaps they rose to make feminist answer to the constricting emphasis in popular culture on heterosexual allure and on women's domestic and childrearing roles. These few voices edged toward insisting on equality with difference, reminding others of what was not being said by a feminism centered on equality of opportunity.[20]

"Today women are in a mighty struggle toward differentiation and individual direction," Beatrice Hinkle judged in 1925, but she saw it as a collective phenomenon: "comparatively few women are aware of the great new issues to which they are contributing any more than the common soldier is aware of what he is fighting for in war. They are consciously concerned only with their individual problems and welfare." Striking the individual pose supplied an interim solution, or substitution, for a more programmatic or collective way of asserting women's simultaneous equality to and difference from men. Women's desires to rise from submergence in family claims, to take the liberty of acting as individuals, to "break into the human race," had vivified Feminism in the 1910s. Like the ideal of equality of opportunity, the ideal of individual achievement had venerable supports in American ideology, and it was newly shored up in the 1920s by state rhetoric as well as private enterprise. (While Herbert Hoover vigorously promoted organizational development and corporate–state cooperation, he heralded "the new individualism.") For women who imagined the resolution of the woman question in terms of individual advances—as did most women who succeeded in business and the professions, and those who gained influence under the New Deal—the individual line was a way to take intragroup diversities among women into account and to sidestep the pitfalls of conceptualizing women as a gender group. Individualism was a progressive but partial demand for women in the mid-twentieth century. The resort to individualism took the feminist standpoint that women's freedoms and opportunities should be no less than men's, but individualism offered no way to achieve the goal except acting as though it had already been obtained. Although it produced outstanding models of individual accomplishment, it could not engender a program for change in the position of women as a group.[21]

In the late 1920s, Miriam Allen de Ford, at age forty, reviewed with satisfaction her now "reasoned and calm" feminism. She was willing to admit there might be some mental differences between the sexes, but she considered more important her operative premise that "the broad unsexual world of activity lies before every human being, and it is not divided into 'his sphere' and 'her sphere.'" She was proud that she had never been economically dependent since childhood, although she had married twice. A writer by trade, she maintained, "I want my work considered as mine, not as some *tour de force* or bit of presumptuous rivalry on the part of an eccentric member of an excluded group. . . . I want to stand before the world and say: 'I am myself. I have defects, weaknesses and faults. I want them judged as mine—not as a woman's. I would rather fail as myself, than succeed because of some accident. And sex is the merest accident of all the tricks that heredity plays upon us.'" Here was the appeal of individualism—and its risks. Rejecting and leaving behind the dependency and limits of woman's sphere, de Ford had no analysis of the sex/gender system with which to replace it. Almost half a century later, interviewed about her political past, de Ford said of the 1920s, "there were plenty of feminists and you knew who they were and

they wrote individually, or spoke individually, but there was no organized movement outside of birth control. There was nothing for them,
they had no organ, no avenue, to speak through. . . . I didn't change any
of my own feelings but there wasn't anything, no movement, nothing to
join. The only thing was that if, individually, anybody had anything to
say, I told them what I thought." [22] If de Ford actually felt in the 1920s
that there was no movement, no organ or avenue for feminists, that was
in part because she preferred to exert herself in the "broad unsexual
world of activity." Similarly, already in 1919 a group of female literary
radicals in Greenwich Village—the very grassroots of Feminism—had
founded a new journal on the thinking, "we're interested in people
now—not in men and women." They declared that moral, social, economic, and political standards "should not have anything to do with sex,"
promised to be "pro-woman without being anti-man," and called their
stance "post-feminist." [23]

Whether de Ford's memory should be seen as accurate (since there
was no one obvious and unified women's movement) or inaccurate (since
she skipped over the many different vortexes of organized women that
there were), it is clear that for her, as for many other "edgy" women at
the time, feminism was an impulse that was impossible to translate into
a program without centrifugal results. For decades after the 1920s, de-
centralization and diversification, competition and even sectarianism
were the hallmarks of efforts to define women's interests and work toward parity between the sexes. The problems and promises made visible
between 1910 and 1930—persistent structures and ideologies of male
dominance, women's assertions of their heterogeneous and conflicting
interests—reverberated through the twentieth century. Without coalescing into one movement, without mobilizing the mass, and often declining the label feminist, individual and group efforts nonetheless
sparked again and again. From Rose Arnold Powell's crusade to have
Susan B. Anthony's head carved on Mt. Rushmore to Mary Inman's internal critiques of the Communist Party, from the Lucy Stone League to
Women Strike for Peace, examples can be cited. [24]

The unfulfilled agenda of 1910s Feminism carrying over the decades
made a subsequent mass women's movement necessary as much as it
made it possible. Modern feminism had defined for itself the problem:
its mandate to see women unbound, its many practitioners' investment
in individual self-expression and realization of individual and intragroup
particularities, warred with the view of the world as divided by sex that
was necessary to power a movement of women. Yet this tension between

heterogeneity and common cause was a vital ambivalence, which needed to be embraced rather than avoided under the name *feminism*. The fracturing of the nineteenth century's singular *woman* was a success of the movement. When feminism sprang vocally to life in the 1960s and 1970s, it took new plural forms: women's rights, women's liberation, the women's movement. The women's liberation movement invoked a new ruling fiction of what women shared, a positive concept that women constituted a "sex-class." The new analysis of sexual politics ended disregard of sex. It was steeped in analogues and models of social group oppression. It required a challenge to sexual hierarchy in private as well as public roles and perception of the interrelation between the two. The path that spokeswomen of the 1960s took to arrive at such findings, over which masses of women also thronged, depended on the predisposing ground of that time just as the mass movement of the 1910s depended on its time and place. Feminism takes part in and comprises part of the general cultural order while it has its own tradition and logic. More than half a century after *feminism* came into American language, women reclaimed it, as a term of unity, to transcend the divisions between women's liberation and women's rights. The story of feminism in the late twentieth century continues, as not only women but also feminisms grow toward the plural.

ABBREVIATIONS USED IN NOTES

Manuscript Collections

BVI: Bureau of Vocational Information Collection, SL
DSC: uncatalogued collection of Doris Stevens's papers at SL (distinct from another collection of her papers there which *is* catalogued). I have cited her original folders as I found them.
JNSC: Jane Norman Smith Collection, SL
NWP #: National Woman's Party Papers, 1913–1974 (Microfilming Corporation of America, 1979), with reel number
WRC: Woman's Rights Collection, SL

Libraries

BL: Bancroft Library, University of California, Berkeley
HI: Hoover Institution Archives, Stanford, California
HL: The Huntington Library, San Marino, California
LC: The Library of Congress, Manuscripts and Archives Division
NYPL: Rare Books and Manuscripts Division, The New York Public Library, Asper, Lenox and Tilden Foundations
SCPC: Swarthmore College Peace Collection, Swarthmore, Pennsylvania
SL: The Arthur and Elizabeth Schlesinger Library on the History of Women in America, Radcliffe College, Cambridge, Massachusetts
SSC: Sophia Smith Collection Archives, Smith College, Northampton, Massachusetts

Journals

AAAPSS: *Annals of the American Academy of Political and Social Science*
AHR: *American Historical Review*
AQ: *American Quarterly*
ER: *Equal Rights* (the journal of the National Woman's Party)
FS: *Feminist Studies*

Indep. W.: Independent Woman (the journal of the National Federation of Business and Professional Women)

JAAUW: *Journal of the American Association of University Women*

JAH: *Journal of American History*

TNR: *The New Republic*

Other

AP OH, JR OH, MV OH, RHR OH, SBF OH; transcripts (at SL) of the Suffragists Oral History Project, Bancroft Library, University of California, Berkeley, as follows:

AP OH: "Conversations with Alice Paul," interview by Amelia R. Fry, © 1976.

JR OH: "Jeannette Rankin: Activist for World Peace, Women's Rights, and Democratic Government," interview by Malca Chall and Hannah Josephson, © 1974.

MV OH: "Mabel Vernon: Speaker for Suffrage and Petitioner for Peace," interview by Amelia R. Fry, © 1976.

RHR OH: "Rebecca Hourwich Reyher: Search and Struggle for Independence," interview by Amelia Fry and Fern Ingersoll, © 1977.

SBF OH: "Sara Bard Field, Poet and Suffragist," interview by Amelia R. Fry (1959–1963), with introduction by Dorothy Erskine, © 1979.

WBB #: U.S. Department of Labor, Women's Bureau Bulletin, with number.

NAW I,II,III: *Notable American Women,* ed. Edward T. James and Janet Wilson James (Cambridge, Harvard University Press, 1971), 3 vols.

NAW IV: *Notable American Women: The Modern Period,* ed. Barbara Sicherman and Carol Hurd Greed (Cambridge, Harvard University Press, 1980).

NOTES

INTRODUCTION

1. Note Sidonie Gruenberg's remark, in a 1916 publication, "It is not so many years since the champions of 'woman's rights' (there were no 'feminists' in those days) felt it incumbent upon them to prove that woman is man's equal in every respect." *Sons and Daughters* (N.Y., Henry Holt, 1916), 55. Chap. 1 discusses the birth of the term *feminism*.

2. An exception is Mari Jo Buhle, *Women and American Socialism, 1870–1920* (Urbana, U. Ill. P., 1981), 290–97. Two historians, Eleanor Flexner, in *Century of Struggle: The Woman's Rights Movement in the United States* (1959; repr. N.Y., Atheneum, 1970), and Aileen S. Kraditor, in *The Ideas of the Woman Suffrage Movement, 1890–1920* (1965, repr. Garden City, Anchor, 1971), scrupulously did not use the term *feminism* in reference to the nineteenth-century woman's rights movement, but virtually all more recent historians do, e.g., William P. O'Neill, *Everyone Was Brave: A History of Feminism in America* (Chicago, Quadrangle, 1969); Ellen Carol Dubois, *Feminism and Suffrage: The Emergence of an Independent Women's Movement in America, 1848–1869* (Ithaca, Cornell U.P., 1978); William Leach, *True Love and Perfect Union: The Feminist Reform of Sex and Society* (N.Y., Basic, 1980). I did so, too, in *The Bonds of Womanhood: "Woman's Sphere" in New England, 1780–1835* (New Haven, Yale U.P., 1977).

In assessing the 1920s, historians have focused on disenchantment with politics after the end of the suffrage movement, and discouragement in the face of continued male resistance to women's gains in politics and the workplace; they have stressed divisions between organized women around the equal rights amendment and have discussed the inhospitable climate for feminist goals because of state authorities' and public opinion's postwar reaction against all efforts that smacked of radicalism. Historians of the period have treated the substitution of heterosexual freedoms for social goals collectively defined by women and have suggested the ways that new uses of psychology and advertising wielded by experts, and new consumer habits encouraged by large corporations, superficially assimilated women's "emancipation" and enforced modern versions of conventional gender bounds. See O'Neill, *Everyone Was Brave*; William H. Chafe, *The American Woman: Her Changing Social, Economic, and Political Roles, 1920–1970* (N.Y., Oxford U.P., 1972), 3–132; J. Stanley Lemons, *The Woman Citizen: Social Feminism in the 1920s* (Urbana, U. Illinois P., 1973); Mary P. Ryan, *Womanhood in America*, 2d ed. (N.Y., Franklin Watts, 1975), 151–82; Sheila Rothman, *Woman's Proper Place* (N.Y., Basic, 1978), 97–220; Estelle Freedman, "Separatism as Strategy: Female Institution-Building and American Feminism, 1870–1930," *FS* 5 (Fall 1979), 512–29; Rayna Rapp and

Ellen Ross, "The Twenties' Backlash: Compulsory Heterosexuality, the Consumer Family, and the Waning of Feminism," in *Class, Race and Sex: The Dynamics of Control*, ed. Amy Swerdlow and Hanna Messinger (Boston, G. K. Hall, 1983), 93–107.

3. *Oxford English Dictionary . . . Supplement* (Oxford, Oxford U.P., 1933), 362–63. The word feminism did not appear in the earlier OED, except as a "rare" equivalent to "womanism." Beatrice Gottlieb warns against using the word *feminism* before the modern period in "Is Feminism the Opposite of Misogyny? A Problem in Historical Methods and Vocabulary," paper presented at the Columbia University Seminar on the Renaissance, Mar. 20, 1984 [in my possession], and in "The Problem of Feminism in the Fifteenth Century," in *Women in the Medieval World*, ed. Julius Kirschner and Suzanne F. Wemple (Oxford, Basil Blackwell, 1985).

4. An essay by Jean Bethke Elshtain, "The Feminist Movement and the Question of Equality," *Polity* 7 (Summer 1975), 452–77, provides a good starting point from which to consider equality in the different arenas of rights, opportunities, and treatment.

5. On historians' employment of the new concept of gender, see Joan W. Scott, "Gender: A Useful Category of Historical Analysis," *AHR* 91:5 (Dec. 1986), 1053–75; and on the historical dynamic within feminism, see Introduction to *A Heritage of Her Own*, ed. Nancy F. Cott and Elizabeth H. Pleck (N.Y., Simon and Schuster, 1979), esp. 11–13.

6. Virginia Sapiro, in "When Are Interests Interesting? The Problem of Political Representation of Women," *Amer. Polit. Science Review* 75 (1981), 710, also uses a tripartite working definition of feminism, differing slightly from mine but not inconsistent with it. In her view feminism is characterized by (1) belief that women's opportunities are limited categorically by sex; (2) desire to release women from such constraints; and (3) belief in group action as well as individual action.

7. Simone de Beauvoir, *The Second Sex* (orig. 1949), trans. H. M. Parshley (N.Y., Vintage, 1974), xxii; Mary Ritter Beard to Florence Kitchelt, Jun. 29, 1950, folder 113, Kitchelt Collection, SL. I allude to the title of Joan Cassell, *A Group Called Women: Sisterhood and Symbolism in the Feminist Movement* (N.Y., David McKay, 1977). Note the useful discussion of stages of women's group consciousness and action in William H. Chafe, *Women and Equality* (N.Y., Oxford U.P., 1977), 3–11, and the discussion of women as a group in history in Hilda Smith, "Feminism and the Methodology of Women's History" in *Liberating Women's History*, ed. Berenice Carroll (Urbana, U. Illinois P., 1976), 368–73.

8. Margaret Fuller, *Woman in the Nineteenth Century* (1855; repr. N.Y., Norton, 1971), 174. The shape of feminism in the United States also reflects the tendency of indigenous American radicalism to be highly individualistic; cf. Eric Foner, "Why Is There No Socialism in the United States?" *History Workshop Journal* 17 (Spring 1984), 63.

9. The otherwise adept survey by Richard J. Evans, *The Feminists: Women's Emancipation Movements in Europe, America and Australasia, 1840–1920* (N.Y., Barnes and Noble, 1977), misses a dimension of its subject by seeing feminism narrowly as a particular expression of liberalism; cf. Zillah Eisenstein, *The Radical Future of Liberal Feminism* (N.Y., Longman, 1981), for analysis of the ways feminism breaks the bounds of liberalism by constituting women as a "sex-class."

10. See chap. 1 for discussion of the suffrage movement in the 1910s.

1. THE BIRTH OF FEMINISM

1. "The Revolt of the Women," *Century* 87 (April 1914), 964; Edna Kenton, "Feminism Will Give—Men More Fun, Women Greater Scope . . . ," *Delineator* 85 (July 1914), 17; Marie Jenny Howe, "Feminism," in "A Feminist Symposium," *The New Review* 2 (Aug. 1914), 441. The *Reader's Guide to Periodical Literature* first indexed the subject heading "Feminism" in the 1910–14 volume, and 40 articles (more than in any of the subsequent five volumes) were listed thereunder, none earlier than 1911.

2. Warner Fite, "The Feminist Mind," *Nation* 96 (Feb. 6, 1913), 123–26, and note an acerbic rebuttal to his review by Charlotte Perkins Gilman under "Comment and Review" in her journal *The Forerunner* 4 (Mar. 1913), 82–84; Floyd Dell, *Women as World Builders: Studies in Modern Feminism* (Chicago, Forbes, 1913); on Rodman, see June Sochen, *The New Woman: Feminism in Greenwich Village, 1910–1920* (N.Y., Quadrangle, 1972); Theda Bara quoted in 1915 in Lary May, *Screening Out the Past* (N.Y., Oxford U.P., 1980), 106; Hughes quoted from the *New York Times*, Aug. 1, 1916, in Christine Lunardini, *From Equal Suffrage to Equal Rights: Alice Paul and the National Woman's Party, 1913–1928* (N.Y., New York U.P., 1986), 92; copy of letter from Missouri Anti-Suffrage League to all candidates for office in St. Louis, Jun. 24, 1918, in folder 14, Edna Gellhorn Coll., SL.

3. Alice Hubbard, "Something New under the Sun," *Harper's Weekly* 58 (Dec. 13, 1913), 7; see also editor Norman Hapgood's essay, "What Women Are After," ibid. (Aug. 13, 1913), 28–29, and Inez Milholland, "The Liberation of a Sex," *McClure's* 40:4 (Feb. 1913), 181; Charlotte Perkins Gilman, "What Is Feminism?" *Boston Sunday Herald*, Sep. 3, 1916, and see also "Is Feminism Really So Dreadful? Listen to Charlotte Perkins Gilman," *Delineator* 85 (Aug. 1914), 6; "Mrs. Catt on Feminism," *Woman's Journal*, Jan. 9, 1915, 12. The same text by Catt was reprinted in 1917 by the NAWSA as a flyer titled "Feminism and Suffrage." Copy in folder 9, box 1, Catt Coll., SSC. The flyer notes, "reprinted from the *New York Times*, Feb. 15, 1914."

4. On early French uses of *feminisme*, I am indebted to personal communications from Claire G. Moses (Feb. 27, 1985) and Steven Hause (Mar. 5, 1985). Though the term is often attributed to Fourier, Moses' search of his works has found no use of it. Hause has completed a biography of Auclert to be published by Yale U.P. in 1987, and is my authority for her early use of the terms *feminisme* and *feministe*. See Steven C. Hause and Anne R. Kenney, "The Limits of Suffrage Behavior: Legalism and Militancy in France, 1876–1922," *AHR* 86:4 (Oct. 1981), 781–806; Steven C. Hause with Anne R. Kenney, *Women's Suffrage and Social Politics in the French Third Republic* (Princeton, Princeton U.P., 1984) esp. 36–42; Claire G. Moses, *French Feminism in the Nineteenth Century* (Albany, SUNY P., 1984). The first usage in English cited in the *Oxford English Dictionary . . . Supplement* (Oxford, Oxford U.P., 1933) for *feminist* (rather than *feminism*), is dated 1894 and refers to a group in the Paris Chamber of Deputies. "Feminism in Some European Countries," *Review of Reviews* [N.Y.] 33 (Mar. 1906), 357–60. (The *Review of Reviews* was a New York branch of the English publication of the same name edited by William Stead.) Another early essay, "Feminism in Politics" by W. M. Lightbody, likewise appeared in an American version of a London serial, the *Westminister Review* 171 (Jan. 1909), 48–53. I owe my awareness of "Suffragism Not Feminism," *The American Suffragette* (Dec. 1909), to Ellen DuBois, who kindly provided me with a photocopy.

5. Kenton, "Feminism Will Give," 17; Winifred Harper Cooley, "The Younger Suffragists," *Harper's Weekly* 58 (Sep. 27, 1913), 7–8.

6. In Gerda Lerner's formulation of "women's rights" and "women's emancipation," the former includes actions to achieve for women the same civil, legal, and economic rights and opportunities men have in existing societal structures and institutions; the latter, more directly threatening existing values and institutions, concerns efforts to gain "freedom from oppressive restrictions imposed by sex; self-determination; and autonomy." "Women's Rights and American Feminism" (1971), in *Majority Finds Its Past* (N.Y., Oxford U.P., 1979), 48–49, and reiterated in the Appendix to *The Creation of Patriarchy* (N.Y., Oxford U.P., 1986), 236–37.

7. The secondary sources most influential on my interpretation of the nineteenth-century background are Olive Banks, *Faces of Feminism* (N.Y., St. Martin's, 1981); Steven M. Buechler, *The Transformation of the Woman Suffrage Movement: The Case of Illinois, 1850–1920* (New Brunswick, Rutgers U.P., 1986); Mari Jo Buhle, *Women and American Socialism* (Urbana, U. Illinois P., 1981); Ellen Carol DuBois, *Feminism and Suffrage* (Ithaca, Cornell U.P., 1978), and *Elizabeth Cady Stanton/Susan B. Anthony: Correspondence, Writings, Speeches* (N.Y., Schocken, 1981); Zillah Eisenstein, *The Radical Future of Liberal Feminism* (N.Y., Longman, 1981); Barbara Epstein, *The Politics of Domesticity* (Middletown, Conn., Wesleyan U.P., 1981); Richard J. Evans, *The Feminists: Women's Emancipation Movements in Europe, America and Australasia 1840–1920* (N.Y., Barnes and Noble, 1977); Eleanor Flexner, *Century of Struggle: The Woman's Rights Movement in the United States* (1959, repr. N.Y., Atheneum, 1970); Dolores Hayden, *The Grand Domestic Revolution* (Cambridge, MIT P., 1981); Aileen S. Kraditor, *The Ideas of the Woman Suffrage Movement, 1890–1920* (1965, repr. Garden City, Anchor, 1971); William Leach, *True Love and Perfect Union* (N.Y., Basic, 1980); William O'Neill, *Everyone was Brave* (Chicago, Quadrangle, 1969); Alice Rossi, ed., *The Feminist Papers* (N.Y., Columbia U.P., 1973).

8. See esp. Dubois, *Feminism and Suffrage;* Buechler, *Transformation;* Jack S. Blocker, Jr., "Separate Paths: Suffragists and the Women's Temperance Crusade," *Signs* 10:3 (Spring 1985), 460–76; and Jeanne Madeline Weimann, *The Fair Women: The Story of the Woman's Building . . . Chicago 1893* (Chicago, Academy, 1980).

9. Mary Austin, *Earth Horizon: Autobiography* (Boston, Houghton Mifflin, 1932), 128. See also Miriam Allen de Ford, "Feminism, Cause or Effect," box 573, de Ford papers, San Francisco Historical Society; Carrie Chapman Catt, "Why I Have Found Life Worth Living," *Christian Century*, Mar. 29, 1928, Catt Papers, LC reel 9; Rheta Childe Dorr, *A Woman of Fifty* (N.Y., Funk and Wagnalls, 1924), 13.

10. Elizabeth Cady Stanton, "Address to the Legislature of New York on Women's Rights," Feb. 14, 1854, in DuBois, ECS/SBA, 50–51; *The Lily* 8:23 (Dec. 1, 1856).

Taking a slightly different slant, Kraditor, in *Ideas*, characterized these two approaches as the natural rights or "justice" argument, and the argument from "expediency." Kraditor's term *expediency* has been taken up by subsequent historians principally as a term of disparagement, but Kraditor implicated in it a full range of meaning about the instrumentality of civic rights for women, including the possibility of social justice and self-protection as well as class domination or social control. Kraditor emphasized that "justice" arguments dominated in the mid-nineteenth century, and "expediency" after the turn of the century but—little noticed—she acknowledged the coexistence of both kinds of arguments all along (38–43, 87–91). More recent historians have made it clear that both kinds of arguments were used throughout, although "justice" arguments may have been deployed more instrumentally in the 1910s. See Leach, *True Love*, esp. 8, 276–87; Carole Nichols, "Votes and More for Women: Suffrage and After in Connecticut," *Women and History* 5 (Spring 1983), 29–30; Buechler, *Transformation*, 99, 193–94; Dale Spender, ed., *Feminist Theorists* (N.Y., Pantheon, 1983), esp. Jenny Uglow, "Josephine Butler: From Sympathy to Theory," 146–64; and Felice Gordon, *After Winning: The Legacy of the New Jersey Suffragists* (New Brunswick, Rutgers U.P., 1986), 9, 18–20.

11. Wallace quoted in Buhle, *Women and American Socialism*, 68. Cf. Mary Livermore, an Illinois veteran of the U.S. Sanitary Commission, who stood for "womanliness" and Christian service, and nonetheless wrote in founding her newspaper the *Agitator* in 1869, "Nothing less than admission in law, and in fact, to equality in all rights, political, civil and social, with the male citizens of the community, will answer the demands now being made for American women." *Agitator*, Mar. 13, 1869, 4, quoted in Buechler, *Transformation*, 77–78.

12. Austin, *Earth Horizon*, 156.

13. Laidlaw quoted in Kraditor, *Ideas*, 91; Elizabeth M. Walling (Victor, N.H.) to Caroline Lexow, Dec. 31, 1907, folder 1, Caroline Lexow Babcock Coll., SL.

14. For introductions to the period, see Richard M. Abrams, "Reform and Uncertainty: America Enters the Twentieth Century, 1900–1918," in William Leuchtenberg, ed., *The Unfinished Century* (Boston, Little Brown, 1973), 1–111; Henry F. May, *The End of American Innocence* (N.Y., Knopf, 1959); Peter Conn, *The Divided Mind: Ideology and Imagery in America, 1898–1917* (N.Y., Cambridge U.P., 1983); Lillian Symes and Travers Clement, *Rebel America* (N.Y., Harper, 1934), 213–312.

15. On women's occupational, educational, and professional advance, see Alice Kessler-Harris, *Out to Work: A History of Wage-Earning Women in the United States.* (N.Y., Oxford U.P., 1982), esp. 108–79; Margaret Rossiter, *Women Scientists in America* (Baltimore, Johns Hopkins U.P., 1982), 1–99; Barbara Solomon, *In the Company of Educated Women* (New Haven, Yale U.P., 1985), 43–140; Kathryn K. Sklar, "Hull House in the 1890s," *Signs* 10:4 (Summer 1985), 658–77; Lynn Weiner, *From Working Girl to Working Mother* (Chapel Hill, UNC P., 1985).

16. Cf. Buhle, *Women and American Socialism*, 161–62. On urban social life, see Lewis Erenberg, *Steppin' Out: New York Night Life and the Transformation of American Culture, 1890–1930* (Westport, Conn., Greenwood, 1981), and Kathy Peiss, *Cheap Amusements* (Philadelphia, Temple U.P., 1986).

17. See Kessler-Harris, *Out to Work*, esp. 151–64; Philip S. Foner, *Women and the American Labor Movement* (N.Y., Free Press, 1979), 1:324–90; and Joan M. Jensen and Sue Davidson, eds., *A Needle, A Bobbin, A Strike: Women Needleworkers in America*, (Philadelphia, Temple U.P., 1984), 81–182. According to Kessler-Harris (152), about 3.3 percent of women industrial workers in 1900 were unionized, and 6.6 percent of all women wage-earners in 1920 (nearly half of these in the clothing trades).

18. Dorr, *A Woman of Fifty*, 164.

19. Gertrude Barnum, in Ida Husted Harper, ed., *History of Woman Suffrage* (N.Y., 1922), 165, quoted in Ellen Dubois, "Harriot Stanton Blatch and the Progressive Era Woman Suffrage Movement," paper presented at the Sixth Berkshire Conference on Women's History, Jun. 1984, 4. My interpretation of

and quotations from Blatch rely on Ellen DuBois, "Working Women, Class Relations, and Suffrage Militance: Harriot Stanton Blatch and the New York Woman Suffrage Movement, 1894–1909," JAH 74 (June 1987). See also "Suffragists and 'Suffragettes': A Record of Actual Achievement," by Winifred Harper Cooley, *The World Today* 15 (Oct. 1908), 1066–67; Harriot Stanton Blatch and Alma Lutz, *Challenging Years: The Memoirs of Harriot Stanton Blatch* (N.Y., G. P. Putnam's Sons, 1940), 93–94, 107–13, 129.

20. On IWSA, see Flexner, *Century*, 238; on European women's movements, see Evans, *Feminists*, 80–84, 90–91, 106–08, 133–35, 161–68; Ann Taylor Allen, "Mothers of the New Generation: Adele Schreiber, Helene Stocker, and the Evolution of a German Idea of Motherhood, 1900–1914," *Signs* 10:3 (Spring 1985), 418–38; Hause and Kenney, "The Limits of Suffrage Behavior"; Susan Groag Bell and Karen Offen, eds., *Women, the Family and Freedom* (Stanford, Stanford U.P., 1983), 2:105–06, 228–32.

21. See DuBois, "Working Women."

22. Breaking windows, setting railway carriages and empty buildings aflame, the WSPU were by 1913 destroying property worth thousands of pounds each month. The pacific forms of militance spread rapidly among suffragists in England: the larger and more moderate National Union of Women's Suffrage Societies joined in mass marches and street demonstrations. Anita Augsberg and Lida Gustava Heymann in Germany, Rosika Schwimmer in Hungary, Hubertine Auclert and Madeleine Pelletier in France inaugurated street marches and publicity-gathering civil disobedience in their own countries, though militance was neither persuasive nor widely adopted by suffragists on the Continent. See Evans, *Feminists*, 190–94; Ray Strachey, *The Cause: A Short History of the Women's Movement in Great Britain* (1929, repr. London, Virago, 1978), chaps. 15–16; cf. Andrew Rosen, *Rise Up, Women! The Militant Campaign of the Women's Social and Political Union, 1903–1914* (London, Routledge and Kegan Paul, 1974); and Antonia Raeburn, *The Militant Suffragettes* (London, Michael Joseph, 1973).

23. Evans, *Feminists*, 189–93; see also Dubois, "Harriot Stanton Blatch." On Catt, see Flexner, *Century*, 254, and Carrie Chapman Catt to Millicent Fawcett, Oct. 19, 1909, Catt Papers, LC reel 3; Inez Haynes Gillmore Irwin, "Adventures of Yesterday," autobiography, esp. 456, folder 11, box 3, Irwin Coll., SL; on Anne Martin, MV OH, 84–86. Joan Dash, in *A Life of One's Own* (N.Y., Harper and Row, 1972), 162, says Milholland was arrested in London; but her biography in NAW does not confirm that. Dorr first met the Pankhursts in London in 1906 and returned to New York determined to emulate them, "fighting" rather than "pleading" for the vote. In her autobiography she reflected that it was the English example that moved American women to see theirs as a movement demanding "political" methods; *Woman of Fifty*, chap. 9, esp. 159. On Mrs. Pankhurst's influence in Hartford, CT see Nichols, "Votes and More," 13–14. Margaret Foley and Florence Luscomb, young Massachusetts suffragists, stopped in England to study the suffragettes on their way to the meeting of the IWSA in Stockholm in 1911 and brought home what they learned; see Sharon Hartman Strom, "Leadership and Tactics in the American Woman Suffrage Movement: A New Perspective from Massachusetts," JAH 62 (1975), 296–315. It was probably then too that Luscomb purchased Olive Schreiner's just-published *Woman and Labor;* the 1911 London imprint with Luscomb's name in it now resides in the SL.

24. DuBois, "Working Women"; Dorr, *Woman of Fifty*, 219–22; Mrs. B.

Boorrman Wells, "The Militant Movement for Woman Suffrage," *Independent* 64 (Apr. 1908), 901–03; Elinor Lerner, "Jewish Involvement in the New York City Woman Suffrage Movement," *American Jewish History* 70 (1981), 444–46.

25. See Flexner, *Century,* 250–54; Anne F. Scott and Andrew M. Scott, *One Half the People: The Fight for Woman Suffrage* (Philadelphia, Lippincott, 1975), 29–30; Rheta Childe Dorr, *What Eight Million Women Want* (Boston, Small Maynard, 1910), 295–96; Strom, "Leadership," 296–315; Nichols, "Votes and More," 12–18; DuBois, "Working Women," and Mrs. B. Boorrman Wells, "Militant Movement."

26. Doris Daniels, "Building a Winning Coalition: The Suffrage Fight in New York State," *N.Y. Hist.* 60 (Jan. 1979), 58–80; Ronald Schaffer, "The New York City Woman Suffrage Party, 1909–1919," ibid. 53 (Jul. 1962), esp. 270; Buechler, *Transformation,* 151–53; and Ronald Schaffer, "The Problem of Consciousness in the Woman Suffrage Movement: A California Perspective," *Pacific Historical Review* 45 (Nov. 1976), 469–93 (quoting Edson on 478–79). Californian Alice Park, never at a loss for a political gesture, for the next several years listed her residence on hotel registers as "Palo Alto, California, where women vote." Alice Park autobiography, HL. For context of other issues on the California ballot in 1911 when the woman suffrage referendum passed, see James Weinstein, *The Corporate Ideal in the Liberal State* (Boston, Beacon P., 1968), 173–78. On that voting day in the Los Angeles mayoral primary, the socialist candidate polled 20,137 votes, the "good government" candidate 16,790, and the Republican 8,009.

The prior gains for woman suffrage can be quickly summarized. As territories, both Wyoming and Utah allowed women to vote before 1870, and when each was granted statehood, in 1890 and 1896 respectively, that provision remained intact. Between 1870 and 1910, women suffragists mounted 480 campaigns, in 33 states, to have referenda offered to the voters; but only 55 referenda were held as a result, and only 2 of the 55 succeeded, in Colorado in 1893 and in Idaho in 1896. Washington, in 1910, was the first state gained since 1896. A referendum the same year in Oregon failed. See Buechler, *Transformation,* 11–13. See also Carl N. Degler, *At Odds: Women and the Family in America from the Revolution to the Present* (N.Y., Oxford U.P., 1980), 328–61, and on woman suffrage in the West, Sandra Myres, *Westering Women and the Frontier Experience* (Albuquerque, U. New Mexico P., 1982), 225–37, 338–39 n. 66; Ruth B. Moynihan, *Rebel for Rights: Abigail Scott Duniway* (New Haven, Yale U.P., 1983) esp. 214–17; Flexner, *Century,* 254–57; and Ronald Schaffer, "The Montana Woman Suffrage Campaign, 1911–14," *Pacific Northwest Quarterly* 55 (Jan. 1964), 9–15.

27. Mary Ware Dennett to Board Members, Dec. 1, 1910, quoted in Buechler, *Transformation,* 225; Olympia Brown to Catharine Waugh McCulloch, Jun. 25, 1911, folder 236, Dillon Coll., SL; Strom, "Leadership." The NAWSA as well as Blatch's Women's Political Union even made pro-suffrage films in the 1910s; see Kay Sloan, "Sexual Warfare in the Silent Cinema: Comedies and Melodramas of Woman Suffragism," *AQ* 33 (Fall 1981), 412–36.

28. Cf. John D. Buenker, "Essay," esp. 45–48, and John Burnham, "Essay," 5–6, in John D. Buenker, John C. Burnham, Robert C. Crunden, *Progressivism* (Cambridge, MA Schenkman, 1977).

29. Cf. Ellen DuBois, "The Radicalism of the Woman Suffrage Movement: Notes toward the Reconstruction of Nineteenth-Century Feminism," *FS* 3 (Fall 1975), 63–71; Marlene Stein Wortman, "Domesticating the Nineteenth-Century

American City," *Prospects* 3 (1977), 531–72; Paula Baker, "The Domestication of Politics: Women and American Political Society, 1780–1920," *AHR*, 89 (Jun. 1984), 620–47.

30. Carrie Chapman Catt, "Why Women Want to Vote," *The Woman's Journal*, Jan. 9, 1915, 11. See n. 10 above. Historians' conclusions about the "conservatism" of the 1910s suffrage movement have been skewed by exaggerating the thesis of Kraditor, *Ideas*, and by concentrating on the NAWSA leadership rather than the grassroots; see, e.g., Degler, *At Odds*, 357–60, and Evans, *Feminists*, 214–47. Buechler's interpretation in *Transformation* is more complicated but falters in defining the components of the suffrage movement consistently over time; it does not reflect the national developments of the 1910s because the study ends with the gaining of suffrage in Illinois in 1913.

31. Judith Smith, *Family Connections* (Albany, SUNY P., 1985), 156–57; Maxine Seller, "The Education of the Immigrant Woman, 1900–1935," *Journal of Urban History* 4 (May 1978), 325; Kathy Oberdeck, "From Wives, Sweethearts and Female Relatives to Sisterhood: The Seattle Women's Label League and *Seattle Union Record* Women's Pages, 1905–1918," unpubl. paper, Yale U., 1984 [in my possession], 15–16; Buhle, *Women and American Socialism*, 214–41.

32. Nancy Schrom Dye, *As Equals and as Sisters* (Columbia, U. Missouri P., 1980), 128–30; Buechler, *Transformation*, 157–62; quotation from Mollie Schepps in *Senators vs. Working Woman* (1912), pamphlet repr. in *America's Working Women*, ed. Rosalyn Baxandall et al. (N.Y., Random House, 1976), 218; Rose Schneiderman, with Lucy Goldthwaite, *All for One* (N.Y., Paul S. Eriksson, 1967), 123–24; Susan Porter Benson, "'The Customers Ain't God': The Work Culture of Department-Store Saleswomen," in *Working-Class America*, ed. Michael H. Frisch and Daniel J. Walkowitz (Urbana, U. Illinois P., 1983), 202, 211 n. 88; quotation from Helen Woodward, *Through Many Windows* (N.Y., Harper and Bros., 1926), 147. See also Flexner, *Century*, 240–93; Lerner, "Jewish Involvement," 442–61. Alice Paul, working with Dora Lewis's Political Equality League in Philadelphia on her return from London in 1911, asked Pauline Newman of the ILGWU to speak; Newman to Rose Schneiderman, Sep. 14, 1911, folder 77, Newman Coll., SL.

33. Anne Firor Scott, *The Southern Lady: From Pedestal to Politics* (Chicago, U. Chicago P., 1970), 177–80; Rosalyn Terborg-Penn, "Afro-Americans in the Struggle for Woman Suffrage," (Ph.D. diss., Howard U., 1977), esp. 265, 275–76, and "Discontented Black Feminists," in *Decades of Discontent*, ed. Lois Scharf and Joan Jensen (Westport, Conn., Greenwood, 1983), 261–66; Paula Giddings, *When and Where I Enter: The Impact of Black Women on Race and Sex in America* (N.Y., William Morrow, 1984), 69–71, 119–31, 159–65, on 121 quoting Nannie Helen Burroughs in the *Crisis* of 1915; Irene Diggs, "DuBois and Women: A Short Story of Black Women, 1910–1934," *A Current Bibiliography on African Affairs* 7 (Summer 1974), esp. 279–92, on 281 quoting Adella Hunt Logan from the *Crisis* of 1912. DuBois believed that "any agitation, discussion or reopening of the problem of voting must inevitably be a discussion of the right of black folk to vote. . . . Essentially the arguments for and against are the same in the case of all groups of human beings." He stressed, too, that "The actual work of the world today depends more largely upon women than upon men . . . it is inconceivable that any fair minded person could for a moment talk about a 'weaker' sex." Diggs, 290, quoting DuBois from the *Crisis* of 1912 and 1915.

34. Dorr, *Eight Million*, 288–90; Rossiter, *Women Scientists*, 102–15; Solomon, *Company*, 111–14; Caroline Lexow to Mamma, Feb. 8, 1909, folder 3,

Babcock Coll., SL; DuBois, "Working Women," 34; Buechler, *Transformation*, 150–51, 163–67; Mary Heaton Vorse to Family, Mar. 10, 1915, folder "1915—Jan.–Mar.," box 55, Vorse Coll., Walter Reuther Library. Vorse continued: "and here I pause to state that if only the Labour Party had a couple of women in it with the slave-driving capacity of Mrs. [Vera] Whitehouse . . . the chance of a social revolution happening within the next five centuries would be greatly increased, for believe me I have never seen any slave-driver able to crack the whip louder than that langorous [sic] southern beauty Mrs. Whitehouse." Whitehouse, an upper-class woman of Southern birth, endorsed the vote for black women rather than weaseling out of the question as did too many white suffragists. (See Diggs, "DuBois and Women.") She became an effective NWP worker.

35. Laidlaw to O'Reilly, Sep. 30, 1912, quoted in Mary Bularzik, "The Bonds of Belonging: Leonora O'Reilly and Social Reform," *Labor History* 24 (Winter 1983), 69; Maud Younger's unpublished autobiography, "Along the Way," NWP #114, and biographical sketch by Eleanor Flexner in *NAW* III, 699–700. See Jane Addams, "The Subjective Necessity for Social Settlements," originally written in 1892 and included in *Twenty Years at Hull House* (N.Y., Macmillan, 1910), chap. 6; Inez Haynes Gillmore, "Confessions of an Alien," and "The Life of an Average Woman," *Harper's Bazaar* 46 (Apr. and Jun. 1912); Christopher Lasch, *The New Radicalism in America: The Intellectual as a Social Type, 1889–1963* (N.Y., Knopf, 1965), and T. Jackson Lears, *No Place of Grace: Anti-Modernism and the Transformation of American Culture, 1880–1920* (N.Y., Pantheon, 1981).

36. Randolph Bourne to Prudence [Winterrowd], Apr. 28, 1913, box 1, Bourne Papers, Rare Book and Manuscript Library, Columbia U. Possibly Edna Kenton was one among the group of young women Bourne observed—his language is very similar to hers. For instance, he continued, "my salon says that their object is to restore 'charm' to life"; Kenton's article title claimed that "Feminism Will Give . . . Life More Charm." Cf. Lasch, *New Radicalism*, 69–103, and the example of Brenda Ueland, who came to New York in the spring of 1913 as a college student, as recalled in her autobiography, *Me* (N.Y., G.P. Putnam's Sons, 1939), esp. 105–06.

37. Sochen, *New Woman*, 28–34; Buhle, *Women and American Socialism*, 265–68, 282–83, 296–97; "A Feminist Symposium," including Marie Jenny Howe, "Feminism," *The New Review* 2:8 (Aug. 1914), 441–50; Mary White Ovington, "Socialism and the Feminist Movement," ibid., 2 (Mar. 1914), 143–47; cf. Linda Gordon, "Archives: Are the Interests of Men and Women Identical?" *Signs* 1 (Summer 1976), 1011–18.

38. "How to Repress the Suffragettes," *Literary Digest* 49:3 (Jul. 18, 1914); also "What to Do with the Raging Suffragettes," ibid., 46:16 (Apr. 19, 1913), 883; "What Should Be Done with the Wild Women," *Outlook*, Jul. 4, 1914, 519–20; Blatch, *Challenging Years*, 183; Edna Kenton, "The Militant Women—and Women," *Century* 87 (Nov. 1913), 13–15; Mary [Heaton Vorse] to Arthur, Feb. 7, 1913, folder "1913—Feb.," box 54, Vorse Coll., Walter Reuther Library. Randolph Bourne, too, delighted in the phenomenon of "finely bred" women shattering expectations to bits, calling them the only thing "alive" in England and a "model for all revolutionary parties the world over." Bourne to Prudence [Winterrowd], Nov. 5, 1913, box 1, Bourne Papers. See also W. L. George, "Feminist Intentions," *Atlantic Monthly* 112 (Dec. 1913), 721–32—an article endorsing the suffragettes' exploits as necessary sex-war—and negative reactions: Edward S. Martin, "Much Ado about Women," ibid. 113 (Jan. 1914), 9–12; Elisabeth Woodbridge, "The Unknown Quantity in the Woman Problem," ibid. (Apr. 1914),

510–20; and Ethel Colquhon, "Modern Feminism and Sex Antagonism," *Quarterly Review* 219 (Jul. 1913), 143–66.

39. Taggard quoted in biography in NAW III, 422; Doris Stevens to Sara Bard Field, May 24, 1916, with handwritten note appended by Field, folder 6, box 202, Wood Coll., HL; see also Buhle, *Women and American Socialism*, 265–68, on "lifestyle radicalism."

In their willingness to act out their revolt against norms of respectability the 1910s feminists had forebears in the radical Quaker women of the mid-nineteenth century, who provoked public condemnation by speaking before mixed audiences, wearing Turkish trousers, illegally voting, and in other ways acting out their belief in the equality of the sexes. As Nancy Hewitt points out, these were "the most accessible forms of social commentary for those with limited resources. The choice then was both pragmatic and ideological. Political statements that were expressed through the events of everyday life required no hierarchy of administration, allowed for independent and decentralized action, and were equally available to all." Hewitt, "Feminist Friends," FS 12 (Spring 1986), 43.

40. Morton G. White, *Social Thought in America: The Revolt against Formalism* (N.Y. Viking, 1952); see also Symes and Clement, *Rebel America*; quotations from Kenton, "Feminism Will Give"; Mary Ritter Beard, *Woman's Work in Municipalities* (N.Y., Appleton, 1915), vi; and Gilman in "Is Feminism Really," 6. Cf. the lesson feminist Madeline Doty hopefully deduced from Jeannette Rankin's election to Congress in 1917: "Woman has ceased to be merely woman. Like man, she has become a personality, but a personality endowed with a woman's spirit." Madeline Z. Doty, "Miss Rankin's Triumph Holds New Promise for Nation's Girls," clipping from the *New York Tribune*, Apr. 4, 1917, in box 1, Doty Coll., SSC. Cf. Warren Susman, "'Personality' and the Making of Twentieth-Century Culture," in *New Directions in American Intellectual History*, ed. John Higham and Paul Conkin (Baltimore, Johns Hopkins U.P., 1979); the Feminist emphasis on personality is not so attuned to pleasing others, in the sense that Susman emphasizes, but toward self-realization. See also a sympathetic male commentary by George Burman Foster, "Philosophy of Feminism," *Forum* 52 (Jul. 1914), 10–22, esp. 17: "she is seeking to be a *self*—and to be *for* herself. In past ideals—secular, servile, aesthetic, angelic, domestic—she has not been a self, and she has not been for herself. . . . It is this most necessary thing—the arrival of free selfhood, the free devotement [sic] of independent personality—that is the big new thing of the new day." W. E. B. DuBois remarked, "The meaning of the twentieth century is the freeing of the individual soul; the soul longest in slavery and still in the most disgusting and indefensible slavery is the soul of womanhood." *Crisis* (Nov. 1915), quoted in Diggs, "DuBois and Women," 290. Some other favorable contemporary commentaries on feminism by men are George Malcolm Stratton, "Feminism and Psychology," *Century* 92 (Jul. 1916), 420–26; and Elias Lieberman, "View of Feminism," *Harper's Weekly* 6 (Mar. 25, 1916), 310. Feminism could be seen to be proposing a "transvaluation of values" on a Nietzschean model, and indeed the English feminist (who called herself a "humanist") Dora Marsden invoked Nietzsche in her journal the *Freewoman*, founded in 1911. See "A Feminist Disciple of Nietzsche," *Current Opinion* 54 (Jan. 1913), 47–48, and "Feminism's New Prophetess," *Review of Reviews* 46 (Dec. 1912), 739–41.

41. Elinor Byrns, "I Resolve to Be Restless," *The Independent* 85 (Jan. 10, 1916), 51. Beatrice Forbe-Robertson Hale cited Wollstonecraft's "classic" text in *What Women Want: An Interpretation of the Feminist Movement* (N.Y., Fred-

erick Stokes, 1914), 30. Both Emma Goldman and Ruth Benedict—very different women both affected by and proponents of Feminism in their separate ways—saw and wrote about Wollstonecraft; see Alice Wexler, "Emma Goldman on Mary Wollstonecraft," *FS* 7:1 (Spring 1981), 113–33; and Margaret Mead, ed., *An Anthropologist at Work: Writings of Ruth Benedict* (Boston, Houghton Mifflin, 1959), esp 511–19. Rodman's Feminist Alliance statement quoted in Sochen, *New Woman*, 47.

42. Irwin, "Adventures of Yesterday," 413–23; Judith Schwarz, *The Radical Feminists of Heterodoxy* (Lebanon, N.H., New Victoria Publishers, 1982), 13, 23–27; Dorr, *Woman of Fifty*, 270–78; George Middleton, *These Things Are Mine* (N.Y., Macmillan, 1947), 128–31. Elizabeth Gurley Flynn quotation from celebratory ms volume (c. 1920), "Heterodoxy to Marie," vol. 1, Irwin Coll., SL; Hale, *What Women Want*; Sochen, *New Woman*, 52–60; Elaine Showalter, *These Modern Women* (Old Westbury, N.Y., Feminist P., 1978), 7. In his autobiography, *Confessions of a Reformer* (1925, repr. New York, 1974), Frederic C. Howe gave no space to his wife's activities, but did remark on his responses, at the time they met, to her convictions about women's independence.

Looking back from the vantage point of 1955, Frances Perkins acknowledged that "feminism" had influenced her to keep her own name when she married at age thirty-three (1913); Perkins's oral history, quoted in Susan Ware, *Beyond Suffrage: Women in the New Deal* (Cambridge, Harvard U.P., 1981), 28. On the history of married women keeping their "own" names, see also Una Stannard, *Mrs. Man* (San Francisco, Germainbooks, 1977).

43. I.e., Elizabeth Oakes Smith, "Men seem resolved to have but one in our sex. Would that women would learn to recognize their own individuality—their singleness of thought," from *Woman and Her Needs* (1851), quoted in Degler, *At Odds*, 343. Stanton, "The Solitude of Self," 1892 ("the best thing I have ever written"), reprinted in Dubois, ECS/SBA, 246–54.

44. Howe quoted in Schwarz, *Radical Feminists*, 25; Elsie Clews Parsons, *The Old-Fashioned Woman* (N.Y., Putnam, 1913), v–vi; quotation from "Heterodoxy to Marie"; see also Rose Young, "What Is Feminism," *Good Housekeeping* 58 (May 1914), 679–84.

45. Hilda Smith, in autobiography, "The Remembered Way," 378–79; see also 196–97, 302–03, 43; Hilda Smith Coll., SL. The conflicts of the period are suggested in the recollection of Rebecca Shelley, a University of Michigan graduate, that in 1915 "women were in a ferment of rebellion against political bondage," and yet Jane Addams was forbidden to speak on campus because her subject, votes for women, was too controversial; Allen Davis, *American Heroine* (New York, Oxford U.P., 1976), 208. Cf. Ellen Hoekstra, "The Pedestal Myth Reinforced: Women's Magazine Fiction, 1900–1920," in Russel B. Nye, ed., *New Dimensions in Popular Culture* (Bowling Green, Bowling Green U.P., 1972).

46. Patricia Albjerg Graham, "Expansion and Exclusion: A History of Women in American Higher Education," *Signs* 3 (1978), 766. Statistic in text pertains to all (male and female) undergraduates. Women in degree-granting colleges and universities in 1910 were 3.8 percent of all eighteen- to-twenty-one-year-old females, and in 1920 were 7.6 percent of same; Solomon, *Company*, 64. Schaffer, "Problem of Consciousness," in a sample of twenty-one California suffrage leaders in the early twentieth century, finds that 52 percent had gone to college or normal school; 29 percent more had postgraduate or professional training. For examples of college students drawn to New York city militance, see Ueland, *Me*, 84, 130–33; Beulah Amidon to Alyse Gregory, Oct. 4, 1948, box 1, Bourne Coll. Almost one-fourth of the National Woman's Party "pickets" arrested and impris-

oned for their suffrage militance had college or professional training, according to the thumbnail sketches in Doris Stevens, *Jailed for Freedom* (N.Y., Liveright, 1920), Appendix.

47. Charlotte Perkins Gilman, *Women and Economics* (1898), Carl N. Degler, ed. (N.Y., Harper and Row, 1966); Mary A. Hill, *Charlotte Perkins Gilman: The Making of a Radical Feminist* (Philadelphia, Temple U.P., 1980); Hayden, *Grand Domestic Revolution*, 183–205.

Not everyone who believed in Gilmanite tenets actually read Gilman. E.g., in 1916 Mabel Vernon, one of the leaders of the Woman's Party, told Sara Bard Field she hadn't had time for reading for two years, and with Gilman's *Women and Economics* on hand for weeks had only read one-third of it. Vernon to Field [1916], folder 9, box 212, Wood Coll., HL.

48. Oberdeck, "From Wives, Sweethearts," on Seattle. Olive Schreiner, *Woman and Labor*, 5th ed. (New York, Frederick Stokes, 1911), 18–19, 172, 271–72; Joyce Avrech Berkman, *Olive Schreiner: Feminism on the Frontier* (St. Albans, Vt., Eden P., 1979), esp. 28–29, 52–56. On Schreiner's relationship with Ellis, Phyllis Grosskurth, *Havelock Ellis: A Biography* (N.Y., Knopf, 1980); on Schreiner's influence, see also Daniel Rodgers, *The Work Ethic in Industrial America, 1850–1920* (Chicago, U. Chicago P., 1979), 199–200, 207–08.

49. Milholland, "Liberation of a Sex," 165. Cf. Nancy F. Cott, "Passionlessness: An Interpretation of Victorian Sexual Ideology," *Signs* 4:2 (1978), 219–36; Linda Gordon, *Woman's Body, Woman's Right* (N.Y., Grossman, 1976), 95–135, 159–85; Kathy Peiss, "Charity Girls and City Pleasures," in *Powers of Desire*, ed. Ann Snitow, Christine Stansell, and Sharon Thompson, (N.Y., Monthly Review P., 1983); Lewis Erenberg, *Steppin' Out*, 7–8, 23–25, 154–57, 237–38; Lois Banner, *American Beauty* (N.Y., Knopf, 1983), 175–201.

50. Miriam Allen de Ford, "Apologia," Feb. 3, 1915, folder 12, box 10, John Collier Coll., Walter Reuther Library. For de Ford's later oral history, see Sherna Gluck, ed., *From Parlor to Prison* (N.Y., Random House, 1976), 125–80.

51. Florence Guy Woolston, "Marriage Customs and Taboo among the Early Heterodites," 1919, quotation from 4–5, folder 2, box 2, Inez Haynes Irwin Coll., SL.

52. "The New Erotic Ethics," *Nation* 94 (Mar. 14, 1912), 261; Louise Bryant to Sara Bard Field, Jun. 12, 1916, folder 39, box 111, Wood Coll., HL; Mary [Heaton Vorse] to Arthur, Feb. 7, 1913, p. 3, folder "1913—Feb.," box 54, Vorse Coll., Walter Reuther Library. See also Sochen, *New Woman*; Buhle, *Women and American Socialism*, 257–68; Leslie Fishbein, *Rebels in Bohemia* (Chapel Hill, UNC P., 1982), 74–112, 127–59; Ellen Trimberger, "Feminism, Men, and Modern Love: Greenwich Village, 1900–1925," in Snitow, Stansell, and Thompson, eds., *Powers of Desire*, 131–52.

53. Austin, *Earth Horizon*, 329. Austin goes on to not-so-veiled criticism of the sexual behavior and values of (unnamed) Inez Milholland. For examples of older suffragists' disapproval see Mrs. O. H. P. Belmont, "The Liberation of a Sex [on Milholland's article so named]," *Hearst's Magazine* 23 (Apr. 1913), 614–16; "Mrs. Catt on Feminism"; and Blanche Wiesen Cook, ed., *Crystal Eastman: On Women and Revolution* (N.Y., Oxford U.P., 1978), 22. Winifred Cooley admitted in 1913 that the question of how to achieve a single standard for the two sexes, whether, in short, to insist that men be virginal, or to relieve women of that necessity, was the source of "violent altercation" in feminist ranks. "Younger Suffragists," 8. Interesting anti-suffragist reactions to feminism, connecting it to sex rights and economic independence, are Edward Sandford Martin, *The Un-*

rest of Women (New York, D. Appleton, 1913), which discourses on Milholland's 1913 *McClure's* article, "Liberation of a Sex"; and Lily Rice Foxcroft, "Suffrage a Step toward Feminism," in *Anti-Suffrage Essays by Massachusetts Women*, ed. Ernest Bernbaum (Boston, Forum, 1916), 141–52. Quotations of Theda Bara in 1914 and 1915 in May, *Screening Out the Past*, 105–109, and see Mary Ryan, "The Movie Moderns," in Scharf and Jensen, eds., *Decades*, 115. Some anti-feminist essays evincing fear of women's sexuality: Henry Walker, "Feminism and Polygamy," *Forum* 52 (Dec. 1914), 831–45; "Phyllis the Feminist," TNR 7 (Jul. 15, 1916), 275–77.

54. At the time (1916), both Stevens's and Field's lovers were men married to other women. Schwarz, *Radical Feminists*, 67–72; Doris Stevens to Sara Bard Field, [1917] in folder 22, [Dec. 7, 1915] in folder 12, [1916] in folder 15, box 202, Wood Coll., HL. See also Cooley, "Younger Suffragists," 8; Kenton, "Feminism Will Give . . . "; Beatrice Harraden, "Women Who Will Help Men: The Meaning and Promise of the Feminist Movement," *Independent* 74 (Jan. 30, 1913), 237–38; Deborah Meredith, "Men, Women, and Marriage in Pre–World War I Greenwich Village: A Study of Neith Boyce and Hutchins Hapgood" (Senior Essay, History Department, Yale College, 1981, in my possession); letters of Madeline Doty to David Graham Phillips and to Roger Baldwin, in Doty Coll., SSC; 1916 letters of Sara Bard Field detailing Ida Rauh's difficulties with Max Eastman, Wood Coll., HL; Trimberger, "Feminism, Men, and Modern Love."

55. Dorr, *Woman of Fifty*, 224–34, 245, 264–66. Ellen Key's works were all published by G. P. Putnam's Sons in New York. *Love and Marriage* and *The Woman Movement* were introduced by Havelock Ellis. See also Key, "Motherliness," *Atlantic Monthly* 110 (Oct. 1912), 562–70; Dell, *Women as World Builders*, 63–79; Madeline Z. Doty, "Women of the Future: In Sweden the Genius," *Good Housekeeping* 67 (Aug. 1918), 32–34, 108–10; Hapgood, "What Women Are After," 28–29; and the worthwhile analysis of Key in Buhle, *Women and American Socialism*, 292–94. On intellectual influences changing sexual morality, Gordon, *Woman's Body*, 159–206, and Christina Clare Simmons, "Marriage in the Modern Manner: Sexual Radicalism and Reform in America, 1914–1941" (Ph.D. diss., Brown U., 1982), are useful.

56. E. S. Dummer, *Why I Think So: The Autobiography of a Hypothesis* (Chicago, 1937), chap. 7, esp. 62–64; quotations from address, "Feminism," to the Chicago Kindergarten Inst., Oct. 30, 1916, folder 232, Dummer Coll., SL. See also correspondence between Dummer and Anthony in folders 431–40, box 26, in Dummer Coll., SL. Katherine S. Anthony, *Feminism in Germany and Scandinavia* (N.Y., Henry Holt, 1915), 99, 108–11, 147–53, 211–14, 230–41, 251. On 92–93 Anthony notes that Freud championed the Bund für Mutterschutz and Die Neue Ethik. Anthony, author of *Mothers Who Must Earn* (1914) and later of biographies of Susan B. Anthony and Margaret Fuller, was not involved in heterosexual venturesomeness herself but shared her life with Elisabeth Irwin, the educator and founder of the Little Red Schoolhouse. See Schwarz, *Radical Feminists*, 67–72.

On Mutterschutz, see Richard Evans, *The Feminist Movement in Germany, 1894–1933* (Beverly Hills, Sage, 1976), 120–39; and Allen, "Mothers of the New Generation." Dorr, who wrote a series of articles on Mutterschutz in 1912, could not find a magazine publisher, for editors maintained that "nice" women were not interested in illegitimacy. *Woman of Fifty*, 224–34, 225.

Cf. to the notion of possessionless sex Milholland's claim that women are fighting for "freedom from the domination of man and property in their lives." "There is no use in blinking the fact that we cannot liberate woman without ultimately finding ourselves facing radical changes in her relations with man as regards the two vital matters of property and sex." "Liberation of a Sex," 188.

57. Margaret Sanger, *An Autobiography* (N.Y., Norton, 1938) esp. 187; David M. Kennedy, *Birth Control in America* (New Haven, Yale U.P., 1970), 13–14, 133; Gordon, *Woman's Body,* 206–45; Crystal Eastman, "Birth Control in the Feminist Program," *Birth Control Review,* Jan. 1918, in Cook, ed., *Crystal,* 47. On Heterodoxites' participation in the birth control movement, see Sanger, *Autobiography,* 229–31; Committee of 100 pamphlet, "The Birth Control Movement" (1917), SL; list of original members of Committee of 100 in folder "Woman Suffrage—Notes," box 132, Vorse Coll., Walter Reuther Library. Where Sanger found in Key's ideas the confirmation she needed, Ruth Benedict, on the other hand, suffered much misery in the 1910s by trying unsuccessfully to fit her experience to Ellen Key's model of female fulfillment. See Benedict's private writings of 1914–17, published in Mead, *Anthropologist at Work,* 130–33, 140.

58. Ellen Key, "Education for Motherhood," *Atlantic Monthly* 112 (Jul. 1913), 48–61, and ibid. (Aug. 1913), 191–97; Charlotte Perkins Gilman, "On Ellen Key and the Woman Movement," *Forerunner* 4 (Feb. 1913), 35–38, and "As to 'Feminism,'" ibid. 5 (Feb. 1914), 45; "Ellen Key's Attack on 'Amaternal' Feminism," *Current Opinion* 54 (Feb. 1913), 138–39; "Charlotte Perkins Gilman's Reply to Ellen Key," ibid. 64 (Mar. 1913), 220–21; "The Conflict Between 'Human' and 'Female' Feminism," ibid. 56 (Apr. 1914), 291. Cf. Havelock Ellis's point, in his Introduction to Key's *Love and Marriage,* xv: "We have been mainly concerned with the rights of women to be like men; we are only now beginning to understand the rights of women to be unlike men, rights which, as Ellen Key understands them, include, although they go beyond, the rights embodied in the earlier claims." See also editorial obituary of Ellen Key (unsigned, but likely written by Freda Kirchwey, who covered women's issues for the journal in the 1920s) in the *Nation* 122 (May 5, 1926), 493–94.

59. Anthony, *Feminism,* 6; Harraden, "Women Who Will Help Men."

2: THE WOMAN'S PARTY

1. Outline of Alice Paul's early life, 1906–12, appearing after correspondence of Apr. 21, 1921, in NWP #7; Antonia Raeburn, *The Militant Suffragettes* (London, Michael Joseph, 1973), 131; Sidney Roderick Bland, "Techniques of Persuasion: The National Woman's Party and Woman Suffrage, 1913–1919" (Ph.D. diss., George Washington U., 1972), 43–51; Eleanor Flexner, *Century of Struggle* (N.Y., Atheneum, 1970), 262–66; Agnes Nestor, *Woman's Labor Leader* (Rockford, Ill., Bellevue Books, 1954), 107, 153 (on Dora Lewis's support of women workers); Sidney R. Bland, "Lucy Burns," in *NAW* IV, 124–25. When Inez Haynes Irwin, author of the "official" history *The Story of the Woman's Party* (N.Y., Harcourt, 1921), requested Paul's comments and corrections on her manuscript before publication, Paul responded that Dora Lewis should look more prominent because she first supported the focus on the constitutional route and she was always the most loyal. Notes of Paul's comments to Irwin, probably recorded by Emma Wold or Florence Brewer Boeckel, Dec. 1920, NWP #5.

2. For the CU/NWP history before 1920, see Flexner, *Century,* 261–70, 275–77, 282–89; Loretta Ellen Zimmerman, "Alice Paul and the National Woman's Party, 1912–1920" (Ph.D. diss., Tulane U., 1964); Bland, "Techniques"; and Christine A. Lunardini, *From Equal Suffrage to Equal Rights: Alice Paul and the National Woman's Party, 1913–1928* (N.Y., N.Y.U.P., 1986). The major ac-

counts by participants are Doris Stevens, *Jailed for Freedom* (New York, Liveright, 1920); Irwin, *Story;* and Caroline Katzenstein, *Lifting the Curtain: The State and National Woman Suffrage Campaigns in Pennsylvania as I Saw Them* (Philadelphia, Dorrance, 1955). Quotations from Alice Paul, during the 1916 campaign, in Irwin, *Story,* 151.

3. Mary R. Beard to Jane Norman Smith, Jun. 23, 1916, folder 55, JNSC; Grace A. Johnson (Cambridge) to Catharine Waugh McCulloch, Jan. 14, 1916, folder 220, Dillon Coll., SL; copy, Clara Ueland (Minneapolis) to Mrs. Orton H. Clarke (Kalamazoo, Mich.), Aug. 3, 1915, in folder "Correspondence 1913–15," box 1, Lucia Voorhes Grimes Coll., Michigan Historical Colls., Bentley Historical Library, U. Michigan. For other NAWSA-affiliated suffragists' comments on CU, see Emma S. E. Green (Boise, Idaho) to Miss Hannah Patterson (NAWSA secretary, New York), May 16, 1916; and Margaret S. Roberts (Boise, Idaho) to C. C. Catt, n.d., in folder 5, Margaret S. Roberts Coll., SL; Gratia Erickson to C. W. McCulloch, Oct. 14 [1915], folder 240, Dillon Coll.; Anna Garlin Spencer to Caroline Lexow, Nov. 4, 1914, folder 8, Caroline Lexow Babcock Coll., SL. On the successful rousing of New Mexico suffragists by the CU, see Joan Jensen, "Disfranchisement Is a Disgrace," *New Mexico Historical Review* 56 (Jan. 1981), 10–23.

To the leaders of NAWSA the political strategy seemed not only disloyal but idiotically counterproductive in the midst of state legislative and referendum campaigns for woman suffrage. It was "common sense," thought Anna Howard Shaw, president of NAWSA in 1914, "that the result of such interference with the States where women vote, would naturally make Democrats everywhere vote against our measure." A. H. Shaw to Caroline Katzenstein, Mar. 27, 1914, in Katzenstein, *Lifting the Curtain,* 141.

4. Bland, "Techniques," 70–71, 185–87; Stevens, *Jailed,* 187–88; Irwin, *Story,* 57–60; on Belmont, see fragmentary autobiography written by Sara Bard Field in 1917, folder 1, box 101, Wood Coll., esp. 50–52 and 61 in first draft, and chap. 5, 5, in second draft; quotation regarding Belmont from Sara Bard Field to Charles Erskine Scott Wood, Dec. 18, [1915], folder 2, box 277; see also Field to Wood, Jan. 22–23, 1916, folder 4, box 277, Wood Coll., HI; and SBF OH; Doris Stevens diary, entry for Dec. 31, 1920, DSC. Belmont's participation in NWP activities is well documented in Doris Stevens's "Notes on Belmont, 1913–1928," folders 269 to 274 in DSC.

On Schneiderman, see Nancy Schrom Dye, *As Equals and as Sisters* (Columbia, U. Missouri P., 1980), 131; Rose Schneiderman with Lucy Goldthwaite, *All for One* (N.Y., Paul Eriksson, 1967), 123–24; Kraditor, *Ideas,* 207 n. 3; on Beard, Bland, "Techniques," 82, and Loretta Zimmerman, "Mary Ritter Beard: An Activist of the Progressive Era," *U. Portland Review* 26 (Spring 1974), 24–26.

5. Alice Paul and Mabel Vernon recalled that the NWP comprised 5 percent or less of the suffrage army; AP OH, 327; MV OH, 190–91. Zimmerman, "Alice Paul," 243, finds that the NWP had no more than 20,000 members in 1917, when Paul claimed 40,000. Elsie Hill, acting chairman in 1921, claimed that the NWP in 1919 had "about 40,000" members; Hill to Mrs. Dorothy C. Rice, Mar. 30, 1921, NWP #7. Inez Haynes Irwin claimed no more than 50,000 for the NWP at its height when NAWSA had about 2 million members; Irwin, *Angels and Amazons: A Hundred Years of American Women* (Garden City, N.Y., Doubleday 1934), 392. Most historians cite 2 million as the membership of NAWSA in 1917 (see Aileen S. Kraditor, *Ideas of the Woman Suffrage Movement, 1890–1920* [1965; repr. Garden City, N.Y., Anchor, 1971], 5), though Maud Wood Park, *Front Door Lobby,* ed. Edna Stantial (Boston, Beacon, 1960), 12, claims more

than that figure for 1915. Kraditor, *Ideas*, 6, asserts that "although the leaders of the NAWSA . . . boasted about the difference in numerical strength, the CU/ NWP was at least as active and effective as the giant NAWSA in the last eight years of the federal amendment campaign."

Doris Stevens envisioned Paul possessing "many of the same qualities that Lenin does," (*Jailed*, 17); and Lavinia Dock referred, tongue-in-cheek, to "our Comrade Alice Paul Lenin"; Dock to Emma Wold, Jan. 1921, NWP #6. For another reference to the NWP as Leninist, see Marjory Nelson, "Ladies in the Streets: A Sociological Analysis of the National Woman's Party, 1910–1930" (Ph.D. diss., SUNY Buffalo, 1976), 315, 320–21. Floyd Dell (reviewing Doris Stevens's *Jailed for Freedom*) in the *Liberator* 3:11 (Nov. 1920), 26, despite distinguishing his goals from Paul's, conceded, "if I were organizing a militant communist movement I think I would invite Miss Paul to come over and show us how to make a go of it." Crystal Eastman, similarly, wrote "Alice Paul does not belong to the revolution, but her leadership has had a quality that only the revolution can understand." "Alice Paul's Convention," ibid. 4 (Apr. 1921), 10. Cf. K. Austin Kerr's description and analysis, applicable to the CU in most respects, of the contemporaneous Anti-Saloon League as a modern single-issue pressure group: "Organizing for Reform: The Anti-Saloon League and Innovation in Politics," *AQ* 32 (Spring 1980), 37–53; and *Organized for Prohibition: A New History of the Anti-Saloon League* (New Haven, Yale U.P., 1985).

6. "How little we know about this laconic person and yet how abundantly we feel her power, her will and her compelling leadership," Stevens continued; *Jailed*, 10–11; Sara Bard Field to Alice Paul, Jan. 7, 1921, NWP #5; Sara Bard Field to Charles Erskine Scott Wood, Jul. 24, [1917], folder 2, box 280, Wood Coll., hl; Irwin, *Story*, 15.

The top-down control exercised early in the CU is emphasized in Bland, "Techniques," 78–79, 178.

7. Historians have maintained the CU's reputation for youthfulness; e.g., Zimmerman, "Alice Paul," 57–59. Alice Paul insisted decades later that of the early CU Executive Board members, only Doris Stevens "could possibly be called young"; AP OH, 211. (The SL collection gives Stevens' birthdate as 1892, but Leila Rupp, who is writing a biography of her, has found that Stevens' passport contradicts other records and puts her birth in 1888. Personal communication from Leila Rupp, Jan. 18, 1987; see also Rupp, "Feminism, Heterosociality, and New Womanhood: The Case of Doris Stevens," 1986, paper to be delivered at the meeting of the Organization of American Historians, April 1987.) Note the equation of youth with radicalism when middle-aged Jane Norman Smith affirmed the NWP's preemption of NAWSA on the federal amendment by saying "the younger women have forced the issue and the conservatives are now stepping up to claim the credit" (Smith to Mr. Levis, Dec. 10, 1917, folder 56, JNSC); or when Lavinia Dock, at sixty, defended the 1917 NWP picketing action in which she joined as evidence of "the fearless spirit of youth"; doc. 8-b in Anne Firor Scott and Andrew M. Scott, *One Half the People* (Philadelphia, Lippincott, 1975), 145.

8. Frank P. Walsh to Mr. Jacob Billikopf, Apr. 29, 1915, box 6, Walsh Coll., NYPL. In a letter of the same date Walsh wrote to Pierce to introduce Billikopf, revealing that his work in Kansas City had been along "social uplift" lines and adding, "please do not throw a fit." According to Irwin, *Story*, 124, the CU/NWP hired three successive groups of organizers as their work expanded. The first hired were Mabel Vernon, Elsie Hill, Margaret Whittemore, Doris Stevens, Ella St. Clair Thompson, and Virginia Arnold; next were Iris Calderhead, Vivian

Pierce, Beulah Amidon, Lucy Branham, Hazel Hunkins, Clara Louise Rowe, Joy Young, Margery Ross, Mary Gertrude Fendall, Pauline Clarke, Alice Henkel, and Rebecca Hourwich; third, Julia Emory, Betty Gram, Anita Pollitzer, Mary Dubrow, and Catherine Flanagan. Since many of them were arrested picketing, one can find thumbnail sketches of them in Appendix 4 to Stevens, *Jailed*. More than three-fourths of these organizers were college graduates. See also recollections of Rebecca Hourwich, a staff organizer in the New York office in 1917–18 at age twenty: RHR OH, 84–85, 91.

9. On Stevens's age, see n. 7 above. On Stevens in the 1910s, see "Notes on Belmont, 1913–16"; and letters from her lovers Frank P. Walsh (1915) and Dudley Field Malone (from 1916 through the 1920s) in DSC; also on Frank P. Walsh, Doris Stevens to Sara Bard Field [March 1916], folder 4, box 202, Wood Coll., HL (in which Stevens refers to herself and Walsh as "firebrands"); see "Sara Bard Field," biographical sketch by Catherine M. Scholten, in *NAW*, I, 232–34; Sara Bard Field to Charles Erskine Scott Wood, Aug. 12, [1916], folder 4, box 278, Wood Coll., and her numerous other letters of 1915–18 in Wood Coll., HL.

10. The fact that Wilson won 10 out of the 12 states where women voted seems to testify to the small impact the NWP campaign had; however, a difference of only four thousand votes in California—the most populous state where women voted and where the Woman's Party put much of its effort—would have lost Wilson the presidency. David M. Kennedy, *Over Here: The First World War and American Society* (N.Y., Oxford U.P., 1980), 12; see also Lunardini, *From Equal Suffrage*, 50–103.

Carrie Chapman Catt to Jane Addams, Jan. 4, 1915, box 4, Catt Coll., LC reel 2; Sara Bard Field to Charles Erskine Scott Wood, Nov. 18, 1916, folder 1, box 279; Helen Marot to Sara Bard Field, Oct. 25 [1916], folder 9, box 170; Field remarks on men allied with Wilson—Gilson Gardener, Amos Pinchot, Richard Lloyd Jones, Dudley Field Malone, William Kent—while their wives or lovers campaigned against Democrats for the Woman's Party, in Field to Wood, Sep. 4 [1916], and [Sep. 21, 1916], folder 5, box 278, Wood Coll., HL. Perhaps the most striking conjunction was Doris Stevens and Dudley Field Malone, who fell in love during this campaign when Malone was managing California for President Wilson and making special appeal to women voters! Besides DSC, on the Stevens–Malone relationship at this time see Sara Bard Field to Charles Erskine Scott Wood, Aug. 14 [1916], folder 4, box 278, and Field to Wood, Aug. 1917, folder 3, box 280, Wood Coll. On Malone's relationship to Wilson, see Bland, "Techniques," 132.

11. Stevens, *Jailed*, and Irwin, *Story*, both describe picketing strategies and prison experiences in detail. On Byrne, David M. Kennedy, *Birth Control in America* (New Haven, Yale U.P., 1970), 83–86. On reactions to picketing, Irwin, *Story*, 220–27; Katzenstein, *Lifting*, 240–41; AP OH, 218. Late in 1917, Mary Beard, who had not been consulted before picketing began, left the NWP Executive Committee because she could not approve the direction the picketing and slogans were taking, even if the tactic would "win"—just as she could not approve using "war work as a cudgel" (NAWSA's approach), even if it would win woman suffrage; Bland, "Techniques," 115, 124.

12. *New York Tribune* quoted in Bland, "Techniques," 116. Kraditor, *Ideas*, 207 n. 32, comments that the abundance of news items and editorials on NWP picketing in 1917–18 gives more importance to the action than secondary works have granted. Stevens, *Jailed*, 229–40; Carole Nichols, "A New Force in Politics: The Suffragists' Experience in Connecticut" (M.A. thesis, Sarah Lawrence College, 1979), 37; Bland, "Techniques," 124–25; Flexner, *Century*, 270–87; C. C.

Catt to Sue Shelton White, May 6, 1918, folder 21, S. S. White Coll., SL. See Grace R. Johnson to Alice Paul, Jul. 2, 1917, and Oct. 22, 1917, folder 135, WRC, SL, for examples of horrified NAWSA reactions to picketing.

Both the Wilson administration and NAWSA tried to diminish media attention to the pickets. See copy, Ethel M. Smith (Press Secretary, NAWSA) to Mrs. Catt, Confidential, Jun. 26, 1917, Catt Papers, LC reel 6. Wilson advised Arthur Brisbane, editor and owner of the *Washington Times*, in Jul. 1917 that the news about the pickets "need not be made interesting reading"; David Morgan, *Suffragists and Democrats* (East Lansing, Mich. State U.P., 1972), 119. On Catt's relationship to Wilson, see ibid., chap. 11, esp. 120–21; Christine Lunardini and Thomas Krock, "Woodrow Wilson and Woman Suffrage: A New Look," *Polit. Sci. Q.* 95:4 (1980–81), 655–71; and Scott and Scott, *One Half*, 149–54. The Wilson administration refused to accept the pickets' claim to be political prisoners; see Janice Law Trecker, "The Suffrage Prisoners," *American Scholar* 41 (1972), esp. 422.

13. When some celebrants and some opponents of woman suffrage attributed the successful 1917 referendum in New York State to the work and votes of socialists (with substantial reason), Catt's close associates took pains to demonstrate that such was not the case. James Weinstein, *Decline of Socialism in America* (N.Y., Monthly Review P., 1967), esp. 133, 182–83; Kennedy, *Over Here*, 27; Stevens, *Jailed*, 82–83; Mari Jo Buhle, *Women and American Socialism* (Urbana, U. Illinois P., 1981), 236–39, 281–82, including quotation from Catt in *Woman Citizen*, Jul. 7, 1917, on 236; John Buenker, "The Politics of Mutual Frustration: Socialists and Suffragists in New York and Wisconsin," in Sally Miller, ed., *Flawed Liberation* (Westport, Conn., Greenwood, 1981), 124–28; Elinor Lerner, "Jewish Involvement in the New York City Woman Suffrage Movement," *Amer. Jewish Hist.* 70 (1981), 459–61. Articles in *The Woman Citizen*, NAWSA's organ, sometimes contended that woman suffrage was a preventive to Bolshevism, e.g., Alice Stone Blackwell, "Notes and Comments," 3:20 (Dec. 14, 1918), 589; "Woman, Bolshevism and the Home," 3:42 (Mar. 15, 1919), 861–63.

14. Marie Louise Degen, *The History of the Woman's Peace Party* (Baltimore, Johns Hopkins P., 1939), 189; "Elinor Byrns," MS by Caroline Lexow Babcock, folder 58, C. L. Babcock Coll., SL; see also copies of letters from Alice Park, Feb. 17, 1917, from the National Board of the Woman's Peace Party, Feb. 22, 1917, and from Mary McHenry Keith, Mar. 19, 1917, to Carrie Chapman Catt, objecting to the policy of NAWSA to take up war service, in Alice Park autobiography, 47–51, box 8, Park Coll., HL, and Alice Park to "my dear children, in duplicate," Dec. 29, 1927, folder "Alice Park," box 11, Keith-McHenry-Pond Families Papers, BL. For examples of radical adventurers, see Dorothy Day, *The Long Loneliness: An Autobiography* (N.Y., Harper and Row, 1952), 72–83; and Sherna Gluck, ed., *From Parlor to Prison* (N.Y., Vintage, 1976), 235–50.

15. *The Woman's Protest*, Apr. 1917, 15, quoted in Elinor Lerner, "American Feminism and the Jewish Question, 1890–1940," in *Anti-Semitism in American History*, ed. David A. Gerber (Urbana, U. Illinois P., 1986), 319; copy of letter sent by Missouri Anti-Suffrage League to all candidates for office in St. Louis, Jun. 24, 1918, in folder 14, Edna Gellhorn Coll., SL; *Woman Patriot* 1:1 (Apr. 27, 1918), 2.

16. Irwin, *Story*, 372–414; Nichols, "New Force," 37–43; Louise Bryant to John Reed, n.d. [Feb. 1919], on *Suffragist* letterhead, folder 302, and see telegrams sent by Reed to Bryant at NWP headquarters in Feb. 1919 in folders 90, 91, 93, John Reed Coll., Harvard College Library; "I.W.W." attribution from

New York Times, Feb. 10, 1919, quoted in Bland, "Techniques," 170; "cannibals" and "Bolsheviks" noted by Stevens, *Jailed*, 33. Over 500 picketers were arrested between 1917 and 1919, and 168 served prison terms, 63 for actions in 1919. In Appendix 4 of *Jailed*, Stevens supplies thumbnail sketches of the 168 imprisoned. Many NWP loyalists were arrested over and over again; Julia Emory (an organizer) 34 times, according to Irwin, *Story*, 472.

17. Despite the NAWSA leadership's conviction that National Woman's Party actions were traitorous in wartime and counterproductive, and despite NWP scorn for the NAWSA's distrust, the two approaches complemented one another. Also lobbying in Washington, the NAWSA insistently pursued its plan to increase, through state referenda and statutory action enabling women to vote, the number of states whose senators and congressmen could be expected to support a constitutional amendment for woman suffrage. The New York victory and statutes in five other states in 1917 doubled the number of women who could vote at least for presidential electors, and through 1918 and 1919 ten more states moved into that column. On the conjunction of NWP and NAWSA strategies, see Stevens, *Jailed*, 250–51; Bland, "Techniques," 134–38; Flexner, *Century*, 290–92; Morgan, *Suffragists and Democrats*, 121–23; and Scott and Scott, *One Half*, 40–42.

When Carrie Chapman Catt read Inez Haynes Irwin's history of feminism, *Angels and Amazons*, in 1933, she was appalled at Irwin's diminution of the NAWSA's work for suffrage as compared to the NWP's, and she wrote to Irwin about it. Irwin's response was "quite square," Catt reported to her former lieutenant Maud Wood Park. "She actually did not know a thing about it [the NAWSA]. She actually believed that everything of consequence that was achieved was done by the Woman's Party! She supposed that they had won the vote and that the rest of us were a lot of old chumps." Copy of Catt to Park, Apr. 18, 1933, Catt Papers, LC reel 5. Irwin's response—unless it was disingenuous—suggests the powerful hold the NWP's worldview had on its members.

18. On the war and Reconstruction period see Burl Noggle, *Into the Twenties* (Urbana, U. Illinois P., 1974), 31–45, 165–68; Allen F. Davis, "Welfare, Reform, and World War I," *AQ* 19 (Fall 1967), 516–33; Stanley Shapiro, "The Great War and Reform: Liberals and Labor, 1917–19," *Labor History*, 7 (Summer 1971), 323–44, and "The Twilight of Reform: Advanced Progressives After the Armistice," *Historian* 33 (May 1971), 349–64; Kerr, *Organized for Prohibition*, 202–10; David Montgomery, "The 'New Unionism' and the Transformation of Workers' Consciousness in America, 1909–22," *Journal of Social Hist.* 7 (1974), 509–29, and "Immigrants, Industrial Unions, and Social Reconstruction in the United States, 1916–1923," *Labour/Le Travailleur* 13 (1984), 101–13. On women workers and World War I, see Maurine W. Greenwald, *Women, War and Work* (Westport, Conn., Greenwood, 1980); Kennedy, *Over Here*, 285–91; WBB #12, *The New Position of Women in American Industry* (Washington, D.C., 1921); J. Stanley Lemons, *The Woman Citizen: Social Feminism in the 1920s* (Urbana, U. Illinois P., 1973), 3–40; Alice Kessler-Harris, *Out to Work: A History of Wage-Earning Women in the United States* (N.Y., Oxford U.P., 1982), 219–24, and "Problems of Coalition-Building: Women and Trade Unions in the 1920s," in *Women, Work and Protest*, ed. Ruth Milkman (Boston, RKP, 1985), 112 (figures for unionization are from 1920 and pertain to nonagricultural workers); William Breen, "Black Women and the Great War," *Journal of Southern Hist.* 44 (Aug. 1978), 421–40; Valerie J. Conner, "'The Mothers of the Race' in World War I," *Labor Hist.* 21 (Winter 1980), 31–54.

19. David Burner, "1919: Prelude to Normalcy," in John Braeman, et al.,

Change and Continuity in Twentieth-Century America; The 1920s (Ohio State U.P., 1968), 3–32; Robert K. Murray, *Red Scare: A Study in National Hysteria, 1919–20* (Minneapolis, U. Minnesota P., 1955), esp. 5–7, 58–67, 92–93, 112–40, 231–44, and *The Politics of Normalcy* (N.Y., Norton, 1973), 3–5; Abraham Pais, *'Subtle is the Lord . . .': The Science and the Life of Albert Einstein* (N.Y., Oxford U.P., 1982), 303–11; Kennedy, *Over Here*, 270–84, 287–92; John D. Hicks, *Republican Ascendancy 1921–1933* (N.Y., Harper, 1960), 11–16; Noggle, *Into the Twenties*, 24–26, 60–65, 98–121, 157–58.

20. Weinstein, *Decline of Socialism*, 224–25; Shapiro, "Twilight"; Crystal Eastman, "Practical Feminism," from *The Liberator*, Jan. 1920, reprinted in *Crystal Eastman: On Women and Revolution*, ed. Blanche Wiesen Cook (N.Y., Oxford U.P., 1978), 51–52; Eugene M. Tobin, *Organize or Perish: America's Independent Progressives, 1913–1933* (Westport, Conn., Greenwood, 1986), 97–130. Historians have paid no attention to the personal links between the NWP and the Committee of 48 and virtually no attention to the latter's equal rights stand. I am greatly indebted to Eugene Tobin for showing me documents from boxes 45 and 67, Mercer Green Johnston Coll., LC, relevant to the Committee of 48, including platform and letterheads, which show that women comprised one-fifth of the National Executive Committee in 1920. See form letter from J. A. H. Hopkins to state and local committees of the 48, Apr. 7, 1920, box 45, advising them to keep in close touch with labor organizations, farmer organizations, women's organizations, "and other organizations having political purposes." In his directions for fund-raising luncheons and dinners, Hopkins specified: "Limit your speakers to three, of which at least one is a woman, and have an equal number of women at your speakers' table"; and suggested that a woman speaker make the "money speech," concluding, "any suffragist will explain how this is done." See also the platform adopted at St. Louis Conference, Dec. 9–12, 1919, box 67; Mercer Green Johnston to the Rev. Olympia Brown, Aug. 13, 1920, box 45.

21. Nichols, "New Force," 78; Doris Stevens to Anne Martin, Oct. 21, 1920 (on letterhead of Women's Independent Campaign Committee), folder "S Miscellany," Anne Martin Coll., BL; Schneiderman, *All for One*, 147–48; Harriot Stanton Blatch and Alma Lutz, *Challenging Years: Memoirs of Harriot Stanton Blatch* (N.Y., G. P. Putnam's Sons, 1940), 318–20; biographical sketch of Elinor Byrns, folder 54, box 4, Babcock Coll., SL; Kathryn Louise Anderson, "Practical Political Equality for Women: Anne Martin's Campaigns for the U.S. Senate in Nevada, 1918 and 1920" (Ph.D. diss., U. Washington, 1978).

22. Doris Stevens to Anne Martin, Oct. 21, 1920, Folder "S Miscellany," and Harriot Stanton Blatch to Anne Martin, May 14 [1918]; Anne Martin Coll., BL.

23. Alice Park to *Suffragist*, Nov. 30, 1920, NWP #4; Mary Heaton Vorse to Florence Brewer Boeckel, May 5, 1920, NWP #4; Florence Brewer Boeckel to Mrs. Lionel Marks, Nov. 2, 1920, NWP #5; Elizabeth Kent to Mabel Vernon, Oct. 24 [1920], folder K, box IV, Mabel Vernon Coll., BL; and Harriet Brewer to Miss Vernon, Jan. 18, 1921, NWP #5.

24. See Minutes of Jul. 9, 1920 (for Belmont's views), Sep. 10, 1920, and Oct. 8, 1920, National Executive Committee, NWP #114. Crystal Eastman's views are also laid out in her article, "Now We Can Begin," *Liberator* 3 (Dec. 1920), 23–24. Lucy Burns did not even attend the NWP convention in Feb. 1921, though she was asked to be a speaker; see [unknown] to Ida Husted Harper, Mar. 22, 1921, NWP #7; and Bland, "Lucy Burns," *NAW IV*, 124–25.

25. *The New York Times*, Jul. 18, 1920, sec. 6, 6, cited in Peter Geidel, "The National Woman's Party and the Origins of the Equal Rights Amendment, 1920–

1923," *Historian* 42 (Aug. 1980), 562, for Paul's view. "I, on thinking it over, am inclined to agree with you," Dr. Caroline Spencer of Colorado wrote to Paul in October, "that the National Woman's Party could only continue its existence on a purely feminist program for the reason you state—women would divide on other issues." Dr. Caroline Spencer to Alice Paul, Oct. 10, 1920, NWP #5. Nat. Exec. Comm. minutes, Sep. 10, Oct. 8, Nov. 16, Dec. 10, 1920, Jan. 21, Feb. 14, 1921, NWP #114. (The words *if desired* were added by hand after *introduced* and *offered* in the portions of the Dec. 10 minutes quoted.) The conclusive meeting was on Jan. 21, 1921.

On impressions of whether Paul was likely to continue her leadership, and on her convictions regarding blanket legislation, see Katherine Fisher to Alice Paul, Nov. 8, 1920, Florence Brewer Boeckel to Madeline Doty, Dec. 21, 1920, NWP #5; Agnes Morey to Alice Paul, Jan. 26, 1921, NWP #6.

26. For invitees, arrangements, and charges for the ceremony, see correspondence Jan.–Feb. 1921, NWP #6; Nat. Exec. Comm. minutes, Jan. 14, 1921, NWP #114; and Geidel, "National Woman's Party," 563. A copy of the program for the Convention is in folder "NWP," box D 341, Belle Case La Follette Papers, LC. It is not clear whether Maud Wood Park for the NLWV addressed the convention. She was invited, as Catt was invited to participate in the installation ceremony. Catt's negative reply is in the NWP records, but there is no reply from Park. National Chairman to Carrie Chapman Catt, Jan. 3, 1921; Carrie Chapman Catt to National Chairman of NWP, Jan. 17, 1921; National Chairman to Maud Wood Park, Jan. 3, 1921; Alice Paul to Maud Wood Park, Jan. 14, 1921, NWP #5. The Convention program does not list Park or her organization among the speakers. Some changes were made from the preprinted program, however, and Belle Case La Follette, in her article, "National Convention of the National Woman's Party," *La Follette's Magazine*, (Mar. 21, 1921), 42–43, recounts that Park spoke for the LWV.

27. Juliet Barrett Roublee (for Sanger) to Paul, Feb. 5, 1921; HQ secretary to Roublee, Feb. 8, 1921; Mary Ware Dennett to Paul, Jan. 31, 1921, Feb. 3, 1921; Mrs. Lawrence Lewis to Dennett, Feb. 4, 1921; Marion May to Paul, Feb. 9, 1921; Emma Wold to Ethel McAdamson, Feb. 12, 1921; Wold telegram to Dennett, Feb. 14, 1921, NWP #6.

28. Walter White to Mary Church Terrell, Mar. 14, 1919, item 615, cont. 4, Mary Church Terrell Papers, LC. On racism in the suffrage movement, Paula Giddings, *When and Where I Enter* (N.Y., Morrow, 1985), 159–63 (including quotation from Paul, in letter to Mary White Ovington, Mar. 31, 1919, on 163); Kraditor, *Ideas*, 163–218; Rosalyn Terborg-Penn, "Discrimination against Afro-American Women in the Woman's Movement, 1830–1920," in *The Afro-American Woman: Struggles and Images*, ed. Sharon Harley and Rosalyn Terborg-Penn (Port Washington, N.Y., 1978), 17–27; Angela Y. Davis, *Women, Race, and Class* (N.Y., 1981), 118. On Paul's decision to segregate marchers by race in the 1913 CU parade in Washington, D.C., see Bland, "Techniques," 53–55. Regarding Ida B. Wells-Barnett's "picket pin," see Ida B. Wells-Barnett to Paul, Mar. 21, 1921, and Paul to Wells-Barnett, Mar. 24, 1921, NWP #7. Though she mentioned the Alpha Suffrage Club, which she founded, Wells-Barnett did not record her NWP participation in her autobiography, *Crusade for Justice: The Autobiography of Ida B. Wells*, ed. Alfreda M. Duster (Chicago, U. Chicago P., 1970). Mary Church Terrell recalled joining the NWP pickets in Mary Church Terrell, *A Colored Woman in a White World* (1940, repr. N.Y., Arno, 1980), 316–17. See also NWP headquarters to Mary Church Terrell, Apr. 24, 1919, item 631, container 5, and NWP headquarters to Terrell, Jan. 1921,

item 214, cont. 6, Mary Church Terrell Papers, LC. Terrell was upbraided by Virginia White Speel, head of Women's Work for a Harding and Coolidge Club she was assisting in 1920, for her connections with the NWP. Speel advised Terrell, who had apparently hosted some NWP speakers, not to get "entangled" with the NWP, who were "unwise and unsafe leaders." Terrell, very surprised, said she had "some very, very dear friends in the NWP," but she agreed not to invite them to speak again. Speel to Terrell, Oct. 15, 1920, item no. 124, and Terrell to Speel, Oct. 19, 1920, item no. 129, cont. 6, Mary Church Terrell Papers, LC.

29. Mary White Ovington to Harriot Stanton Blatch, Dec. 3, 1920; Ovington to NWP Advisory Council members, Dec. 6, Dec. 23, 1920; Emma Wold to Blatch, Dec. 29, 1920, with appended handwritten note by Blatch to Ovington, "National Woman's Party 1920–21" folder, cont. 384, series C, NAACP Papers, LC; Ovington to Lucy Burns, Dec. 17, 1920, with appended handwritten note by Burns to NWP headquarters; Wold to Burns, Jan. 14, 1921; Hallie Brown to Paul, Jan. 22, 1921, NWP #5; Mrs. Lizzie McPherson to Paul, Feb. 2, 1921; Wold to Mrs. Sophie Meredith, Feb. 3, 1921; Wold to McPherson, Feb. 4, 1921; McPherson to Wold, Feb. 11, 1921; Paul to Mrs. William Spencer Murray, Jan. 24, 1921; Paul to Hallie Brown, Jan. 24, 1921; Hallie Brown to Paul, Jan. 31, 1921, NWP #6; Giddings, *When and Where*, 164–66.

The National Association of Colored Women's Clubs was not one of the forty-four women's organizations individually named on the Convention program under "Laying of tributes . . . etc."; it was (presumably) left under the grouping "And Over Forty Other Organizations."

30. Giddings, *When and Where*, 166–69; Mary Talbert to Ovington, Jan. 15, 1921; Ovington to Mrs. William Spencer Murray, Jan. 12, 1921, "National Woman's Party 1920–21" folder, cont. 384, series C, NAACP Papers; Inez Richardson (secretary of delegation) to Paul, Feb. 2, 1921, NWP #6.

Paul defended her actions, stressing that she had ensured that black delegates could present their views from the floor just like everyone else although some white Southern delegates were hostile, in letters to Mrs. Lawrence Lewis, Mar. 23, 1921, and to Mrs. John Rogers, Mar. 24, 1921; see also Dora Lewis to Mrs. Brannan, Mar. 9, 1921, Elsie Hill to Olympia Brown, Mar. 8, 1921, and Dora Lewis to "Dearest Paulie," Apr. 11, 1921, NWP #7. Paul reported that the entire white delegation from North Carolina, protesting black women's presence, at first refused to register and only with difficulty were persuaded to attend; they stayed away from the ceremonial dinner, where they would have had to eat with black women, and one member refused to accept her picket pin because Terrell was awarded one at the same ceremony.

When Florence Kelley intervened on behalf of the black women's demand, Paul told her that she feared a black spokeswoman's "inflaming" the Southerners at the convention, and thus preventing the next and "by far the most important item" on the NWP "immediate program," which, according to Paul, was to push for federal penal sanctions against state registration or election officials who discriminated against women. The sanctions were presumably aimed at Southern states which disfranchised black women. Kelley generously concluded that "Miss Paul, as a Quaker woman is of course entirely in sympathy with Mrs. Talbert and her work" but "as a tactician" denied the request to speak from the podium. In fact, the NWP did have an "enforcement" bill introduced to Congress, on Dec. 30, 1920, by Wesley Jones, Republican senator from Washington. Florence Kelley to Ovington, Dec. 22, 1920, "National Woman's Party 1920–21" folder, cont. 384, series C, NAACP Papers. For the enforcement bill, see

Congressional Record, 66 Cong., 3 sess., Dec. 30, 1920, p. 808; Mary Winsor to Ovington, Dec. 31, 1920, and clipping sent by Mary Talbert to Ovington, "National Woman's Party 1920–21" folder, cont. 384, series C, NAACP Papers; Anna A. Clemons to Secretary of the NWP, Oct. 10, 1920; Headquarters Secretary (Wold) to Miss Clemons, Oct. 20, 1920; Clemons to Wold, Oct. 24, 1920; Wold to Clemons, Oct. 28, 1920; and Wold to Clemons, Nov. 2, 1920, NWP #5. (Anna A. Clemons, a black woman from Southport, North Carolina, wished to register to vote.)

31. *The Nation* sent questionnaires (probably on Freda Kirchwey's initiative) to top members of the NWP, asking their views of enforcement of the Nineteenth Amendment for Southern black women, and published some answers. Alice Paul, characteristically, managed to sound entirely neutral. Florence Kelley, Harriet Stanton Blatch, Sara Bard Field, and Mary Winsor emphatically voiced the need for special efforts to ensure black voting rights, Winsor urging socialism as a solution. Alva Belmont and Susan Pringle Frost (both Southern-born) opposed any intervention in the states' management of election procedures. "The White Woman's Burden," *Nation*, 112 (Feb. 16, 1921), 257–58. Mabel Vernon much later reported that Paul was prejudiced against blacks and Jews, though always polite to individuals of both groups. Vernon saw Paul's intimacy with Anita Pollitzer, a Jew, as an exception. MV OH, 157–58.

32. Ella Rush Murray, "The Woman's Party and the Violation of the 19th Amendment," *The Crisis* 21 (Apr. 1921), 259–61; Transcript of NWP Convention (Feb. 18–21, 1921), 61, folder 18, Alma Lutz Coll. MC 182, SL.

33. Lillian Kerr to Mabel Vernon, Sep. 19, 1920, folder "K", box 4, Mabel Vernon Coll., BL; for debate on minority resolution see Transcript of NWP Convention, 106–22 (quotation on 117); La Follette, "National Convention," 42; SBF OH, 425. La Follette cited a "farmer" who "had come all the way from Oklahoma, at heavy expense, in the belief that her party was going to help women use their ballots to end war, and . . . dreaded to go home and report that the convention had refused to support disarmament."

34. Transcript of NWP Convention, 129–34. The vote against Crystal Eastman's proposal was 170 to 95. Many years later Paul described Eastman's proposal as "a very involved feminist program . . . , embracing everything that Russia was doing and taking in all kinds of things that we didn't expect to take in at all. . . . We didn't give a second thought to it." AP OH, 259.

Eastman, "Alice Paul's Convention," 9–10; Freda Kirchwey, "Alice Paul Pulls the Strings," *Nation*, Mar. 2, 1921, 332–33; La Follette, "National Convention," 42. Quite a few NWP members were offended by Freda Kirchwey's snide and condemnatory tone in her article, which focused on Paul's dismissal of the black women; even Ella Rush Murray and Florence Kelley, who disapproved of what had happened, found Kirchwey's report too "flippant" and one-sided. Kelley to Mrs. Dora Lewis, Feb. 28 and Mar. 7, 1921, NWP #6; Ella Rush Murray to editor, *Nation*, Mar. 23, 1921, 434. See also Olympia Brown to Paul, Feb. 28, 1921, NWP #6; Lavinia Dock to Paul, Mar. 31, 1921, and Mary Austin to Paul, Mar. 3, 1921, NWP #7.

35. Paul to Mrs. Lawrence Lewis, Mar. 23, 1921, and to Mrs. John Rogers, Mar. 24, 1921; see also Dora Lewis to Mrs. Brannan, Mar. 9, 1921, Elsie Hill to Olympia Brown, Mar. 8, 1921, and Dora Lewis to "Dearest Paulie," Apr. 11, 1921, NWP #7. Cf. Nelson, "Ladies in the Streets," 201–06, who makes the point that the way black women's concerns were resolved constituted the NWP's first step toward elitism.

36. Florence Kelley to Mrs. Lawrence Lewis, Feb. 28, 1921, NWP #6; Agnes

Chase to Elsie Hill, Apr. 2, 1921, NWP #7; Ella Rush Murray to Temporary Secretary, Apr. 7, 1921, NWP #7. Kelley had earlier expressed her views to Ovington thus: "the only ground for having a Woman's Party is that it shall be *every* woman's Party, black, brown and yellow as well as white, alien as well as native. A Native White American Ladies' Party would be an amusing spectacle!" Kelley to Ovington, Dec. 17, 1920, folder "NWP 1920–21," NAACP Papers. After the NWP February convention the enforcement bill slipped from sight and was dropped entirely at a meeting of the National Executive Committee in May, 1921, attended only by Hill and three Southerners; Nat. Exec. Comm. minutes, May 16, 1921, NWP #114.

On black women's activism in the 1920s, see Rosalyn Terborg-Penn, "Disillusioned Black Feminists," in Lois Scharf and Joan Jensen, eds., *Decades of Discontent* (Westport, Conn., Greenwood, 1983), 261–78.

37. See chap. 8 for a discussion of women's efforts toward disarmament. Anne Martin to Miss Anita L. Pollitzer, Mar. 4, 1921; Jessie Hardy MacKaye to Elsie Hill, Mar. 21, 1921, NWP #7.

38. Hill to Willystine Goodsell, Apr. 1, 1921; Hill to Marie Ernst Kennedy, Mar. 21, 1921, NWP #7.

39. Mabel Raef Putnam to Anita L. Pollitzer, Apr. 14, 1921; Katherine Morey to Alice Paul, Mar. 17, 1921, NWP #7.

Fewer than two thousand copies of Doris Stevens's book on the militants, *Jailed for Freedom*, sold in 1920 and 1921, suggesting that there was no widespread appetite to recall women's direct action on the streets. By 1922 *Jailed for Freedom* was being "remaindered." Horace Liveright to Doris Stevens, Jan. 26, 1921, folder "Correspondence *re* Jailed for Freedom, 1920–32," DSC.

40. Rebecca Hourwich to Elsie Hill, May 6, 1921, NWP #8; Agnes B. Leach to Alice Paul, Mar. 25, 1921, NWP #7; Leach to Mrs. [Elizabeth] Rogers, Feb. 25, 1921, NWP #6; Sylvia Thygeson to Elsie Hill, Mar. 30, 1921; Beulah Amidon to NWP, n.d. [Apr. 1921]; Emma Bancroft to Elsie Hill, Mar. 24, 1921; Hill to Bancroft, Mar. 26, 1921, NWP #7.

Katherine Fisher, who was working in the labor movement in Denver, held back her "disgust" at the party's "association with the wives of plutocrats and politicians" at the convention only because she firmly imagined that "after we had shaken them down for contributions, we should do something to send them into fits, and make them all resign." Fisher to Mabel [Vernon], Feb. 12, 1921, NWP #6.

41. On Stokes, see Buhle, *Women and American Socialism*, 318–24; Lerner, "American Feminism and the Jewish Question," 321; Joan Jensen, "All Pink Sisters: The War Department and the Feminist Movement in the 1920s," in Scharf and Jensen, eds., *Decades*, 204–06; Rheta Childe Dorr, *A Woman of Fifty* (N.Y., Funk and Wagnalls, 1924), chaps. 18–22, esp. 214–19, 315. Sarah Rozner is an example of a socialist (an East European immigrant garment worker) who despite her sympathies did not want to be associated with feminism because the NWP dominated the instrumental meaning of the term; the NWP's behavior at the 1926 Women's Bureau Conference convinced her that such feminism was at odds with her socialist commitment to end capitalism. Sherna Gluck, "Socialist Feminism between the Two World Wars," in Scharf and Jenson, eds., Decades, 279–98. Cf. history of Ernestine Hara Kettler, in Gluck, ed., *From Parlor to Prison*, 227–70. See Cook, ed., *Crystal*, 24–34, on Eastman's exceptional position as a socialist and feminist.

On results in the 1930s of the split between feminism and the left, see Sharon

Hartman Strom, "Challenging 'Woman's Place': Feminism, the Left, and Industrial Unionism in the 1930s," *FS* 9: 2 (Summer 1983), 359–86.

To appropriate audiences, NWP leaders occasionally presented theirs as "one of the most radical movements," but their radicalism pertained solely to the priority given to their conception of gender equality. In a letter signed by Edith Houghton Hooker and Mary Winsor, the party appealed to the American Fund for Public Service (the Garland Fund)—a foundation run by left-wing liberals and socialists—for financial support for *Equal Rights*. Calling themselves "a small group of radical feminists," they urged, "it is especially the feminist movement that should be supported by radicals." To dispute the "false" notion of the Party's wealth, they said that the NWP was not sufficiently well off to keep open the whole of the mansion Mrs. Belmont had donated, nor to pay the taxes owed on it. Their request was turned down. Hooker and Winsor to American Fund, Jan. or Feb. 1925, and Roger M. Baldwin to Hooker and Winsor, Mar. 5, 1925, box 47, American Fund for Public Service Coll., reel 29, NYPL.

42. On number of members, Anita Pollitzer to Mrs. Dora Lewis, Apr. 13, 1921. See n. 4 above, on membership figures. Katherine B. Day to Paul, Mar. 22, 1921; Dora Lewis to Mrs. Alva Belmont, Mar. 9, 1921. NWP #7. Dunning letters appear throughout NWP #7 and #8. The *New York Times*, reporting that NWP membership had doubled during the three months preceding the dedication of a new headquarters in April 1922 (without saying what it had started from), stressed the New York society women who were enlisting as "founders." May 29, 1922, 10.

To raise funds to pay the debt accrued during the suffrage campaign, Paul charged each women's organization the inflated sum of $25 for banners and wreaths for the convention ceremony, eliciting furious complaint from Lavinia Dock (see undate letters of Jan. and Feb. 1921 from "LLD" to Emma Wold and to Alice Paul, NWP #6). She also auctioned off chairs which had been loaned, not donated, to headquarters (see Caroline Katzenstein to Alice Paul, Mar. 30, 1921, NWP #7).

The U.S. government in the mid-1920s claimed the mansion Belmont had donated to the party; the NWP received a high settlement, bought a new headquarters, and had $163,500 remaining in 1929 to invest in a capital fund. In 1933 Belmont's will left $100,000 to the Party and M. Carey Thomas's will added $50,000 in 1935. This information is contained in Susan D. Becker, *The Origins of the Equal Rights Amendment: American Feminism Between the Wars* (Westport, Conn., Greenwood, 1981), 38–41, which also reports that NWP income averaged $46,000 annually between 1923 and 1929, with approximately $6000/yr. coming from Belmont, and averaged $13,500 annually between 1930 and 1936, with approximately $5000/yr. coming from Belmont. A few other sources raise doubts about these figures, however. In a letter to Anna Kelton Wiley of Jan. 8, 1931, Alva Belmont cited the fact that she had donated $23,242 in 1930 alone to NWP efforts; folder "B", cont. 55, Wiley Coll., LC. In her recollection of Belmont, Doris Stevens claimed that Belmont had paid Alice Paul a salary of $1,000 per month during the decade; and, further, that the Women's Research Foundation was incorporated on Jul. 31, 1923, so that the money could be funneled to Paul without her paying income tax; see "Notes on Belmont 1920–21," folder 269, and "Notes—1922–23," folder 270, DSC.

Mimeographed letter, Edith Houghton Hooker to "Member of the National Council," Jan. 15, 1935, Lutz Coll. MC 182, SL, reports that Donald Hooker, Edith's husband, had donated 65 percent of the income of *Equal Rights*, a total of $28,384, between 1923 and 1934.

43. Activities of the occupational councils can be followed in *Equal Rights*. In the mid-1920s, the NWP claimed 10,000 members. However, Dora Ogle, business manager, reported in Dec. 1927 that the NWP newspaper *Equal Rights* had only 1,425 subscribers. That may have been in addition to members, for nine years later Ethel Adams Crosby wrote to Alma Lutz that *Equal Rights* went to 739 "subscribers" in addition to 1,971 "members" and 179 "founders." National Council minutes, Dec. 5, 1927, NWP #114; E.A. Crosby to Alma Lutz, May 23, 1936, folder 68, Lutz Coll., SL. Lutz, who became national organization chairman for the NWP in 1930, concluded after a survey that "our 9000 members are a myth." "Report of Organization Chairman," draft, folder 23, Lutz Coll.

Opponents of the NWP in the National Women's Trade Union League and the League of Women Voters thought NWP membership claims were exaggerated by a factor of ten. Ethel Smith to Belle Sherwin, May 10, 1926, folder 42, NWTUL Papers, SL; Mary Anderson to Mary Mundt, Sep. 24, 1926, folder 11, Mary Anderson Papers, SL.

44. Burnita Shelton Mathews to Doris Stevens, Dec. 7, 1932, folder "Burnita Mathews," box 4, DSC; Caroline Spencer to Anita Pollitzer, Apr. 30, 1921, NWP #7; Stevens, "False Social Barriers to Women's Psychic Release," speech for the Sixth International Malthusian and Birth Control Conference, Mar. 30, 1925, N.Y., folder "ts., ms. by DS," box 8, and folder "Birth Control," box 4, DSC.

45. Editorial, ER, Apr. 21, 1923, 76; Edith Houghton Hooker, Editor's Note, ER, Dec. 22, 1928, 365.

46. "The New Religion," ER, 1 (Jun. 16, 1923), 140. As editor, Hooker frequently wrote the unsigned editorials, but not always. "The Significance of the Woman's Party," ER (Sep. 18, 1926), was written by Jane Norman Smith; see folder 11, JNSC. On social movement theory and practice, including "solidary" motives and "encapsulated" formations, see Jo Freeman, ed., *Social Movements of the Sixties and Seventies* (N.Y., Longman, 1983), esp. 60–62, 283.

47. Doris Stevens, "Tribute to Alva Belmont," ER, Jul. 15, 1933. Becker, *Origins*, 161–86, describes the NWP's international work. Though president was an honorary more than a working office, the NWP National Council responded affirmatively and ingratiatingly to Belmont's 1928 query to ascertain that she was the head of the party's international as well as national work; see National Council minutes, Oct. 9, 1928, and Jan. 15, 1929, part C, NWP #114. Notes by Doris Stevens describe Belmont's pressure on the NWP to take up international work beginning in 1923—"only done because Mrs. B. so insistent . . . by no means whole-hearted interest and support of int'l [sic] work by officers of NWP," folder "Notes re Belmont, 1922–23," DSC. See note 42, above, on Belmont's financial contributions to the NWP.

48. Stevens's life and feminist work is best documented in the uncatalogued collection of her papers at SL. Her work for the Inter-American Commission on Women is catalogued in a separate collection also at SL. Because she was (by a last-minute codicil, which she blamed on Alice Paul's machinations) cut out from Belmont's will, which she had expected to reward her, and she sued to break the will, she compiled for her lawyer extensive notes on her own and Belmont's intertwined activities for the NWP between 1913 and 1933, filed under "Notes on Belmont" in DSC. Quotations in text are from MV OH, 178; Ruby Darrow to Doris Stevens, n.d., box 4, DSC; Maud Younger, autobiography, "Along the Way," chap. 41, NWP #114. (Younger also called Stevens "brilliant, dominating, untiring, dauntless," all in reference to her performance at the 1928 conference of the Pan-American Union.) On Rambouillet, Doris Stevens to Jane Norman Smith, Apr. 15, 1932, folder 125, JNSC.

49. Becker, *Origins*, provides a history of the NWP derived principally from *Equal Rights*.

50. Doris Stevens's quotation from "Littleton" folder, box IV, DSC. The papers of the NWP, but even more clearly the private papers of individuals, reveal numerous small and large controversies in which Paul had her way. Some of the more remarkable ones are Paul's break with Anne Martin over the latter's campaigns for the U.S. Senate in 1918 and 1920 (Paul claimed Martin was withdrawing woman power from the suffrage campaign); a dispute which alienated Harriot Stanton Blatch (a possible contender for NWP leadership) in 1921; the 1924 departure of the headquarters housekeeper; Mabel Vernon's resignation as executive secretary in 1930; and of course the major schisms in 1933–35 and 1946–47. See letters and telegrams between Blatch and Paul dated Nov. 1920, NWP #4 and NWP #5. On the 1924 HQ problem, Emma C. Johnson (District Treasurer of NWP) to Mrs. Evelyn Wainwright, May 29, 1924, folder "G", cont. 56; on Mabel Vernon's resignation, *New York Times* clippings, Mar. 19, 1930, and Wiley to Miss Fisher, Mar. 21, 1930, folder "F", cont. 56; Anna Kelton Wiley to Member of the National Council of the National Woman's Party, Feb. 27, 1930, folder "S", cont. 57–58; Jane Norman Smith to Mrs. Anna Kelton Wiley, Mar. 26, 1930, "S", cont. 57–58; Wiley to Miss Leila Enders, Mar. 21, 1930, "F", cont. 56, Anna Kelton Wiley Papers, LC; Mabel Vernon to Rilla Nelson, Mar. 25, 1930, folder "Corr. 1930;" Grimes Coll., Michigan Hist. Collections, Bentley Library, Univ. of Mich. The major schisms are discussed in Becker, *Origins*. Cf. this portrait of Alice Paul in 1932, written "from the heart" by Helen Archdale, an English feminist who shared Paul's goal of equal rights: "It breaks my heart to see her here in Geneva, with a handful of stray followers; with all the women's organizations with their hackles and bristles out and up against her; with the delegates being horrid about her; with the secretariat rigid to oppose her. Why? With all it is not that they disagree with her proposals but that they are upset by her methods. I wish I knew her reasons for believing in the value of antagonising people. Is it possible . . . that she has given so many years to an unpopular fight that she feels things are wrong when they become less so and even popular?" Archdale to Doris [Stevens], May 22, 1932, "Archdale" folder, box IV, DSC.

51. JR OH, 54; on Paul's strategy, AP OH, 441–42. See Nancy F. Cott, "Feminist Politics in the 1920s: The National Woman's Party," *JAH* 71 (Jun. 1984), 66–67, on the NWP and the woman's rights legacy of deliberative and collective process; cf. Ellen Dubois, *Feminism and Suffrage* (Ithaca, Cornell U.P., 1978), esp. 18, 24, and Sara Evans, *Personal Politics* (N.Y., Pantheon, 1979). Felice Gordon confirms the NWP preference for elite-run operations and neglect of grassroots organizing at the state level in New Jersey, in *After Winning: The Legacy of the New Jersey Suffragist* (New Brunswick, N.J., Rutgers U.P., 1986), 109–11.

52. Peter Geidel, "The National Woman's Party and the Origins of the Equal Rights Amendment" (M.A. thesis, Columbia U.), chap. 1, 5, quoting "Women Urge Amendment," *New York Times*, Apr. 13, 1914, 6.

3: VOLUNTARIST POLITICS

1. Catt's remarks at the NAWSA/LWV victory celebration quoted in Carrie Chapman Catt and Nettie R. Shuler, *Woman Suffrage and Politics* (N.Y., Scribner's, 1923), 382. Inez Haynes Irwin, chronicler of the Woman's Party, similarly felt "a sense of satisfaction so soul-warming" in her suffrage involvement she

could find no adjective adequate: "What fights I joined! How many speeches I made! How many words I wrote! But best of all, what women I met! How I pity any generation of women who cannot know that satisfaction!" Irwin, "The Adventures of Yesterday" (autobiography), 463, folder 12, box 3, Irwin Coll., SL. Cf. Frances Perkins's recollection, recorded in an oral history interview in 1955, "the friendships that were formed among women who were in the suffrage movement have been the most lasting and enduring friendships—solid, substantial, loyal—that I have seen anywhere. The women learned to like each other in that suffrage movement." Quoted in Susan Ware, *Beyond Suffrage: Women in the New Deal* (Cambridge, Harvard U.P., 1981), 31.

2. Inez Haynes Irwin, *Angels and Amazons* (Garden City, N.Y., Doubleday, 1934), 408–11, and Appendix. The nineteenth-century voluntary tradition in women's politics has been stressed by some historians, but with little carryover past 1920; see Mary P. Ryan, *Cradle of the Middle Class* (Cambridge, Cambridge U.P., 1981), 105–44; Anne Firor Scott, *Making the Invisible Woman Visible* (Urbana, U. Illinois P., 1984), 259–94; Paula Baker, "The Domestication of Politics: Women and American Political Society, 1780–1920," AHR 89 (Jun. 1984), 620–48. For historians' view that women's organizations waned in the 1920s, see William O'Neill, *Everyone Was Brave: A History of Feminism in America* (Chicago, Quadrangle, 1969), 225–94, and Estelle Freedman, "Separatism as Strategy: Female Institution Building and American Feminism, 1870–1930," FS 5 (Fall 1979), 512–29.

3. The League had branches in 45 states in 1931, with total membership probably under 100,000, according to Sophonisba Breckinridge, *Women in the Twentieth Century: A Study of their Political, Social and Economic Activities* (N.Y., McGraw Hill, 1933), 66–68; on the LWV program, J. Stanley Lemons, *The Woman Citizen: Social Feminism in the 1920s* (Urbana, U. Illinois P., 1973), 49–55; Louise Young, "The Excursion," Dorothy Kirchwey Brown Coll., SL; "Ten Years of Growth: The NLWV, 1920–1930," pamphlet, folder 1046, WRC, SL; on Feickert, Felice D. Gordon, *After Winning: The Legacy of the New Jersey Suffragists, 1920–1947* (New Brunswick, N.J., Rutgers U. P., 1986), 79.

Some examples of conflict between partisan priorities and the LWV: Margaret S. Roberts, a NAWSA suffragist, chaired the Idaho LWV for a short time after its founding, but she resigned because she (a loyal Republican) saw it as a Democratic plot (after Catt's predilections). Roberts to Mrs. Gifford Pinchot, Apr. 29, 1921, folder 11, Margaret S. Roberts Coll., SL.

In 1922, 42 prominent Clarksdale, Mississippi, women resigned from the local LWV because the editor of the LWV paper had sold a great deal of advertising space to Senate candidate James K. Vardaman—making it look, they thought, like a partisan sheet supporting a candidate they opposed. See Vinton M. Price, Jr., "Will Women Turn the Tide? Mississippi Women and the 1922 U.S. Senate Race," *Journal of Mississippi History* 42:3 (Aug. 1980), 212–20.

Charles Edward Russell noted in 1924 that "at its last convention" the LWV "was assailed in unmeasured terms by ladies of a strong partizan [sic] sympathy because it had not compelled all its members to be either Republicans or Democrats." "Is Woman Suffrage a Failure?" *Century Magazine* n.s. 35 (Mar. 1924), 730.

4. Margaret Gibbons Wilson, *The American Woman in Transition: The Urban Influence 1870–1920* (Westport, Conn., Greenwood, 1979), 98, 100–01, 107 n. 26; O'Neill, *Everyone Was Brave*, 256–62; Breckinridge, *Women in the 20th Century*, 39, 53–54, 79–80.

5. Folder 2, International Federation of Working Women Coll., SL; Clarke

A. Chambers, *Seedtime of Reform* (Minneapolis, U. Minnesota P., 1963), 7; Allis Wolfe, "Women, Consumerism, and the National Consumers League in the Progressive Era, 1900–23," *Labor History* 16 (Summer 1975), 378–92; Nancy Schrom Dye, *As Equals and As Sisters: Feminism, Unionism, and the Women's Trade Union League of New York* (Columbia, U. Missouri P., 1980); Lemons, *Woman Citizen*, 25–30, 122–23; O'Neill, *Everyone Was Brave*, 231–49; Pauline Newman, transcript of interview by Barbara Wertheimer, in The Twentieth Century Trade Union Woman, Oral History Project, Program on Woman and Work, Institute of Labor and Industrial Relations, U. Michigan and Wayne State U., SL.

    6. Breckinridge, *Women in the 20th Century*, 56–57; Alice Kessler-Harris, *Out to Work: A History of Wage-Earning Women in the U.S.* (N.Y., Oxford, 1982), 243–45; Theresa Wolfson, "Trade Union Activities of Women," AAAPSS 143 (May 1929), 130–31; Philip S. Foner, *Women and the American Labor Movement* (N.Y., Free Press, 1980), 2; 126–28; Mary Frederickson, "The Southern Summer School for Women Workers," *Southern Exposure* 4 (Winter 1977), 70–75, and "'I know which side I'm on': Southern Women in the Labor Movement in the Twentieth Century," in *Women, Work and Protest*, ed. Ruth Milkman (Boston, Routledge Kegan Paul, 1985), 169–71; Mary Anderson, "Summer Schools for Women in Industry," *JAAUW*, 21 (Apr. 1928), 77–78; Hilda Worthington Smith, "Schools for Women Workers in Industry," *JAAUW*, 23 (Apr. 1930), 115–21; Dolores Janiewski, *Sisterhood Denied: Race, Gender and Class in a New South Community* (Philadelphia, Temple U.P., 1985), 83, 151; Rita R. Heller, "The Bryn Mawr Workers' Summer School, 1921–1933: A Surprising Alliance," *History of Higher Education Annual* (1981), 110–31, and "The Women of Summer: The Bryn Mawr Summer School for Women Workers, 1921–1934" (Ph.D. diss., Rutgers U., 1986), esp. 97 on YWCA Industrial Clubs as recruitment mechanism and 186 for quotation from college student, Elizabeth Lyle Huberman. Barbara Solomon, *In the Company of Educated Women* (New Haven, Yale U.P., ;1985), 165–66, reports decline in membership in college YWCAs in 1920s and 1930s.

    7. Report, "Business Women's Convention [1919]," box 1, and Phillips' essay of 1921 regarding founding and goals of NFBPW in folder "1918–1921–1925," box II, Lena Madesin Phillips uncatalogued coll., SL; see Lemons, *Woman Citizen*, 43–45, and 58–59 n. 8 for a listing of women's professional associations formed in the World War I era.

    8. Breckinridge, *Women in the 20th Century*, 63–64, 54–55, 79. The NFBPW membership were 40 percent clerical workers in the latter 1920s, according to a survey of 14,000 representative NFBPW members conducted between 1926 and 1929 by Margaret Elliott, "What Women Earn," *Indep. W.*, Dec. 1930, 536. The proportion increased to almost 45% in a 1936 study of the membership reported on "Sarah Matthews' Page" in folder "1918 [sic], Rep'ts," box I, L. M. Phillips Coll., SL. Elliott's survey also yielded information about the educational background of BPW members in the late 1920s. About 40 percent of them had more than a high school education: 13 percent had attended normal school, 14 percent some college, and 13 percent held a college degree or advanced degree; 11 percent had finished grade school only; the remaining half had attended or graduated from high school. Margaret Elliott and Grace Manson, "Some Factors Affecting Earnings of Business and Professional Women," AAPSS 143 (May 1929), 142.

    9. Elisabeth Israels Perry, "Training for Public Life—ER and Women's Political Networks in the 1920s," in Joan Hoff Wilson and Marjorie Lightman, eds.,

Without Precedent: The Life and Career of Eleanor Roosevelt (Bloomington, Indiana U.P., 1984), 28–44; and Paula J. Dubeck, "Influential Alliances? Cincinnati Women in the Political Arena, 1920–45," in Dana V. Hiller and Robin Ann Sheets, eds., *Women and Men: The Consequences of Power* (Office of Women's Studies, U. Cincinnati, 1976), 287–97.

10. Joan Jensen, "The Evolution of Margaret Sanger's *Family Limitation* Pamphlet, 1914–21," *Signs* 6:3 (Spring 1981), 548–67; David Kennedy, *Birth Control in America* (New Haven, Conn., Yale U. P., 1970), 100–01, 221–22; Linda Gordon, *Woman's Body, Woman's Right* (N.Y., Grossman, 1976), 274–87, 295–98; [Mrs. Leonard D. Adkins] to Mrs. Day, Jul. 21, 1928, in folder "Birth Control—Correspondence, A. G. Porritt, 1924–1932," box 2, Annie G. Porritt Coll., SSC.

11. I depend here on the work of Steven L. Schlossman, esp. "Before Home Start: Notes Toward a History of Parent Education in America, 1897–1929," *Harvard Educational Review* 46 (Aug. 1976), 436–67; "Philanthropy and the Gospel of Child Development," *Hist. of Educ. Q.* 21 (Fall 1981), 275–99; and "The Formative Era in American Parent Education: Overview and Interpretation," in Ron Hoskins and Diane Adams, eds., *Parent Education and Public Policy* (Norwood, N.J., Ablex, 1983), 7–38.

12. Breckinridge, *Women in the 20th Century*, 54–56, 79.

13. Breckinridge, *Women in the 20th Century*, 49–51, 58–59; June Sochen, *Consecrate Each Day: The Public Lives of Jewish American Women 1880–1980* (Albany, SUNY P., 1981), chaps. 4 and 5; Norma Fain Pratt, "Transitions in Judaism: The Jewish American Woman Through the 1930s," in Janet James, ed., *Women in American Religion* (Philadelphia, U. Pennsylvania P., 1978), 222.

14. Breckinridge, *Women in the 20th Century*, 77–79; Rosalyn Terborg-Penn, "Disillusioned Black Feminists," in Lois Scharf and Joan Jensen, eds., *Decades of Discontent* (Westport, Conn., Greenwood, 1983), 269–70, 272–73; Paula Giddings, *When and Where I Enter: The Impact of Black Women on Race and Sex in America* (N.Y., William Morrow, 1984), 177, 183–85, 203–04, 211–12, including quotation from Elise J. MacDougald, "The Double Task: The Struggle of Negro Women for Race and Sex Emancipation," *Survey Graphic*, Mar. 1925, on 183; Evelyn Brooks, "In Politics to Stay: Mobilization of the Black Female Electorate During the 1920s," paper prepared for the Russell Sage Foundation Project, "Women in 20th Century American Politics," 9 Jun. 1986 [in my possession].

15. Breckinridge, *Women in the 20th Century*, 43–49F42 58.

16. Charles DeBenedetti, *Origins of the Modern American Peace Movement, 1915–1929* (Millwood, N.Y., KTO P., 1978), esp. 90–97; Charles Chatfield, *For Peace and Justice: Pacifism in America, 1914–1941* (Knoxville, Tennessee U.P., 1971); Florence Brewer Boeckel, "Women in International Affairs," *AAAPSS* 143 (May 1929), 231–32; Breckinridge, *Women in the 20th Century*, 85–87; Joan Jensen, "All Pink Sisters: The War Department and the Feminist Movement in the 1920s," in Scharf and Jensen, eds., *Decades*, 199–222; on the National Congress of Parents and Teachers' legislative programs, see folders 15, 17, 33, 36, Elizabeth Tilton Coll., SL. The memberships affiliated with the NCCCW amounted to 8 million women by 1930, when the adult female population was 37 million; the assertion regarding one in five does not take overlapping memberships into account. See Merle Curti, *Peace or War* (N.Y., Norton, 1936), 272.

17. Gordon, *After Winning*, 122–23, confirms that the level of organization among New Jersey women at the end of the 1920s compares favorably to suffrage days. Census figures for women over 20 in Gertrude Bancroft, *The American*

Labor Force: Its Growth and Changing Composition (N.Y., Wiley, 1958), table D-1, 203; on Ames, Jacquelyn Dowd Hall, *Revolt Against Chivalry: Jessie Daniel Ames and the Woman's Campaign Against Lynching* (N.Y., Columbia U. P., 1979).

18. Anne O'Hagan, "The Serious-Minded Young—If Any," *The Woman's Journal* 13 (Apr. 1928), 6; Julia Adams, "The 'Serious Young' Speak Up," *The Woman's Journal* 13 (May 1928), 8–9; Mildred Adams, "Did They Know What They Wanted?" *The Outlook* 147 (Dec. 28, 1927), 544. See also Margaret Culkin Banning, "The Lazy Thirties," *Harper's Monthly Magazine* 154 (Feb. 1927), 357–65.

19. Marion Cannon Schlesinger's recollections [*Snatched from Oblivion* (Boston, Little Brown, 1979)] of her mother, Cornelia James Cannon (the wife of a university professor in Cambridge), offer a fascinating example of a 1920s voluntarist "type" of home-occupied woman, always writing letters to the newspapers and to city politicians, a birth control activist, often on the school board.

20. See Edward B. Logan, "Lobbying," AAAPSS 144, suppl. (Jul. 1929), 32; Dorothy Johnson, "Organized Women as Lobbyists in the 1920s," *Capitol Studies* 1 (Spring 1972), 41–58.

21. Breckinridge, *Women in the 20th Century*, 259–61, quotation on 264; Lemons, *Woman Citizen*, 55–56; Johnson, "Organized Women as Lobbyists," 46–48; Sheila Rothman, *Woman's Proper Place* (N.Y., Basic, 1978), 136–42; Charles Selden, "The Most Powerful Lobby in Washington," *Ladies Home Journal*, Apr. 1922, 5, 93–96. Constituents of WJCC not mentioned in text were the AAUW, PTA, National Council of Jewish Women, and American Home Economics Association. Felice Gordon confirms that among New Jersey suffragists after 1920 the voluntarist, lobbying mode of women's politics persisted; see *After Winning*.

After the Keating-Owen Act of 1916 prohibiting child labor in interstate commerce was declared unconstitutional in 1918, Florence Kelley led the effort to put a 10 percent surtax on products manufactured by child labor, which was passed in 1919 but struck down in 1922. Chambers, *Seedtime of Reform* 33–37.

22. Lemons, *Woman Citizen*, 63–68 (quotation from Park, 66), 235–37; Virginia Sapiro, "Women, Citizenship and Nationality: Immigration and Naturalization Policies in the U.S.," *Politics and Society* 13:1 (1984), 1–26; see also Sophonisba Breckinridge, *Marriage and the Civil Rights of Women* (Chicago, U. Chicago P., 1931).

23. [Mary Anderson,] "Organized Women and their Program," c. 1924, folder 84, Mary Anderson Coll., SL.

24. Quotations from Shaw, CU, and Kelley cited by Aileen S. Kraditor, *The Ideas of the Woman Suffrage Movement, 1890–1920* (1965, repr. Garden City, N.Y., Anchor, 1971), 50; Ronald Schaffer, "The New York Woman City Suffrage Party, 1910–1919," *N.Y. History* 43 (Jul. 1962), 273; quotation from Catt's letter of Oct. 9, 1915 to speakers, in Doris Daniels, "Building a Winning Coalition: The Suffrage Fight in New York State," ibid. 60 (Jan. 1979), 71.

25. On political science, Edward A. Purcell, Jr., *The Crisis of Democratic Theory* (Lexington, U. P. Kentucky, 1973), 95–114. Cf. a work of contemporary political cynicism by a journalist, Frank Kent, *Political Behavior* (N.Y., William Morrow, 1928). On voter turnout, Walter Dean Burnham, "The Changing Shape of the American Political Universe," *American Political Science Review* 59 (Mar. 1965), 10; see also E. E. Schnattsneider, *The Semisovereign People* (Hinsdale, Illinois, Dryden, 1960), William H. Flanigan and Nancy H. Zingale, *Political Behavior of the American Electorate*, 4th ed. (Boston, Allyn and Bacon, 1979).

318 NOTES TO PAGES 102–04

26. The literature on the meaning of Progressivism is vast; a good survey of recent trends is Daniel T. Rodgers, "In Search of Progressivism," *Reviews in American History* 10 (Dec. 1982), 113–32. Especially relevant are Samuel Hays, "The Politics of Reform in Municipal Government in the Progressive Era," *Pacific Northwest Quarterly* 55 (1964), 157–69; James Weinstein, *The Corporate Ideal in the Liberal State, 1900–1918* (Boston, Beacon, 1968), esp. 92–116; J. Morgan Kousser, *The Shaping of Southern Politics* (New Haven, Yale U.P., 1974); David W. Eakins, "The Origins of Corporate Liberal Policy Research, 1916–1922: The Political Economic Expert and the Decline of Public Debate," in Jerry Israel, ed., *Building the Organizational Society: Essays on Associational Activities in Modern America,* (N.Y., Free Press, 1972), 163–79, 288–91. Cf., above, the Cable's Act function in closing off marriage as a route to citizenship for immigrant women; Sapiro, "Women, Citizenship and Nationality."

State-level woman suffrage campaigns in the 1910s moved progressively away from popular decision-making and toward more elite forums: before 1915 all had sought popular referenda, but the later state campaigns, with rare exceptions, sought to obtain woman suffrage through the statutory actions of state legislatures. See Eileen L. McDonagh and H. Douglas Price, "Woman Suffrage in the Progressive Era: Patterns of Opposition and Support in Referenda Voting, 1910–1918," *American Political Science Review* 79 (Jun. 1985), 415–435.

27. Suzanne La Follette, *Concerning Women* (N.Y., Boni, 1926), 268; Schattsneider, *Semisovereign People;* Burnham, "Changing Shape."

28. "Is Woman Suffrage Failing?" *Woman Citizen,* n.s. 8 (Apr. 19, 1924), 14–16. Susan C. Bourque and Jean Grossholz, in "Politics an Unnatural Practice: Political Science Looks at Female Participation," *Politics and Society* (Winter 1974), 225–66, very effectively show that early 1920s analyses of female nonvoting—especially from Merriam and Gosnell, discussed below—were still being repeated in political science texts of the 1960s.

29. Charles Edward Merriam and Harold Foote Gosnell, *Non-Voting: Causes and Methods of Control* (Chicago, U. Chicago P., 1923), see esp. 5–8, 25–26, 37–38, 109–201, 236–61, quotations on 145–47. With regard to choice of investigators, there is an intriguing footnote, p. 3, stating that "in 1922, some 1,000 observations of non-voters were made by the National League of Women Voters under the direction of Mr. Merriam, but it proved impossible to carry on this work successfully without trained observers under close supervision." See Purcell, *Crisis,* esp. 96–98, on the point that voting behavior became a prime subject in the 1920s and 1930s for political scientists who aimed to use scientific methodology.

30. Stuart A. Rice and Malcolm M. Willey, "American Women's Ineffective Use of the Vote," *Current History* 20 (Jul. 1924), 641–47. Cf. Hugh L. Keenleyside, "The American Political Revolution of 1924," *Current History,* 21 (Mar. 1925), 833–40, which adopts Rice's and Willey's estimates. Recent treatments are Paul Kleppner, "Were Women to Blame? Female Suffrage and Voter Turnout," *Journal of Interdisciplinary History* 12 (Spring 1982), 621–43; Sara Alpern and Dale Baum, "Female Ballots: The Impact of the Nineteenth Amendment," ibid. 16 (Summer 1985), 43–67; Kristi Anderson, "Women and Citizenship in the 1920s," paper prepared for the project "Women in Twentieth-Century American Politics," Russell Sage Foundation, Jun. 7, 1986.

In Richmond, Virginia, in 1920, despite the fact that white women's applications were processed six times faster than blacks', as many black women as black men registered to vote while white women were outnumbered by white men three to one. Still, the absolute number of black women registered was too small to make an appreciable difference in black political power. Suzanne Lebsock, "Woman Suffrage and White Supremacy: A Virginia Case Study," paper presented at the Woodrow Wilson International Center for Scholars, Washington, D.C. Jul. 18, 1985, 9. In Baltimore, the black electorate more than doubled, increasing from 16,800 to 37,400, in 1921. Ida B. Wells-Barnett credited the votes of black women organized by her Alpha Suffrage Club (enfranchised in 1913) for the election in 1915 of Oscar de Priest as Chicago's first black alderman; and political scientist Harold Gosnell's several studies of Chicago politics likened black women's involvement in politics to black men's; Terborg-Penn, "Discontented Black Feminists," 265, 275, and Brooks, "In Politics To Stay," 4–5, 8.

In *Recent Social Trends*, by the President's Committee on Social Trends (N.Y., McGraw Hill, 1934), 738, Breckinridge reported more figures on women voters' participation. In Chicago in 1914, 32 percent of people registering to vote were female; in 1928, 43%; in 1931, 42%. Secretaries of State of Pennsylvania and Rhode Island supplied the following figures (percentages of voters who were female):

	Percentages of voters who were female:
Pennsylvania	
1925	41.8
1931	44.0
Rhode Island	
1922	40.2
1924	44.1
1926	42.8
1930	45.4

31. Ida M. Tarbell, "Is Woman's Suffrage a Failure?" *Good Housekeeping* 79 (Oct. 1924), 18. Tarbell also remarked, similarly to Suzanne La Follette, whose politics she did not share, "it is one of the tragic features of the case that women have got their hands on political machinery and formulas when a good part of the world is realising that they are not the fundamentals of salvation" (240). E.g., Russell, "Is Woman Suffrage a Failure?" 724–30; "Woman Suffrage Declared a Failure," *Literary Digest* 81 (Apr. 12, 1924), 12–13; Ida Clyde Clarke, "Why Pick on the Women?" *Pictorial Review* 25 (Jun. 1924) 1–2; Edna Kenton, "Four Years of Equal Suffrage," *Forum* 72 (Jul. 1924), 37–44; Carrie Chapman Catt, "What Women Have Done with the Vote," *Independent* 115 (Oct. 17, 1925), 447–48; "Is Woman Suffrage Failing?" *Woman Citizen*, n.s., 8 (Mar. 22, 1924), 7–9, 29–30—includes Lifshitz and Schneiderman comments; ibid., Apr. 5, 1924, 8–10, 30; ibid., Apr. 19, 1924, 14–16; ibid., May 3, 1924, 17, 26.

32. Lemons, *Woman Citizen*, 92–93; Elizabeth Tilton, entry for Jul. 16, 1919, Journal vol. 1, 255, Tilton Coll., SL; John D. Buenker, "The Urban Political Machine and Woman Suffrage," *The Historian* 33 (1970–71), 264–79; William Ogburn and Inez Goltra, "How Women Vote: A Study of An Election in Portland, Oregon," *Political Science Q.* 34 (Sep. 1919), 413–33; Rice and Willey, "American Women's Ineffective Use," 641–47. Rice and Willey contributed some interesting, if fragmentary, evidence that women's electoral choices leaned toward "moral" and "civic" concerns and shunned radical economic proposals in local politics. In a 1919 vote whether to oust saloons from Chicago, while voters of both sexes defeated the question, men were against it four to one, women only two to one. In the 1920 presidential race, Illinois women voted slightly

Table 3.1: Party Vote for President in Illinois, 1920

Party	Total Vote	Women's Vote	Proportion of Women's Vote to Total
Republican	1,420,480	564,557	39.0
Democratic	534,395	192,005	35.9
Socialist	74,747	18,976	25.4
Prohibition	11,216	6,336	56.5
Farmer-Labor	49,630	12,342	24.9
Single Tax	775	258	33.3
Socialist Labor	3,471	979	28.2
Total	2,094,714	795,453	37.9

more strongly Republican and more weakly Democratic than men, but varied broadly in their choices among the five minor parties. Rice and Willey made little of it, but a "gender gap" was visible, for women cast only a quarter of the votes for left-wing parties and more than half of those for the Prohibition candidate (see table 3.1).

33. Maud Wood Park, *Front Door Lobby*, ed. Edna Stantial (Boston, Beacon, 1960), 260; Carole Nichols, "Votes and More for Women: Suffrage and After in Connecticut," *Women and History*, 5 (Spring 1983), 34–38; Lemons, *Woman Citizen*, 93–95; on 1918 campaigns to defeat incumbent Senators, see ibid., 91–92, and Eleanor Flexner, *Century of Struggle* (N.Y., Atheneum, 1968), 310–11. Connecticut ratified the Nineteenth Amendment after the requisite 36th state (Tennessee) had done so, but when there still was some challenge being raised against the Tennessee ratification.

34. Lemons, *Woman Citizen*, 90, 93–96, 98–100 (quotation from Miller, 99); Jean Burnett Tompkins, "Women's Void in Politics," *New York Times*, Nov. 21, 1920, 22; "Are Women a Menace?" *Nation* 112 (Feb. 9, 1921), 198.

35. Martin continued through the mid-1920s to view the NWP's effort at equal rights legislation as insufficient because "nothing less than woman's actual and equal participation in government, and in all the business of life will establish her equality." No doubt some lingering resentment about the NWP's refusal to divert womanpower to her own campaigns in 1918 and 1920 figured there. Quotations from Martin, "Woman's Inferiority Complex," TNR 27 (Jul. 20, 1921), 210–12; "Woman's Vote and Woman's Chains," *Sunset Magazine* (April 1922), 14; and "Feminists and Future Political Action," *Nation* 120 (Feb. 18, 1925), 185. See also her "Equality Laws vs. Women in Government," *Nation* 115 (Aug. 16, 1922), 165–66; "Political Methods of American and British Feminists," *Current History* 20 (Jun. 1924), 396–401; "Women and Their Magazines," TNR (Sep. 20, 1922), 93; and Kathryn Louise Anderson, "Practical Political Equality for Women: Anne Martin's Campaigns for the U.S. Senate in Nevada, 1918 and 1920" (Ph.D. diss., U. Washington, 1978), 223.

Rice and Willey, in "American Women's Ineffective Use," pointed to many of the same inequities Anne Martin decried. They admitted "party politics is a man's game." They pointed out that a woman was able to land a major party nomination for U.S. senator only when "there was not even a remote chance of victory." They contrasted the 84 women state legislators elected in 30 states in 1922 with the nearly 10,000 men holding such offices. They observed that women gained appointive positions in counties and states only if those were "lacking in one or both of the two features which make officeholding attractive to men—salary and power." Unlike Martin, they made no proposals to address those inequities, positing instead that as women "learned to use" the ballot box and gained "experience," they would participate in all of political life on terms of "actual equality" with men.

36. Schneiderman in *Woman Citizen*, n.s. 8 (Mar. 22, 1924), 29–30; Frances Kellor, "Women in British and American Politics," *Current History* 17 (Feb. 1923), 831–35; Gordon, *After Winning*, esp. 37–38, 85.

37. Park, *Front Door Lobby*, 179–80.

38. In 1920, 7 women ran on major party tickets for the U.S. House of Representatives, all but one under the aegis of the party habitually defeated in her district. In 1922, 6 women candidates tried for the office of U.S. senator, 2 as Democrats against popular Republican incumbents, the other 4 on minor party tickets. There were 21 candidates for the U.S. House of Representatives, 5 Republicans (all but one in Democratic districts), 10 Democrats (all in Republican districts), 2 on the Prohibition Party, one on the Socialist, and three on the Socialist/Farmer-Labor tickets. The only victor was Winifred Mason Huck of Illinois, who had been nominated by the Republican Party to fill her deceased father's seat. Breckinridge, *Women in 20th Century*, 296–303, quoting *Woman Citizen*, Nov. 18, 1922, on 302; Martin Gruberg, *Women in American Politics* (Oshkosh, Wisc., Academia, 1968), 121; cf. Marguerite Arnold, "Politics—A Profession for Women," *Journal of the Association of Collegiate Alumnae* 14:2 (Nov. 1920), 34–39. Joan Jensen discusses the Republican campaign of Adelina Otero-Warren for the U.S. House of Representatives in New Mexico in 1922, "'Disfranchisement is a Disgrace': Women and Politics in New Mexico, 1900–1940," *N. M. Historical Rev.* 56 (Jan. 1981), 26–27.

39. William Chafe, *The American Woman: Her Changing Social, Economic and Political Roles, 1920–1970* (N.Y., Oxford U.P., 1972), 25–47; Breckinridge, *Women in 20th Century*, 301–311; Lemons, *Woman Citizen*, 101–12; Louise Young, *Understanding Politics: A Practical Guide for Women* (N.Y., Pellegrini and Cudahy, 1950), 48, 205–206; for examples of women gaining local and state office only when on the dominant party slate, see Nichols, "Votes and More," 47–50; see also Paul C. Taylor, "The Entrance of Women into Party Politics: the 1920s" (Ph.D. diss., Harvard U., 1966). Partisan barriers showed up strongly in Florence Ellinwood Allen's political career in Ohio. Elected as judge of common pleas in Cuyahoga County, Ohio, in 1920, and then as the first female justice of the Supreme Court of Ohio two years later, through the mobilization of women's support in nonpartisan elections, Allen tried for the Democratic nomination for U.S. senator in 1926. At the last minute the male incumbent, an anti-suffragist who had promised to retire, entered the primary race and was restored to place by 20,000 votes. Allen prospered in her judicial career, however; she was re-elected to the Supreme Court in 1928 and appointed by Franklin Delano Roosevelt to the U.S. Circuit Court of Appeals in 1934. See Florence E. Allen, *To Do Justly* (Cleveland, P. Western Reserve, 1965), 39–78.

40. On Robertson and on Coe, Lemons, *Woman Citizen*, 71, 103, 158; Johnson, "Organized Women as Lobbyists," 47. Mary Anderson to Harriet Taylor Upton, Jan. 16, 1925, folder 8, Mary Anderson Coll., SL; Sue Shelton White to Molly Dewson, Nov. 23, 1928, vol. 1, Sue Shelton White Coll., SL; Emily Newell Blair quoted in Breckinridge, *Women in the 20th Century*, 336–37. A different path in Democratic politics was taken by Belle Moskowitz, who, in contrast,

gained her great importance to Democratic governor of New York and presidential nominee Alfred Smith by working behind the scenes and accepting as her principal priority Smith's and the Democratic Party's welfare. See Elisabeth Israels Perry, *Belle Moskowitz: Social Reform and Politics in the Age of Alfred E. Smith* (N.Y., Oxford U.P., 1987).

The problem of "the wrong woman" was not a passing one. Cf. Mary Anderson to Louise Franklin Bache (Exec. Sec. of NFBPW), Jul. 24, 1942, regarding appointments of women to the Labor Advisory Committee of the Manpower Board, "if women are going to get anywhere, women will have to tell men whom they think would represent them best, and I think that is perfectly fair. If men are left to choose we usually get the kind of woman who doesn't know what it is all about and will misrepresent us rather than represent us." Folder 40, Mary Anderson Coll., SL.

41. Blair was a greater advocate of forming a woman's bloc in 1931 than she had been ten years earlier, when she had imagined that the political parties were open to women's self-defined interests. See her articles, "Wanted: A New Feminism," *Indep. W.* 10 (Dec. 1930), 498; "Discouraged Feminists," *The Outlook* 158 (Jul. 8, 1931), 302–03, 318; and "Putting Women into Politics," *Woman's Journal* 16 (Mar. 1931), 14–15, 29. Cf. Freedman, "Separatism as Strategy." Lillian Feickert experienced similar bitterness over "official women" embraced by the New Jersey Republican Party and an evolution similar to Blair's toward the notion of a woman's bloc; see Gordon, *After Winning*, esp. 90.

42. See "Women for Congress" [1924], folder 6, Mary Winsor Coll., SL.

43. Mary Garrett Hay, quoted from *New York Tribune*, Dec. 1, 1918, in Marie Louise Degen, *The History of the Woman's Peace Party* (Baltimore, Johns Hopkins U.P., 1939), 220; cf. the hope of a NWP suffragist, a Philadelphia newspaperwoman, that the party after suffrage would not be "a separate women's political organization," which she thought "would only antagonize the men and jeopardize woman's influence in politics." Constance Drexel to Florence Brewer Boeckel, Sep. 6, 1920, NWP #4.

44. Quotations of 1920s spokeswomen are cited in Alpern and Baum, "Female Ballots," 60–62; John W. Furlow, "Cornelia Bryce Pinchot: Feminism in the Post-Suffrage Era," *Pennsylvania Hist.* 95 (Oct. 1976), esp. 337–40.

45. *New York Times*, Nov. 30, 1918, 16; "The Interlocking Lobby Dictatorship," *The Woman Patriot* 6 (Dec. 1, 1922); "Organizing Women for Class and Sex War," ibid. 7 (Apr. 15, 1923).

46. William Hard, quoted in "What the American Man Thinks," *Woman Citizen*, Sep. 8, 1923, cited by O'Neill, *Everyone Was Brave*, 264.

4: EQUAL RIGHTS AND ECONOMIC ROLES

1. Crystal Eastman, "Birth Control in the Feminist Program," *Birth Control Review*, Jan. 1918, repr. in *Crystal Eastman on Women and Revolution*, ed. Blanche Wiesen Cook (N.Y., Oxford U.P., 1978), 46–47. On women and eighteenth-century natural rights philosophy, see Linda K. Kerber, *Women of the Republic: Intellect and Ideology in Revolutionary America* (Chapel Hill, UNC P., 1980), and Ellen Dubois, *Feminism and Suffrage* (Ithaca, Cornell U.P., 1978), esp. 42–46. On the meaning of independence in republican ideology, see J.G.A. Pocock, *The Machiavellian Moment* (Princeton, Princeton U.P., 1975); on nineteenth-century "free labor" ideology, see Eric Foner, *Free Soil, Free Labor, Free Men* (N.Y., Oxford U.P., 1970).

2. Detroit Association statement quoted in Maurine W. Greenwald, *Women,*

War and Work (Westport, Conn., Greenwood, 1980), 156; lawyer's remark in response to question on BVI questionnaire, "Has suffrage increased women's opportunities in law?" folder 133, BVI Coll., SL.

3. Doris Stevens, "Women in Industry" [1923], box IV, DSC; figure on unionization among women in industry cited in Alice Kessler-Harris, "Problems of Coalition-Building: Women and Trade Unions in the 1920s," in *Women, Work and Protest*, ed. Ruth Milkman (Boston, Routledge Kegan Paul, 1985), 112; among all women employed outside of agriculture, the proportion organized was much lower, under seven percent. On World War I, see Greenwald, *Women, War, and Work*; and cf. Sandra M. Gilbert, "Soldier's Heart: Literary Men, Literary Women, and the Great War," *Signs* 8:3 (1983), 422–50, on reactions in English fiction to women's wartime gains.

4. See Mari Jo Buhle, *Women and American Socialism* (Urbana, U. Illinois P., 1981), esp. 50–60, 176–84; Susan Levine, "Labor's True Woman: Domesticity and Equal Rights in the Knights of Labor," *JAH* 70 (Sep. 1983), 323–40; Dubois, *Feminism and Suffrage*, esp. 105–62; *Elizabeth Cady Stanton/Susan B. Anthony: Correspondence, Writings, Speeches*, ed. Ellen Carol Dubois (N.Y., Schocken, 1981), esp. 98–101; Melusina Fay Pierce quoted in Daniel T. Rodgers, *The Work Ethic in Industrial America 1860–1920* (U. Chicago P., 1974), 196. As it was linked to the labor theory of value (the reasoning that all wealth derived from labor), insistence on woman's right to labor could be turned either to uphold capitalist entrepreneurial values or to decry those values. On the range contained within the labor theory of value, see Sean Wilentz, *Chants Democratic* (N.Y., Oxford U.P., 1984), 157–58.

5. See Leslie Woodcock Tentler, *Wage-Earning Women: Industrial Work and Family Life in the U.S., 1900–1930* (N.Y., Oxford U.P., 1979), chap. 1, on industrially employed women's wages, keyed below subsistence. Tentler argues that industrial wage-earning reinforced gender hierarchy and domestic expectations among female adolescents rather than suggesting any notions of economic independence.

6. Katherine Fisher to Paul, (also mentioning that Mary Beard "fears the effect of your amendment and bills on women workers") Nov. 8, 1920, NWP #5; Paul to Elsie Hill, telegram, Jan. 4, 1921; Eva Epstein Shaw to Paul, Jan. 4, 1921; Florence Brewer Boeckel to Mr. Brigham, Jan. 28, 1921, NWP #6. Deputation to Harding, and versions of state legislation are discussed in correspondence of Mar. 1921, NWP #7.

7. Paul to Katherine Morey, Mar. 20, 1921, NWP #7. For similar sentiments see also Paul to Katherine Morey, Mar. 22, 1921; Anita L. Pollitzer to Izetta Jewel Brown, Mar. 30, 1921, NWP #7; Elsie Hill to Florence Kelley, n.d. early 1921, NWP #6; Elsie Hill to Mrs. Florence Kennedy [sic—should be Kelley], Mar. 21, 1921; Temp. Sec. Anita L. Pollitzer to Shippen Lewis, Apr. 1, 1921; Elsie M. Hill to Shippen Lewis, Apr. 7, 1921; rough draft, Paul to Florence Sanville, Apr. 2, 1921, NWP #7. Peter Geidel, in "The National Woman's Party and the Origins of the Equal Rights Amendment, 1920–1923," *Historian* 52 (Aug. 1980), 561–62, notes that articles critical of protective labor legislation for women first appeared in *The Suffragist* in the spring of 1920, written by Florence Brewer Boeckel, Rheta Childe Dorr, and Marie Obenauer.

On the Wisconsin Equal Rights Bill, see Edwin E. Witte, "History and Purposes of the Wisconsin Equal Rights Law," Dec. 1929, Mabel Raef Putnam Coll., SL; and Peter Geidel, "The National Woman's Party and the Origins of the Equal Rights Amendment" (M.A. thesis, Columbia U., 1977), chap. 3.

8. Harriot Stanton Blatch to Anne Martin, May 14, [1918], and see Blatch to

Martin, Jul. 4, [1918], Anne Martin Coll., BL; Blatch to Elsie Hill, Mar. 22, 1921, and Blatch to NWP Headquarters, Apr. 8, 1921, NWP #7; Harriot Stanton Blatch and Alma Lutz, *Challenging Years: Memoirs of Harriot Stanton Blatch* (N.Y., G. P. Putnam's Sons, 1940), 287–89, 324–25; obituary of Dr. Caroline Spencer in ER, Oct. 6, 1928, 275; Paul to Jane Norman Smith, Nov. 29, 1921, folder 110, JNSC, SL. Paul recalled, in AP OH, 47678, that Laughlin had alerted her to the risks in sex-based labor legislation. On Laughlin's prickliness in the NFBPW, see typescript attached to Lena Madesin Phillips to Miss Florence Crawford, folder "National Federation 1921," box 1, Lena Madesin Phillips un-cat. coll., SL. On NWP persistence with safeguarding clauses, see Anita L. Pollitzer to Jane Norman Smith, Jan. 5, 1922, folder 110, and Jane Norman Smith to Hon. Salvatore A. Cotillo, Mar. 4, 1922, folder 196, JNSC.

9. Maud Wood Park, *Front Door Lobby*, ed. Edna Stantial (Boston, Beacon P., 1960), 23. Catharine Waugh McCulloch, for example, a former NAWSA suf-fragist and attorney who in the 1920s worked on the LWV's legal rights effort, would not take NWP materials seriously nor work with NWP lawyers. See her papers in the Dillon Coll., SL.

10. On NWTUL, Nancy Schrom Dye, *As Equals and as Sisters: Feminism, the Labor Movement, and the Women's Trade Union League of New York* (Columbia, U. Missouri P., 1980); copy of Ethel M. Smith (Press Secretary, NAWSA) to Mrs. Catt, Confidential, Jun. 26, 1917, Carrie Chapman Catt Coll. LC, reel 6. Kelley to Mrs. Dora Lewis, Mar. 7, 1921, NWP #6; Kelley to Elsie Hill, Mar. 21, 1921, NWP #7, and see Nora Stanton Blatch Barney's remarks in Transcript of NWP Convention, Feb. 15–18, 1921, 67, folder 18, Alma Lutz MC 182 Coll., SL; see also Nora Stanton Barney to Mrs. [Dora] Lewis, Jan. 26, 1921, NWP #6. On Kelley's "apprenticeship" in reform, see Kathryn Kish Sklar, "Hull House in the 1890s: A Community of Women Reformers," *Signs* 10 (Summer 1985), 658–77; and on Barney, Ellen Dubois, "Spanning Two Centuries: The Autobiography of Nora Stanton Barney," *History Workshop* 22 (Autumn 1986), 131–52.

11. "Conference on So-called 'Equal Rights' Amendment Proposed by the Na-tional Woman's Party Dec. 4, 1921," NWTUL Papers, reel 2; "Conference Held December 4, 1921," NWP #116; Kelley to Hill, Mar. 23, 1921, NWP #7. Ethel Smith reported that no consensus had been reached, and it was believed none could be, "largely because of the *known opposition of several members* of the Executive Board of the National Woman's Party *to the very laws we desire to protect*." Ethel Smith to Members and Friends, Dec. 12, 1921, folder 378, Con-sumers League of Massachusetts Coll., SL.

12. Anita L. Pollitzer to Mrs. Jane Norman Smith, Jan. 5, 1922, folder 110, JNSC; National Council (which replaced the National Executive Comm. as of Mar. 1921) minutes, Dec. 17, 1921, Feb. 14, 1922, April 11, 1922, NWP #114; Geidel, "NWP," *Historian*, 576–77; Paul to Jane Norman Smith, Feb. 20, 1923, folder 111, JNSC. In her unpublished autobiography, Maud Younger confessed it took a great wrench to let go her advocacy of protective legislation, but she came to believe that such laws were "among the greatest handicaps" to women seeking employment. She was convinced that male labor leaders saw women workers as competitors and approved "protective" legislation for women in order to protect *men's* jobs. "Along the Way," autobiography (c. 1936), NWP #114.

13. Cf. "Summary of the Woman's Party Legislative campaign, 1921–23," ER, 1 (Jul. 21, 1923), 183, showing 39 bills in 14 states passed, and ER, 1 (Dec. 29, 1923), 364, showing more than twice that number defeated; National Council Minutes, Jun. 19, 1923, NWP #114. Before 1923 the ERA went through scores of drafts, recorded in part F, NWP #116. Versions akin to the suffrage amend-

ment—e.g., "Equal rights with men shall not be denied to women or abridged on account of sex or marriage"—were considered in 1922, but not until 1943 was the amendment introduced into Congress in the form, "Equality of rights under the law shall not be denied or abridged by the United States or by any state on account of sex," modeled on the Nineteenth Amendment, which in turn was modeled on the Fifteenth Amendment.

14. M. Carey Thomas to Mary Anderson, Feb. 5, 1924, folder 4, Mary Anderson Coll., SL. Printed sources for NWP views include Elsie Hill, "Shall Women Be Equal before the Law? Yes!" *Nation* 114 (Apr. 12, 1922), 419–20; Doris Stevens, "The Blanket Amendment—A Debate: I—Suffrage Does Not Give Equality," *Forum* 72 (Aug. 1924), 145–52; Harriot Stanton Blatch, "Do Women Want Protection? Wrapping Women in Cotton-Wool," *Nation* 116 (Jan. 31, 1923).

15. On Casey, see Dye, *As Equals*, 68; Blatch and Lutz, *Challenging Years*, 251; Doris Stevens to Alva Belmont, Apr. 13, 1928, folder "Notes and Correspondence *re* Belmont, Jan.–Aug. 1928," DSC. At a Conference on Women in Industry sponsored by the Women's Bureau in 1926, Casey offended the labor unionists by saying they had wasted their time on legislation and were now standing in the way of progress. "I am sure that you would not have recognized Josephine as what she used to be," Mary Anderson, director of the Women's Bureau, lamented to Margaret Dreier Robins, longtime leader in the WTUL. Mary Anderson to Margaret Dreier Robins, Feb. 4, 1926, folder 67, box 3, Mary Anderson Coll., SL. See also Alma Lutz to Jane Norman Smith, Mar. 7, 1932, folder 98, and Casey correspondence to Lutz, 1936–37, folder 89, Lutz Coll., SL. There are also papers regarding Casey's attempts to organize women workers in Providence, Rhode Island, in 1930–31 in the Anne Kelton Wiley Coll., LC. See copy of Mary Murray's resignation from Amalgamated Association of Street and Railway Employees of America, May 7, 1920, NWP #4; Jane Norman Smith to Alma Lutz, Dec. 29, 1933, folder 98, Lutz Collection, SL. See also Mary Anderson (as told to Mary N. Winslow), *Woman at Work: The Autobiography of Mary Anderson* (Minneapolis, U. Minnesota P., 1951), 159–172; Susan D. Becker, *The Origins of the Equal Rights Amendment: American Feminism Between the Wars* (Westport, Conn., Greenwood, 1981), 198–234.

16. Alice Kessler-Harris, *Out to Work: A History of Wage-Earning Women in the United States* (N.Y., Oxford U.P., 1982), 200–05, and "Coalition-Building," 132, for the argument about convergence of trade union men's and trade union women's views. On labor and business attitudes toward protective legislation, see James Weinstein, *The Corporate Ideal in the Liberal State* (Boston, Beacon P., 1968), 43–45. Fannia Cohen, a Jewish union organizer active in the 1920s and 1930s, and Florence Thorne, special assistant to Samuel Gompers, were two women unionists who suspected protective legislation for women for the same reasons male unionists avoided it for themselves; see Alice Kessler-Harris, "Organizing the Unorganizable," *Labor History* 17 (Winter 1976), 19; and (on Florence Thorne), interview of Margaret Scattergood by Alice Hoffman, © 1978, 21–22, the 20th Century Trade Union Woman Oral History Project, Institute of Labor and Industrial Relations, University of Michigan and Wayne State University.

Clara M. Beyer, a labor economist who opposed the ERA because she thought it would harm labor legislation for women, acknowledged in a study for the Women's Bureau that organized labor had been "probably the largest single factor" precipitating such legislation, and that its motives had been mixed and had included self-interested aims to keep women out of some trades. Beyer, *History of Labor Legislation for Women in Three States* [Mass., N.Y., Calif.,] WBB #66-1 (Washington, D.C., 1932), 1–2.

17. Ethel Smith, "Working Women's Case Against 'Equal Rights,'" *New York Times*, Jan. 20, 1924, 12; Pauline Newman, debate with Heywood Broun, c. 1931, folder 130, Pauline Newman Coll., SL; Alice Hamilton to Alice Paul, May 7, 1926, folder 19, Alice Hamilton Coll., SL. The controversy over the ERA in the 1920s sparked a great outburst of writing, public and private. Printed sources for my summary on the anti-ERA side include Florence Kelley, "The New Woman's Party," *Survey* 47 (Mar. 5, 1921), 828, "The Blanket Equality Bill," *Women's Home Companion* 49 (Aug. 1922), 4, "Shall Women Be Equal before the Law?" (debate with Elsie Hill), *Nation* 144 (Apr. 22, 1922), 421, and "Why Other Women [sic] Groups Oppose It," *Good Housekeeping* 78 (Mar. 1924), 19, 162–65; Mrs. Raymond Robins, "The Progress of Industry: Standards Raised through Legislation," NWTUL pamphlet, folder 41, NWTUL Coll., SL; Silas Bent, "The Women's War," *New York Times*, Jan. 14, 1923, 4, 4; Ethel M. Smith, "The Women's Industrial Conference," *Woman Citizen*, Feb. 1926, "Professional Women, Business Women, Industrial Women: Their Common Cause—But Different Needs," *Life and Labor Bulletin*, Nov. 1928, and "What Is Sex Equality and What Are the Feminists Trying to Accomplish?" *Century Monthly Magazine* 118 (May 1929), 96–106; Mary Van Kleeck, "Women and Machines," *Atlantic Monthly* 127 (Feb. 1921), 250–60; editorial, "Women's Equality in Industry," *TNR* 57 (Nov. 28, 1928), 31–32; editorial, "Doctrinaire Equality," *TNR* (Jul. 24, 1929), 249; Lorine Pruette, "Equal Rights or Easier Work? The Women's Bureau Answers," *Woman's Journal*, n.s. 14 (Jun. 1929), 14–15, 44.

18. Elisabeth Christman to Pauline Newman, Feb. 18, 1938, folder 31, Newman Coll., SL. Working women's support for protective legislation appears in Bertha Wallenstein, "The Working-Woman's Idea," *Nation* 116 (May 30, 1923), 627–28; Mary D. Blankenhorn, "Do Working Women Want It [legal limitation to 48-hour week]?" *Survey* 57 (Feb. 15, 1927), 630–31; Louise Gugino, Buffalo, N.Y., to Jane Norman Smith, Jan. 25, 1926, folder 196, JNSC. Kessler-Harris, *Out to Work*, 189–94, reveals ambivalent assessments of labor legislation by working women.

19. Elizabeth Glendower Evans, "The Woman's Party—Right or Wrong?" *TNR* Sep. 26, 1923, 123; Clara M. Beyer, "Do Women Want Protection?: What Is Equality?" *Nation* 116 (Jan. 31, 1923), 116; Mary Anderson, "Should There Be Labor Laws for Women? Yes," *Good Housekeeping*, Sep. 1925, 16 (reprint, Jun. 1927), folder 93, Mary Anderson Coll., SL; Alice Hamilton, "The Blanket Amendment—A Debate," *Forum* 72 (Aug. 1924), 156.

Some more impartial contemporary assessments are Elizabeth F. Baker, "At the Crossroads in the Legal Protection of Women in Industry," AAAPSS 143 (May 1929), 265–79, and Edwin Witte, "The Effects of Special Labor Legislation for Women," *Quarterly Journal of Economics* 42 (Nov. 1927), 153–164.

Secondary sources on the controversy over the ERA in the 1920s include J. Stanley Lemons, *The Woman Citizen: Social Feminism in the 1920s* (Urbana, U. Illinois P., 1973), 184–99; William Chafe, *The American Woman: Her Changing Social, Economic and Political Roles* (N.Y., Oxford U.P., 1972), 112–32; William N. O'Neill, *Everyone Was Brave* (Chicago, Quadrangle, 1969), 274–94; Becker, *Origins of the Equal Rights Amendment*, 121–51; Judith Sealander, *As Minority Becomes Majority* (Westport, Conn., Greenwood, 1983); Geidel, "NWP," thesis; Sheila M. Rothman, *Woman's Proper Place: A History of Changing Ideals and Practices, 1870 to the Present* (N.Y., Basic, 1978), 153–65; Kessler-Harris, *Out to Work*, 194–95, 205–12; Josephine Goldmark, *Impatient Crusader* (Urbana, U. Illinois P., 1953), 180–88; Martha Swain, "Organized Women in Mississippi: The Clash over Legal Disabilities in the 1920s," *Southern Studies* 23 (Spring 1984), 91–102.

20. Gertrude F. Brown, "Editorially Speaking," *Woman Citizen*, Jul. 1926, 24.

21. Lavinia Dock, "A Sub-Caste," *ER* 11 (May 31, 1924), 125; Blatch and Lutz, *Challenging Years*, 288–89, 324–25.

22. Sophonisba Breckinridge, "The Activities of Women Outside the Home," in *Recent Social Trends*, by the President's Committee on Social Trends (N.Y., McGraw Hill, 1934), 735; Lois Scharf, *To Work and To Wed: Female Employment, Feminism, and the Great Depression* (Westport, Conn., Greenwood, 1980), 15–16, 41; Valerie K. Oppenheimer, *The Female Labor Force in the U.S.* (Westport, Conn., Greenwood, 1976), 8; Elizabeth K. Nottingham, "Toward an Analysis of the Effects of Two World Wars on the Role and Status of Middle-Class Women in the English-Speaking World," *Amer. Sociol. Rev.* 12 (Dec. 1947), 670n; Winifred D. Wandersee, *Women's Work and Family Values, 1920–1940* (Cambridge, Harvard U. P., 1981), 68; Agnes L. Peterson (Assistant Director of Women's Bureau), "What the Wage-Earning Woman Contributes to Family Support," *AAAPSS* 143 (1929), 74–93, also reprinted as WBB #75; see also *Short Talks About Working Women*, WBB #59 (1927), 22–23. On films, see Lary May, *Screening Out the Past* (N.Y., Oxford U.P., 1980), 219.

23. Lorine Pruette, *Women and Leisure: A Study of Social Waste* (N.Y., E. P. Dutton, 1924), 66; Breckinridge, "Activities," 735; Peterson, "What the Wage-Earning Woman Contributes"; Tentler, *Wage-Earning Women*, chap. 1.

24. Frank Stricker, "Affluence for Whom?—Another Look at Prosperity and the Working Classes in the 1920s," *Labor History* 24 (Winter 1983), 5–33; Dolores Janiewski, "Flawed Victories: The Experiences of Black and White Women Workers in Durham During the 1930s," in *Decades of Discontent*, Lois Scharf and Joan Jensen, eds. (Westport, Conn., Greenwood, 1983), 90–92; Mary Frederickson, "The Southern Summer School for Women Workers," *Southern Exposure* 4:4 (1977), 73; Ethel Johnson, "Present-Day Problems of Women in Industry," *The Nation's Health* 9 (Jul. 1927), 2; Judith E. Smith, *Family Connections* (Albany, SUNY P., 1985), 76. In eight "special" studies, which focused on such low-paying sites as laundries, canning industries, domestic service, candy factories, and cotton mills, the Women's Bureau found that only 43 percent of the female wage-earners were single; Peterson, "What the Wage-Earning Woman Contributes," Table 6. Wandersee, *Women's Work*, 60–66, discusses the decline of child labor and rise in married woman's labor but does not posit a causal relationship between them.

25. See U.S. Census figures on female labor force as tabulated by Oppenheimer, who calls women's labor force changes "supertypical," *Female Labor Force*, 3, 149; Scharf, *To Work and To Wed*, 15–16; Wandersee, *Women's Work*, 85, 89; Pruette, *Women and Leisure*, 67; Sharon Hartman Strom, "'We're No Kitty Foyles': Organizing Office Workers for the CIO," in *Women, Work and Protest*, ed. Milkman, 208–09. On problems with 1910 census, see Oppenheimer, *Female Labor Force*, 2–5, Wandersee, *Women's Work*, 130–31. On black women's employment patterns, Jacqueline Jones, *Labor of Love, Labor of Sorrow* (N.Y., Basic, 1985), 166–67, 177–80. The point that black women were twice as likely to be in the labor force is another way of saying that black women's representation in the female labor force was twice as high as their proportion in the female population. Native-born white women of American parentage were relatively underrepresented but were the fastest-growing presence among women at work:

in 1920 they formed 45 percent of the female labor force and 55% of the female population overall. Foreign-born women composed only 13% of the female labor force in 1920, the same as their proportion in the population. Kessler-Harris, *Out to Work*, 347 n. 20.

Throughout this period female enrollments in high school outnumbered male by four to three among whites, and by three to two among blacks. Those proportions suggest working-class families' rational apprehension that where a son might learn a skilled trade outside of high school, the white-collar sector was girls' main chance for earning power, and a high school diploma was the qualification needed. On high school attendance, Clarke N. Chambers, *Seedtime of Reform* (Minneapolis, U. Minnesota P., 1963), 52; Paula Fass, *The Damned and the Beautiful: American Youth in the 1920s* (N.Y., Oxford U.P., 1977), 124–25; Susan B. Carter and Mark Prus, "The Labor Market and the American High School Girl, 1890–1928," *J. Econ. Hist.* 42 (Mar. 1982), 163–71.

26. E.g., Helen Woodward, who became successful in the advertising field after entering as a secretary early in the century, advised that stenography was "a woman's shortest cut to a big job." *Through Many Windows* (N.Y., Harper and Bros., 1926), 89. In 1916, an investigator for the Intercollegiate Bureau of Occupations (an employment agency for female college graduates) conceded that there was some dissent from the majority opinion that stenographic work was the best route to promotion in business—one camp held that it "queered" a girl for advancement and kept her in routine work—but the consensus was optimistic. Miss Cummings of Intercollegiate Bureau of Occupations, May 9, 1916, "Summary," 12–13, vol. 2, box 1, BVI.

27. Grace Coyle, "Women in the Clerical Occupations," AAAPSS 143 (May 1929), 185–87. A contemporary study by F. G. Nichols, *A New Conception of Office Practice*, cited by Coyle, found office workers full of divergent opinions about how promotional opportunities might occur, highlighting the absence of any certain career ladder. More ominously, it found that 90 percent of office managers wanted "clerks who are satisfied to remain clerks." A Bureau of Vocational Information study of the mid-1920s, in which almost 1,500 secretaries gave an opinion on their chances of advancement, showed that almost two-thirds expected no promotion. A fifth of the group did expect to advance beyond a secretarial job, and half that many again expected to move up within the secretarial ranks. "The Woman Secretary," pt. 2, last page, vol. 6, BVI. Cf. Kessler-Harris, *Out to Work*, 225–36; Harry Braverman, *Labor and Monopoly Capital* (N.Y., Monthly Review P., 1974), esp. 293–358; Margery Davies, *Woman's Place Is at the Typewriter* (Philadelphia, Temple U. P., 1982); Ileen DeVault, "Sons and Daughters of Labor: Class and Clerical Work in Pittsburgh" (Ph.D. diss., Yale U., 1985); Rosabeth Kanter, *Men and Women of the Corporation* (N.Y., Basic, 1977), esp. 69–103.

28. Economist Paul Douglas's study of real wages from the 1890s through the 1920s, which showed that the average earnings of clerical workers had remained the same while average earnings of manual workers had advanced by almost 30 percent, is discussed in Stricker, "Affluence," 15, and Sophonisba P. Breckinridge, *Women in the Twentieth Century: A Study of their Political Social and Economic Activities* (N.Y., McGraw Hill, 1933), 173–81.

A "high-grade" clerical worker averaged $1,908, according to the National Education Association. Its findings are cited in Charl Williams, "The Position of Women in the Public Schools," AAAPSS 143 (May 1929), 156. In a survey (conducted between 1926 and 1929) of 14,000 representative NFBPW members, the median salary was $1,548. Of those surveyed, 40 percent were in clerical work,

20% in teaching, 10% in sales and publicity, the remainder scattered in various fields, and the clerical workers were as a group the lowest paid. Margaret Elliott, "What Women Earn," *Indep. W.* (Dec. 1930), 536. Similarly, a study undertaken by the AAUW in 1926–27 surveyed 3,000 of its single members employed full-time and showed that the clerical workers were the lowest paid among them, with a median salary of $1,500 despite their college degrees. Chase G. Woodhouse, "The Occupations of Members of the AAUW," *JAAUW* 21 (June 1928), 120, 122. The bulk of the clerical workers in the AAUW study were employees with less than five years' experience.

29. Guion G. Johnson, "Feminism and the Economic Independence of Woman," *Journal of Social Forces* 3 (May 4, 1925), 615; cf. Tentler, *Wage-Earning Women*, esp. 25, 45–46, and Wandersee, *Women's Work*, on motivations and psychological results of women's wage-earning.

30. Cornelia S. Parker, "feminists and Feminists: They Join Battle in Paris on the Issue of Protective Laws," *Survey* 56 (Aug. 1, 1926), 502, 505; Smith, "What Is Sex Equality," 96; Anderson, "Should There Be Labor Laws for Women? Yes."

31. Baker, "At the Crossroads," 277. See also Baker's study *Protective Labor Legislation* (N.Y., 1925). Summary of protective legislation in 1925 in Edward Clark Lukens, "Shall Women Throw Away Their Advantages," reprint from the *Amer. Bar Assoc. Journal*, Oct., 1925, folder 744, WRC, SL.

Recently historians have stressed the regressive potential of sex-based protective laws. See Rothman, *Woman's Proper Place*, 162–64; Dye, *As Equals*, 159–60; Olive Banks, *Faces of Feminism: A Study of Feminism as a Social Movement* (N.Y., St. Martin's, 1981), 115; and Judith A. Baer, *The Chains of Protection: The Judicial Response to Women's Labor Legislation* (Westport, Conn., Greenwood, 1978). Kessler-Harris, *Out to Work*, 212, is especially succinct and conclusive: "protective labor legislation joined with limited labor force opportunities and virtual exclusion from labor unions to institutionalize women's isolation from the mainstream of labor."

32. T. K. Cory to Mary Wiggins, Nov. 10, 1922, folder 378, Consumers' League of Mass. Coll., SL. See n. 16, above.

33. Printed release from the National Association of Manufacturers, "Defend American Womanhood by Protecting their Homes, Edgerton Tells Women in Industry," Jan. 19, 1926, in folder 1118, and speech by James Davis, U.S. Sec. of Labor, Jan. 18, 1926, in folder 1117, Box 71, Mary Van Kleeck Coll., SSC. Although defenders of labor legislation accused the NWP of being in cahoots with the National Association of Manufacturers, I have not been able to find any positive link between them.

34. Quotations are from Alice Stone Blackwell to Carrie Chapman Catt, May 16, 1927, Catt Papers LC reel 2; Mary Anderson to Mrs. [Margaret Dreier] Robins, Feb. 4, 1926, folder 67, Mary Anderson Coll., SL; Anderson, *Woman at Work*, 168; Olive A. Colton (Toledo, OH) to Mary Anderson, Jan. 23, 1926, folder 10, Mary Anderson Coll., SL.

35. There is a valuable discussion of the differing meanings of equality between the sexes in Jean Bethke Elshtain, "The Feminist Movement and the Question of Equality," *Polity* 7 (Summer 1975), 452–77.

36. Kelley, "Shall Women Be Equal," 421; NLWV pamphlet [1922], 10, in folder 744, WRC, SL; Hamilton, "The Blanket Amendment"; Kelley, "The New Woman's Party." See also Felice D. Gordon, *After Winning: The Legacy of the New Jersey Suffragists* (New Brunswick, N.J., Rutgers U.P., 1985), 60–61.

37. One observer in Durham, North Carolina, recalled that when the mills let out, young men and women chatted and strolled, older men smoked and

talked, but "the older women walk[ed] quickly, anxious to get home where the evening meal must be prepared and the ironing must be finished before they can sit down." Travis Jordan, "Life in Erwin Village," Durham, N.C., 21 Nov. 1938, quoted in Dolores Janiewski, *Sisterhood Denied: Race, Gender and Class in a New South Community* (Philadelphia, Temple U.P., 1985), 135; and see also 30–32, 127–150; Table 26 (134) showing less than 40 percent of Durham women over the age of twelve engaged only in unpaid housework.

38. Quotations from Parker, "feminists and Feminists," 502, 505; Anne Martin to Sara Bard Field, Feb. 4, 1925, folder 42, box 170, Wood Coll., HI; Harriot Stanton Blatch, "Can Sex Equality Be Legislated?" *The Independent* 3 (Dec. 22, 1923), 301. "Such naive proposals as the 'Equal Rights Amendment' show a bland disregard of the realities of child-bearing and rearing," wrote one social worker; it was an "overcompensating" attempt of women "to extricate themselves from the tangles of domesticity." Helen Glenn Tyson, "The Professional Woman's Baby," *TNR* 46 (Apr. 7, 1926), 190.

39. Mary Anderson quoted in unidentified newspaper clipping, Nov. 25, 1925, in folder 349, BVI. Cf. Ethel Smith's objection that the NWP's feminism required that "men and women must have exactly the same things, and be treated in all respects as if they were alike," as distinguished from her own view that "men and women must each have the things best suited to their respective needs, which are not all the time, nor in all things, alike." Smith, "What Is Sex Equality," 96.

40. National Council of Catholic Women testimony at U.S. Congress (House of Representatives) subcommittee of Committee on the Judiciary, hearings, 1925, quoted in Robin Whittemore, "Equality vs. Protection: Debate on the Equal Rights Amendment, 1923–1937" (M.A. thesis, Boston U., 1981), 19; mill worker quoted in Frederickson, "Southern Summer School for Women Workers," 73.

41. A recent acute analysis of immigrant (Jewish and Italian) women and men in family and community context in an East Coast city in the early twentieth century is Smith, *Family Connections;* for a summary interpretation of recent historical literature on immigrants, see also John Bodnar, *The Transplanted* (Bloomington, Indiana U. P., 1985).

42. For the history of the NWP in the 1930s and 1940s see Becker, *Origins of the Equal Rights Amendment.* The papers of Alma Lutz, Jane Norman Smith, Caroline Lexow Babcock, and Doris Stevens, all at SL, are highly enlightening about the NWP's internal and external difficulties. In the 1930s the NFBPW took much more initiative than it had earlier in forwarding the ERA, and local non-NWP groups also formed to lobby for it. See Lemons, *Woman Citizen,* 202–04; Gordon, *After Winning,* 144; and the papers of Lena Madesin Phillips and Florence Kitchelt at SL.

On the long-standing enmity from advocates of protective legislation, the tone of Mary Anderson to her long-time associate Mary Dreier, Mar. 10, 1943, is instructive: "I have a letter from Mrs. Wiley, who is legislative chairman of the Woman's Party, in which she says she thinks we are getting closer and closer together! She has been saying that to me for the last 20 years, and that all we have to do now, since the Supreme Court decision on the Wage and Hour law, is to extend the legislation to men and then we will be helping them too. I am going to answer her letter by pointing out to her that she certainly has had enough experience as to how long it takes to get through any kind of legislation, in trying to get through the amendment for the last 20 years! That we have always had in mind to extend the legislation to men but so far have not been able to do it, that the States work slower than the Federal Government—but what is the use of telling them! They only have a one-track mind." Mary E. Dreier Collection, box 5, SL. Anna Kelton Wiley (who was almost seventy at the time!) believed that the NWP would get the ERA passed in 1946; see Anna Kelton Wiley to Lena Madesin Phillips, Dec. 22, 1945, folder "National Woman's Party," box 3, L. M. Phillips Coll., SL.

5: MODERN TIMES

1. Advertisements from the *Sat. Eve. Post*, Sep. 8, 1928, 93, and May 5, 1928, 184; *Good Housekeeping*, Oct. 1927, 145, quoted in Roland Marchand, *Advertising the American Dream* (Berkeley, U. California P., 1985), 169.

2. On urbanization, suburbanization, and homeownership, see Valerie Oppenheimer, *The Female Labor Force in the U.S.* (Westport, Conn., Greenwood, 1976), 38; Kenneth Jackson, *Crabgrass Frontier* (N.Y., Oxford U.P., 1985), 174–76; Gwendolyn Wright, *Building the Dream: A Social History of Housing in America* (N.Y., Pantheon, 1981), 195–97; Charles N. Glaab, "Metropolis and Suburb: The Changing American City," in *Change and Continuity in 20th-Century America: the 1920s*, John Braeman, et al. eds. (Columbus, Ohio State U. P., 1968), 403–05. (Suburbs' populations were growing twice as fast as those of center cities.) On household change and mass consumption, Heidi I. Hartmann, "Capitalism and Women's Work in the Home, 1900–1940," (Ph.D. diss., Yale U., 1974), 78–87, 120–28, 135, 148–71, 264, 329, 350. Brookings Institute Survey of 1929 (*American's Capacity to Consume*, publ. 1934), cited in Hartmann, 142, characterized 41 percent of population at subsistence or below, 36% at minimum comfort, 14% in moderate circumstances, and 9% comfortable, well-to-do, or wealthy. For Durham counterexample, see Dolores Janiewski, "Flawed Victories: The Experiences of Black and White Women Workers in Durham During the 1930s," in *Decades of Discontent*, Lois Scharf and Joan Jensen, eds. (Westport, Conn., Greenwood, 1983), 92–93, and *Sisterhood Denied: Race, Gender and Class in a New South Community* (Philadelphia, Temple U. P., 1985), esp. 32.

On the decline of servants, David Katzmann, *Seven Days a Week: Women and Domestic Service in Industrializing America* (N.Y., Oxford U.P., 1978), 55–61, finds that in the North the ratio of female servants and laundresses per 1,000 families dropped from 92 to 47 between 1900 and 1920. In the South, where the black population was still concentrated and women had few options outside domestic service, the ratio fell less, from 104 to 81. In the West, where the proportion of employed women in domestic service had always been lower than the rest of the country (although it grew rapidly in the late nineteenth century), the ratio decreased from 59 to 32. Large cities, always the sites of the greatest disparities of wealth and the greatest frequency of domestic service, showed the most pronounced change. In Boston, where there had been 239 servants and laundresses per 1,000 families in 1880 and 192 in 1900, there were only 82 in 1920. In Chicago, the ratio went from 153 in 1880 to 68 in 1920. In Denver in 1920, there were 58 servants and laundresses per 1,000 families; in Los Angeles, 48. Among Southern cities in 1920, Atlanta had the highest availability of servants and laundresses—249 per 1,000 families—but only 20 years earlier there had been 452. According to experts meeting at the U.S. Bureau of Home Economics in 1928, domestic servants—or, as the experts preferred to call them, "household employees"—labored in only about 5 percent of American homes;

see Amey Watson, "Employer-Employee Relationship in the Home," *AAAPSS* 143 (May 1929), 49–60.

3. See Robert Sklar, *The Plastic Age, 1917–1930* (N.Y., Braziller, 1970), 1–2, 13–19; James Shideler, "Flappers and Philosophers and Farmers: Rural-Urban Tensions of the Twenties," *Agric. Hist.* 47:4 (Oct. 1973), 283–99; Mary P. Ryan, "The Projection of a New Womanhood: The Movie Moderns in the 1920s," in *Decades of Discontent*, eds. Scharf and Jensen, 114; Hartmann, "Capitalism and Women's Work," 330–32; Jacqueline Dowd Hall, *Revolt Against Chivalry: Jessie Daniel Ames and the Women's Campaign Against Lynching* (N.Y., Columbia U. P., 1979), 168–70; J. F. Steiner, "Recreation and Leisure Time Activities," in *Recent Social Trends*, by the President's Committee on Social Trends (N.Y., McGraw-Hill, 1934), 2: 921, 940–42; Joann Vanek, "Household Technology and Social Status: Rising Living Standards and the Status and Residence Difference in Housework," *Technology and Culture* 19 (Jun. 1978), 361–75. Loren Baritz, "The Culture of the 1920s," in *The Development of an American Culture*, Stanley Coben and Lorman Ratner, eds. (Englewood Cliffs, N.J., Prentice-Hall, 1970), 150–62, maintains to the contrary that provincial culture ruled.

4. John Modell, et al., "The Timing of Marriage in the Transition to Adulthood," Table 1, in John Demos and Saranne Boocock, eds., *Turning Points: Historical and Sociological Essays on the Family* (Chicago, U. Chicago P., 1978), 12; Paula Fass, *The Damned and the Beautiful: American Youth in the 1920s* (N.Y., Oxford U.P., 1977), 66–68.

The significance of the marrying trend depends on how it is viewed. An increase in the marrying proportion of the population from 90–91 percent to 93–94 percent may not seem very much of a change. Another way to describe the trend is to say that the portion of the population that never married was reduced by almost one-third.

5. Clipping, "Modern Business Woman Held All Right Except for Husbands," *New York Herald Tribune*, Apr. 5, 1924, in folder 350, BVI; Sophonisba Breckinridge, "The Activities of Women Outside the Home," in *Recent Social Trends*, 715.

6. Roberta Wein, "Women's Colleges and Domesticity, 1875–1918," *History of Education Quarterly* 14 (Spring 1974), 31–48; Barbara Miller Solomon, *In the Company of Educated Women* (New Haven, Yale U.P., 1985), 119–22; Fass, *Damned*, 124 and 407–08, note 4. Solomon cautions that marital statistics on women college graduates around the turn of the century cannot necessarily be taken at face value, because the investigations were often done fairly soon after graduation and may not have registered marriages that occurred later in life.

7. Jane Addams, *Second Twenty Years at Hull House* (New York, MacMillan, 1930), 195–96. Alfred Kinsey, et al., *Sexual Behavior in the Human Female* (Philadelphia, W. B. Saunders, 1953), 242–45, 298–301, 339, 422–24, 461–62, 529, 553. Kinsey notes that the increase in premarital coitus is not due to change in age at marriage (299) and also records (301–02) that the cumulative proportion of females who reached orgasm in premarital coitus remained "remarkably" constant over four decades, going from about 50 percent at age 20 to over 75% by age 35. Kinsey's analysis was based on a sample of 5,940 white females, skewed toward more highly educated, upper white-collar and professional groups; only 12% of the sample were linked to blue-collar occupational status (their own or husbands'). The birth cohort pre-1900 numbered 456, the 1900–09 cohort numbered 784 (see 31–37). On married women's sexual satisfaction, Kinsey's table 160 shows that at ages 21–25, among those born before 1900, 80% had reached orgasm through coitus; of those born in the successive three decades, 86%, 90%,

and 92% had done so. Differences between birth cohorts are slighter at later ages, e.g., by ages 41–45, 93% of the women born before 1900 and 95% of those born 1900–09 had reached orgasm through marital coitus.

A study by Lewis Terman and associates undertaken in the late 1930s showed that 74% of the women born between 1890 and 1900 were virgins at marriage, while only 31% of those born after 1910 were; William Chafe, *The American Woman: Her Social, Economic and Political Roles, 1920–1970* (N.Y., Oxford U.P., 1972), 94–96. Cf. Erwin O. Smigel and Rita Seiden, "The Decline and Fall of the Double Standard," *AAAPSS* 376 (March 1968), 7–10; William O'Neill, *Everyone Was Brave* (Chicago, Quadrangle, 1968), 296–304; G. V. Hamilton and Kenneth MacGowan, *What Is Wrong with Marriage* (N.Y., Boni, 1929), 245; Robert S. Lynd and Helen Merrell Lynd, *Middletown: A Study in Modern American Culture* (N.Y., Harcourt Brace, 1929), 169.

8. Fass, *Damned*, chap. 6, esp. 276–78, 307–10; Solomon, *Company*, 99–102, 159–62; Helen Lefkowitz Horowitz, *Alma Mater* (N.Y., Knopf, 1984), 282–93; Eleanor Wembridge, "Petting and the Campus," *Survey* 54 (Jul. 1, 1925), 393–95. Dr. Clelia Mosher's diary quoted in the introduction by Carl Degler to James Maltood and Kristine Wenburg, eds., *The Mosher Survey* (N.Y., Arno P., 1980), xvii; cf. Rosalind Rosenberg, *Beyond Separate Spheres: Intellectual Roots of Modern Feminism* (New Haven, Yale U. P., 1982), 178–206. In 1870, 59 percent of degree-granting colleges and universities in the United States were all male and 29% coeducational; by 1911 these proportions were almost exactly reversed; Solomon, *Company*, 44.

9. Charlotte Perkins Gilman, "The New Generation of Women," *Current History* 18 (Aug. 1923), 735; Addams, *Second Twenty Years*, 197–98. Cf. Molly Dewson to Sue Shelton White, Oct. 13, 1939, folder 8, White Papers, SL, "After all, us old maids have been repaid in our secret hearts for what we sacrificed to some principles and standards thro' which I suppose we sublimated the sex instinct!" cited in Peter Filene, *Him/Her/Self* (N.Y., NAL, 1974), 64–65. On the sexual ideology and behavior of the latter nineteenth-century generations, see Carroll Smith-Rosenberg, "The Female World of Love and Ritual," *Signs* 1 (Autumn 1975), 1–29; Nancy F. Cott, "Passionlessness: An Interpretation of Victorian Sexual Ideology, 1790–1850," ibid. 4 (Winter 1978), 219–36; Blanche Wiesen Cook, "Female Support Networks and Political Activism," *Chrysalis*, no. 3 (1977), 43–61; Nancy Sahli, "Smashing: Women's Relationships Before the Fall," ibid. no. 8 (1979), 17–28; Carl N. Degler, *At Odds* (N.Y., Oxford U.P., 1980), 211–97; William Leach, *True Love and Perfect Union* (N.Y., Basic, 1980); Ellen Rothman, *Hands and Hearts: A History of Courtship in America* (N.Y., Basic, 1984); Peter Gay, *The Bourgeois Experience: Victoria to Freud* (N.Y., Oxford U.P., 1984).

10. Lynd and Lynd, *Middletown*, 266. On changing sexual ideology and its implications, see Christina Simmons, "Purity Rejected: The New Sex Freedom of the Twenties," paper delivered at the Third Berkshire Conference on the History of Women, Jun. 1976, esp. 1–6, SL; Linda Gordon, *Woman's Body, Woman's Right*, (N.Y., Grossman, 1976), 186–206; James P. McGovern, "The American Woman's Pre-World War I Freedom in Manners and Morals," *JAH* 55 (Sep. 1968), 315–33; Lois W. Banner, *American Beauty* (N.Y., Knopf, 1983), 175–201; Lewis Erenberg, *Steppin' Out* (Westport, Conn., Greenwood, 1981), esp. 7–8, 23–25, 60–91; Kathy Peiss, *Cheap Amusements* (Philadelphia, Temple U. P., 1985).

11. Quoted from *Ohio Lantern*, Jan. 9, 1922, in Fass, *Damned*, 307. Discussion of popular novels in Christina Clare Simmons, "Marriage in the Modern

Manner" (Ph. D. diss., Brown U., 1982), 80–87, 130–34, is especially useful on views of older women's morality current among 1920s youth; see also Carroll Smith-Rosenberg, *Disorderly Conduct* (N.Y., Knopf, 1985), 245–96.

12. Gordon, *Woman's Body,* 95–135. See chap. 1, n. 53 and concomitant text.

13. Lillian Symes, "Still a Man's Game: Reflections of a Slightly Tired Feminist," *Harper's Magazine* 158 (May 1929), 678–79. Note that she loosely and retrospectively applied the term feminists to those in the woman movement before.

14. "Divorce Papers," Jun. 21, 1927, folder 43, DSC. Letters in the collection make clear Steven's relationship with Jonathan Mitchell, perhaps beginning as early as 1923 and certainly by 1924. The divorce went through in 1929. Symes, "Still a Man's Game," 679.

"Where the women tried to achieve a genuinely emancipated status," recounted the young social scientist Caroline Ware with respect to Stevens's cohort in Greenwich Village: "difficulty often arose out of the fact that the men gave only lip service to the principle of equality and took advantage of the girls' seriousness to exploit them." In deceptively neutral language she concluded, "the changed attitudes toward sex were much more of a wrench for the girls. . . . when the girls talked about sex equality they really meant it, while the men often did not." Thus "the whole brunt of an uncertain position in a shifting culture" fell upon the seriously intentioned "emancipated woman" who "embodied in herself much of the break with tradition." Caroline Ware, *Greenwich Village, 1920–1930* (Boston, Houghton Mifflin, 1935), 258.

15. Edward A. Purcell, Jr., *The Crisis of Democratic Theory: Scientific Naturalism and the Problem of Value* (Lexington, U. P. Kentucky, 1973), 16–23; Dorothy Ross, "The Development of the Social Sciences," in *The Organization of Knowledge in Modern America, 1860–1920,* Alexandra Oleson and John Voss, eds. (Baltimore, Johns Hopkins U. P., 1979), 125–29.

16. Bessie Bunzel, "The Woman Goes to College: After Which, Must She Choose Between Marriage and a Career?" *The Century Monthly Magazine* 117 (Nov. 1928), 26–32, quotations from 26 and 31.

17. On psychology in 1920s, Purcell, *Crisis,* 34–35, and John C. Burnham, "The New Psychology: From Narcissism to Social Control," in *Change and Continuity,* John Braeman, et al., eds., 351–98. Cf. Rosenberg, *Beyond Separate Spheres,* on the earlier generation of women social scientists. I am especially indebted here to two essays by Jill Morawski: "Not Quite New Worlds: Psychologists' Conceptions of the Ideal Family in the 1920s," in *In the Shadow of the Past: Psychology Portrays the Sexes,* Miriam Lewin, ed., (N.Y., Columbia U.P., 1984), 97–125, on psychologists' utopias; and "The Measurement of Masculinity and Femininity: Engendering Categorical Realities," *Journal of Personality* 53:2 (Jun. 1985), 196–223, which discusses Terman's and subsequent masculinity-femininity scales, with quotations on 205–06. Although Terman's research, conducted with Catherine Cox Miles, was not published in book form until 1936, it was begun in the early 1920s, and its attempt to quantify masculinity and femininity documents the pervasive psychological concern with both items. For some contemporary resistance by feminists to emplacement of "masculinity" and "femininity," see Alice Beal Parsons, *Woman's Dilemma* (N.Y., Thomas Crowell, 1926), esp. 9, 11, 73–78; and Beatrice Hinkle, "Arbitrary Use of the Terms 'Masculine' and 'Feminine,'" *Psychoanalytic Review* (Jan. 1923).

18. Ernest Groves, "The Personality Results of the Wage Employment of Women Outside the Home and Their Social Consequences," AAAPSS 143 (May 1929), 339–48. Cf. the important 1964 critique of social science's impact on

women's self-estimation by a leading female sociologist, Alice Rossi, "Equality Between the Sexes: An Immodest Proposal," *Daedalus* 93:2 (Spring 1964), 611–13, 616–23.

19. Essays and commentaries reprinted in *These Modern Women: Autobiographical Essays From the Twenties,* Elaine Showalter, ed. (Old Westbury, N.Y., Feminist P., 1978), quotations on 3, 140–41, 142–43, 147; I have benefited from Showalter's perspicacious essay on the autobiographies, 3–29. See also letter to the editor from Floyd Dell, [Jul. 1, 1927], *Nation* 125, no. 3238, likening both male experts' responses to the voice of "the poolroom." On Watson's utopia, Morawski, "Not Quite New Worlds."

20. Herrick, "The Limitations of Science," *Journal of Philosophy* 26 (Mar. 28, 1929), 187, quoted in Purcell, *Crisis,* 21. Purcell emphasizes the positivistic approach and naturalistic attitude of social scientists from about 1910 to the mid-1930s: "Sharply skeptical of all nonempirical concepts and theories, they accepted a highly particularistic, nominalistic epistemology. Exasperated with *a priori* systems and rationalistic schematizations, they declared that knowledge must be based on empirical functions, not on logical necessities. Those assumptions of objectivism, particularism, and functionalism uniquely characterized the social science that blossomed after 1910."

On women in the social sciences between 1870 and the 1920s see Leach, *True Love* (which stresses the coincidence of bourgeois reformist aims, women's rights efforts, and the ideology of social science between 1850 and 1880), Margaret Rossiter, *Women Scientists in America* (Baltimore, Johns Hopkins U. P., 1982), and Rosenberg, *Beyond Separate Spheres* (which stresses the advance on the equalitarian women's rights front in the generation of women social scientists of the 1890s and the rollback of their intents by the 1920s). On the development of the social sciences, and the seesaw between overt reform aims and claims to neutrality, see Mary Furner's aptly titled *Advocacy and Objectivity* (Lexington, U.P. Kentucky, 1975), Ross, "Social Sciences" and Thomas Haskell, *The Emergence of Professional Social Science* (Urbana, U. Illinois P., 1977), as well as Purcell. These treatments together span the generations from the post–Civil War to post–World War II eras. Ross observes a repetition of successive waves of scientism and advocacy in the social science community over several generations.

21. John C. Burnham discusses the convergence of differing interest groups in the sexual hygiene movement in the 1910s in "Medical Specialists and Movements Toward Social Control in the Progressive Era: Three Examples," in *Building the Organizational Society: Essays on Associational Activities in Modern America,* Jerry Israel, ed., (N.Y., Free Press, 1972), 19–30. Cf. Steven Schlossman and Stephanie Wallach, "The Crime of Precocious Sexuality: Female Juvenile Delinquency in the Progressive Era," *Harvard Educational Review* 48 (Feb. 1978), 65–94.

22. Inez Milholland's conviction, expressed to her husband in 1916 after three years of marriage, might have been a model for 1920s and 1930s marital advice: "I read everything I can lay hands on about married people and compare them to us—and I swear our love must always be full of color. We must study of course how to keep it warm and thrilling and take pains." Her unusual husband also believed that "my plans shall not and may not interfere with your ambitions and your work or search for work—that I will not have." Such appreciation and room for a wife's autonomy outside of her marriage did not persist in the prevailing mores of companionate marriage. Inez to Eugen [Apr. 1916], folder 2; Eugen to Inez, Oct. 17, 1916, folder 8, Milholland uncat. Coll., SL.

My portrayal of companionate marriage ideology is greatly indebted to Christina Simmons, "Companionate Marriage and the Lesbian Threat," *Frontiers* 4 (Fall 1979), 54–59, and see also her dissertation, "Marriage in the Modern Manner," 186–88. Ellen Kay Trimberger discusses the lapse or retraction of feminist men of the 1910s into woman-subordinating companionate marriage ideology in the latter 1920s in "Feminism, Men, and Modern Love," in *Powers of Desire*, Ann Snitow, Christine Stansell, and Sharon Thompson, eds. (N.Y., Monthly Review P., 1983), 131–52. Cf. Rayna Rapp and Ellen Ross, "The Twenties' Backlash: Compulsory Heterosexuality, the Consumer Family, and the Waning of Feminism," in *Class, Race and Sex: the Dynamics of Control*, Amy Swerdlow and Hanna Lessinger, eds. (Boston, G. K. Hall, 1983), 93–107. Michael Gordon provides an analysis of marital advice literature in "From an Unfortunate Necessity to a Cult of Mutual Orgasm: Sex in American Marital Education Literature, 1830–1940," in *Studies in the Sociology of Sex*, James M. Henslin, ed. (N.Y., Appleton-Century-Crofts, 1971), esp. 68–69.

23. Robert C. and Frances W. Binkley, *What Is Right with Marriage* (N.Y., Appleton, 1929), 216, quoted in Gordon, "From an Unfortunate Necessity," 68; Phyllis Blanchard and Carolyn Manasses, *New Girls for Old* (N.Y., Macaulay Co., 1930), 179–80, 196. See Blanchard's brief autobiography in Showalter, *These Modern Women*, 105–09; Elsie Clews Parsons, "Changes in Sex Relations," in *Our Changing Morality*, Freda Kirchwey, ed. (N.Y., Boni, 1924), 40; cf. Fass, *Damned*, 72–78.

24. Cornelia Bryce Pinchot to Ruth [Pickering Pinchot], Jan. 10, 1927, box 105, Pinchot Papers, LC. Hollingworth herself was married but had no children; see Rosenberg, *Beyond Separate Spheres*, 84–86, 95–113.

25. Madeleine Doty, chap. 2, autobiography, "Tap on the Shoulder," box 2, Doty Coll., SSC; Floyd Dell, "Can Men and Women Be Friends?" in Kirchwey, ed., *Our Changing Morality*, 184. See also Sahli, "Smashing"; Mary McIntosh, "The Homosexual Role," *Social Problems* 16 (Fall 1968), 182–92; Lillian Faderman, *Surpassing the Love of Men: Romantic Friendship and Love Between Women from the Renaissance to the Present* (N.Y., Morrow, 1981), 227–377; Paul Robinson, *The Modernization of Sex* (N.Y., Harper and Row, 1976), 1–41; and, on changing patterns of domitory design at women's colleges, Horowitz, *Alma Mater*, 314–15.

26. From John F. W. Meagher, M.D., "Homosexuality: Its Psychobiological and Psychopathological Significance," *The Urologic and Cutaneous Review* 33 (1929), 511, quoted in Simmons, "Companionate," 57.

27. Blanchard and Manasses, *New Girls*, 198. Editorial, "What's in a Name?" *Indep. W.* 11 (Jan. 1927), 3. An advertising flyer for the journal (of the same year) states that 78 percent of its subscribers are single or widowed, a statistic based on a sample of 1,000 respondents. Folder "National Federation Convention, 1927" box II, Lena Madesin Phillips Coll., SL. See also Faderman, *Surpassing*, 227–394; George Chauncey, Jr., "From Sexual Inversion to Homosexuality: Medicine and the Changing Conceptualization of Female Deviance," *Salmagundi* 58–59 (Fall 1982–Winter 1983), 114–46; Smith-Rosenberg, "New Woman as Androgyne"; Blanche Wiesen Cook, "'Women Alone Stir My Imagination': Lesbianism and the Cultural Tradition," *Signs* 4:4 (Summer 1979), 718–39; Esther Newton, "The Mythic Mannish Lesbian: Radclyffe Hall and the New Woman," ibid. 9:4 (Summer 1984), 557–75; Sheila Jeffreys, *The Spinster and Her Enemies* (London, Pandora P., 1985).

See chap. 6 on feminists' incorporation of companionate marriage ideology into proposals for combining career with marriage.

28. Vern Bullough and Bonnie Bullough, "Lesbianism in the 1920s and 1930s: A Newfound Study," *Signs* 2 (1977), 895–904; Christina Simmons, "Women's Sexual Consciousness and Lesbian Identity, 1900–1940," paper delivered at Sixth Berkshire Conference on Women's History, Smith College, Jun. 3, 1984 [in my possession]; Leila Rupp, "'Imagine My Surprise': Women's Relationships in Historical Perspective," *Frontiers* 5 (Fall 1980), 61–71. Blanchard and Manasses, *New Girls*, chap. 7, treats lesbianism with equanimity. Cf. Cook, "'Women Alone,'" and Newton, "Mythic Mannish Lesbian," on lesbian circles in the 1920s. Two examples of women engaged in sexual relationships with both men and women in the interwar years have recently been revealed in Elinor Langer, *Josephine Herbst* (Boston, Little Brown, 1983), and Catherine Mary Bateson, *With A Daughter's Eye: A Memoir of Margaret Mead and Gregory Bateson* (N.Y., Morrow, 1984).

29. On proposals for wages for wives in the 19th century, Leach, *True Love*, 194–95. See also, for 1910s and 1920s, "Shall We Place Wives on a Salary Basis," *Current Literature* 53 (Oct. 1912), 413–14; William Johnston, "Should Wives Be Paid Wages?" *Good Housekeeping*, Mar. 1925, 30–31, 202–04; Doris Stevens, "Wages for Wives" (c. 1925), folder "ms.ts.," box 8, DSC, published in *Nation* 122, No. 3160 (Jan. 27, 1926), 81–83. Stevens debated lawyer Arthur Garfield Hays on the issue of wages for wives in an event staged by the *Nation* on Feb. 4, 1926, chaired by Freda Kirchwey, and attended by 400 or more. F. L. Kellogg, "Feminists and Family Income," *ER* 13 (Feb. 27, 1926), 21–22. Stevens aided in staging a debate on wages for wives in London in 1927, between two international journalists: her lover, Jonathan Mitchell, and Raymond Gram Swing, husband of Betty Gram Swing (one of Stevens's best friends). See J. Mitchell to "dearest beloved," Mar. 29 [1927], box 5, DSC. Home economist Hildegarde Kneeland devoted much of her article on "Woman's Economic Contribution in the Home," *AAAPSS* 143 (May 1929), 35–40, to refuting the feasibility of the "solution . . . which is frequently heard of late . . . that of 'wages for wives.'"

30. Hildegarde Kneeland, "Is the Modern Housewife a Lady of Leisure?" *Survey* 62 (Jun. 1, 1929), 301–02, reports her time-budget studies; Mrs. Abel J. Gregg, "What Women are Thinking: the YWCA Talks It Over," *Survey* 57 (Dec. 1, 1926), 300. See also Anna E. Richardson, "The Woman Administrator in the Modern Home," *AAAPSS* 143 (May 1929), 22, 28; and, for summary and interpretation of the decades 1920s–1960s, Joann Vanek, "Time Spent in Housework," *Scientific American* (Nov, 1974), 116–20.

31. See Hartmann, "Capitalism and Women's Work," particularly on the marketing of washing machines, 213–16, 249–59; Dolores Hayden, *The Grand Domestic Revolution* (Cambridge, MIT P., 1981)—which maintains that a "material feminist" tradition dating from the nineteenth century, and intending to transform women's private household labor through collective projects, was overturned by the late 1920s; Rapp and Ross, "The Twenties' Backlash"; Christine Bose, et al., "Household Technology and the Social Construction of Housework," *Technology and Culture* 25:1 (1984), 63, 74; Ruth Cowan, "The Industrial Revolution in the Home: Household Technology and Social Change in the Twentieth Century," *Technology and Culture* 17 (1976), 1–23, and *More Work for Mother* (N.Y., Basic, 1983), esp. 172–91. Cowan argues that the important innovation of the gas stove did not necessarily reduce women's labor, since the chores it eliminated—chopping and lugging wood or filling the coal scuttle—were more likely done by men of the household. Vanek, in "Time Spent," shows that the only factor correlating positively with reduction of time spent in house-

work (from the 1920s through 1960s) is the housewife's gainful employment outside the home.

32. C. G. Woodhouse, "The New Profession of Homemaking," *Survey* 57 (Dec. 1, 1926), esp. 316–17, 336; Lillian Gilbreth, "Efficiency of Women Workers," *AAAPSS* 143 (May 1929), 61–64, and interview by Lillian Budd, "Housekeeping: An Industry," *Woman Citizen* n.s. 11:21 (Aug. 1926), 19, 41–42; Hildegarde Kneeland, "Is the Modern Housewife . . . ?"; see also her "Woman's Economic Contribution," 33–40; Amey Watson, "The Reorganization of Household Work," *AAAPSS* 160 (1932), 168. Margaret Rossiter discusses the gender dynamics that created a female monopoly in home economics as in no other science or social science, and points out that the U.S. Department of Agriculture was the largest single employer of women scientists in the 1920s and 1930s, in "Women's Work in Science," 395–96, and *Women Scientists in America* (Baltimore, Johns Hopkins U.P., 1982), 199–203, 228–29, 258–59.

33. Woodhouse, "New Profession," quotation on 316; Watson, "Reorganization," 169–72. It is an interesting commentary on changing middle-class occupational ideals that mid-nineteenth-century prescriptions drew analogies between running a household and running a business (or, occasionally, ruling a state), whereas twentieth-century prescriptions likened women's domestic performance to carrying on a profession (or being in a managerial position).

34. Richardson, "Woman Administrator," 32.

35. Of women born 1900–09 and marrying approximately in the 1920s, 18.6 percent married but remained childless and 7.3% stayed single and childless. A greater proportion of that cohort remained childless than of women who were born in the 1910s and married during the Great Depression of the 1930s, when the economic motive to avoid children was especially strong. The average number of children born *per mother* for those marrying in the 1920s was greater than for those marrying in the 1930s (3.1 compared to 2.9), but because of the high proportion of childless wives, the average number of children born per woman and per wife was lower for the generation marrying in the 1920s than in the Depression decade. (Among the 1940s birth cohort, marrying in the 1960s, only 9.4 percent remained childless although married; 4.4% remained single and childless.) Table 2 in Paul C. Glick, "Updating the Life Cycle of the Family," *Journal of Marriage and the Family* 39 (Feb. 1977), 8.

36. On the fall of the birth rate during the nineteenth century see Daniel Scott Smith, "Family Limitation, Sexual Control, and Domestic Feminism in Victorian America," *FS* 1 (Winter-Spring 1973), 40–57; Degler, *At Odds*, 178–248; James Mohr, *Abortion in America* (N.Y., Oxford U.P., 1978); Gordon, *Woman's Body*, 47–115; and on birth control in the 1920s, ibid., esp. 270, 288–89, 308–11; James Reed, *From Private Vice to Public Virtue* (N.Y., Basic, 1978), esp. 121; Winifred D. Wandersee, *Women's Work and Family Values* (Cambridge, Harvard U.P., 1981), 56; Margaret Sanger, *An Autobiography* (N.Y., Norton, 1938), 361, 429–30; Lynd and Lynd, *Middletown*, 123. Details regarding Manhattan clinic are found in Anne Kennedy [Executive Secretary, Amer. Birth Control League] to Roger Baldwin [Secretary, Amer. Fund for Public Service], Jan. 23, 1924, American Fund for Public Service Coll., box 9, reel 5, NYPL, and see other letters in that collection from the American Birth Control League asking for funds to send a birth control organizer to labor groups (1923–24) and to fund new clinics. On causes of the drop in the birth rate in the 1920s, Richard A. Easterlin, *The American Baby Boom in Historical Perspective* (N.Y., National Bureau of Economic Research, Occasional Paper #79, 1962), 6–12, 15–21.

37. See Burnham, "The New Psychology," 360–66, 378–79, 381–84; Fass, *Damned*, 96–101; quotation from Lorine Pruette, "The Married Woman and the Part-Time Job," *AAAPSS* 143 (May 1929), 315.

38. Quotation from Charlotte Perkins Gilman, *The Home, Its Work and Influence* (1903, repr. Urbana, U. Illinois P., 1972), 55, in Mary M. Ladd-Taylor, "Mother-work: Ideology, Public Policy, and the Mothers' Movement" (Ph.D. diss., Yale U., 1986), 18, and see ibid., chap. 1, on changes in childrearing advice from 1890 to the 1920s; on the brief rise and demise of "instinct" psychology, see Purcell, *Crisis*, 36–37.

39. Lynd and Lynd, *Middletown*, 131–52; Pruette, "The Married Woman and the Part-Time Job," 305; Gwendolyn Hughes Berry, "Mothers in Industry," *AAAPSS* 143 (May 1929), 315; estimate of Children's Bureau's outreach cited in Ladd-Taylor, "Mother-work," 12. More than three-quarters of 300 young mothers surveyed by sociologist Ruth Lindquist about 1930 said they wished they had had courses in "child training" in college; Hornell Hart, "Trends of Change in Textbooks on the Family," *Am. Journal of Sociology* 39 (1933), 229. For an evocative sampling of letters sent to the Children's Bureau, see Molly Ladd-Taylor, *Raising a Baby the Government Way: Mothers' Letters to the Children's Bureau* (New Brunswick, N.J., Rutgers U. P., 1986).

40. My discussion of parent education is indebted to Steven L. Schlossman, "Before Home Start: Notes Toward a History of Parent Education in America, 1897–1929," *Harvard Educational Review* 46:3 (1976), 436–67, "Educating the Modern American Parent: Perspectives on the 1920s and 1930s," paper presented at the annual meeting of the History of Education Society in Toronto, Ontario, Oct. 16, 1977 [in my possession]; "Philanthropy and the Gospel of Child Development," *History of Education Quarterly* 21 (Fall 1981), 275–99, and "The Formative Era in American Parent Education: Overview and Interpretation," in Ron Hoskins and Diane Adams, eds., *Parent Education and Public Policy* (Newark, N.J., Ablex, 1983), 7–38. I have also benefited from reading two unpublished essays [in my possession] by Debra D. Schwartz, "The Professionalization of Parenthood: The Child Study Association of America and the Movement for Parent Education, 1923–32," senior essay, Yale College, Apr. 1984; and "Becoming Professional: A History of Chicago's Association for Family Living and Its Women, 1916–65," History 485b tutorial paper, May, 1984, in which oral histories provide several examples of Chicago women's career paths developing from their involvements as mothers in child study. On "parent education" in colleges, see Eva von B. Hansl, "Parenthood and the Colleges," *JAAUW* 15:2 (January 1922), 36–45; Helen Merrell Lynd, "Parent Education and the Colleges," *AAAPSS* 160 (Mar. 1932), 197–204; and Ernest R. Groves, "Parent Education," ibid., 204–17. Cf. Sheila Rothman, *Woman's Proper Place* (N.Y., Basic, 1978), 152–53; and Rossiter, *Women Scientists*, 203–04. On expansion of government-sponsored agencies dealing with children in 1930s, see Sonya Michel, "Children's Interests/Mothers' Rights: American Women Professionals and the Family, 1920–1945" (Ph.D. diss., Brown U., 1986).

41. Interview with Sidonie Gruenberg by Mary Jacobs, "Has Mother's Career Helped the Child?" *Indep. W.* 9 (Sep. 1930), 365, 400. See also biographical sketch of Gruenberg, by Roberta Wollons, in *NAW* IV, 295–96. Estimate of 22,500,000 women keeping house without pay in 1920 from Wesley Clair Mitchell, *Business Cycles* (National Bureau of Economic Research, Publ. 10, 1920), 83–85, cited in Watson, "Reorganization," 169.

42. On *Parents' Magazine*, see publicity material in *Survey* 57 (Dec. 1, 1926),

329, and in folders 1 and 20 (including reprint from *Sales Management*, Feb. 15, 1934) in Clara Savage Littledale Coll., SL. The papers of the Boston Parents' Council, 1930–38, SL, document a parent education group.

43. A. M. McMahon, "An American Courtship: Psychologists and Advertising Theory in the Progressive Era," *Am. Studies* 13 (Fall 1972), esp. 3–8, 15; Marchand, *Advertising*, 5–7; Robert Atwan, et al., *Edsels, Luckies and Frigidaires* (N.Y., Dell, 1979), 3; Hartmann, "Capitalism and Women's Work," 351–55; Stuart Ewen, *Captains of Consciousness* (N.Y., McGraw Hill, 1976), 54–56; George Burton Hotchkiss and Richard B. Franken, *The Leadership of Advertised Brands* (Garden City, N.Y., Doubleday, 1923); Robert S. Lynd, "The People as Consumers," in *Recent Social Trends*, 867–68, 911.

44. Quotation from *Printer's Ink*, Nov. 7, 1929, in Marchand, *Advertising*, 66; Woodhouse, "New Profession," 339. For the advocacy of women's power as consumers, cf. Hayden, *Grand Domestic Revolution*, 57; Rhoda McCulloch, *The War and the Woman Point of View* (pamphlet, N.Y., Religious Outlook Series, Association P., 1920), 28–29; Benjamin Andrews, "The Home Woman as Buyer and Controller of Consumption," *AAAPSS* 143 (May 1929), 41–48; Editorial, "Woman's Responsibility," *JAAUW* 22:4 (Jun. 1929), 212; Wandersee, *Women's Work and Family Values*, 52; Barbara Ehrenreich and Deirdre English, *For Her Own Good* (Garden City, N.Y., Doubleday Anchor, 1978), 162–63. See also Marchand, *Advertising*, 34, 66–69, 162–63, 342–45.

45. "Contacts of the Home with Economics," *JAAUW*, 18:3 (1925), 31; quotation from *Chicago Tribune*, 1930, reported in Marchand, *Advertising*, 186; Judith Williamson, *Decoding Advertisements* (London, Marion Boyars, 1978), 42; see also Wright, *Building the American Dream*, 208–10; Ewen, *Captains*, 159–84; Christopher Lasch, *Haven in a Heartless World* (N.Y., Basic, 1977), 19–20. Some feminist theorists have argued that the individualizing realm of choice proffered to women as consumers can lay the groundwork for women to seize more significant political choices; e.g., Juliet Mitchell, *Woman's Estate* (N.Y., Vintage Books, 1971), 71; "Consumerism and Women," by a Redstocking Sister [Ellen Willis], in *Woman in Sexist Society*, ed. Vivian Gornick and Barbara K. Moran (N.Y., NAL, 1972), 658–64; cf. William Leach, "Transformations in a Culture of Consumption: Women and Department Stores, 1890–1925," *JAH* 71 (Sep. 1984), 319–42.

46. Anne Martin, "Women and 'Their' Magazines," *TNR* 32 (Sep. 20, 1922), 91–93; Silas Bent, "Woman's Place Is in the Home," *Century* 116 (Jun. 1928), 204–13; see also Elizabeth Schlesinger, "They Say Women Are Emancipated," *TNR* 77 (Dec. 13, 1933), 125–27, and "The Women's Magazines," ibid., 114 (Mar. 11, 1946), 345–47. On advertising volume, Lynd, "People as Consumers," 874, 889.

47. Faith Baldwin, "Love and Romance," in Fred Ringel, ed., *America as Americans See It* (N.Y., Literary Guild, 1932), 88–97 (quotation, 95); Lynd, "People as Consumers," 874, 889. In consumer responses to advertising as surveyed in the 1930s and summarized by Neil Borden, housewives were the least critical of all occupational groups. E.g., only 31 percent of housewives' comments about ads sampled in a study of almost 15,000 consumers (of whom housewives comprised more than one-third) were complaints, whereas 85 percent of all students' comments were complaints. It can be inferred from Borden's study that gainful employment raised women's skepticism, for 66 percent of the clerical workers' assessments were complaints, and 45 percent of the domestic employees' were. Neil H. Borden, *The Economic Effects of Advertising* (Chicago, Richard D. Irwin, 1942), chap. 26, esp. 744–45, 763–65, 768–97.

6: THE ENEMY OF SOCIETY

1. "Has Modern Woman Disrupted the Home?" *Indep. W.*, 8:1 (Jan. 1929), 6–7.

2. Crystal Eastman, "What Shall We Do with the Woman's Page," *Time & Tide*, 20 May 1927, reprinted in *Crystal Eastman; On Women and Revolution*, Blanche Wiesen Cook, ed. (N.Y., Oxford U.P., 1978), 99.

3. See William Leach, *True Love and Perfect Union* (N.Y., Basic, 1980), esp. 158–212. Jane Croly and Antoinette Brown Blackwell were two white women who spoke up on married women's right to work in the late nineteenth century. Some black club women justified married women's paid employment in the 1890s not simply on grounds of economic duress but on grounds of individual scope; the economic duress of the majority did not prevent black women intellectuals from proclaiming the justice and legitimacy of married women's non-domestic occupations on grounds of right as well as need. Paula Giddings, *When and Where I Enter* (N.Y., Morrow, 1984), 108–09, 196–97.

4. Katherine Anthony, *Feminism in Germany and Scandinavia* (N.Y., Henry Holt, 1915), 200–01; Charlotte Perkins Gilman, "Maternity Benefits and Reformers," *The Forerunner* 7 (1916), 66.

5. *Smith College Weekly* 10 (Dec. 3, 1919), 2, quoted in Peter Filene, *Him/Her/Self* (N.Y., NAL, 1974), 128; Phyllis Blanchard and Carolyn Manasses, *New Girls for Old* (N.Y., Macaulay, 1930), 5; Elizabeth Read's draft for AAAPSS Convention session, 1924, in folder "Civil Disabilities of Women," AAAPSS, in Yvette Eastman Accession 81–M175, SL. The articles named can be found in *Literary Digest* 75 (Nov. 11, 1922), 40–63; by Nancy Mavity, in *Harper's Magazine* 153 (Jul. 1926), 189–99; by Anne Byrd Kennon in *JAAUW*, 20 (Jun. 1927), 100–06; by Eunice Richardson, in *JAAUW* 20 (Jun. 1928), 113–15; by Eleanor D. Coit and Elsie G. Harper, in *Survey* 64 (Apr. 15, 1930), 79–80; *Woman Citizen* 15 (Mar., May 1926) 15–16, 45 (a serial instituted in response to great interest); by Margaret Lane, in *The Suffragist* 8 (Nov. 1920), 275–76; John Macy and Lena Madesin Phillips, *Indep. W.*, 11 (May 1927), 4–5; the last is a book of stories by Florence Seabury Woolston. See also "How Would You Solve It? The Modern Woman's Greatest Problem: Economic Independence," *Delineator* 90 (Jan. 1917), 2; "Should Married Women Work? By One of Them," *Indep. W.* 6 (Oct. 1922), 20; Edith Clark, "Trying to Be Modern," *Nation* 125 (Aug. 17, 1927), 153; Helen Glenn Tyson, "The Professional Woman's Baby," *TNR* 46 (Apr. 7, 1926) 190–92; Jane Littell, "Meditations of a Wage-Earning Wife," *Atlantic Monthly* 134 (Dec. 1924). Note two favorable articles from husbands' points of view: "I'm Glad I Married a Business Woman," *Indep. W.* 11 (Oct. 1927), 12–14; and "The Way My Husband Feels About It," ibid. 1 (Sep. 1927), 8–9, 38–39. Journals with recurrent articles include *Harper's, Atlantic Monthly, Current History, Century, Outlook, Nation, TNR*.

6. Quotations from Dorothy Dix in Gilman Ostrander, *American Civilization in the First Machine Age* (N.Y., Harper, 1970), 248–49, and Lois Scharf, *To Work and to Wed* (Westport, Conn., Greenwood, 1980), 21–23; M. Carey Thomas to Millicent Carey McIntosh, May 22, 1932, in M. H. Dobkin, ed., *The Making of a Feminist: Early Journals and Letters of M. Carey Thomas* (Kent, Ohio, Kent State U.P., 1979), xiv. Under Thomas, 45 percent of Bryn Mawr graduates (1889–1908) got married and only 65 percent of these had children, according to Roberta Wein, "Women's Colleges and Domesticity," *Hist. of Educ. Q.* 14 (Spring 1974), 37–38.

7. See Filene, *Him/Her/Self*, 128–39, Elaine Showalter, *These Modern*

Women (Old Westbury, N.Y., Feminist P., 1978), 3–29, and Scharf, *To Work*, 21–42, all of which discuss the combination of career and marriage as a 1920s feminist proposition. Descriptive brochures, 1929, folder 1, Institute of Women's Professional Relations Coll., SL; Emilie Hutchinson, "The Economic Problems of Women," *AAAPSS* 143 (May, 1929), 136.

8. See table 6.1. In 1930, 32.1 percent of female clerical workers and 33.5 percent of saleswomen were married. Winifred D. Wandersee, *Women's Work and Family Values, 1920–1940* (Cambridge, Harvard U.P., 1981), 89, 100; Elizabeth Nottingham, "Towards an Analysis of the Effects of Two World Wars on the Role and Status of Middle-Class Women," *Am. Sociol. Review* 12 (Dec. 1947), 670n.; Scharf, *To Work*, 41–42. Wandersee, 89, finds 32.5 percent of gainfully employed married women were in white-collar work in 1930 (up from 21.5 percent in 1920). Census figures, however, understate the number of married women working in the home, keeping boarders and lodgers, doing laundry and other similar work that could be income-producing and yet invisible to the census-taker. According to the calculation of Lynn Weiner, *From Working Girl to Working Mother* (Chapel Hill, UNC P., 1985), 89, the proportion of black married women who were employed rose not at all between 1920 and 1940, while the proportion of white married women with paid jobs doubled, from 7 percent to 14 percent. In 1940 the proportion of black wives in the labor force (32 percent) was still more than twice that of whites. See table 6.1.

The attention given the "two-career couple" in the 1970s, when a miniscule proportion of working people achieved that category, is a similar phenomenon; i.e., even by 1982, married women in the elite professions of law, medicine, and college teaching comprised less than three-quarters of 1 percent of all married women in the labor force; if architects, computer systems analysts, engineers, and physical scientists are added, still wives in the seven high-level professions constituted only slightly over 1 percent of all wives in the labor force. Harold Benenson, "Women's Occupation and Family Achievement in the U.S. Class System," *British Journal of Sociology* 35 (Mar. 1984), 19–41.

9. Blanchard and Manasses, *New Girls*, tables 4, 5, 7, pp. 260–61; Lorine Pruette, *Women and Leisure: A Study of Social Waste* (N.Y., Dutton, 1924), chap. 7, esp. 124–35; Gregg, "What Women Are Thinking," *Survey* 57 (Dec. 1, 1926), 300.

10. Lorine Pruette, "The Married Woman and the Part-time Job," *AAAPSS*, 143 (May 1929), 301; Hutchinson, "Economic Problems of Women," 136. Robert Lynd and Helen Lynd, *Middletown in Transition* (N.Y., Harcourt Brace, 1937), 181. The assumption that the intrinsic and extrinsic pulls are sociologically separable is perpetuated in Wandersee, *Women's Work*.

11. Grace Coyle, "Women in the Clerical Occupations," *AAAPSS* 143 (May 1929), 183.

12. Cf. Ellen Dubois, "The Radicalism of the Woman Suffrage Movement," FS 3 (Fall 1975), and *Feminism and Suffrage* (Ithaca, Cornell U.P., 1978); Carl Degler, *At Odds* (N.Y., Oxford U.P., 1980), 328–61.

13. Joseph Warren, "Husband's Right to Wife's Services," *Harvard Law Review* 38 (Feb. 1925), quotations from 433, 446. My awareness of the difference between the earnings statutes and judicial interpretations of them was first provoked by Amy Dru Stanley, "Status or Free Contract: Marriage in the Age of Reconstruction," paper delivered at the 1986 Annual Meeting of the Amer. Hist. Assoc., N.Y., and by Reva Siegel, "Of Status and Contract, Marriage and Market: Nineteenth-Century Reform of Coverture: Judicial Construction of the Earnings Statutes," unpubl. paper, Aug. 1986 (in my possession). I am greatly

indebted to the latter for references to cases and summaries of the 1920s and 1930s that form the basis for my interpretation here, esp. Warren (above) and Blanche Crozier, "Marital Support," *B.U. Law Review* 15 (1935). Mary Phlegar Smith, "Legal and Administrative Restrictions Affecting the Rights of Married Women to Work," *AAAPSS* 143 (May 1929), 255–64, is also helpful but not as forceful as the law review articles. See also Norma Basch, *In the Eyes of the Law* (Ithaca, N.Y., Cornell U.P., 1982), 200-32. Siegal argues—against the usual view that coverture was reformed through the nineteenth-century legislation—that wives' common-law status was very little reformed by the early twentieth century; judges interpreted the content of wives' services in less palpable, more emotional forms, but kept intact the service relation as essential to marriage. Her reasoning is supported by language such as that of the Supreme Court of Arkansas, 1915, quoted in Warren, 623: "The word 'services' does not contemplate merely what wages should be paid the wife for the work actually performed by her, but it rather implies whatever assistance, aid or comfort she would be expected to render her husband in all the relations of domestic life." Siegal also makes the point (12–14) that judges grappling with the married women's earnings statutes from the 1880s to the 1920s did not want to upset the social order based on the wife's owing her labor to her husband; their efforts to avoid and evade the statutes' contradiction of principles of coverture resulted in the tremendous variation between statutes and decisions as well as in variations from state to state.

14. Paul Sayre, "A Reconsideration of Husband's Duty to Support and Wife's Duty to Render Services," *Va. Law Review* 29 (1943), 871, still cites Warren (1925) as valid on the general case that the wife is not permitted "to collect for services rendered within the home . . . since the wife is under a common law duty to render services within the home and there would be no consideration for the latter contract to do the same thing." On wives' awareness of economic dependence, cf. Rebecca Hourwich, "Money, Money, Everywhere and Not a Cent to Spend," *ER*, 27 March 1926.

15. Quotations from Smith, "Legal and Administrative Restrictions," 255, and Crozier, "Marital Support," 37. Crozier points out that the statutory recognition of the wife's ownership of her own earnings, and the husband's obligation to support his wife financially—the necessary corollary of which was his ownership of her labor power—were two concepts in equally good legal standing, and in flat contradiction of one another.

16. Crozier, "Marital Support," 40.

17. This series was provoked by Ethel Puffer Howes's intent to start cooperative schemes among housewives. On the number of letters received, Howes, "True and Substantial Happiness," *Women's Home Companion* 50:9 (Sep., 1923), 32; quotations from ibid., 2 (Feb. 1923), 15; 7 (July 1923), 25; 6 (June 1923), 30; 7 (July 1923), 25; 6 (June 1923), 30.

18. *The New York Times*, Jan. 7, 1909, 9. The event was sponsored by the WTUL, and "union girls" acted as ushers, but the newspaper report does not indicate whether the audience was working class. A mention in Aileen S. Kraditor, *Ideas of the Woman Suffrage Movement* (Garden City, N.Y., Anchor, 1971), 97, alerted me to the debate.

19. Dorothy M. Brown, *Mabel Walker Willebrandt: A Study of Power, Loyalty, and Law* (Knoxville, U. Tennessee P., 1984), 135.

20. First quotation, from an Oregon attorney with her own firm, who had begun law practice in an office with her father and brother; the second, from a woman in practice sixteen years with her father, doing commercial, probate, and title law; the third, from an Arizona woman in practice for three years. There

are 93 questionnaires, from 1918 and 1920–21, on which this question is answered, in folders 133 and 134, BVI. Of the 93, 5 said they did not know; 21 reserved judgment on such a personal decision; 26 mentioned a variety of arrangements and concessions to facilitate the combination; 12 more also mentioned arrangements but were more insistent that motherhood should take precedence over career; only 6 perceived no conflict. Internal evidence indicates that 23–25 of the respondents were married. These lawyers (especially the older ones) had not necessarily attended law school or even college; they might simply have apprenticed to a male relative before passing the bar exam. It is probable that the younger ones had attended law school, however.

21. The thousands of questionnaires administered by the BVI to secretaries are in boxes 29–35 of the BVI. In my random sample of 1,021 (every tenth questionnaire, covering fifteen states), 501 contained an answer to the question, "what are the advantages and disadvantages of secretarial work for a married woman?" Of those who responded, 74 percent were single women, but of those who expressed general approval of married women as secretaries, only 64 percent were single. Single women were 87 percent of those expressing general disapproval of married women in the field. Of those who mentioned only advantages in secretarial work for married women, 58 percent were single, but 83 percent of those who mentioned only the disadvantages for married women were. An advertising flyer for *Independent Woman*, NFBPW's magazine of 1927, states that 78 percent of its subscribers were single or widowed (based on a survey of 1,000 members); folder "National Federation Convention, 1927," box 2, Lena Madesin Phillips Coll., SL.

Helen Woodward, a one-time secretary who worked her way up in the advertising business, reserved her highest praise (jaundiced as it was) for "the year-after-year stenographer who without title and without pay runs the boss's job and the boss's business. There are thousands of such women in the United States. . . . Many of these women, quite unconsciously, are in love with their employers, and think them a little like gods. Others do it because it is their nature to run things, and modern business is not yet modern enough to give them the opportunity they need." Trying to be sympathetic and to acknowledge capable women blocked by irrational barriers, Woodward nonetheless typified a much more widespread reductionist tendency to see women in the office as potential lovers or wives rather than as potential executives. Woodward, *Through Many Windows* (N.Y., Harper and Bros., 1926), 88–89. Cf. Rosabeth Kanter, *Men and Women of the Corporation* (N.Y., Basic, 1977), 69–103.

22. Smith, "Legal and Administrative Restrictions," esp. 261–62, 263 (quotation). Cf. "Railroad Attempts to Oust Married Women," ER, Sep. 29, 1928, 270.

On the clustering of college-educated women in the teaching field: Kennon, on a sample of 243 married and 135 unmarried and gainfully employed alumnae drawn from 12,000 Boston-area alumnae, found almost three-fourths of the single women and slightly more than a third of the married women in the educational field. Woodhouse, in an analysis of 6,535 questionnaires returned to the AAUW, found that 76 percent of the single and 70 percent of the married women employed were in the educational field. Anne Byrd Kennon, "College Wives Who Work," *JAAUW* 20:4 (Jun. 1927), 100–06; Chase Going Woodhouse, "The Occupations of Members of the *AAUW*," *JAAUW* 21:4 (Jun. 1928), 119–22, and "Married College Women in Business and Professions," *AAAPSS* 143 (May 1929), 325–38.

23. *Survey* 57 (Dec. 1, 1926), 263–67. The long-standing position of male craft unionists was opposed to wives' earning wages; cf. an earlier piece by Samuel

Gompers, "Should the Wife Contribute to the Family Support? My Answer Is Emphatically No!" *Women's Home Companion*, 1905, cited in Kathryn Oberdeck, "From Wives, Sweethearts, and Female Relatives to Sisterhood: The Seattle Women's Label League and *Seattle Union Record* Women's Pages, 1905–1918," unpubl. paper, 1984, 6. See summary of negative views of working wives in 1920s and 1930s in Weiner, *From Working Girl to Working Mother*, 98–110.

24. Alice Beal Parsons, *Woman's Dilemma* (N.Y., Crowell, 1926), esp. 211–12, 226–85, and see 247–48 for point that household work is not naturally woman's; Suzanne La Follette, *Concerning Women* (N.Y., Boni, 1926), esp. 92–126, 194 (quotation). Both were ERA supporters and pacifists. La Follette was a cousin of Robert La Follette and had worked for him in Congress in 1918; see the small collection of hers in La Follette Family Papers, LC. For Pruette's support of part-time work, see *Women and Leisure*, 91–96, 195–96; and "The Married Woman and the Part-Time Job"; and on Howes, see below.

25. My summary of the career/marriage position is based on articles cited in n. 5, with exception of Coit and Tyler, and also Emily Newell Blair, "The Married Feminist's Predicament," *Outlook* 153 (Sep. 4, 1929), 7–9; Virginia MacMakin Collier, *Marriages and Careers; A Study of One Hundred Women Who Are Wives, Mothers, Homemakers and Professional Workers* (N.Y., BVI, 1926); writings of Ethel Puffer Howes discussed later in this chapter; Cecile Tipton La Follette, *A Study of the Problems of 652 Gainfully Employed Married Women Homemakers* (N.Y., Teachers College, Columbia U., 1934); and Pruette, *Women and Leisure*, and "The Married Woman and the Part-Time Job."

26. Vera Brittain, "Home-Making Husbands," ER 13 (Jan. 29, 1927), 403; Louise Rice, graphologist, to Miss Emma Hirth, Nov. 17, 1924, folder 350, BVI.

27. Quotation from "Reflections of a Professor's Wife," *Journal of the Association of Collegiate Alumnae* 14 (Jan. 1921), 91. In her case, her husband took a job at a small-town university with anti-nepotism regulations. Cf. Blair, "Married Feminist's Predicament"; and an aggrieved male response to "two-career" couples, Henry Carey, "This Two-Headed Monster—The Family," *Harper's Magazine* 156 (Jan. 1928), 162–71. Littell, "Meditations," is an unusual example of a wife who becomes the family breadwinner so that her husband can be freed from his distasteful job in order to write; nonetheless, her major consideration justifying the pattern is the quality of the relationship between husband and wife.

28. My thinking on the failure to critique marriage was furthered by an unpublished seminar paper by Sabina Piatzer, "The Changing Concept of Marriage," Yale U., 1985.

29. Poll of men in Pruette, *Women and Leisure*, 99–108; prescription closes La Follette, *A Study*.

30. Kennon, "College Wives Who Work," 100–06; Woodhouse, "The Occupations of Members of the AAUW," 119–22, and "Married College Women in Business and Professions," 325–38. Both of Woodhouse's essays use the same database, the first analyzing single women, the latter, married.

31. The difference in economic resources between La Follette's and Collier's groups was not due solely to onset of the Depression, but also to the kind of selection Collier had made. Collier, *Marriages and Careers*, 27–29, 54–59, 69–70, 87, 113; Kennon, "College Wives," 103; La Follette, *A Study*, esp. 34, 78, 86, 87–88, 170–71, 173–74. Categories of help which husbands contributed may overlap. Amount of husbands' help in any category was not detailed.

32. Two-thirds of the women La Follette surveyed, for instance, had borne no children (although a small proportion cared for stepchildren or adopted chil-

dren), and the remaining third averaged fewer than two children per family. Childless wives predominated in Kennon's study and represented probably 40 percent of Woodhouse's career groups. Among the more than 500 married women with low-level service, clerical, and factory jobs surveyed by Eleanor Coit and Elsie Harper in 1930, one-third were childless. Collier, *Marriages and Careers*, 27–29, 45; La Follette, *A Study*, 52–53; Coit and Harper, "Why Do Married Women Work?" 79–80. Which was the independent and which the dependent variable—the employment or childlessness—remains unclear. A high proportion of the "modern women" whose biographical sketches appeared in the *Nation* in 1926–27 were childless; see Showalter, *These Modern Women*. All of these studies covered women of a wide age span, so their childlessness cannot be attributed simply to youth.

33. Bessie Bunzel, "The Woman Goes to College—After Which Must She Choose Between Marriage and a Career?" *Century Monthly Magazine* 117 (Nov. 1928), 32; Tyson, "Professional Woman's Baby," 192. Both the lawyer and secretary respondents to the BVI's questions, discussed above, clearly distinguished between the wife with career and the mother with career; and cf. young women's responses, Blanchard and Manasses, *New Girls*, table 5, 260. Elizabeth Brandeis [Raushenbush] to Clara Beyer, Dec. 7, 1931, folder 40, Clara Beyer Coll., SL. (Beyer, also the mother of several children, curtailed her professional activities while they were young and later picked up a full-time career in the Bureau of Labor Statistics; see her papers in SL.) Another example of a professional woman able to take child psychologists' strictures with many grains of salt: Elizabeth Dickens, "If Mother Has a Profession," *Indep. W.* 9:4 (Apr. 1930), 154–56.

34. Eva Von Baur Hansl, "What About the Children? The Question of Mothers and Careers," *Harper's Magazine* 154 (Jan. 1927), 220–27, 223 (quotation). Hansl reasoned syllogistically (225, 227) that educated women's conflicts would abate because the training and intellect required for mothering were becoming better acknowledged, women were more accepted in the professions, and "a new science of child study and education" was creating new occupations consistent with family responsibilities for women. She concluded optimistically that "as soon as women assume a professional attitude toward everything they do—from housekeeping to business—their problems of combining careers and motherhood will begin to adjust themselves more easily."

35. "Confessions of an Ex-Feminist," *TNR* 46 (Apr. 14, 1926), 218–20; Diana Freeman, "The Feminist's Husband," ibid. 52 (Aug. 24, 1927), 15–16; Worth Tuttle, "Autobiography of an Ex-Feminist," *Atlantic Monthly* 152 (Dec. 1933), 641–49, and "A Feminist Marries," ibid. 153 (Jan. 1934), 73–81, 80 (quotation). Cf. R. Phillips, "The Problem of the Educated Woman," *Harper's Magazine* 154 (Dec. 1926), 57–63, and "The Harm My Education Did Me," by an Ex-Feminist, *The Outlook* 147 (Nov. 30, 1927), 396–97.

36. Collier, *Marriages and Careers*, 23–24, 35–37, 46–48. On Lucy Sprague Mitchell; see Joyce Antler, "Feminism as Life Process," *FS* 7:1 (Spring 1981), 134–57, and *Lucy Sprague Mitchell: The Making of a Modern Woman* (New Haven, Yale U.P., 1987). The move of professionally trained women toward child-oriented work might be considered "overdetermined" by sex-segregation and proclivity, but the personal inclinations of professionals who were mothers should also not be ignored. See Margaret Rossiter, *Women Scientists in America* (Baltimore, Johns Hopkins U.P., 1982), on sex-segregation in social science professions.

37. Clipping from *The New York World Telegraph*, Aug. 25, 1931, folder 3,

and 1951 publicity material about *Parents' Magazine*, folder 1, Clara Savage Littledale Coll., SL.

38. Collier, *Marriages and Careers*, 34. Cf. U.S. Secretary of Labor Frances Perkins's remarks, probably about 1936: "It is difficult to generalize as to whether marriage and the home interfere with woman's achievement in the professional field or any other. It all depends on the circumstances of the particular woman. If her income is large enough to provide for skilled and reliable household assistance; if her husband is cooperative and objective about her wage-earning activities; if she is strong physically; if her job is one in which she can utilize valuable experience and consciously make a rich contribution to social welfare—surely close home and family ties serve to realize the type of integrated personality that contributes so largely to professional achievement." Quoted in Susan Ware, "Political Sisterhood in the New Deal: Women in Politics and Government, 1933–1940" (Ph.D. diss., Harvard U., 1978), 46. Ware criticizes the New Deal women's individualistic resolutions of the career–marriage issue.

39. Quotations taken from clippings, "College Expands to Reach Wives," *The New York Times*, Nov. 1, 1925, 6, and "An Institute to Coordinate Women's Interests Launched," *The Christian Science Monitor*, Oct. 22, 1925, 9, in folder 138, Morgan-Howes Coll., SL; Ethel Puffer Howes, "The Progress of the Institute for the Coordination of Women's Interests," pamphlet report, Oct. 12, 1928 (Northampton, Smith College), SSC; Howes, "The Women's Orientation Course—What Shall Be Its Basic Concept?" *JAAUW* 20 (Jun. 1927), 106–09; Howes, "The Meaning of Progress in the Woman Movement," *AAAPSS* 143 (May 1929), 14–20 (quotation, 19); see also collection of reports and documents on the institute in SSC. I have benefited from the discussion of Howes in Dolores Hayden, *The Grand Domestic Revolution* (Cambridge, MIT P., 1981), 267–71, where Howes appears as the last voice in the "material feminist" tradition.

40. Documentation on the Laura Spelman Rockefeller Memorial Fund's reasons for terminating the institute is sparse; see Hayden, *Grand Domestic Revolution*, 276–77. On the contemporary struggle over home economics in elite women's colleges and home economics, see Mary E. Woolley, "Changing Ideas of Home Life," *JAAUW* 19 (Jan. 1926), 4–7; Chase Going Woodhouse, "Modern Homemaking in Relation to the Liberal Arts College for Women," ibid., 7–10; Elizabeth E. Wellington, "Re-Routing Women's Education," ibid. (Jun. 1926), 4–8; Louise Stanley (chief of the U.S. Dept. of Agriculture's Bureau of Home Economics), "Home-Making Education in the Colleges," *AAAPSS* 143 (May 1929), 361–67; see also Emma Weigley, "It Might Have Been Euthenics," *AQ* 26 (1970), 79–96; Barbara Solomon, *In the Company of Educated Women* (New Haven, Yale U.P., 1985), 85–87; Helen Horowitz, *Alma Mater*, (N.Y., Knopf, 1984), 295–301.

41. Maurine W. Greenwald (History Dept., U. Pittsburgh), "The Case for Working-class Feminism: Seattle Wage Earners and Married Women's Right to Work in the 1920s," unpubl. paper, 1986, esp. 18–25. The workers of Seattle in 1919—the city that shocked the nation with its general strike that year—cannot be assumed to be "average American" workers, but neither can they be assumed to be entirely unrepresentative.

42. Judith Sealander, *As Minority Becomes Majority* (Westport, Conn., Greenwood, 1983) esp. 7–9, 58–62, 153–164, on the Women's Bureau bureaucrats as "insiders" who remained "outsiders"; Mary Anderson, as told to Mary N. Winslow, *Woman at Work: The Autobiography of Mary Anderson* (Minneapolis, U. Minnesota P., 1951), 157–58.

43. Ethel Best and Ethel Erickson, "A Survey of Laundries and Their Women Workers in Twenty-Three Cities," WBB #78 (1930), cited in Jacqueline Jones, *Labor of Love, Labor of Sorrow* (N.Y., Basic, 1985), 178. Examples of opponents to the ERA citing its danger to the legal requirement for husbands' support include Ethel Smith, "Working Women's Case Against 'Equal Rights,'" *The New York Times*, Jan. 20, 1924, 12; and editorial by Carrie Chapman Catt in *Women's Home Companion*, Aug. 1922.

44. A Women's Bureau study of wage-earning women in four cities in 1920 (a reasonably representative national sample) showed that more than half had children under six years of age; see Agnes Peterson, "What the Wage-Earning Woman Contributes to Family Support," *AAAPSS* 143 (May 1929), 89. Lathrop quotation from a 1919 speech cited in Mary M. Ladd-Taylor, "Mother-work: Ideology, Public Policy, and the Mothers' Movement, 1890–1930" (Ph.D. diss., Yale U., 1986), 343, and see 318–21 for Children's Bureau correlation of maternal employment with infant death rates. The highest infant death rate correlated with maternal employment outside the home, a middle rate with maternal earning through work performed at home, and the lowest rate with mothers who earned no wages.

45. See Martha May, "The Historical Problem of the Family Wage," *FS* 8:2 (1982), esp. 400–05, and Martha May, "Bread Before Roses: American Workingmen, Labor Unions and the Family Wage," in *Women, Work and Protest*, ed. Ruth Milkman (Boston, RKP, 1985), 1–21.

46. Coit and Harper, "Why Do Married Women Work?"; Collier, *Marriages and Careers*, 87–88. Cf. Helen Tyson, "Mothers Who Earn," *Survey* 57 (Dec. 1, 1926), 275–83, Beulah Amidon, "They Must Work," ibid., 311, 340–32, and Leslie Woodcock Tentler, *Wage-Earning Women* (N.Y., Oxford U.P., 1979), 137–47, for views similar to the Women's Bureau's.

47. Eudora Ramsay Richardson, "From Pram to Office," *JAAUW* 21 (Jun. 1928), 115. As much as married women were driven by economic need, it was an interpretive category just as "adequate standard of living" was. The prejudice in favor of economic-familial rationales for married women's employment must have shaped women's responses to investigators, although it is impossible to say just how far such self-assessments were shaped and how far real. Cf. evidence cited by Viva Boothe, "Gainfully Employed Women in the Family," *AAAPSS* 160 (1932), 78, that of 345 married women applying to the employment service of the Denver, Colorado, YWCA in the summer of 1928, almost three-quarters said they had no support from their husbands, another 15 percent said they had inadequate support, and only 10 percent mentioned a preference for working outside the home. Of more than 100 women applying to one department store, more than four-fifths—almost half of whom were widowed, divorced, or separated—gave economic necessity, and only 8 percent gave preference for outside employment as their reason.

48. Woodhouse, "Married College Women in Business and Professions."

49. Boothe, "Gainfully Employed Women in the Family," 78, 79, 85; Dean Virginia Gildersleeve quoted in Margaret Speer, "Education, Business and Babies," *Indep. W.* 12 (Jun. 1926), 245. As shown by the dates of Gildersleeve's remark and Woodhouse's reasoning, explicit disavowal of feminist aims by some career–marriage advocates predated the Depression; nonetheless, Scharf has grounds for her contention in *To Work and to Wed* that Depression conditions were instrumental in exhausting the 1920s form of career–marriage feminism.

Cecile Tipton La Follette used economic reasoning in more than one way in her 1932 *Study of 652 Gainfully Employed Married Women Homemakers*. She not only demonstrated her subjects' economic need, but also pointed out that they were creating employment for 540 household service workers (thus easing rather than exacerbating the economic crisis); they also created business for the baker, merchant, laundryman, and prepared food industry. *A Study,* 34, 78, 86, 170.

50. Scharf, *To Work,* esp. 44–45, 76, 85, 107. Scharf's is the fullest discussion of the Depression's impact on married women's employment and shows its effect of demoting women in, rather than removing them from, the work force. See also Mary W. M. Hargreaves, "Darkness Before the Dawn: Women in the Depression Years," in *Clio Was a Woman,* ed. Mabel E. Deutrich and Virginia C. Purdy (Washington, D.C., Howard U.P., 1980), 181; Wandersee, *Women's Work,* 66–102, esp. 90, 100–01. Alice Kessler-Harris argues that there were "some benefits of labor segregation [for women] in a decade of Depression" in *Out to Work* (N.Y., Oxford U.P., 1982), 250–73.

51. Ruby Black, "Common Problems of Professional Women," ER, Aug. 4, 1928, 207; Smith, "Legal and Administrative Restrictions," 263. Reasoning of this sort lay behind not only school boards and private employers' discriminations but also the policies instituted during the Depression in many states and at the federal level (in sec. 213 of the Economy Act of 1932), prohibiting more than one member of a family from holding a government job. Although superficially sex-neutral, such legislation stemmed from reasoning of a family wage sort and, together with the economic fact that women earned less than men, it became equivalent to a requirement that the wife resign her job if her husband were also employed by the state. Such regulations sparked the most concerted and united women's activism during the Depression, spanning career–marriage feminists and Women's Bureau allies. See Scharf, *To Work,* esp. 46–53.

7: PROFESSIONALISM AND FEMINISM

1. On Gertrude Ederle, see Paul Carter, *Another Part of the Twenties* (N.Y., Columbia U.P., 1977), 116–19; Robert Daniel, *American Women in the Twentieth Century: The Festival of Life* (N.Y., Harcourt Brace, 1986), 60; biographical sketch of Amelia Earhart by Katherine A. Brick, NAW I, 538–50; Pickford quoted in Lary May, *Screening Out the Past* (N.Y., Oxford U.P., 1980), 119. Note Florence Guy Seabury's objection that despite such firsts, earlier female stereotypes persisted: "Stereotypes," in *Our Changing Morality,* ed. Freda Kirchwey, (N.Y., Boni, 1924), 219–31.

2. Olive Schreiner to Mrs. Francis Smith, Jul. 1912, quoted in Joyce Avrech Berkman, *Olive Schreiner: Feminism on the Frontier* (St. Albans, Vt., Eden, 1979), 65.

3. There is a large literature, mainly sociological, on professionalization; the historical literature is growing. For historical perspective, a good starting place is Alexandra Oleson and John Voss, eds., *The Organization of Knowledge in Modern America, 1860–1920* (Baltimore, Johns Hopkins U.P., 1979); see especially in that volume the definition of professionalism by Dorothy Ross, in "The Development of the Social Sciences," 117–18. Burton Bledstein, *The Culture of Professionalism* (N.Y., Norton, 1976); William Leach, *True Love and Perfect Union* (N.Y., Basic, 1980); Rosalind Rosenberg, *Beyond Separate Spheres* (New Haven, Yale U.P., 1982); and Virginia Drachman, *Hospital with a Heart* (Ithaca, Cornell U.P., 1984), are all helpful on the appeal of scientific ideology to nineteenth-century middle-class women with reform aims. There are perceptive re-

views of the literature of professionalism from the point of view of female professionals in Penina Glazer and Miriam Slater, *Unequal Colleagues* (New Brunswick, N.J., Rutgers U.P., 1986), chap. 1, and in Barbara Melosh, *'The Physicians' Hand'* (Philadelphia, Temple U.P., 1982), 15–19. I have also benefited from Joyce Antler, "Women and the Professions: Emerging Historical Perspectives," paper presented at the Conference on the 40th Anniversary of the Arthur and Elizabeth Schlesinger Library, Cambridge, Mar. 1984.

4. Alice Kessler-Harris, *Out to Work: A History of Wage-Earning Women in the United States* (N.Y., Oxford U.P., 1982), 116.

	1900	1910	1920	1930	1940	1950
Women as % of labor force	—	21.2	20.5	22.0	25.4	—
Women as % of professional and kindred workers	35.2	41.3	44.1	44.8	41.5	39.6
Professional women as % of all women in labor force	8.2	9.1	11.9	14.2	12.3	—

Statistics based on U.S. Census data as presented in Elizabeth K. Nottingham, "Towards an Analysis of the Effects of Two World Wars on the Role and Status of Middle-Class Women in the English-Speaking World," *Amer. Sociol. Rev.* 12 (Dec. 1947), 669–70; Frank Stricker, "Cookbooks and Lawbooks: The Hidden History of Career Women in Twentieth-Century America," in *A Heritage of Her Own*, ed. Nancy F. Cott and Elizabeth H. Pleck (N.Y., Simon and Schuster, 1979), 482; Valerie K. Oppenheimer, *The Female Labor Force in the United States* (Westport, Conn., Greenwood, 1976), 149.

5. See table 7.1. Disputing Graham (a), whose figures were based on the U.S. Dept. of Health, Education and Welfare *Digest of Education Statistics* (1976), Carter (b) has based her figures on more detailed publications of the Office of Education, annual and biennial reports based on questionnaires sent out to institutions. According to Carter's figures, women's proportional hold on the field of college teaching did not decline until the 1940s, although it was in stasis during the 1920s and 1930s.

6. On numbers of women lawyers, Joyce Antler, "The Educated Woman and Professionalization: The Struggle for a New Feminine Identity, 1890–1920" (Ph.D. diss., SUNY, Stony Brook, 1977), 269; and Lorine Pruette, *Women and Leisure: A Study of Social Waste* (N.Y., Dutton, 1924), table 5, 68. Stricker, in "Cookbooks and Lawbooks," points out the importance of the comparison group—whether all professionals or all women—in assessing proportional gains by professional women. Similarly, in *Women Scientists in America* (Baltimore, Johns Hopkins U.P., 1982), 130–32, Margaret Rossiter points out that the number of women earning Ph.D.s in science rose (unevenly) from about 50 annually in the early 1920s to about 165 per year in the late 1930s; but since the number of men doing the same grew faster, women's proportion of the degrees declined after 1932. From a 1920s high of 15.5 percent it slipped to 11.5 percent in the late 1930s and 10 percent in 1940. Stricker notes (484) that if one defines career women as all the women in the U.S. Census categories of "Professional, Tech-

nical and Kindred" workers and "Managers, Officials and Proprietors," then there were 3 career women per 100 adult women in 1920, 4 in 1930, and 5 in 1940. The female population aged twenty to sixty grew by 11 percent between 1930 and 1940; see U.S. Bureau of the Census, *Statistical Abstracts of the United States* (Washington, D.C., 1965).

7. See n. 4.

8. Mary Roth Walsh, *Doctors Wanted: No Women Need Apply* (New Haven, Yale U.P., 1977), esp. 185–86; 218–25; see also Drachman, *Hospital with a Heart*, and Regina Markell Morantz-Sanchez, *Sympathy and Science* (N.Y., Oxford U.P., 1985), 232–350.

9. Rossiter, *Women Scientists*, 160–217; Marion O. Hawthorne, "Women as College Teachers," *AAAPSS* 143 (May 1929), 146, 153.

10. Inez Milholland, "A Woman Lawyer's Difficulties," c. 1912–15, temporary folder 30, Milholland Collection, SL.

11. On academic salaries, see Susan B. Carter, "Academic Women Revisited: An Empirical Study of Changing Patterns of Women's Employment as College and University Faculty," *Journal of Social History* 14 (Summer 1981), 687, and Frank Stricker, "Affluence for Whom?—Another Look at Prosperity and the Working Classes in the 1920s," *Labor Hist.* 24 (Winter 1983), 15, showing a decline in college professors' salaries by 35 percent during 1914–20 and its rise by 64 percent during 1920–27; on anthropology, Rossiter, *Women Scientists*, 139.

12. "Although most of the barriers to women's advancement that one finds documented are administrative or procedural," in historian Margaret Rossiter's judgment, "at root they were cognitive and perceptual": that was the least palpable but perhaps the most important circumstance holding back women's continued advance in the scientific professions. Rossiter, *Women Scientists*, 167 (quotation), 278–79. Cf. Paul Lauter, "Race and Gender in the Shaping of the American Literary Canon: A Case Study from the Twenties," *FS* 9:3 (Fall 1983), 435–64.

13. E.g., William H. Chafe, *The American Woman: Her Changing Social, Economic and Political Roles* (N.Y., Oxford U.P., 1972), 90–93; Walsh, *Doctors Wanted*, 260–63; Rosenberg, *Beyond Separate Spheres*, 244.

14. Scharf, *To Work and to Wed*, (Westport, Conn., Greenwood, 1980), chap. 5, esp. 90–91.

15. Doris Fleischman, *An Outline of Careers for Women: A Practical Guide for Achievement* (Garden City, N.Y., Doubleday, 1929), 1; Norris quoted, 271.

16. Journalist questionnaires (collected in 1917), in folder 337, BVI. Two-thirds of the respondents were from the Northeast. Lawyer questionnaires (33 collected in 1918, 111 collected in 1920–21), in folders 133–34. Miriam Simons Leuck, surveying "Women in Odd and Unusual Fields of Work," *AAAPSS* 143 (May 1929), 166–79, found that these women testified that once in the field, whether it was electrical engineering or heading a taxi fleet, their sex was an advantageous recognition factor rather than a handicap.

17. Ella Lonn, "Academic Status of Women on University Faculties," *JAAUW* 17 (Jan. 1924), 5; college teachers' salaries in Chase Going Woodhouse, "Occupations of Members of the American Association of University Women," *JAAUW* 21 (Jun. 1928), 121; Rossiter, *Women Scientists*, 197–98. In Woodhouse's survey, the *median* salary of those with Ph.D. and 15 years experience ($3,500) was higher than median of those with B.A. and some experience ($2,600); but the maximum for both was $6,500.

18. Emilie Hutchinson, *Women and the Ph.D.* (Greensboro, N.C., Institute

of Professional Relations, 1929), 99, 101 (quotation), 113, 174–212, esp. 181 (quotation); Hawthorne, "College Teachers," 153.

19. Rossiter, *Women Scientists*, 129–30, 156–59, 165–67, 249–51; Hutchinson, *Ph.D.*, 191; Victoria Schuck, "Sexism and Scholarship: A Brief Overview of Women, Academia, and the Disciplines," *Social Science Q.* 55 (Dec. 1971), 581; Helen Hamilton Gardener, "Women in Government Work," *JAAUW*, 19 (Oct. 1925), 17–20. Rossiter calls the hidden catch of the professional double standard "the Madame Curie syndrome"—i.e., Curie's outstanding accomplishments did not revise male scientists' general view of women in science; rather, she was regarded as the exception. Cf. Ruth Hahn, "When the Boss Has a Grudge Against Women in Business," *Indep. W.* 11:3 (Mar. 1927), 7–8, 34; and see also the contemporary comment with respect to a woman in political office, "if she fails, she closes, to some extent, a new avenue which is just opening out to her sisters," written by Eleanor Roosevelt under the entry "Politics," in Fleischman, *Outline of Careers*, 382.

20. Ella Lonn, "Academic Status," 10; Rossiter, *Women Scientists*, 306–07.

21. Quotation from Phi Delta Delta law fraternity in Ruby Black, "Common Problems of Professional Women," *ER*, Aug. 4, 1928, 207; Elizabeth Kemper Adams, *Women Professional Workers* (N.Y., MacMillan, 1921), 19, 28–29. See also Anne W. Armstrong, "Seven Deadly Sins of Women in Business," *Harper's Magazine* 153 (Aug. 1926), 295–303, citing sins ranging from "taking themselves too seriously" to "imitating men's standards," with "talking too much" and "antagonizing male associates" in between.

22. Adams, *Women Professional Workers*, 19, 28–29.

23. On women's professional organizations, see J. Stanley Lemons, *The Woman Citizen: Social Feminism in the 1920s* (Urbana, U. Illinois P., 1973), 41–43, 58–59; Rossiter, *Women Scientists*, chap. 11; Walsh, *Doctors Wanted*, 216–19.

24. Black, "Common Problems," 205–07; Lena Madesin Phillips, "A Challenge to the Business Woman," *Indep. W.* 8: (Aug. 1929), 344; see also "Let Us Build Our Work Lives Frankly and Freely as Women," ibid. 6 (Apr. 1927), 4–5, 41, and Agnes Von Zahn-Hurnuck, "University Women and the Woman's Movement," *JAAUW* 23:1 (Oct. 1929), 1–3.

25. Ella Lonn, "Academic Status," 8, 9, 10.

26. Fleischman, "Public Relations," in *An Outline of Careers*, 392; A. Ruth Hahn, "But I Won't Work for a Woman!" *Indep. W.* 6 (Nov. 1927), and "When the Boss Has a Grudge," 34; Adams, *Women Professional Workers*, 441. Cf. Dr. Martha Tracy, "The Profession of Medicine and Women's Opportunity in This Field," *JAAUW* 21 (Oct. 1927), 5–10: "The subject is no longer to be dealt with as an issue in a feminist program. Today one need not hark back to the struggle of the pioneer women who demonstrated against great odds the capacity of their sex for useful service in medical practice, as in other professional and business fields."

27. Lawyers' quotations from 1887 letters of Laura de Force Gordon, Lelia J. Robinson, and Martha K. Pearce, in "Equity Club" papers, folder 405, Dillon Coll., SL; see also Antler, "Educated Woman," 211–12, 247–51; Drachman, *Hospital with a Heart*, esp. 151–75; Morantz-Sanchez, *Sympathy and Science*, esp. 90–202.

28. Rosenberg, in *Beyond Separate Spheres*, has elucidated the tensions of academic women (social scientists) at coeducational universities around the turn of the century. Having isolated themselves from the nurturing and domestic culture of women behind them in order to take advantage of professional and

academic opportunities, and yet not comfortable or fully accepted in the male-structured world of professional expertise, they balanced unevenly between two worlds.

29. Questionnaire in folder 133, BVI.

30. See Dorothy Ross, "Development of the Social Sciences," esp. 125–29; Rosenberg, *Beyond Separate Spheres*, 49; and cf. Mary O. Furner, *Advocacy and Objectivity* (Lexington, U.P. Kentucky, 1975).

31. Regarding credentialing, see Susan B. Carter, "Education Was for Women What the Frontier Was for Men," paper presented at the Sixth Berkshire Conference on the History of Women, Smith College, Jun. 1984.

32. Cf. also Mabel Walker Willebrandt, who was appointed assistant attorney-general by President Harding in 1921 and was probably the most successful woman lawyer in the early twentieth century. Responsible for prosecuting offenders against Prohibition, by 1929 she was fourth among all members of the bar in the total number of cases she had argued before the U.S. Supreme Court. Throughout the 1920s she paid attention to advancing women lawyers: she devoted time to the women's legal "fraternity," Phi Delta Delta (serving as its president for six years), admitted frankly that women had a much harder row to hoe in the professions than men, and urged that women be given a "fighting chance." In her role as a professional, however, identification with women meant to her only the "girlie-girlie stuff" she deplored. She advised aspiring professionals to "refrain from argument on the woman question" and to make their strategy "insisting on a fair field for all." Dorothy M. Brown, *Mabel Walker Willebrandt: A Study of Power, Loyalty, and Law* (Knoxville, U. Tennessee P., 1984), 47, 75, 138–43.

33. Tentative draft Report of Committee on Standards for Promotion and Tenure, as presented at the Annual Convention, Apr., 1925, AAUW, dated Mar. 30, 1925, in folder 546, box 29, Mary Van Kleeck Coll., SSL. On the committee were, besides Van Kleeck, Marion E. Park, Willystine Goodsell, and Mina Kerr.

34. See Glazer and Slater, *Unequal Colleagues*, on the point that marginal groups seeking access to professions can embrace no other than meritocratic standards. Cf. Anne Armstrong on the inability of women in the business world to protest openly, though "seething" (esp. the "abler" ones) with dissatisfaction over unequal treatment: "business women do not feel themselves strong enough yet, as a class, to force the issue." "Are Business Women Getting a Square Deal?" *Indep. W.* 7: (Jan. 1928), 30. The impact of the Civil Rights Act of 1964 in effectuating feminist protests within and about the professions in the 1960s and 1970s cannot be minimized; women in the earlier generations had no such support from outside the professions themselves.

On female clients, the BVI's questionnaires to women lawyers provided some interesting data. Ninety-eight respondents answered the question, "what proportion of your clients are female?" Answers were as follows:

Proportion cited	N
75%	16
60%–74%	9
50%	21
15%–40%	28
10% or less	21
Don't know	3

(No respondents used figures between 51% and 59%, between 41% and 49%, or between 11% and 14%.) An increasing tendency for men to hire women lawyers was cited by 67 percent of the respondents, but only 57 percent felt there was a corresponding tendency among women. Judge Jean Hortense Norris claimed that women lawyers faced worse prejudice from their own sex than from men, in Fleischman, *Outline of Careers*, 271. Lonn, "Academic Status," 8–9, found evidence from all her university respondents that female students preferred men to women as professors, as much as or more than male students did.

35. See chap. 3. Cf. the essential "behind the scenes" character (rather than overt feminist stance) of the network among women prominent in the New Deal, in Susan Ware's portrayal, *Beyond Suffrage* (Cambridge, Harvard U.P., 1981).

36. Nina Asher, "Dorothy Jacobs Bellanca: Women Clothing Workers and the Runaway Shops," in *A Needle, A Bobbin, A Strike*, ed. Joan Jensen and Sue Davidson (Philadelphia, Temple U.P., 1984), esp. 197–218; quotation from Bellanca to Mamie Santora, Aug. 5, 1925, on 217–18. In the retrospective judgment of Julia Maietta, who was born in 1909 in Pennsylvania, began to work in a sweatshop at fifteen, joined the ACW and then became an organizer, women organizers were treated as second-class citizens and were paid less than men; she also felt that the women who rose to the executive boards of both the ACW and ILGWU were tokens and that women had to shout (metaphorically) to be heard by the leadership. Transcript of interview with Maietta by Alice Hoffman, in "The Twentieth-Century Trade Union Woman: Vehicle for Social Change," Oral History Project, Institute of Labor and Industrial Relations, U. Michigan and Wayne State U., 30–38, 55–56.

37. Alice Kessler-Harris, "Problems of Coalition-Building: Women and Trade Unions in the 1920s," in *Women, Work and Protest*, ed. Ruth Milkman (Boston, RKP, 1985), esp. 121–33; on 126, quotation from Craton, "Working the Women Workers," *The Nation* 124 (Mar. 1927), 312.

38. *The Advance*, Sep. 3, 1926, quoted in Kessler-Harris, "Problems of Coalition-Building," 130.

39. Joan Brumberg and Nancy Tomes, "Women in the Professions: A Research Agenda for American Historians," *Reviews in American History* 10 (Jun. 1982), 286. Cf. a young social worker's remark: "being a professional soc. [sic] worker, I suppose I do prefer to work with a recognized professional agency than with the dear ladies who volunteer"; Lucia to Dorothee [sic], Sep. 17, in folder "correspondence, 1920–22," Dorothy Kirchwey Brown uncat. coll., SL.

40. Account of C. G. Woodhouse line in Mary Ritter Beard to Florence Kitchelt, Jun. 29, 1950, folder 113, Kitchell Coll., SL. Mary Beard deplored Woodhouse's sentiment; in response to it she wrote, "women can't avoid being women whatever they do," quoted in Introduction.

In 1933, Woodhouse—head of the Institute of Women's Professional Relations at Greensboro, North Carolina—was hoping to be appointed assistant commissioner of the federal Office of Education. Among other attempts to foster her appointment, she tried to get the recommendation of Anna Kelton Wiley, aging stalwart in the NWP and widow of Dr. Harvey Wiley, leader in the Food and Drug Administration early in the century. In her request to Wiley, Woodhouse described herself thus: "while I have not been a member [of the NWP] I lived in the house and have always done what I could for large sections of the Program. My own belief is that a strong feminist in the Office of Education could do a great deal. After all what we need is more social science in our education and more understanding of the economic order and women's relation to it." Woodhouse to Mrs. Wiley, Mar. 31, 1933, folder W, box 58, Anna Kelton Wiley Coll., LC. (Wiley refused to write the recommendation because Woodhouse was not an NWP member, but she returned a sympathetic and admiring letter.)

41. Dr. Caroline Spencer to Mrs. Jane Norman Smith, Apr. 20, 1928, NWP

#39; Mary Gertrude Fendall to Jane Norman Smith, Sep. 1, 1927, folder 64, JNSC.

42. Only women whose death dates fell between 1955 and 1970 appeared in this volume; thus the numbers for the birth cohorts are as follows: 1850s, 8; 1860s, 38; 1870s, 93; 1880s, 134; 1890s, 91; 1900s, 54; 1910s, 20. Interestingly, almost half of the 1860s birth cohort were noted to be suffragists; one-third of the 1870s cohort were; but for only 17.5 percent of the 1880s birth cohort and 6 percent of the 1890s birth cohort was belief in and/or advocacy of woman suffrage mentioned. I have used only information supplied by the biographical sketches, even if other information was available, in order to keep the sources as uniform as possible. Of course there must be a great deal of variation in points found interesting by all the different authors of the sketches, but each was following a set of queries set out by the editors of the volume. There were difficulties in coding, in distinguishing "woman's rights" from "women's issues," but the proportions in the two categories, as it turns out, reinforce the same pattern of decline. Cf. Eileen L. McDonagh, "Profiles of Achievement: Women's Entry into the Professions, the Arts, and Social Reform," *Sociological Inquiry* 53:4 (Fall 1983), 343–67, an analysis of the biographical sketches in the first three volumes of NAW, which asks somewhat different questions about generational change. McDonagh finds the proportion of women in social reform decreasing while the proportion of those in the arts increases, from the 1841–70 birth cohort to the 1871–1900 birth cohort. The proportion in professions remains about the same over these two generational cohorts (362–63).

8: IN VOLUNTARY CONFLICT

1. Newspaper clipping quoting Alice Park's plans to attend WILPF convention, attached to diary entry Mar. 24–25, 1924, box 24; fragment tucked in 1927 diary; clipping pasted in Mar. 5, 1929, diary page; fragment tucked in Jul. 1, 1929, diary page, box 25, Alice Park Diary, Park Coll., HI.

2. Chap. 3 describes the founding of women's peace associations and peace departments. See Charles DeBenedetti, *Origins of the Modern American Peace Movement, 1915–1929* (Millwood, N.J., KTO, 1978), 86–97; and Felice D. Gordon, *After Winning: The Legacy of the New Jersey Suffragists* (New Brunswick, N.J., Rutgers U.P., 1986), 67. Feminist–pacifist connections carrying over from the 1910s are clearest in the women's societies founded explicitly to further disarmament, pacifism, or nonresistance, that is, the WCWD the WILPF, the Women's Peace Society, and the WPU. The general women's organizations with peace departments perhaps deserved the appraisal from the left made by Roger Baldwin and Stuart Chase in 1923, that they "all mean well, but they have no program translatable into political or international action." "International Peace," pt. B, #5, in "Survey of Enterprises in the Liberal, Labor, and Radical Movements in the U.S.," prepared for the American Fund for Public Service, Jul. 1923/Feb. 1924, by Roger N. Baldwin and Stuart Chase, box 7, Amer. Fund. Coll., NYPL.

3. C. Leonard Hoag, *Preface to Preparedness: The Washington Disarmament Conference and Public Opinion* (Washington, D.C., American Council on Public Affairs, 1941), esp. 35–37, 45, 68–69, 73–79, 89–98, 81–82 (Fried quotation). In Hoag's judgment, the WCWD was the "pioneer" of public sentiment in favor of disarmament. Cf. the judgment of Yale law professor Irving Fisher, prominent in the peace movement: "I regard the women as politically the most important factor in the situation. I believe it was through the women's sentiment

that the disarmament movement made such rapid headway." Irving Fisher to President A. Lawrence Lowell (Harvard University), Jul. 20, 1921, box 9, Fisher Papers, Sterling Memorial Library, Yale U. See folders labeled "Women's Committee for World Disarmament," in box D15, Belle Case La Follette Papers, LC, and in Swarthmore College Peace Collection. Letterheads from May 1921 and Nov. 1921 reveal leadership by NWP members. I have followed their usage of the title "chairman." Charles Chatfield, *For Peace and Justice: Pacifism in America, 1914–1941* (Knoxville, U. Tennessee P., 1971), 147; and DeBenedetti, *Origins*, 86, following Hoag, *Preface*, 92, state that founders of WCWD "withdrew" from the NWP, which is not the case for all. Joan Jensen, in "All Pink Sisters: The War Department and the Feminist Movement in the 1920s," in *Decades of Discontent*, ed. Lois Scharf and Joan Jensen (Westport, Conn., Greenwood, 1983), 207, notices their error.

Feminist peace activists' willingness to ally with Borah is interesting, since he was a diehard opponent of the Nineteenth Amendment (see Maud Wood Park, *Front Door Lobby*, ed. Edna Stantial [Boston, Beacon, 1960], 236, 260) and an opponent of the Sheppard-Towner bill (see J. Stanley Lemons, *The Woman Citizen: Social Feminism in the 1920s* [Urbana, U. Illinois P., 1973], 160).

4. They were Mrs. Thomas Winter, Mrs. Charles Sumner Bird, Mrs. Eleanor Franklin Egan, and Mrs. Katherine Phillips Edson. See "Women's Part in the Washington Conference," *The Literary Digest*, Nov. 26, 1921, 48–53.

5. Gertrude Bussey and Margaret Tims, *The Women's International League for Peace and Freedom, 1915–1965* (London, George Allen and Unwin, 1965), 37–41; Harriet Connor Brown, "Women to the Rescue," *Nation* 112 (Feb. 16, 1921), 261–62; folder "National Council on Limitation of Armaments," in box D33, Belle Case La Follette Papers, LC; DeBenedetti, *Origins*, 86–87; Chatfield, *For Peace and Justice*, 148–50. Generally, the WCWD's formative influence in the National Council on Limitation of Armaments has been ignored, although more members of that group than of any other constituent attended the preliminary meeting of the coalition. See press release entitled "Disarmament Workers Confer" re meeting of Sep. 8, 1921, "National Council on Limitation of Armaments" folder, box D33, Belle Case La Follette Papers, LC.

6. Hoag, *Preface*, 163–86; Jensen, "All Pink Sisters," 209.

7. I am indebted here to Jensen's analysis of the military backlash to the gains made by WILPF in the early 1920s in "All Pink Sisters," esp. 210–14.

8. On the WPU see DeBenedetti, *Origins*, 93–94; and folders 47 and 58, box 4, Caroline Lexow Babcock Coll., SL. The WPU letterhead contains their oath; on war-resisters' oath and WILPF-U.S. see E. G. Balch to Mrs. Mead [copy], May 26, 1924, box 2, ser. C1, WILPF-U.S. Papers, SCPC.

9. The Grange also withdrew from the NCPW at this time. Lemons, *Woman Citizen*, 214–16; Frederick Wile quotation from *Washington Herald*, March 22, 1922, in Hoag, *Preface*, 167; military officer's comment (precipitated by fear that women college students were being taught pacifism to instill in their children) quoted in Jensen, "All Pink Sisters," 212.

10. Elizabeth H. Tilton to Miss Bottomley, Apr. 13, 1923, folder 22; Tilton to Mrs. [Florence] Watkins, Mar. 3, 1923, folder 19; and see also other letters between Tilton and Watkins, Mar.–Apr. 1923, folder 22, Tilton Coll., SL.

11. Copy of "The Notorious Spider-Web Chart" as printed in *The Dearborn Independent* in folio + box 1, Mary Anderson Coll., SL; Lemons, *Woman Citizen*, 215–18; Jensen, "All Pink Sisters," 213; NWTUL press release, Jun. 10, 1924, in container 27, Catt Papers, LC reel 17; Anna Garlin Spencer to Emily Greene Balch, Jun. 11, 1924, box 1, ser. C1, WILPF-U.S. Papers, SCPC; Chatfield, *For*

Peace and Justice, 156–57; DeBenedetti, *Origins*, 88. For a later version of Spider-Web, see Allen Davis, *American Heroine: The Life and Legend of Jane Addams* (N.Y., Oxford U.P., 1973), 262–67. Jensen reports that the DAR was included in Maxwell's first chart but not in published versions, and, indeed, in the version I cite and reprint, there is a blank space where the DAR's name might have been. Lemons brought the impact of the Spider-Web Chart to light in an informative discussion which, however, concentrates on social welfare reformers and thus misses both the context of the military's intents to counter the disarmament movement (revealed by Jensen) and the Spider-Web Chart's attention to NWP feminists.

Henry Ford bought the *Dearborn Independent* to use as a vehicle for his anti-Semitic views in the early 1920s, at which time its circulation reached half a million. Albert Lee, *Henry Ford and the Jews* (N.Y., Stein and Day, 1980), 14–15. My thanks to Beth Wenger for this reference.

12. Norman Hapgood, *Professional Patriots* (N.Y., Boni, 1927); Paul L. Murphy, "Sources and Nature of Intolerance in the 1920s," *JAH* 51:1 (1964), 67–68; Mrs. Lawrence Lewis to Miss K. Morey, Mar. 19, 1921, NWP #7; Mary Kilbreth to President Harding, Nov. 25, 1921, quoted in Lemons, *Woman Citizen*, 160; "The Interlocking Lobby Dictatorship," *The Woman Patriot* 6 (Dec. 1, 1922); "Organizing Women for Class and Sex War," ibid. 7 (Apr. 15, 1923); Elizabeth Tilton to Florence Watkins, confidential memo [1923], folder 22, Tilton Coll., SL; on groundswell of pacifist sentiment in 1923–24, DeBenedetti, *Origins*, 104–06, 111–12. See Jensen's perceptive discussion, to which I am indebted, of the function of right-wing groups in United States politics and the timing of the 1923–24 defamation of women's groups, in "All Pink Sisters," 212–13.

13. Isabelle Kendig (Executive Secretary, Women's Committee for Political Action) to Women Voters, Apr. 9, 1924, folder "Women's Committee for Political Action," box 23, Alice Park Coll., HI; this folder contains the most complete documentation of the WCPA's existence I have found.

14. William Johnston, president, International Assoc. of Machinists, to Rev. Mercer Greene Johnston, Feb. 4, 1922; Johnston to "Dear Sir and Brother," Mar. 15, 1922; pamphlet, "Producers of Wealth Unite," by CPPA [1920–21], box 47, M. G. Johnston Coll., LC. I am indebted to Eugene Tobin for showing me these documents. See also Eugene Tobin, *Organize or Perish: America's Independent Progressives, 1913–1933* (Westport, Conn., Greenwood, 1986), 131–66; and Robert Zieger, *Republicans and Labor, 1919–1929* (Lexington, U. Kentucky P., 1969), 159–99.

15. See printed program, National Conference, WCPA, May 8–11, 1924, Washington, D.C.; Report on the National Conference of the WCPA Held in Washington, May 8–11, 1924; WCPA press release, May 9 [1924]; and clippings, WCPA folder, box 23, Alice Park Coll., HI.

See also Harriet Connor Brown to Mrs. [Belle] La Follette, May 31, 1924, folder "1924, Brown, Harriet Connor," and Zona Gale to Mrs. La Follette, Apr. 25 [1924], folder "1924, Gale, Zona," box D16, Belle Case La Follette Papers, LC. The *Washington Post* reported that "radical" members of the WILPF—notably, Harriet Connor Brown—were circulating the so-called "slacker's oath" of nonresistance at the WCPA conference.

16. Winifred Van Duser, "Women at Cleveland Active in Convention," unidentified clipping (dateline Cleveland, Jul. 4 [1924]), in WCPA folder, box 23, Alice Park Coll., HI; Sophonisba P. Breckinridge, *Women in the Twentieth Century: A Study of their Political, Social and Economic Activities* (N.Y., McGraw-Hill, 1933), 262; *ER* 9 (Jul. 19, 1924), 181, re Socialist Party's and Progressive

Party's equal rights planks. See also H. S. Blatch to Fola La Follette, Jan. 8, 1925, folder "Harriot Stanton Blatch," box E2, Fola La Follette Papers; and Meta Berger to Mrs. La Follette, Jul. 5, 1924, folder "1924, Victor and Mega Berger," D16, Belle La Follette Papers, LC16.

17. Kendig quoted in Van Duser clipping; Mary Winsor, "Women for Congress," folder 6, Mary Winsor Coll., SL; Anne Martin, "Feminists and Future Political Action," *Nation* 120 (Feb. 18, 1925), 185; Anne Martin to John M. Nelson, Esq., Aug. 28, 1924, and Oct. 25, 1924, folder "1924," box 9, Anne Martin Coll., BL; Tobin, *Organize or Perish*, 143–58; Kenneth C. MacKay, *The Progressive Movement of 1924* (N.Y., Columbia U.P., 1947), 9–22, 227–28; Hugh L. Keenleyside, "The American Political Revolution of 1924," *Current History* 21 (Mar. 1925), 834; David Burner, "The Democratic Party in the Election of 1924," *Mid-America* 46 (Apr. 1964), 111.

Two NWP members appealing to the left-wing American Fund for Public Service for money for *Equal Rights* said that the NWP's backing of women candidates on the Progressive ticket in 1924 "angered and alienated some of our wealthy supporters." Edith Houghton Hooker and Mary Winsor to American Fund, [Jan.–Feb.] 1925, box 47 (reel 29), American Fund for Public Service Papers, NYPL.

18. "The Need for a League of Progressive Women," in WCPA folder, box 23, Alice Park Coll., HI; Isabelle Kendig, "Women in the Progressive Movement," *Nation* 119 (Nov. 19, 1924), 544; Kathryn Louise Anderson, "Practical Political Equality for Women: Anne Martin's Campaigns for the United States Senate in Nevada, 1918 and 1920" (Ph.D. diss., U. Washington, 1978), 228.

19. DeBenedetti, *Origins*, 93–94; [unknown, signature page missing] to Members of the Women's Peace Union, Sep. 19, 1924, and Mary Gertrude Fendall for the Working Committee, to Member of the Women's Peace Union, Feb. 19, 1925, folder 47, box 4, Caroline Lexow Babcock Coll., SL. According to biographical sketch "Elinor Byrns" written by Caroline L. Babcock (in folder 58, box 4), Elinor Byrns composed the "Frazier amendment."

20. Bussey and Tims, WILPF, 45–49; Carrie Foster-Hayes, "The Women and the Warriors: Dorothy Detzer and the WILPF" (Ph.D. Diss., U. Denver, 1984), 150; Davis, *American Heroine*, 273–74. Bussey and Tims, WILPF, 45–49, also report that the foreign WILPF delegates on the Pax Special were subject to harrassment and even physical abuse; some meetings to welcome them were cancelled, but some brave goodwill also showed up, as in Detroit, where auto workers greeted the Pax Special with a line of automobiles placarded for peace.

21. "Patriotic Societies Co-operate," *Woman Patriot* 8 (Jul. 15, 1924), 7–8; Helena Huntington Smith, "Mrs. Brosseau and the DAR," *Outlook and Independent*, Mar. 20, 1929, 460; "Our Threatened Heritage: A Letter to the DAR," by a Member [Helen Tufts Baillie], pamphlet (Cambridge, 1928), 6–8, folder 1, box 1; and report, "National Defence Committee," prepared by the Palo Alto, California, chapter of the DAR (and including quotations from DAR annual reports), [1929], 6–7, folder 9, box 1, DAR Blacklist Controversy Coll., Stanford University Archives.

22. Jensen, "All Pink Sisters," 214–15; Amy Woods to Eva Perry Moore, Apr. 24, 1924, box 3, ser. C1, WILPF-U.S.; Papers, SCPC;*Women in a Changing World: The Dynamic Story of the International Council of Women since 1888* (London, Routledge and Kegan Paul, 1966); clipping, "Anger over DAR Action Flames in Women's Council" *Evening Star* (Washington, D.C., May? 1925), in folder "1925, Research Materials, Suffrage," box D36, Belle Case La Follette

Papers, LC; Eva Perry Moore to Amy Woods, Sep. 13, 1924, and Moore to Hannah Clothier Hull, Dec. 6, 1924, box 3, ser. C1, WILPF-U.S. Section Papers, SCPC.

23. Clipping, "Women of 36 Lands Will Confer Here," *Christian Science Monitor,* Apr. 21, 1925, folder "1925, Research Materials, Suffrage," box D36, Belle Case La Follette Papers, LC; Mary Church Terrell, *A Colored Woman in a White World* (1940, repr. N.Y., Arno, 1980), 370–71; Lucia Ames Mead to Hannah Clothier Hull, Sep. 16, 1924, box 6, Hull Papers, DG 16, SCPC. My thanks to Nancy Robertson for further information about the singers' incident.

24. "Anger over DAR Action Flames in Women's Council," 1; "Women Destroy Pacifist Tracts at Quinquennial," *Evening Star,* (Washington, D.C., May 7, 1925), 1, 5; "Women Cast Vote for Disarmament," ibid., May 9, 1925; "Pleads for Union in Peace Efforts," ibid., May 12, 1925; "Mrs. Moore Flays Ultra-Patriots," and "Accuses Alien Women," ibid.? (probably May 14, 1925), all clippings in folder "1925, Research Materials, Suffrage," box D36, Belle Case La Follette Papers, LC.

25. Jensen, "All Pink Sisters," 215–17; Carrie Chapman Catt to Lucia Ames Mead, Jan. 9, 1924, folder 5, box 6, Papers of Edwin D. and Lucia Ames Mead, SCPC; Catt to Maud Wood Park, Jan. 21, 1924, Catt to Josephine Schain, n.d. [summer 1925], and (attached) Catt to Presidents of Cooperating Associations, and other letters in folder "Catt, Carrie Chapman, 14 L.S. 1924–25 to Josephine Schain," box 5; Josephine Schain to Catt, May 19, 1925, Jun. 20, 1925, Jun. 24, 1925, and other letters in folder "Josephine Schain to Carrie Chapman Catt, 1924–25," box 5; Catt to the Committee on the Cause and Cure of War, May 27, 1926; Catt to Schain, Jul. 15, 1926, Catt to Catherine Gerwick, Dec. 14, 1926, in folder "Carrie Chapman Catt, 10 L.S. to Josephine Schain, 1926," box 5; Josephine Schain Coll., SSC; Mary Anderson to Mary Van Kleeck, Jan. 19, 1925, folder 1107, box 71, Mary Van Kleeck Coll, SSC. Cf. "United for World Peace: The Conference on the Cause and Cure of War," *The Woman Citizen* 9, n.s. (Feb. 7, 1925), 7–9, noting that it was not a "pacifist conference," "not opposing Army and Navy." Inez Haynes Irwin, in *Angels and Amazons* (Garden City, N.Y., Doubleday, 1934), 419–20, claimed that Catt formed the NCCCW in order to counter the right-wing Women's Patriotic Council.

Catt's method of amassing peace sentiment in the NCCCW by coalescing the memberships of existing women's organizations was similar to Alice Paul's method of amassing sentiment for the ERA by working on the leadership of existing women's organizations to endorse the amendment. Se AP OH, 440–41.

26. Jensen, "All Pink Sisters," 216; "Doubtful Speakers" lists circulated in Kansas and Massachusetts, folder 2, box 1, DAR Blacklist Controversy Collection, Stanford University Archives. The collection at Stanford offers extensive documentation of the matter in published and unpublished documents from the viewpoint of DAR dissenters, especially Helen Tufts Baillie of Massachusetts, and the Palo Alto chapter (which resigned from the DAR in May 1930, after a struggle). Catharine W. McCulloch to Miss Mary McDowell, Jun. 15, 1927, folder 79, Dillon Coll., SL; Catt to Anna Garlin Spencer, Sep. 13, 1927, folder "Correspondence 1860–1931, and n.d.," box 1, Papers of Anna Garlin Spencer, DG 54, SCPC. See also Catt, "Lies at Large," *Woman Citizen,* Jun. 1927, and *Woman Patriot* 9 (Jul. 15, 1927), in folder 9 of NWTUL Coll., SL; 1927–28 correspondence of Carrie Chapman Catt, and folders "Women's Organizations, attacks on," Catt Papers, LC reels 2, 17.

27. Dorothy Johnson, "Organized Women as Lobbyists," *Capitol Studies* 1

(Spring 1972), 46–48; Lemons, *Woman Citizen*, 146–47, 172–74, 219–25. Johnson points out that the DAR had supported the Sheppard-Towner legislation in 1921, when it was first passed, and only turned against it in mid-decade.

28. Lemons, *Woman Citizen*, 222; Louise Young, "The Excursion" (Apr. 1956), 9, folder 25, Dorothy Kirchwey Brown Coll., SL; Jensen, "All Pink Sisters," 217; Foster-Hayes, "The Women and the Warriors," 318–21.

29. See chap. 3.

30. Valborg Fletty, *Public Services of Women's Organizations* (Menasha, Wis., Banta, 1951), 10; Jensen, "All Pink Sisters," 217; see Caroline Lexow Babcock Coll., SL, on WPU.

31. "The Woman's Party and Communism," and "Woman's Party Organizing 24 Soviets," *The Woman Patriot* 6 (Oct. 1, 15, 1922), 12–13; "Petition Submitted by the 'Woman Patriot' Against Miss Dell," ER 13 (Mar. 6, 1926), 30–31. The origin of claims about the NWP's intentions of "dictatorship" may have been Mrs. Belmont's article, "Women as Dictators," *Ladies Home Journal*, Sep. 1922, 7, 43.

32. Doris Stevens to Alva Belmont, Apr. 13, 1928, folder "Notes and Correspondence *re* Belmont and NWP, January–August 1928," DSC; NWP organization for D.C. to Mrs. Alfred J. Brosseau (president-general of the DAR), Apr. 9, 1928, NWP #39. Asked in the 1970s whether the NWP had ever been accused of being Bolshevik, Alice Paul replied, "No. Maybe people accused us, but I never heard of it. No; we were much more apt to be accused of being too conservative, you see. Because so many, almost all our members seemed to be of the conservative school." AP OH, 436. Certainly her memory was foreshortened on this point.

33. ER, Jun. 23, 1928, 155; Jul. 7, 1928, 171; Jul. 14, 1928, 181–82; Sep. 22, 1928, 258–61; Sep. 29, 1928, 269; Nov. 3, 1928, 306; National Council minutes, Sep. 11, 1928, NWP #114; Jane Norman Smith to Member of the Woman's Party, Oct. 8, 1928, NWP #40; Mabel Vernon to Mrs. Rilla Nelson, Sep. 17, 1928, box 1, Lucia Voorhes Grimes Coll., Michigan Historical Collections, Bentley Historical Library, U. Michigan. Jane Norman Smith to Lutz, Feb. 6, 1932, folder 58, Lutz Collection, SL. See also Smith to Alice Paul, Jan. 19, 1934, folder 116, JNSC. Vernon's letter says that the decision was made at a conference at headquarters, 34 to 8, with all of those "who take a really active part in our work," except 2, in favor. But when the endorsement was brought up and discussed favorably at the National Council meeting, Sep. 11, 1928, according to the Minutes, only 10 people beside Jane Norman Smith were present. No record remains in the NWP papers of another conference at headquarters before Sep. 17. In "Meeting at the Headquarters of the Natl. Woman's Party, Sunday, Sept. 30, 1928," folder "S," cont. 58, Anna Kelton Wiley Papers, LC, a conference meeting on Sep. 12 at which the decision was voted is described; there is no mention of how many were present. The NWP's position was that it had always pressured parties strictly in relation to its own goal, whether suffrage or equal rights, and that the current endorsement was a typical instance of "remaining independent to use our votes in the way we decide will be of greatest help to Equal Rights." Sidney R. Bland argues in "Techniques of Persuasion: The National Woman's Party and Woman Suffrage, 1913–1919" (Ph.D. diss., George Washington U., 1972), that Paul was Republican at heart (in the 1910s) and would never have campaigned against the party in power in 1914–16 had the Republicans been in power.

Jane Norman Smith's activities in New York in the 1920s can be followed in her correspondence in box 2, JNSC. On the New York network of anti-ERA social reformers in the 1920s, see Susan Ware, *Beyond Suffrage* (Cambridge, Harvard

U.P., 1981), 33–38, and Clarke Chambers, *Seedtime of Reform* (Minneapolis, U. Minnesota P., 1963), 260–61.

34. Sue Shelton White to Jane Norman Smith, Sep. 15, 1928, folder 35, Sue Shelton White Coll., SL; White to Member of the Woman's Party, Nov. 20, 1928, and White to Miss Lucia V. Grimes, Dec. 28, 1929, box 1, Lucia Voorhes Grimes Coll., U. Michigan; Lavinia L. Dock to Party, Oct. 2, 1928; Emma C. Johnson to NWP, Oct. 18, 1928; Ruby Black to Mrs. Jane Norman Smith and Mabel Vernon, Oct. 26, 1928, NWP #40; National Council minutes, Oct. 31, 1928, NWP #114. See also Florence Bayard Hilles to Edith Houghton Hooker, Oct. 21, 1928, and NWP Nebraska Organization to Jane Norman Smith, Oct. 21, 1928, NWP #40; and Susan D. Becker, *The Origins of the Equal Rights Amendment: American Feminism between the Wars* (Westport, Conn., Greenwood, 1981), 93–96.

35. For Paul's thought about 1928, see MV OH, 87–88.

36. Harriot Stanton Blatch and Anne Martin had been standoffish since the early 1920s; for dispute between Blatch and Paul, see their correspondence of Nov. 1920, NWP #4, #5. After 1928 Sue Shelton White pursued Democratic politics; see folder 35, Sue Shelton White Coll., SL. RHR OH, 221 (quotation), and 221–31 on Vernon and Pierce; on Florence Brewer Boeckel's resignation, National Council minutes, Mar. 14, 1930, NWP #115; on Mabel Vernon's resignation, *New York Times* clippings, Mar. 19, 1930, Anna Kelton Wiley to Miss Fisher, Mar. 21, 1930, and Wiley to Miss Leila Enders, Mar. 21, 1930, folder "F," box 56; Wiley to Member of the National Council of the National Woman's Party, Feb. 27, 1930, and Jane Norman Smith to Mrs. Anna Kelton Wiley, Mar. 26, 1930, folder "S," box 57–58, Anna Kelton Wiley Papers, LC. On Mary Gertrude Fendall, see her letter to Wiley, Nov. 3, 1931, folder "F," box 56, ibid. On Stevens, see "Notes on Belmont," DSC. See also Becker, *Origins*, 37–38, on changing membership of NWP in the late 1920s and 1930s.

37. David Kyvig, "Women Against Prohibition," *American Quarterly* 28 (Fall 1976), 465–82, and *Repealing National Prohibition* (Chicago, U. Chicago P., 1979), 118–27; Paul A. Carter, *Another Part of the Twenties* (N.Y., Columbia U.P., 1977), 96–99. Gordon, in *After Winning*, 163–65, confirms that anti-Prohibition sentiment created disruption within women's political groupings in New Jersey. Cf. a correspondent of Elizabeth Tilton, who remained dry to the end, "sad to relate, not many of our women are interested in, or care to work in the W.C.T.U." Mrs. Virginia Kick, Blytheville, Arkansas, to Miss [sic] Elizabeth Tilton, Sep. 25, 1931, folder 35, Tilton Coll., SL.

38. On women's actions regarding ratification of the Kellogg-Briand Pact, Florence Brewer Boeckel, "Women in International Affairs," AAAPSS 143 (May 1929), 245; Edward B. Logan, "Lobbying," ibid. 144, suppl. (Jul. 1929), 32; Robert H. Ferrell, *Peace in Their Time: The Origins of the Kellogg-Briand Pact* (New Haven, Yale U.P., 1952), 231–50; DeBenedetti, *Origins*, 213, 227–30.

39. Hearings of Mar. 6, 1930, Sophonisba Breckinridge, *Marriage and the Civil Rights of Women* (Chicago, U. Chicago P., 1931), 145. The changes being made were: native-born women who had lost their U.S. citizenship by marriage could be repatriated by a simple affirmative action in court, with no preceding residence requirement; native-born women who had married aliens and lived abroad could return to the United States outside the immigration quota while still married. On mobilization against Sec. 213 of the federal Economy Act, see Lois Scharf, *To Work and to Wed* (Westport, Conn., Greenwood, 1980), 47–53.

In the early 1930s, the NWP national leadership missed or rejected the opportunity to organize women locally about economic issues and reiterated the single goal of the ERA; this led to a schism in the organization between 1933 and 1936. See, e.g., form letter, NWP headquarters to State Chairmen, Jan. 4, 1931, folder "Correspondence 1931," box 1, Grimes Coll., U. Michigan; Becker, *Origins*, 87–92; Gordon, *After Winning*, 168–71; Edith Houghton Hooker to Alma Lutz, Mar. 13, 1935, folder 67, Mary W. Williams to Lutz, Apr. 22, 1934, folder 76, Jane Norman Smith to Lutz and Marguerite Smith, Dec. 9, 1933, folder 98, Alma Lutz Coll. MC182, SL; Edith Houghton Hooker to Doris Stevens, Nov. 19, 1934, folder "H," Betty Gram Swing to Stevens, Nov. 20, 1934, folder "Betty Gram Swing," box 4, DSC; Doris Stevens to Jane Norman Smith, Aug. 2, 1934, folder 126, JNSC.

40. Walter Lippmann, "Lady Politicians: How the Old-Fashioned Illusion that Women Would Redeem Politics Has Been Destroyed," *Vanity Fair* 29 (Jan. 1928), 43, 104. Lippmann's starting point was the case of Florence Knapp, a Republican elected secretary of state in New York (the highest woman state official), who had been discovered by Democrats to have handed out some of the jobs connected with the taking of the state census to her relatives and many to the Republican machine, through the recommendations of the state and county chairmen. She was, Lippmann noted tongue-in-cheek, a woman "charged with being an ordinary politician." Frank R. Kent, *Political Behavior* (New York, William Morrow, 1928), 281–93, quotations 282, 292; George E. Anderson, "Women in Congress," *The Commonweal* 9:17 (Mar. 13, 1929), 532–34, quotation 534.

CONCLUSION

1. For claims or intimations that feminism is archaic, see Elizabeth Kemper Adams, *Women Professional Workers* (N.Y., MacMillan, 1921), 441; Julia Adams, "The 'Serious Young' Speak Up," *The Woman's Journal* 13 (May 1928), 8–9; Dorothy Dunbar Bromley, "Feminist—New Style," *Harper's Magazine* 155 (October 1927), 552–60; Mary Ross, "The New Status of Women in America," in *Woman's Coming of Age*, ed. Samuel D. Schmalhausen and V. F. Calverton (N.Y., Liveright, 1931), 536–49; for criticisms that feminism has gone too far, see Avrom Barnett, *Foundations of Feminism* (N.Y., Robert McBride, 1921); "Feminism and Jane Smith," *Harper's Magazine* 155 (Jun. 1927), 1–10; John Macy, "Equality of Women a Myth—A Challenge to Feminism," ibid., 153 (Nov. 1926), 705–13; Gina Lombroso Ferrero, "Feminism Destructive of Woman's Happiness," *Current History* 25:4 (Jan. 1927) 486–92; Hugh McMenamin, "Evils of Woman's Revolt Against the Old Standards," ibid., 27:1 (Oct. 1927), 30–32; Anthony Ludovici, "Woman's Encroachment on Man's Domain," ibid., 21–25; and Joseph Collins, "Woman's Morality in Transition," ibid., 33–39.

2. Alice Beal Parsons, *Woman's Dilemma* (N.Y., Thomas Crowell, 1926); Suzanne La Follette, *Concerning Women* (N.Y., Boni, 1926). See also Beatrice Forbes-Robertson Hale, "Women's Revolution," *Current History* 19 (Oct. 1923), 16–32; Lorine Pruette, "Should Men Be Protected?" *The Nation* 125 (Aug. 31, 1927), 200–01; Miriam Allen de Ford, "The Feminist Future," TNR 56 (Sep. 19, 1926), 121–23; Freda Kirchwey, ed., *Our Changing Morality* (N.Y., Boni, 1924); Edna Kenton, "Four Years of Equal Suffrage," *Forum* 72 (Jul. 1924), 37–44; Josephine Bacon, "In 1979: The American Woman," *Forum* 117 (Jan. 1929), 269–74. Cf. the commentary of eternal progressive and optimist Alice Park at age 72: "just think what progress *we* have seen in progressive movements of special interest. Votes for women first of course, child labor forbidden (of course the end can't come at once), the recent pronouncement of 6 hour day and shorter

hours besides. The dread of war—Kellogg peace pact—and hope of peace even while wars go on. The SHORT SKIRTS—*hurra* for those. Every step a new freedom. Health a topic for every newspaper and ever person. *Hurra* for us—US. It is great to count up some progress and to know we gave it a shove." Park to Mary McHenry Keith, Jul. 29, 1933, folder "Alice Park," box 11, Keith-McHenry-Pond Families Papers, BL.

3. See n. 1 and Carrie Chapman Catt, "Woman Suffrage Only an Episode in Age-Old Movement," *Current History* 27:1 (Oct. 1927), 1–7; Charlotte Perkins Gilman, "Woman's Achievements Since the Franchise," ibid., 7–14; Leta S. Hollingworth, "The New Woman in the Making," ibid., 14–20.

4. Besides items mentioned in n. 1, see Creighton Peet, "What More Do Women Want?" *Outlook and Independent* 158 (Aug. 5, 1931), 433–34; Henry R. Carey, "This Two-Headed Monster—The Family," *Harper's Magazine* 156 (Jan. 1928), 162–71, a retort, in part, to Bromley's "Feminist-New Style"; Albert Jay Nock, "A Word to Women," *Atlantic Monthly* 148 (Nov. 1931), 545–54. Ferdinand Lundberg and Marynia Farnham's *Modern Woman: The Lost Sex* (N.Y., Harper, 1947) topped the genre of works seeking to blame the dislocations of the modern world on feminism's misplaced goals for women.

5. Lillian Symes, "Still a Man's Game: Reflections of a Slightly Tired Feminist," *Harper's* 153 (May 1929), 678–86, and "The New Masculinism," ibid. 161 (Jun. 1930), 98–107. Cf. Elizabeth Onativia, "Give Us Our Privileges," *Scribner's* 87 (Jun. 1930), 593–98; Margaret Culkin Banning et al., "The Future of Marriage," *Forum* 86 (Aug. 1931), 74–78; Emily Newell Blair, "Discouraged Feminists," *The Outlook* 158 (Jul. 8, 1931), 302–03, 318; Carey, "This Two-Headed Monster," and Nock, "A Word to Women." The economic crisis of the Depression deepened the vein of attitudinal conservatism; see Hornell Hart, "Changing Social Attitudes and Interests," chap. 8 in *Recent Social Trends*, vol. 1, by the President's Committee on Social Trends (N.Y., McGraw-Hill, 1934); Genevieve Parkhurst, "Is Feminism Dead?" *Harper's* 176 (May 1935), 735–45; Elizabeth Schlesinger, "They Say Women Are Emancipated," *TNR* 77 (Dec. 13, 1933), 125–27.

6. Hale, "Women's Revolution," 16; Ferrero, "Feminism Destructive," 486; Martha Bensley Bruere, "The Highway to Woman's Happiness," *Current History* 27:1 (Oct. 1927), 26; Marcia Leach, "Feminine Modernism: The Economics of the Situation," *The Century* 118 (Jun. 1929), 226. See also Viva Boothe, "Gainfully Employed Women in the Family," *AAAPSS* 160 (1932), 75–85, discussed in chap. 6. Cf. Hollingworth, "New Woman," 18, which attributed the making of the "new woman" principally to discoveries by "men of science, inventors, and philosophers," which had abolished the need for female industrial labor in the home and had allowed control over reproduction; secondarily she credited the propaganda value of Feminism, which "hastened the change" by calling attention to it. Mary Ross, who had been trying to sort out the relation between women's wage-earning and pronouncements of feminism since the 1910s, and who by 1931 considered feminism passé, regarded women's presence in the labor force as the most important fact reorienting male–female relationships and social hierarchy. "This new adaptation of the old status of women—" (by which she meant that women, married or not, took economically productive roles in the labor force while they also ran households and reared children) "looked at closely—has little of the glamour of 'emancipation.' It bristles with a thousand questions," she observed. Ross, "New Status"; see also her "Some Unsheltered Daughters," Letter to the Editor, *TNR* 8 (Sep. 2, 1916), 116–17.

7. See Dorothy Ross, "American Social Science and the Idea of Progress," in

The Authority of Experts, ed. Thomas Haskell (Bloomington, Indiana U.P., 1984), 167–70, on cultural lag theory in the 1920s and 1930s.

8. "Where Are the Pre-War Radicals?" *Survey*, Feb. 1, 1926, 556–66. Howe's autobiography was no better at remembering Feminism; see above, chap. 1, note 42 (p. 297). Catt cited another example of disremembering in "Woman Suffrage Only an Episode," 1, noting that a man who had been an active suffragist only in the last five years of the campaign had in 1927 exhorted a group to be as energetic as the suffragists in order to win "as quickly and easily" as they did.

9. Cf. Carl N. Degler, "Revolution without Ideology: The Changing Place of Women in America," *Daedalus* 93 (Spring 1964), 653–71.

10. Ida Clyde Clarke, "Feminism and the New Technique: Strike for High Places," *The Century* 117 (Apr. 1929), 753. Clarke contrasted "the impassioned reformer of three generations ago whose life and work were dedicated to one all-absorbing cause." Note here, interestingly, the passion of the woman movement has been moved back *three* generations. Catt, "Woman Suffrage Only an Episode," 5. Political commentator (unnamed) cited by Ernestine Evans, "Women in the Washington Scene," *The Century* 84 (Aug. 1923), 508. Evans also recounted a prescient remark by W. E. B. DuBois, whom she interviewed about the question of black women political leaders. He made an analogy to the expectation in Reconstruction that blacks would migrate North. "Social change comes slowly, like molasses from jugs. The negroes did begin to migrate, but only after forty years," he said, implying that in forty years [1963] one would know something about women in politics.

11. Copy of Susan Kingsbury to Mrs. Catherine Filene Shouse, Feb. 28, 1934, folder 35, Institute of Women's Professional Relations Collection, SL; Catt, "Woman Suffrage Only an Episode," 5.

12. Dorothy Dunbar Bromley, "Feminist—New Style." On ex-feminists, see chap. 6.

13. Hollingworth, "New Woman," 19.

14. Cf. *A Portrait of Marginality: The Political Behavior of the American Woman*, ed. Marianne Githens and Jewel L. Prestage (N.Y., David McKay, 1977); Rosalind Rosenberg, *Beyond Separate Spheres* (New Haven, Yale U.P., 1982), 144; Carroll Smith-Rosenberg, *Disorderly Conduct* (N.Y., Knopf, 1985), 245–96.

15. Doris Stevens, "Tribute to Alva Belmont," *ER*, July 15, 1933.

16. Dewson to Marvin McIntyre, Feb. 5, 1934, quoted in Susan Ware, *Beyond Suffrage* (Cambridge, Harvard U.P., 1981), 45. Transcript of interview with Sara Fredgant, 98, in "The Twentieth-Century Trade Union Woman Oral History Project," Program on Women and Work, Institute of Labor and Industrial Relations, U. Michigan/Wayne State U., Ann Arbor. Fredgant was born in 1900 in Russia and came to the United States as a child.

17. Eleanor Roosevelt, "Women in Politics," *Good Housekeeping* 110 (Apr. 1940), 45, quoted in Ware, *Beyond Suffrage*, 16. It is interesting to note that Alice Paul dispatched a very effective NWP recruit, Helen Hunt West, a Florida lawyer and active Democrat, as an intermediary to "have a real discussion of the equality program with Mrs. Roosevelt." "As one observes her work in the White House," Paul wrote to West, "one cannot but feel that she belongs with us and not against us." Paul to West, May 9, 1936, folder 9, Helen Hunt West Coll., SL.

18. Julia Adams, "'Serious Young' Speak Up," 8–9.

19. Blair, "Discouraged Feminists"; and "Wanted: A New Feminism," *Indep.*

W. 10 (Dec. 1930), 498; see also Estelle Freedman, "Separatism as Strategy: Female Institution-Building and American Feminism, 1870–1930," *FS* 5 (Fall 1979), 512–29. Mary R. Beard, "University Discipline for Women—Asset or Handicap?" *JAAUW* 25:3 (Apr. 1932), reprinted in *Mary Ritter Beard: A Sourcebook*, ed. Ann J. Lane (N.Y., Schocken, 1977), quotation 149 (and see Beard's other important essays of the 1930s reprinted in the volume). See also Bonnie Smith, "Seeing Mary Beard," *FS* 10 (Fall 1984), 399–416. Beard's views had a great deal in common with the contemporary views of Virginia Woolf in *Three Guineas*.

20. Beatrice Hinkle, "Woman's Subjective Dependence on Man," *Harper's* 164 (Jan. 1932), 193–205 (quotation 194); Olga Knopf, *The Art of Being a Woman*, ed. Alan Porter (Boston, Little Brown, 1932), *Women on Their Own*, ed. Alan Porter (Boston, Little Brown, 1935), 10, 15 (quotations). Cf. also "Let Us Build Our Work Lives Frankly and Freely as Women," *Indep. W.* 11 (Apr. 1927), 4–5. The alternative NWP weekly edited by Edith Houghton Hooker reviewed Knopf's *Women on Their Own* and recommended it, but with the warning that "no submerged group can win rights for itself except by organized activity"—noted in Susan D. Becker, *Origins of the Equal Rights Amendment* (Westport, Conn., Greenwood, 1981), 67.

21. Beatrice Hinkle, "The Chaos of Modern Marriage," *Harper's* 152 (Dec. 1925), 1–12. On Hoover see Joan Hoff Wilson, *Herbert Hoover: Forgotten Progressive* (Boston, Little Brown, 1975), and *Herbert Hoover as Secretary of Commerce: Studies in New Era Thought and Practice*, ed. Ellis Hawley (Iowa City, U. Iowa P., 1981). See Ware, *Beyond Suffrage* for portrayal of New Deal women; Ware similarly critiques their individualist tenets. The introduction to *Decades of Discontent* (Westport, Conn., Greenwood, 1983), ed. Lois Scharf and Joan Jensen, points out the irony of individual successes and collective problems of women in the 1920s and 1930s.

22. Miriam Allen de Ford, "Feminism, Cause or Effect?" c. 1928, folder 25, box 2, de Ford Coll., California Historical Society; and interview with de Ford in *From Parlor to Prison*, ed. Sherna Gluck (N.Y., Vintage, 1976), 176–77. Cf. the emphasis on individualism found by Elaine Showalter in "modern women" sketched in the *Nation* in 1926–27, in *These Modern Women* (Old Westbury, N.Y., Feminist Press, 1978).

23. *Judy* 1:1 (Jun. 1919); 2:3 (1919), n.p., SL.

24. See Rose Arnold Powell Collection, SL; on Mary Inman, Robert Shaffer, "Women and the Communist Party U.S.A., 1930–1940," *Socialist Review* 45 (May 1979), 73–118; on Lucy Stone League, scattered items in Ruth Hale Scrapbook and in DSC, SL; on Women Strike for Peace, Amy Swerdlow, "Ladies' Day at the Capitol: Women Strike For Peace vs. HUAC," *FS* 8 (Fall 1982), 493–520. See also Leila Rupp and Verta Taylor, *Survival in the Doldrums: The American Women's Rights Movement, 1945 to the 1960s* (N.Y., Oxford U.P., 1987).